# To Seek & To Serve

Forward Movement Publications
Cincinnati, Ohio
1991

*The publication of this book was assisted by a grant from the Church Missions Publishing Company, Hartford, Diocese of Connecticut.*

Copyright © 1991, by The Domestic and Foreign Missionary Society of the Protestant Episcopal Church in the United States of America.

All rights reserved.

Published by Forward Movement Publications, 412 Sycamore Street, Cincinnati, Ohio 45202 USA

Printed in the United States of America

# CONTENTS

Preface ................................... vii

Acknowledgments ......................... ix

Foreword by the Presiding Bishop ............ 1

Introduction ................................. 3
   *The Mission Discernment Project*

## STORIES OF MISSION DISCERNMENT

**1. A Beautiful Bowl of Colors** ............. 15
   *Story of a Multicultural Congregation*
   *St. Philip's Church, San Jose, California*

**2. People Embody the Message** ............ 36
   *Story of a Program-Sized Ministry in the World*
   *St. George's Church, Fredericksburg, Virginia*

**3. Intimacy and Small Groups** ............. 53
   *Story of a Catechumenal Process*
   *St. Luke's Church, Madison, Wisconsin*

**4. Hoosier Hospitality** ..................... 71
   *Story of Wage Earners in Community Service*
   *St. Mark's Church, Plainfield, Indiana*

**5. Creating a Village** ..................... 88
   *Story of the Transformation of an*
     *Inner-City Community*
   *Church of the Messiah, Detroit*

**6. A Public Church** ....................... 110
   *Story of a Corporation-Sized Congregation*
   *St. Luke's Church, Atlanta*

7. **Gumbo Stew** .............................. 130
   *Story of Community Service*
   Baskervill Ministries, Pawleys Island, South Carolina

8. **Grapefruit and Good News** ............. 153
   *Story of a Hispanic Jubilee Ministry*
   Santa Fe Episcopal Church, San Antonio, Texas

9. *Mitakuye Oyasin:* **Partners on the Prairie** ............................... 175
   *Story of a Native American Lutheran-*
       *Episcopal Ministry*
   Pine Ridge Indian Reservation, South Dakota

10. **Joyfully Serving God and Country** ...... 199
    *Story of a Charismatic/Evangelical Congregation*
    St. Stephen's Church, Oak Harbor, Washington

11. **God's House: Build It Up** ............... 223
    *Story of a Program-Sized Congregation*
        *in New England*
    Church of the Nativity, Northborough, Massachusetts

12. **High-Country Calling** ................... 249
    *Story of a Congregation Using Professional*
        *Consulting Services*
    Christ Church, Cody, Wyoming

13. **Sowing the Seed, Yielding a Harvest** .... 274
    *Story of a Regional Cluster Ministry*
    Hudson Valley Ministry, Greater Newburgh, New York

14. **Faith Under Fire: A Witness of Hope** ... 299
    *Story of Two Congregations Staying Faithful in a*
        *Country at War with Itself*
    Congregación San Juan Evangelista, San Salvador, and
    Congregación Santa María Virgen, Ilopango

15. **Common Threads: A Discussion of the Stories** ........................... 324

# DIOCESAN STORIES, USE GUIDES, RESOURCES, AND PROJECT DOCUMENTS

**Appendix 1. Diocesan Stories of Mission Discernment** .................... 345

**Appendix 2. Use Guides** ................... 363

**Appendix 3. Selected Resources** ............ 388

**Appendix 4. Documents of the Mission Discernment Project** .................... 398
 *A Summary Description of the Mission Discernment Project*
 *Planning Guide for Site Visits*
 *Guidelines for Site Visits*
 *Getting the Story—Site Visitors as Midwives*

# PREFACE

General Convention in 1988 called for helping congregations discern their mission (Appendix 4a). An Episcopal Church Center team decided to respond by telling the stories of congregations that had already identified their mission and were living it out. Their stories could then help other congregations discern their own mission.

Here, then, are fifteen stories of congregations in mission. They reflect the rich diversity of Episcopal life. Some diocesan stories are included as well (Appendix 1). Two use guides suggest ways to use the stories (Appendix 2). Other resources (Appendix 3) suggest the breadth of experience available.

Churches are encouraged to reproduce various parts of this work. Simply cite the author, the title, and the publisher, and note that it was produced by the Episcopal Church Center.

We look for more stories to tell in the years ahead. The mission to reconcile all people to unity with God and each other in Jesus Christ is unchanging. The world in which we carry on the mission and the ways in which we carry it on will change and grow as God's reign continues among us.

| | | |
|---|---|---|
| A. Wayne Schwab | Anne Rowthorn | John T. Docker |
| *Project Director* | *Project Coordinator* | *Staff* |

# ACKNOWLEDGMENTS

The Mission Discernment Project has been a truly collegial undertaking, involving the help, hard work, advice, and good will of dozens of people. The project staff is grateful for all those in the congregations visited—parish leaders, vestry members, community leaders, clergy and staff, and all others who planned the visits at their locations and offered hospitality to site visiting team members. We are thankful for all the mission discernment team members who took time out of their busy lives to visit the various sites. Many Episcopal Church Center staffers suggested locations to visit and contributed to the design of the project. Administrative staff made arrangements, copies, and telephone calls and obtained visas. Friends and contacts throughout the Episcopal Church also helped.

In particular, we say thank you to the following: Dr. Owanah Anderson, the Rt. Rev. Craig B. Anderson, Ruth Asher, Nancy Axell, the Rev. Herman Badecker, Lindy Baker, the Rev. Charles E. Bennison, Joan Bray, Dr. Gloria Brown, the Rev. Canon Jervis Burns, Virginia Bernel de Cabezos, Julie Campbell, the Rev. Antoine L. Campbell, Nancy Cannon, Susie Casto, José Ramiro Chavez, Tom Chu, the Rev. Judy Cirves, the Rev. Susan Clark, the Rev. Kevin Coffee, Dawn E. Conley, Judith G. Conley, Jane Cosby, the Rev. Canon William Coyne, Ann Cramer, Scotland Davis, Carol Dietmeyer, the Rt. Rev. Herbert Donovan, Bill Drake, the Rev. Jerry W. Drino, Sandy Elledge, Ethel Felh, the Rev. Santiago Garcia, Alan George, Ana Emelia Gomez, the Rev. Fred Goodwin, the Rev. Linda Grenz, the Rev. Daphne B. Grimes, Dr. Richard Groepper, the Rev. Francisco Guardado, the Rev. Carmen B. Guerrero, the Rev. Edwin Gulick. the Rev. Abigail Hamilton, John Hannan, the Rev. Robert Hansel, the Rt. Rev. Barbara C. Harris, Mary Hassell, Frank Hemlin, Val Hillsdon-Hutton, the Rt. Rev. Harold Hopkins, Bryant Hudson, Dr. Charles Huttar, Joan Irvin, Dr. Irene Jackson-Brown, the Ven. Victoriano Jimeno, Edward Jones, Janet King, the Rev. Sheryl Kulawa, the Rt. Rev. Robert Ladehoff, Diana LaMee, Ellen Little, the Rev. Nathanael Lizarazo, Phil MacVean, Nancy Marvel, Diane May, the Rev. Lynde E. May, the Rev. Ted McEachern, the Rev. Thomas McElligott, the Rev. Jacqueline A. Means, Berry Meaux, Rosa Elia Mejia, the Rev. Fred Mesteth, Warren Murphy, the Rev. Henry

L. H. Myers, the Rev. Henry Myers, Linda Nichols, the Rt. Rev. James Ottley, the Rev. David W. Perry, the Rev. Ricardo Potter-Norman, the Rev. Wilfrido Ramos-Orench, John Ratti, the Rt. Rev. George Reynolds, Elizabeth and Brian Rixham, the Rev. Creighton Robertson, the Rev. John A. Rollins, the Rev. Sylvestre Romero, the Rev. Arlin J. Rothauge, Dr. David Rowe, the Rt. Rev. Jeffrey Rowthorn, the Rev. Wayne Schmidt, Alecia Schuster, Doug and Ellen Scott, the Rev. Luis Serrano, Ann Smith, Mary Smith, Barbara Somers, the Rev. Ronald Spann, the Rev. J. David Stanway, the Rev. Linda Strohmier, the Rev. Nancy Baillie Strong, Jane Trent Surles, the Rev. Charles Syndor, Frank L. Tedeschi, the Rev. Jack M. Tench, Liliana E. Tressera, Charles Turner, the Rev. Benjamin R. Tyon, Doug VanDemark, the Rev. Wenifredo Veraga, Jeanne Vetter, Shirley Viall, the Rt. Rev. Orris Walker, the Rt. Rev. Arthur E. Walmsley, Marcy Walsh, the Rev. Barbara Wangsness, the Ven. Robert N. Willing, the Rev. Charles R. Wilson, the Rev. Charles Wilson, LaDonna M. Wind, the Rt. Rev. Andrew F. Wissemann, the Rev. Paul Worley, and Tyler Zabriskie.

# FOREWORD

The 1988 Lambeth Conference of Anglican Bishops called for "a shift to a dynamic missionary emphasis going beyond care and nurture to proclamation and service" (Resolution 044). In this Decade of Evangelism, we are called to respond to God's call to mission. In response to God's searching and inescapable call, the church of Jesus Christ moves from nurture to mission.

I rejoice that these stories of response to God's call have been told, and know that individuals and congregations will benefit from the rich stories of mission. This book is commended as a resource for individual study by every Episcopalian and for corporate study by every Episcopal congregation. It provides many new ideas, which may be adapted for each mission situation.

There are more stories to be told, and more stories are unfolding. May the Holy Spirit continue to renew us for mission.

The Most Rev. Edmond L. Browning
*Presiding Bishop*

> *Christians are formed and nurtured as followers of Jesus Christ through their participation in the total life and mission of local congregations. . . . Each congregation has the responsibility to discern what it is uniquely called to be and do in order to fulfill its mission. . . .*
> —Res. A066a

## INTRODUCTION

# THE MISSION DISCERNMENT PROJECT

### IN THE BEGINNING

The General Convention of the Episcopal Church meeting in Detroit in July, 1988, resolved

> That the Episcopal Church renew and strengthen its educational ministry by advocating a clear focus on mission at every level of its life faithful to the standard of biblical word and baptismal covenant, and . . . . That the Executive Council provide the necessary structures and funding so that the Mission Operations Team can enable congregations, with diocesan support, to continue or initiate a process of discernment, challenge, leadership and resource development, and action. (Res. A 066a)

The resolution was the result and the product of the Presiding Bishop's Task Force on Christian Education in Congregations, selected and appointed by Bishop Browning in 1986 to examine the educational ministry of the Church—including current practices—and to make recommendations to strengthen it.

The resolution was directed to congregations, was expected to involve all members of congregations, and anticipated actions and results. Such an emphasis was timely, since, as we are poignantly reminded in the closing words of the Anglican Consultative Council's (ACC) "Progress in Partnership" report,

> Today there is no shortage of pious words, affirmations of faith, discussions about hunger or expressions of spirituality. But the world is still waiting for the demonstration, in costly and practical terms, of what we proclaim with our lips.
>
> I was hungry and you formed a committee to investigate my hunger . . . . I was sick, and you held a seminar on the situation of the underprivileged . . . . You have investigated all aspects of my plight. Yet I am still hungry, homeless and sick.[1]

## *THE MISSION DISCERNMENT PROJECT*

The Education and Training interunit working group of the Episcopal Church Center began to carry out the resolution by adopting the following working definitions of mission discernment:

- Mission discernment is a process for helping a congregation to discover its particular call to mission.
- The mission of the Church is to restore all people to unity with God and each other in Christ (BCP, p. 855).
- Congregations that effectively educate their members convey a clarity of mission; cultivate a shared vision of what the Church is called to be; involve and value all their members; affirm, celebrate, and utilize their diversity—racially, culturally, and linguistically; enable a strong sense of community centered in God; and balance the nurture of their membership with their ministry in the larger community in which they live and in the world (Report of the Christian Education Task Force to General Convention—1988).
- Mission discernment is a continuing process for a congregation to discern with its community what God is doing in the

community; how to join God's action; and how to empower everyone to share in God's action.²

According to A. Wayne Schwab, the Mission Discernment Project's director, a process of mission discernment includes the following:

- Analyzing the community of which the congregation is a part and its needs;
- Identifying the resources in the community and the gifts of the congregation and its members;
- Making specific plans for mission;
- Developing ways for the congregation to support the ministry of the members in their daily lives; and
- Evaluating the effectiveness of specific efforts in mission.³

A "Mission Discernment Survey" was then devised and sent to bishops and leaders of education networks throughout the Episcopal Church. It cited the following eight areas, in which they were asked to provide examples, resources, and materials to support their responses:

1. Analyzing and assessing community needs
2. Identifying the gifts of members and the resources of the community
3. Making specific plans for mission
4. Building the competence and confidence of people engaged in mission
5. Providing congregational support for the ministry of people in their daily lives
6. Evaluating the effectiveness of the mission effort
7. Describing mission discernment as you see it
8. Specifying areas of mission discernment as you see them.⁴

The Mission Discernment Project staff was then asked to develop models for mission discernment. They soon realized that the most effective models of mission discernment were actually stories of congregations where mission discernment was already working, where congregations had discerned their mission and were already making a decided difference in their communities and in the lives of their members.

At the same time, it was recognized that although many congregations may effectively do what we would call "mission discernment," they may never have heard of the phrase, never have read a book on the subject, never developed a plan of mission discernment. As these matters were discussed, the project staff and the members of the Education and Training interunit working group were readily able to identify many congregations that—whether or not they termed it as such—were clearly engaged in mission discernment. The question then became—How do we bring into conversation and dialogue that which is being done quite naturally and unself-consciously in such a way as to make it available to others?

It became evident that certain questions needed to be asked of congregations:

What are the key political, social, and economic issues facing a particular community or area? Where do people in the community live and work? Who is moving into the community? Who is moving out? What is the ethnic, racial, or cultural makeup of the community? What is its personality? What are the community's needs? What is going on in the lives of the members of the congregation? And how, under all these circumstances, does the congregation go about its mission and ministry in the community? And how do its members personally carry out Christ's ministry in their daily lives—in their families and households, in their communities and workplaces?

To ask these questions of congregations, it would be necessary to visit them, to hear and see their stories, and with them to determine the steps they took, and are taking, in the development of their ministries. Mission discernment: What are you doing, and how do you do it?—that is what the project staff needed to have answered in a whole range of congregations.

## *SELECTING THE SITES*

In developing a list of congregations that exemplified effective mission discernment, it was not enough simply to identify locations that had good ideas and even excellent education plans and programs. Nor was it enough for the local congregation to have a mission program appended to, but in effect unrelated to, the total ministry of the congregation, however effective that program might be. This project is about the total mission of the total congregation. Congregations selected had to have demonstrated that they had been so effective that even the impartial observer could point to them and declare unequivocally: There surely is a family of Christian people at work in mission, actively engaged in extending the reign of God. There truly is a congregation that is making a difference—a difference in the lives of its members, and a difference in the wider community beyond the parish.

In developing a list of congregations to visit, the project staff endeavored to include congregations of varying sizes. In this, they followed Arlin Rothauge's classification of family-, pastoral-, program-, and corporation-sized churches. The family-sized congregation has an average of fewer than 50 adult Sunday worshipers, the pastoral-sized an average of 50 to 150 Sunday worshipers, the program-sized an average of 150 to 350, and the corporation-sized an average of more than 350. It was important to select congregations that would represent and celebrate the Episcopal Church's racial, cultural, and ethnic diversity, as well as its different styles of ministry. In making the choices, geography and location were accounted for, so that congregations were identified in cities, in the country, and in towns large and small. Every province of the Episcopal Church is represented in the project.

While the project staff attempted to be as inclusive as possible, they were limited by time and money to only fourteen locations. Hence congregations selected for site visits *represent* the best in their categories in the Episcopal Church. We say *represent* because for every congregation selected there were dozens of others that could equally well have been chosen. The project staff also acknowledge that not every style or type of congregation is represented, and even that having one congregation represent a certain size or type of ministry—such as one corporation-sized church—is less than desirable. Nor is one congregation in all the vast and varied dioceses of the Ninth Province adequate. Nonetheless, the congregations whose stories are presented in this Mission Discernment Project have all demonstrated a successful process of mission discernment. They have all, in their own ways, responded to the question, What is Christ calling us to be and do at this time and in this place? and planned their ministries accordingly.

# VISITING TEAMS

The visiting teams were composed of the project staff (Anne Rowthorn and either John Docker or Wayne Schwab where possible) and from one to three representatives drawn from the following groups: Education and Training Network, Total Ministry Task Force, the Executive Council, and the Standing Commission on Evangelism.

The visiting teams, which were different for each location, spent from one to three days in the congregations. At each location their function was to serve as a vehicle through which the congregation's members could tell their story of mission discernment. Although the timing and specific agenda were shaped by each setting, the visit always included the following four components: 1) Hearing the story in the words of the congregation's members; 2) Seeing the story—observing examples of mission discernment; 3) Reflecting on the story; and 4) Understanding the story—how mission is discerned, developed, and maintained.

Site visits usually included a tour of the community and conversations with community and political leaders, local news reporters, and others who were knowledgeable about the area. Some of these community leaders were members of Episcopal congregations, others were not. Site visitors often attended a local community event. They read local newspapers, listened to local television. Their goal was to get the flavor and the context of the particular ministry.

The same procedure was followed in the congregations. Vestry members, wardens, and clergy were interviewed, as were newcomers to the congregations and recipients of the congregation's ministry in the community. The site visitors talked to as many of the congregation's members as was possible. They visited them at their places of employment. They encouraged them to talk about their own ministries and the collective ministries of the congregation. Team members interviewed the matriarchs and patriarchs in an attempt to tap their knowledge of earlier times to learn the key people, circumstances, and events in the development of the congregation's present ministry and mission.

It did not matter in what order or in what way the four basic components of the visit were covered, just so long as they were covered. What did matter profoundly was that the team members listen carefully, that they ask questions in such a way as to stimulate thought and discussion. It was very important that team members see examples of ministry. The documents of the project detailing these procedures are included in Appendix 4.

Copious notes were taken, and conversations tape-recorded. At the conclusion of each visit, members of the visiting teams shared what they had learned, and discussed what they thought were the key steps the congregation had taken in evolving its process of mission discernment. They then completed individual site visitor reports, in which they stated what they most wanted to have included in the congregation's story and passed on to the wider Episcopal Church.

## *TELLING THE STORY*

The principal writer was Anne Rowthorn, and she visited every location. Immediately following each visit, while it was still fresh in her mind, she transcribed the tapes, ordered her notes, and wrote the mission discernment story of the congregation just visited. More correctly, she—with the help of the other visiting team members—was the vehicle through which each congregation *told its own story of mission discernment*. The draft was then sent back to the congregation for its approval, corrections, and modifications. The project's other staff members—Wayne Schwab and Jack Docker—also read through the chapters and suggested changes and modifications. Chapters were then rewritten in final form to incorporate these revisions.

## *RESOURCES*

The leaders of each congregation were asked to supply their own lists of resources. They were asked to include 1) those that best describe their ministry; 2) those that have been most helpful in shaping the style of ministry in their location; and 3) those that are making a real difference in the life and depth of their church community. These resources are listed after each chapter.

In addition to the references cited by members of the congregations, there are a number of other resources the Mission Discernment Project staff wish to bring to the readers' attention. These are listed in Appendix 3.

## PROJECT STAFF

The Rev. A. Wayne Schwab, Evangelism Ministries Coordinator at the Episcopal Church Center, was the project director; Dr. Anne Rowthorn was the project coordinator and principal writer; and the Rev. Dr. John T. Docker, Deputy for Program to the Executive for Education for Mission and Ministry and Coordinator for Ministry Development, served as staff. They planned and executed the project in consultation with members of the Education and Training Interunit Working Group of the Episcopal Church Center and the Rev. David Perry, Executive for Education for Mission and Ministry at the Episcopal Church Center. As they developed the project, they received the advice and assistance of many others whose names are listed in the Acknowledgments.

The Rev. A. Wayne Schwab and George Lewis, a consultant, researched and wrote the diocesan stories of mission discernment and the user guides included in Appendices 1 and 2. Members of the Total Ministry Task Force, most of whom had served on the visiting teams, read the drafts of all the chapters and made suggestions about the recurring themes and common threads that were revealed. The Rev. Dr. John Docker contributed to the writing of Chapter 15.

## CALLED TO MISSION

The Mission Discernment Project is not a study. Neither is it plans, programs, or models of mission discernment that can be lifted from one setting and planted in another. It is fourteen stories of congregations that have demonstrated a process of mission discernment.

Readers will recognize through the stories that mission discernment is a process that quite naturally occurs within congregations that are faithful and responsive to the communities in which they are located. If there is *one* major lesson from this project that stands out above all others, it is that mission discernment grows out of the context of the local area and the textures of the lives of the people who make up the local congregation. So these stories cannot be taken and used as models for processes of mission discernment elsewhere. Each congregation must engage in its own process of mission discernment. On the other hand, an inspired idea, a style of ministry, a concrete suggestion or course of action, a certain approach to looking at the community and the lives of a congregation's members—these can be gleaned by reading the stories of others. St. Ignatius of Loyola is said to have been converted by reading the lives of the saints!

## NOTES

[1] David Watson, from his book, *Discipleship,* as quoted by Simon E. Chiwanga, in Anglican Counsultative Council, *Progress in Partnership,* Report of the Mission Agencies Conference, 1987, p. 96.
[2] Education and Training Interunit Working Group, quoted from a letter sent by David Perry to bishops, education networks, and related agencies, April 27, 1989.
[3] Education and Training Interunit Working Group Memo, A. Wayne Schwab, October 11, 1989.
[4] "Mission Discernment Survey," April 27, 1989.

# STORIES OF MISSION DISCERNMENT

> *We are co-creators of new religious forms. In the process, our understanding of God is expanded. We are laying foundations for an unknown future.*
>
> —Jerry Drino
> Rector,
> St. Philip's, San Jose

―――― CHAPTER 1 ――――

# A BEAUTIFUL BOWL OF COLORS

## STORY OF A MULTICULTURAL CONGREGATION

### SAINT PHILIP'S CHURCH
### SAN JOSE, CALIFORNIA

## *INTRODUCTION*

The future is now in California. The day after the Mission Discernment Project's visiting team concluded its visit to St. Philip's, *Time* magazine appeared on the newsstands bearing on its cover a red, black, brown, blue, yellow, and white American flag and announcing the lead story, "America's Changing Colors." *Time* asks the question, "What will the U.S. be like when whites are no longer the majority?"

Already 25 percent of Americans describe themselves as nonwhite or Hispanic. By the middle of the next century the typical U.S. resident will trace his or her roots to Africa, Asia, a Spanish-speaking country, the Pacific Islands, or Arabia. In New York State right now, 40 percent of the school children are non-white; in ten years it is expected to be 50 percent. In California white pupils are already in the minority.

California is where the population changes are most visible. There whites account for only 58 percent of the total population. In San Jose the Vietnamese surname *Nguyen* outnumbers *Smith* fourteen pages to eight in the local telephone directory. Bob Lawrence, an African-American, recalled that when he first came to San Jose it was virtually impossible for anyone of color to get an entry-level job in the San Jose Police Department. Now the director of traffic is an African-American, and many other key city positions are held by African-Americans as well as by Americans of virtually every other ethnic and racial group. He recalls the days when ethnic quotas kept all but a few Chinese students out of the University of California. Now the president of the University of California at Berkeley is a Chinese-American, along with 20 percent of the student body.

In Silicon Valley alone, 400 electronics firms are owned by Asian-Americans. And they keep coming—from Vietnam, Laos, Cambodia, Thailand, Korea, Japan, the People's Republic of China, Taiwan. There are one million Filipinos—the state's second largest ethnic group—in California, and they come in at the rate of 50,000 a year.

But the newly arrived to American shores do not usually find the "streets paved with gold." Fear and racism abound, and new arrivals must struggle with employment and language. Ethnic rivalries often explode in the quest for a "piece of the pie." There is great diversity among Asian groups—as there is among Hispanic groups. New immigrants from Cambodia, Vietnam, and Laos are still suffering the pain of refugee camps and of separation—often by death—from their families. In contrast, the descendants of the Chinese who built the intercontinental railway a century ago, and of the Japanese who were forced into detention camps during World War II, have long since made a place for themselves, and they often resent being lumped together with and mistaken for new Asian arrivals. There are the African-Americans, who still have to fight for equal opportunity, and Hispanics of various cultures, who are often left behind as newer groups claim for themselves wealth and status. And then there are the Native Americans—the original Americans—who still rank at the top of some scales—unemployment, school dropout rates, infant mortality rates—and at the bottom of such others as per capita income, percentage of high school and college graduates, longevity. And finally there are the Americans of European descent, who still run the show but do so with increasing unease in a browning America. They sometimes forget that their ancestors too were once immigrants to these shores.

According to *Time,*

> The deeper significance of America's becoming a majority nonwhite society is what it means to the national psyche, to individuals' sense of themselves and their nation—their idea of what it is to be American . . . . Becoming a conspicuously multiracial society is bound to be a somewhat bumpy experience for many ordinary citizens. For older Americans, raised in a world where the numbers of whites were greater and the visibility of non-whites was carefully restrained, the new world will seem even stranger . . . [but] the new world is here. It is now.[1]

For the Episcopal Church, as well as for other mainline churches of Euro-American tradition, the "writing on the wall" ought to be apparent. Either the churches will embrace the enormous challenges presented by the changing, multicultural face of America or they will not survive. If we fail to respond, sheer demographics will spell our fate and possibly our doom. Although we have our "ethnic desks" at the Episcopal Church Center, there is a limit to how many ethnic desks the Church can sustain. Thus the multicultural church gives us a vehicle through which we can respond to the rapidly evolving missionary opportunities in urban centers where the population is culturally diverse. St. Philip's is one such congregation.

## *THE CONTEXT OF MISSION DISCERNMENT: INTRODUCING SAN JOSE*

San Jose, the nation's fourteenth largest city, with a population of 730,000, lies in the Santa Clara Valley between the Mount Hamilton Range on the east and the Santa Cruz Range on the west. Founded by the Spanish as Pueblo de San José de Guadalupe in 1777, the settlement was established to raise crops and cattle to feed soldiers encamped at the nearby presidios of San Francisco and Monterey. Vineyards also found their way into the fertile soil of the San Jose area, which now includes 50 wineries ranging from family-run establishments to large international corporations.

Today San Jose is the commercial center of Santa Clara County, and its crops are mainly technological. Popularly known as "Silicon Valley," Santa Clara County has one of the heaviest concentrations of high-tech industries in the world. Just as immigrants of past decades—from Europe, China, and Mexico—built an agricultural empire in Santa Clara County, so today's immigrants—from Southeast Asia, Mexico and other Central American countries, the Philippines, India, Hong Kong, and Taiwan—are building and reaping a technological harvest. They have fueled Silicon Valley's economy with laboratory brain-power and assembly-line dexterity.

The result of these migrations has been not only a technological revolution but a cultural revolution as well. The editor of the *San Jose Mercury News* has said,

> A demographic revolution has changed the face of Santa Clara County in the 1980s. At the beginning of the decade more than two thirds of the residents of San Jose were Anglo. When the 1990 U.S. census is taken more than half the people counted will be Hispanic, Asian or black. There will be no ethnic majority.
>
> This amazing diversity affects all of us, day in and day out. In our schools, some five dozen languages are spoken. At the offices, immigrants from India work shoulder to shoulder with immigrants from Mexico and Taiwan. At home five-generation Californians live next door to Vietnamese families who came five years ago . . . .
>
> Such change is profound. While it is true we live peacefully alongside one another, we also exist in ignorance of one another. A community such as ours can avoid ethnic strife in the future only by understanding who we are, where we've come from and what we value.[2]

# A BEAUTIFUL BOWL OF COLORS: SAINT PHILIP'S CHURCH TODAY

St. Philip's is a multicultural congregation on the east side of San Jose which has welcomed the opportunity of opening wide its doors to respond, receive, celebrate, and build upon the rich cultures present on its doorstep. The rector of St. Philip's, the Rev. Jerry W. Drino, has said,

> The vast cultural, economic, and social changes taking place in Santa Clara County must compel us to re-examine our own retreating into a "private and privatized religion" that will result in a white enclave in the 21st century or join with other forces of change that seek to "incarnate the Gospel" into the new social context in which the Church finds itself.[3]

In effect, St. Philip's is composed of five separate and distinct ethnic and cultural congregations within the larger parish, each with its own warden, services, and leaders. The numbers and cultural heritages of its members are as follows: 45 Hispanic, 150 Laotian, 25 African-American, 175 Anglo (Euro-American), 100 Filipino, and 15 other members—Native Americans, Indians, Pacific Islanders.

Each congregation meets for services and activities consistent with its cultural heritage, personal needs, traditions, and tastes. For example, the Lao are organized in home groups, where they sit without shoes (which are left outside on the doorstep) on woven floor mats in a dimly lit room to share a meal, discussion, the Eucharist, and a shared sermon participated in by members of the community. The Bible is older than Berlitz as a language course, and the Lao practice their English skills while learning the Scriptures of their new religion.

In 1973 a ministry among seniors was developed in a retirement community called the Villages nine miles away from the Parish Center. The model of separate congregations but one parish was born as the Villagers created a semi-self-determining congregational lifestyle.

Recently a ministry probe has been initiated to explore with ten Episcopal Indians and Inuits (Eskimo) the possibility of starting an Indian, Inuit, and Native Alaskan ministry. The San

Francisco Bay area has the second largest concentration of American Indians in the country. The natural meeting place for urban Indians is either at a powwow or a basketball or baseball game. The natural strategy, then, is to reach them through picnics and baseball games. A group of Anglicans from Belize have also begun to attend, and there is a possibility of a West Indian ministry presenting itself.

St. Philip's vestry is composed of a senior warden and five junior wardens, each of which is elected by members of his or her congregation.

The various congregations find their focus as a single parish in the All Parish Eucharist, which is held on the first Sunday of each month at the Parish Center. Usually the other Eucharists are canceled for that day, so that everyone is drawn into the one Eucharist. However, seldom does a month go by without another excuse to get together. The usual feasts and festivals of the liturgical calendar are occasions of special celebration. In addition, on approximately two Sundays a month the parish Eucharist is expanded to include a cultural festival commemorating a holiday or significant tradition of one of the cultures present at St. Philip's. These liturgies find their culmination in a fiesta following the service and featuring the cuisine of the particular culture that was highlighted in the liturgy. St. Philip's members have learned a deep and heartfelt appreciation for a variety of cultures, and needless to say, they and their friends eat very well!

Martin Luther King's birthday and death are occasions for liturgies that celebrate African-American tradition. The martyrdom of Oscar Romero, Las Posadas (the night before Christmas), the feast of the Three Kings (Epiphany), and Carnival have special significance for Central American members. The Romero and King services are also used as occasions to remember all martyrs who died for the cause of a more just and loving society. The Lao have a New Year Festival during which members of the congregation—some of them former Buddhist monks—intone the ancient chants of the East.

The "Kirking of the Tartan," the oldest cultural feast day of the parish (18 years), revives an old American colonial custom linking members of Scottish clans to the Highlands. Today the bagpipes sound and a Celtic liturgy is chanted, but members of other cultures are invited to bring pieces of cloth representing their own cultures and traditions to be placed on the altar along with 30 or more clan tartans. There are batiks and prints of Africa, silks of Southeast Asia, ponchos from Latin America, and tapa from the Pacific. The colorful collection is then blessed ("kirked"), and outwardly the congregation is once more linked to the world of their origins.

Icons and symbols present in the Parish Center reinforce the multicultural traditions of members. There is the Santo Niño (Holy Child), an icon important to the Filipino members. The Holy Child also speaks to Anglos and Hispanics. The Virgin of Guadalupe brings together Anglo and Hispanic symbols. The reclining Buddha (the Buddha close to Nirvana) is there along with the Lao candle tree. The use of many of the cross-cultural icons of Robert Lentz (bridge-building icons) enhances the seasonal processions and festival celebrations.

The sanctuary is arranged with seating on four sides to represent the four corners of the world. The Jerusalem altar (with a central stone from Golgotha) at the heart of the sanctuary is a sign of the inclusion of all symbols, cultures, and traditions in Holy Communion—the holy community of every race and culture gathered around the throne of Almighty God.

During the service the eucharistic prayer is recited in English, Spanish, Lao, and Tagalog to further express the reality that although we come from every corner of the globe, from a multitude of human families and tongues, we are all one in the body and blood of Christ.

Irene Hendy, warden of the Hispanic congregation, described St. Philip's as "a beautiful bowl of colors"—a bowl of colors that St. Philip's members have stirred up. The Asian missioner, the Rev. Winifredo (Fred) Vergara, uses another image from his native Philippines, the image of the milkfish in brackish water. The milkfish, according to Father Vergara, grows at the borders of fresh and salty water, in neither fresh water nor salty water, but where the waters converge. He says the Filipinos at St. Philip's are the milkfish, but actually all the cultural groups are both the beautiful bowl of colors stirred up and the milkfish in brackish water. They are people who thrive in the meeting of cultures, who see the diversity of their traditions enhancing both the personal lives of members and the quality of their community life, which spills over into daily life and work.

The clergy mirror the cultural diversity of the congregation. The rector, the Rev. Jerry W. Drino, is also the executive director of Province VIII Coalition for Cross-Cultural Ministry Development (CCMD). He is a Euro-American of Italian descent who first "touched the Divine" as a high school student working on a Ute Indian reservation. Other clergy on the staff include the Hispanic missioner, the Rev. Sylvestre Romero, a Guatemalan who was born in Belize, and the Rev. Fred Vergara from the Philippines and Singapore. A seminarian, Holly Hudson-Louis, is taking an intern year at St. Philip's and is responsible for the Villages, a retirement community for the largely Anglo elderly. Another seminarian, Jan Meikle, is responsible for Christian education. Barbara Somers, an aspirant to the diaconate, has worked closely with the Lao since 1983, helping to develop this ministry.

The Parish Center is located in an attractive but not prosperous neighborhood. It consists of several one-story buildings in a courtyard with attractive flowers and shrubbery. The parish offices are located in one building; another building consists of the sanctuary (the church building proper) with an adjoining meeting room and kitchen. Because of the area's year-round fine weather, the courtyard is used frequently as a meeting and gathering space, with an easy flow between inside and outside. Also located on the property are the Alum Rock Counseling Center, a multilingual, multicultural crisis counseling center for teenagers, established by the parish in 1972 and now operating as a separate corporation so that it can receive county, state, and federal funding. Approximately 4,000 new cases are seen each year. The Mandala Children's House is a Montessori preschool of 150 students from fifteen cultural groups, with half of the children's fees subsidized by the state. It was established in 1973 and, like the counseling center and for the same reasons, is now a separate corporation.

Through preserving the unique cultural identities in the five congregations, through service to the community, through the bonds of unity with one another and oneness as the people of God, celebrated and symbolized by weekly parish Eucharists and festivals, St. Philip's lives a vibrant congregational life. It is also making a difference in the lives of its members and in the community in which it is situated. To Ray Sagon, warden of the Filipino congregation, "St. Philip's promotes friendship. It's like one whole family, whether you are Filipino, black, or white. We *love* being with each other." Gaylord Fischer, the senior warden, is convinced that if the Church is to be faithful in its enrolment it must reflect and mirror the society that it is called to serve.

> I came from a black Episcopal church in Detroit in which I felt comfortable and which gave me the values I have today. When I left Detroit there weren't that many black Episcopal churches and I never felt good in an all-white church. St. Philip's allows me to bridge the gap between what I was and what I am now.[4]

Fischer, a top-level executive in a leading aerophysics corporation, claims that he has been helped in his business by his grounding in St. Philip's multicultural atmosphere. The experience of St. Philip's gives him an understanding of and deep respect for his business peers which he might not otherwise have. He agrees with the sentiment expressed in the television situation comedy "Cheers," "I want to be in a place where everyone knows your name." "St. Philip's is a place where everyone knows my name."[5]

For John LeSchofs, an industrial photographer who is warden of the Euro-American congregation, St. Philip's is a place to start breaking down the barriers. Because of his grounding in the St. Philip's parish family, LeSchofs was able to give several examples of instances in which he and his wife, Sally, were able to counter negative racial and cultural attitudes among their white friends and peers.

Although the members of the congregation claim that the multicultural makeup of St. Philip's is the reason they are there, Father Drino believes that "seldom do they come because they are looking for a multicultural parish. Rather they come to meet personal needs." But having met personal needs, he believes, they stay because they are attracted to the multicultural character of the parish. According to Drino,

> They see the image of the human family as it is emerging in the urban area. They are those who have a sense of the future. Something deep in the soul knows that this is the image God intends.[6]

St. Philip's is a beautiful bowl of colors stirred by the loving hand of God. It is milkfish in brackish water. It feeds and nourishes its members, strengthening them and upholding them in their daily lives and ministries.

# *UNDERSTANDING THE STORY*

The Rev. Jerry Drino has modestly said that in his first eleven years as rector of St. Philip's, very little happened. Of course the Alum Rock Counseling Center and the Mandala Children's House were established during these years, as was the Village congregation, the prototype of a satellite congregation. Nonetheless, Drino maintains that a fairly traditional, ordinary ministry was being carried out.

The congregation had begun in 1957 on the east side of San Jose, and the bishop and founding members had hoped to attract the small but wealthy population that lived in the country club area of the surrounding hills.[7] However, the parish was poorly located to attract its intended members, since the east side of San Jose was, and continues to be, largely inhabited by members of nonwhite cultures. Then came the Civil Rights Movement of the 1960s, which divided the parish.

Into that uncertain environment the present rector was called. He was young. He had only four years of parish ministry under his belt. But he had cut his teeth for a year and a half in South Los Angeles, where, after the Watts riots, he had had some success at getting leaders of rival street gangs to sit down and talk with each other and become one youth group. He had been a seminarian in an all-black parish in Oakland and had worked on three Indian reservations during summer breaks while in college. As an associate priest he had worked to develop an educational opportunities program in California for thirty-six Sioux teenagers from South Dakota. He had organized an ecumenical tutorial program for children of migrant workers while working with youth in a parish in the Diocese of California. Nonetheless, during Drino's first decade very little happened at St. Philip's to indicate what St. Philip's would become.

> The first eleven years were an inner journey for me and the parish. I put a lot of emphasis on adult education and community development. But I was also having to face my own racism, especially against my own cultural group. I was having to face my own need to control. I looked back at my life since Utah in 1958 and all the experiences among Indians and blacks, Pacific Islanders and Hispanics and wondered where this was going to lead. I was

fed up with trying to move the parish to see that what they had touched inwardly had to have some social manifestation. When the Lao arrived in 1982 I was [he now admits] fed up and ready to move. I was just fed up![8]

Thus the arrival of the Lao marked the first turning point in the process that would ultimately make St. Philip's the multiracial, multicultural congregation it is today. Barbara Somers, a laywoman who has been instrumental in the development of ministry among the Lao, explains it this way:

> Everything and nothing in my life prepared me to enter "cross-cultural ministry." All I know is that I was called upon to prepare the Laotians for baptism and [deal with] any problems which they had, and there they were sitting with the rector in his office.
>
> I had no choice but to respond. St. Philip's had no choice. The Lao were here, wanting to know more about God, about Christianity, about American religion and about baptism. The Episcopal Church had produced no educational materials in Lao, even though it had been very active, nationally and locally, in the resettlement of Southeast Asian refugees following the conflict in Vietnam. I listened to the stories of their lives, their escapes, their suffering in the camps in Thailand, their eventual resettlement in California. Much of our time was spent trying to understand one another, working on pronunciation, explaining the complexities of the English language . . . . Bounnam, Chanpheng and Souphat were learning very fast. As time went on, the level of trust increased and their ability to share their stories at a deeper level put me in touch with a world of small villages, war, constant upheaval, pain and a persistent joy for life accompanied by a deep knowing of what family and community can be at its deepest level.
>
> Another turning point came a year and a half after beginning the class. The Lao wanted

to use St. Philip's facilities for a Lao New Year Celebration. They asked that we invite a few people from the parish, and when we arrived, we discovered not just the Lao we knew, but many we had not seen before, including some from the Lao Association. WE WERE NOT IN CONTROL. For many, that was a strange and revealing feeling. We, the "old timers" of the parish, had nothing to do with the planning, preparation and execution of an event! Many of the Lao who were present expressed an affection for our Church because we were open to their cultural celebrations. Some asked whether they could attend services. Our numbers suddenly increased significantly![9]

Soon the Diocese of El Camino Real declared itself solidly behind St. Philip's and other emerging cross-cultural ministries and wished to encourage the development of even more cross-cultural ministries in the diocese. The 1985 evaluation includes an imperative to "pursue ministry among the culturally diverse population of the Diocese and to become ethnically representative of the total population."[10]

So the Lao had settled into St. Philip's. Being sensitive to their needs, serving them, and helping them in innumerable practical ways was involving most of the members of the congregation. Euro-Americans, African-Americans, and a few Hispanics continued to participate in parish life as always. But it was the Euro-Americans who held control and made the important decisions in the parish. All the others more or less had to fall in with choices that were being made for them by what was more and more a white minority. Such control kept St. Philip's—despite its changing color—in effect an Anglo parish.

At this point the rector took a rather unusual and risky step. The main Sunday service began just like every other, except that on the particular Sunday in question, the rector stopped the action and explained that he could no longer defend the right of the "English congregation" to maintain a monocultural structure in a setting that was clearly multicultural. To be faithful to the reality apparent in every pew, the old would "have to give way to the new." Starting "right now" members of the congregation would meet in their separate culture groups. It was as abrupt as that. Somewhat stunned, no doubt, members the congregation filed out of the sanctuary right then and there and went to different rooms for the Liturgy of the Word and a "shared reflective sermon." They returned to be reconciled at the passing of the peace. For the next three months the pattern of the culture groups meeting by themselves continued to evolve.

In 1987, the Rev. Sylvestre Romero, a priest from Guatemala, arrived, bringing twenty-four Hispanic people with him, significantly increasing that part of the congregation. He is quoted as saying,

> You see, I was born in Belize, and worked in Guatemala, and just look at my features! People confuse me with someone from the Philippines, or from China, or . . . what? So I really think I fit in well because of my background. Roy, Bayardo and their families [black-Hispanics]—we are in a dialogue in three different languages, Spanish, English and Creole. My mother worked for a Chinese person in Belize for sixteen years, so just being there as a kid . . . and being at St. Philip's does bring back a lot. But other than that, what has attracted me most has been the liturgy. It is not the same Sunday after Sunday. The liturgy helps us go back to our traditions. Just to fix up the Guadelupe altar, and celebrate that feast day is so meaningful to us, and the Episcopal Church has ignored the festival in Latin America. Doing it here in San Jose reminds us that we depend upon God for a lot of things. We need to do these things together to bring unity.[11]

At that point Sandra Bright, executive director of the Coalition for Cross-Cultural Ministry Development (Province VIII), and Val Hillsdon-Hutton, the provincial evangelism officer, met with parish members to help them develop the structure and organization of ministry that is essentially what is described in this account.

In 1988 the Rev. Winifredo Vergara, a priest on loan from the Philippine Independent Church, joined the staff to serve as Asian missioner. Father Vergara's past—from the age of thirteen, when he ran away from his island home as a stowaway to

Manila, where he lived and roamed the streets for three months as a street urchin—could fill a book. A thriller at that! In himself he carries a diversity of cultures and experiences that includes working on the World Council of Churches' Commission on Dialogue with People of Other Faiths and Cultures. His presence at St. Philip's is a sign that the Church takes very seriously the lives of some 75,000 Filipinos who make their home in the Santa Clara Valley. But people of all Asian culture groups are of special concern to Father Vergara, and in that connection he edits a newsletter called *Bamboo Church: Asian Ministry in Santa Clara County*. However, like Fathers Drino and Romero, Father Vergara enjoys working with all culture groups.

    The change from a monocultural to a multicultural parish has naturally been the most difficult for the English-speaking members. Perhaps they have not had to endure the upheavals of migration; but they have nonetheless witnessed enormous disruption of their social and cultural contexts, both in the Church and in society. And some of them quit the Church. However, in order to make way for the new, some of the old ways, especially the inclinations of the old guard to hold the reins of control, had to give way so that the new thing God was doing in the midst of St. Philip's could emerge. For those who have stayed it has been nothing short of a conversion of attitude, since it is never easy to willingly give up what one once took for granted. The English-speaking members have quite literally had to stand by and let the congregation as they had known it from the beginning die. Acknowledging the process these members were going through, Father Drino used the process of dying and grief, as documented by Dr. Elisabeth Kübler-Ross in her work with patients who were actually, physically dying. Father Drino is quoted as saying,

> The principles of facing death and dying apply to all aspects of our life. It is God who leads us into death for the sake of transformation and the sharing of the final stage, rebirth. He wants us to share in the fullness of his joy and new creation. But the decisions are ours. The choices are ours. He only brings us death. It is up to us what we do with it.
> 
>     God has given us great opportunities to find a living birth through the challenges of liv-

ing in a multi-cultural parish. This cannot happen to you unless you make choices to be committed to the process that leads to rebirth through the necessary grief work, which includes recognition of denial, anger, depression, that leads us to acceptance as the threshold to rebirth.[12]

To the English-speaking members, Jesus' words, "Whoever would save his life will lose it; and whoever loses his life for my sake, will save it" (Luke 9:24), spoke to their situation. Indeed, those who have stayed have been given back their life more gloriously than they could possibly have imagined. Indeed, one of the Euro-American members commented to site visitor Nancy Axell, "Here I learn more about myself, and some things lose their importance by knowing others' perspectives."[13] And their numbers have grown.

In February, 1989, St. Philip's vestry wrote a mission statement. In a phrase it summarized their work over the previous six years as well as the way they see themselves now.

> The mission of St. Philip's is to present the basic teachings of Jesus and to encourage persons to see themselves as pilgrims seeking to do and to know the will of God and to enter into communities of acceptance and care committed to serving God in the needs of the world.

St. Philip's is an evolving story of God becoming incarnate in new forms. In Father Drino's words, "We are co-creators of new religious forms. In the process our understanding of God is expanded. We are laying foundations for an unknown future."[14]

## *DISTINCTIVE FEATURES*

There are a number of factors that come together to make St. Philip's a highly effective one-parish multicultural example of ministry:

- ***Contextual Theology:*** Theologically, one visiting St. Philip's feels as if he or she is stepping into both a Roland Allen laboratory and a Latin American ecclesial base community. Roland Allen's ideas about indigenous ministry are there, along with the social analysis characteristic of liberation theologies.

Roland Allen, the British missionary writer, saw in China in the early days of this century that what was being presented to the Chinese people was not only a faith but English culture as well. Since Jesus Christ was and is for all cultures, faith in Jesus Christ must be transmitted through the forms and symbols of particular cultures. At St. Philip's one is constantly faced with such questions as "What is the nature of our faith?" "What is the essence of Christianity?" "What is essentially Anglican?" But at St. Philip's the faith is being indigenized through the forms of *a variety of cultural traditions,* and thus it goes beyond the forms Roland Allen envisioned. But faith is not only being indigenized, it is being synthesized as it is blended through the many cultures included in the one fellowship.

Contextual liberation theology comes to mind also. In liberation theology, particularly Latin American liberation theology, there is a key element of social analysis in which the context of ministry is examined and the Gospel applied in that context. St. Philip's members have examined the sociology of their multicultural location in the heart of Santa Clara County and are responding accordingly.

While these strands of theology and ministry are very obvious to those who care to notice, the members of the congregation talk about God and culture and serving Christ in each other, without ever bothering with theological labels or imagining that they are "doing theology." But they are, and in the course of it contributing to a vibrant dynamic that can be readily felt by even the most casual visitor to St. Philip's.

- ***Preservation of Cultural Traditions:*** The pattern of meeting in cultural groups has benefits in terms of preserving cultural traditions and meeting personal needs.

    In small groups, individuals know and are known to each other. Trust develops among members who help each other out in material as well as spiritual ways. The people are "there for each other," as the saying goes, just like family.

    At the same time cultural traditions are preserved. In the small culture groups, members can relate to each other in the forms with which they are comfortable. They do not have to translate either language or modes of expression.

- ***Lively Liturgy:*** The liturgies are so varied that they are rarely boring and can do what all good liturgy ought to. They express the connections between ordinary life and worship while they allow particular cultural expressions of the faith to flow through them.

- **Articulate Laity:** Although the laity are no better or worse educated than any other Episcopalians, they are very articulate about the faith. One gets the impression that they have learned how to talk about their faith by practicing it and by taking considerable responsibility in exercising it both within the congregation and without.

    A case in point: one of the Lao children was tragically drowned. Beside themselves with grief and shock, the family called Barbara Somers. Barbara was their friend. She had taught them English and helped them out in practical ways. Barbara and her husband, Dick went right over to the house, helped the family with the undertaker and the legal processes, and took a large part in planning the funeral.

- **Well-Matched Clergy:** With the exception of the lack of an African-American priest, the cultural makeup of the congregation's clergy mirrors the cultural makeup of the congregation. But more than that, all three priests are well suited to this congregation by their personal backgrounds and experience as well as by their personalities and personal sense of security. They are people very secure in their personal identities, who appreciate their own cultures as well as the diversity of cultures. They obviously thrive in the bowl of colors that is St. Philip's. It is important to members of the congregation that their clergy are racially and culturally just like them. Unfortunately the Episcopal Church has a severe shortage of African-American, Hispanic, and Asian clergy. As the United States becomes a technicolor, multicultural society, this raises the issue for the Episcopal Church of whom it needs as its ordained leaders, how they are recruited, and how they are trained.

- **Bending Anglican Traditions:** St. Philip's members exhibit a willingness to bend Anglican traditions to do what makes sense. If Scripture, tradition, reason, and experience are the heart of the Anglican ethos, only Scripture is a common cultural link. The challenge is how to enter into dialogue with the tradition, reason, and experience of the various cultural groups. For example, at the Great Vigil of Easter, instead of reading the assigned text of Hebrew Scripture from Genesis, etc., creation myths from various cultures of the parish are retold in the circle around the Jerusalem altar. It is not unusual for twelve or more myths to be retold by candlelight, recalling the movement of God throughout the world from the beginning of human memory.

Another example, in the simplest of terms, is the very important issue of financial support of the Church. Each congregation begins with their own tradition. Western stewardship is a long way off for the Filipino, who will sponsor special fund-raising events, such as bingo, while getting used to offering envelopes. The "money tree" of the Lao gives them a tie to their temple traditions while they are exposed to a Biblical sense of stewardship.

Both Asian congregations have huge extended families, and they want them all involved in important family occasions. Thus one Lao baby was baptized recently with twenty-four godparents! The Hispanics celebrate quinceañeras (fifteenth birthday's for girls). Both African-Americans and Euro-Americans are breaking out of their former homogenized understanding of the Episcopal Church to expand Anglican tradition by developing special feast days that reclaim aspects of their cultural heritage.

- ***Sensitive Handling of the European-Americans' Feelings of Loss:*** The realistic confrontation of the issues of the English-speaking members and helping them through their grief.
- ***A Sense of Fun, Good Times, and Community:*** In our Eucharistic Prayer C we say, "Risen Lord, be known to us in the breaking of the Bread." At St. Philip's the Lord is indeed known through the breaking of bread, both at the liturgies and afterwards. Cultural festival liturgies are usually followed by parties and fiestas, so that the liturgies continue over the dinner tables. These regular occasions build community and strengthen links across the cultures. They contribute to making St. Philip's a happy church in which everyone has a good time.
- ***The Welcome and Incorporation of Visitors:*** Visitors are easily incorporated into the fellowship. At the start of each Sunday's parish Eucharist, first-time visitors are introduced and given a Hawaiian shell lei, an aloha greeting, and a kiss. From that moment on they are neither strangers nor outsiders.
- ***Outside Assistance:*** The congregation has gotten outside help when it has been needed. For example, staff from what is now

the Coalition for Cross-Cultural Ministry Development were invited in to work with parish leaders in creating the necessary structures for multicultural ministry. And when the extent of Lao needs became apparent, St. Philip's called upon the diocese for help. Thus in 1985 ministry with the Lao moved towards being a diocesan ministry. In the following year the Hispanic ministry moved in that direction. In the course of obtaining assistance, St. Philip's was able to help the diocese understand that part of its mission is to support the people and ministry in their particular locations.

## THE DOWNSIDE

St. Philip's experience has not been without its difficulties as well. Among them are the following:

- *Few Models and Mentors:* Father Drino has commented that "the risk of being a trail-blazer is that you have no one ahead of you to learn from." There is now a printed resource available (see the resource section at the end of the chapter), developed in part from this ministry, but when St. Philip's got started there was virtually no other parish with the experience of doing this type of ministry to which they could turn for help.
- *Finances:* Finances are a continuing problem for St. Philip's. The non-Euro-American culture groups do not have traditions of financial stewardship (pledges, tithing, etc.), and in addition, many of the newer immigrants are very poor and just barely managing financially. St. Philip's has had to seek outside financial help, because on its own it could not support its ministry. Demographics, and the fact that the number of Anglo members will continue to decline as these congregations change, raise the issue of diocesan financial priorities—and even national Church priorities—and how this and similar ministries will be supported as they develop. There are also issues of financial dependency: how are congregations such as St. Philip's going to educate their own members for stewardship?
- *Complexity:* A multicultural ministry is a complex operation. Father Vergara has said, "If you can't stand the mess, don't try it." And Father Drino adds:

> When you have two cultures with their own sets of meanings and ways of doing things, you have

built-in stress. When you have five cultures, not to speak of two and three generations, you have a real challenge on your hands. But if the Church is to be a laboratory in which the conditions of the world have an opportunity to be worked out, then the sixty-three different cultures that make up the East Side of San Jose are only being touched lightly by St. Philip's. A central question is whether the sacrifice of a mono-cultural, self-contained congregation to maintain a single parish, even with multiple congregations, is worth the energy and time given over to communications and planning.

It is one thing to affirm the canticle that God has called us from many nations, tongues, and peoples to be a royal priesthood; but it is quite another thing to really try to make it work on a day-to-day basis.[15]

## RESOURCES

Coalition for Cross-Cultural Ministry Development (CCMD). *Cross-Cultural Ministry: A Developing Resource.* San Francisco: CCMD, 1989. Write to the CCMD Office, 399 San Fernando Way, San Francisco, CA 94127.

Elizondo, Virgil. *The Future Is Mestizo: Life Where Cultures Meet.* Bloomington, IN: Meyer-Stone Books, 1988.

## NOTES

[1] William A. Henry III, "Beyond the Melting Pot," *Time,* Vol. 135, April 9, 1990, pp. 30-31.
[2] Bob Ingle, *San Jose Mercury News,* "Not a Simple Majority," October 8, 1987.
[3] Jerry W. Drino, "Proposal for a Jubilee Ministry Partnership 1990—Diocese of El Camino Real," p. 2.
[4] Gaylord Fischer, interview in San Jose, April 1, 1990.
[5] *Ibid.*
[6] Jerry Drino, interview in San Jose, April 1, 1990.
[7] *Ibid.*
[8] *Ibid.*

[9] Barbara Somers, quoted in *Cross-Cultural Ministry* (San Francisco: The Coalition for Cross-Cultural Ministry Development, 1989), p. 48.

[10] Jerry W. Drino, "Proposal for a Jubilee . . . Partnership," p. 3.

[11] Sylvestre Romero, quoted in *Cross-Cultural Ministry*, p. 50.

[12] Jerry W. Drino, quoted in *Loaves and Fishes*, St. Philip's parish newsletter, November, 1987, pp. 2-6.

[13] A parish member as reported to Nancy Axell, Site Visitor Report.

[14] Jerry Drino, interview in San Jose, April 1, 1990.

[15] Jerry Drino, correspondence to Anne Rowthorn, August 23, 1990.

*Visiting Team:* Nancy Axell and Val Hillsdon-Hutton
*Date of Visit:* March 30-April 1, 1990

*Behold,
I make
all things new.*
—Revelation 21:5

---------- CHAPTER 2 ----------

# PEOPLE EMBODY THE MESSAGE
## STORY OF A PROGRAM-SIZED MINISTRY IN THE WORLD
### SAINT GEORGE'S CHURCH
### FREDERICKSBURG, VIRGINIA

## *THE CONTEXT OF MISSION DISCERMENT: FREDERICKSBURG, VIRGINIA*

Fredericksburg, Virginia, has been rated the best small city in the East and the third best in its size category in the nation in terms of climate, economics, education, sophistication, transportation, and housing.[1]

Fredericksburg has a history that goes back almost three hundred years. It was founded and given its present name in 1728, but settlers had built a fort there as early as 1676. The name *Fredericksburg* honors Prince Frederick, the father of England's King George III. Its location on the Rappahannock River led to the city's becoming a prosperous port.

Fredericksburg was George Washington's boyhood home. James Monroe, who practiced law in Fredericksburg, was a vestry member of St. George's. Thomas Jefferson wrote what eventually became the Virginia Statute of Religious Liberty in Fredericksburg—a document that later became the basis for the First Amendment of the United States Constitution.

The history of Fredericksburg has sometimes been violent. Between 1861 and 1865 Fredericksburg was an armed camp, and there were more Civil War deaths in Fredericksburg than anywhere else in the United States.

The old city area is packed with historic red brick buildings, some of them—like St. George's—built around a cobblestoned market square. Historic houses and quiet, tree-shaded neighborhoods lead off from the square. Fredericksburg is the natural center of four Virginia counties and the center of the counties' planning district. Although it has a population of only 21,000, Fredericksburg is the fastest-growing area in the state of Virginia. The consequences of this growth are the most important issues now facing the city. The local paper's five-part series on Fredericksburg began its lead article dealing with growth thus:

> Few issues have been as important to the Fredericksburg area in the last twenty years as growth. Within a generation, the area's population has doubled, transforming the largely rural landscape into a suburban mix of houses and shopping centers.[2]

Fredericksburg's location on Interstate 95, about an hour and a half from Washington, is an important factor in its growth. One in four workers commutes to the nation's capital every day. A recent study of the area noted that economics is pushing the workers farther and farther from their jobs:

> For the most part, they're not moving here to be closer to their jobs or to get away from them. They simply can't afford anything else.[3]

But there are many who do not commute to Washington. There are two hundred major employers in the Fredericksburg area today. The old-time occupations of logging, milling, fishing, farming, and mining are being joined by service industries. Computer-related firms are on the rise, and there are a number of defense-related industries (those dealing in lasers, artificial intelligence, and "Star Wars" technology). The Army, Navy, and Marine Corps maintain three major military installations close to Fredericksburg, the best known of which is the Quantico Marine Corps Base. These military sites employ thousands of area residents.

The city is governed by a mayor, who is one of the seven members of the city council. The council is said to be the longest-running form of municipal government in Virginia. The mayor, who is also pastor of Shiloh Baptist Church, was Fredericksburg's first African-American elected to the city council (1966). He has been mayor since 1976. Two members of the city council are parishioners of St. George's, Bill Greenup and Robert Wheeler.

## SAINT GEORGE'S TODAY, WHERE PEOPLE EMBODY THE MESSAGE

St. George's is a historic parish located at the Market Square in the old center of Fredericksburg, with a booming congregation. Over thirty people were recently baptized, confirmed, and received. In the past year the parish has experienced a 10-percent increase in membership and a 42-percent increase in pledged income. Currently the parish has 637 members in good standing, representing 587 households.

The parish has its roots in a settlement that goes back to 1714, when a reformed congregation was established to serve the German settlers. The Anglican Church of St. George's was established in 1721, and the present structure dates from 1849. It contains three original Tiffany windows.

The congregation has a long tradition of service in Fredericksburg. In the colonial period the vestry, by law, had responsibility for the welfare of orphans, widows, the sick, and the needy. Even after the Anglican Church's civil authority was dissolved following the American Revolution, the parish continued to take care of the poor. The church served as a military hospital during one of the Civil War battles. In this century, the parish provided a recreation room for servicemen who were located in the area during the World War II period.

The tradition of service to and in the city of Fredericksburg continues. In 1985, members of the congregation noticed an increase in the number of homeless people in the vicinity. The church's response began in an unexpected and dramatic way. As Fritz Leedy, a local realtor, tells it,

> We arrived at the church on a miserably cold Tuesday morning at 7:00 for our Brotherhood of St. Andrew's Bible study. There we found Roger, crouched in the doorway. So we said, "Let's invite him in," and we gave him a doughnut and sat with him while he got warm. He seemed an educated and literary fellow and he set off in us an interest in his situation. He told us about the problems of homelessness and those who sleep under the Falmouth Bridge.[4]

This incident sparked the initiation of an area-wide group, the Rappahannock Refuge, which one year later opened Hope House, a shelter large enough for twelve people. Later a small building on the property was renovated to provide space for another twelve. When *The Virginia Episcopalian* reported the project, it titled the story "Strangers and Angels," since "an angel aware or unaware" had motivated the brotherhood members to act. The shelter initiative begun by the church has helped raise the congregation's awareness of other housing needs. Various parish members are now working to provide affordable housing in the community with public funds and through Habitat for Humanity. Tim Melton, a newly baptized member of the congregation, works with the Central Virginia Housing Coalition. Tim had no previous church background at all but was attracted to St. George's because he saw what the congregation was doing in the community. Recently he organized a "housing summit" that included everyone involved in housing—realtors, members of the Home Builders Association, the Chamber of Commerce. After many years of activism without the benefits of Baptism, he was asked what difference his Baptism made and why he felt he needed it. Melton responded:

> I had been very confrontational. I began to think that maybe there was a part of the whole equation that I was missing out on. I began to feel a more spiritual calling. I felt a calling to understand Christ as my Savior. Now my prayers are more meaningful. My work is done with more overall

love, love that is carried over into my work even more.[5]

For Tim, "It is people who embody the message of Jesus Christ."

Chip Willis, a lifelong Episcopalian and chair of the church's Service Commission, now admits that he first came to St. George's because of the Tiffany windows, but he stayed because,

> There is room here for me to make a difference. This place calls forth talent and you don't have to earn it through longevity. Here they're looking for talent.[6]

Chip has been building Section 8 (low-income) housing and is a member of the Virginia Housing Development Authority as well as the Home Builders Association. He has worked to get Habitat for Humanity started in Fredericksburg and has been successful in establishing a housing trust fund, which helps those in need with rent deposits. Chip took it as a compliment that one of his associates said he was "one of the nicest Republicans I've ever met." Why does Willis do it?

> It's important to give something back to the community. It's important to help other people make it themselves.[7]

Linda Grigsby, former director of Hope House, the shelter for the homeless, like Tim Melton, came to St. George's because of its members' commitment to improving the community and serving those who need help.

According to Janet King, chair of the Pastoral Care Commission, St. George's has always been a caring parish. "From the early days we had trust funds to provide fuel, shoes for orphans, and money for widows."[8] One way or another, as Chip Willis said,

> St. George's has been able to bring together under a common roof many divergent people and opinions, from Tim Melton, one of the guys who "works in the trenches," to the "Ducks Unlimited crowd" [that is, the socially elite].[9]

St. George's is a congregation that helps people make the links between their work and their faith. Take, for example, the case of Edward Jones, the managing editor of *The Free Lance-Star*, Fredericksburg's daily newspaper. Jones had been editorial page editor for ten years, responsible for writing ten editorials a week and handling the 1,600 letters to the editor that arrived on his desk every year. Still on the young side of his middle years and still on the paper's editorial board, Jones feels that the Church supports him in his public role. Jones thinks that most people consider those in the newspaper business secular, cynical, thick-skinned, hard-nosed. They *are* people who have to get a story fast:

> A newspaper is not a magazine; it's not a book. We don't have the time for polished editorials. We are governed by the clock and the nightmare of a blank space.
>
> For the first couple of years it was hard. You see [Jones explains], this paper is "left of center" in a city which is "right of center." So I used to get a flood of angry people calling at home and the office. There are three Joneses in town. I'm the first one listed in the phone book so I got all the calls. I had to deal with people who were overly defensive, and it was hard.
>
> I feel I have learned to deal with people in a compassionate way. I've learned an appreciation for people who feel passion for an issue. An editorial writer is trying to be an instant expert in a thousand topics. He or she doesn't have the luxury of time. It's fear that drives you, fear that gets you going. It's the clock that moves the adrenaline.
>
> In my writing I tried to be sharp and pointed. What an editorial writer wants, at all costs, is to avoid saying "... on the other hand." It loses the power of the point. The art is to develop a style of making a strong point yet suggesting a tolerance of other points of view.[10]

Jones feels that his involvement at St. George's has helped him develop a feeling of compassion for those who hold opposing opinions, and he believes he's learned to be fair in presenting a diversity of opinions. He has a deep understanding of the place of the newspaper in the community and the responsibilities that go with it.

Linda Grigsby, like Ed Jones, is encouraged by the Church to make the important connections in her life:

> Charles' [Sydnor, the rector] preaching connects with me. He addresses reality. He relates to what you're doing in your own life through his teaching and preaching.[11]

Catherine Hicks, the chair of the Christian Education Commission, agrees:

> The sermons are always thought-provoking. Entering into them you can't remain in the same place. You take that empowerment and use it.[12]

She continued, "In this very old place, I've become new."[13]

Does this commentary suggest a parish that just three years ago was plagued with low morale, one that was divided and polarized between the "traditionals" and the newer members? A parish that was not attracting new members? A parish and rector that were at odds with each other?

On one side were the members who felt that,

> The dignity and the reverence of the traditional 11:00 service have been lost, with the emphasis geared to young families with accompanying children. We have been subjected to slang, asides, guitars, children clomping up and down the aisles and organ music approaching the level of pain. The decline of dignity and reverence in our services is upsetting . . . . [The approach] to our Sunday services is steadily becoming more unpleasant, causing increasing dissatisfaction among older members—those whose families have worshiped at St. George's for generations . . . .

On the other side were those, mostly young, many from other areas of the nation, who felt that the old-time Fredericksburg Episcopalians were too rigid and were unwilling to budge on anything:

> If the liturgy is not Rite I or Morning Prayer, they are unwilling to accept it. *Any change* seems to be met with hostility. This group uses backroom in-

timidation to get their way . . . . New ideas in worship such as liturgical dance, guitars, folk music and drama are always accompanied by cries of anguish the next week. Several times in church meetings, children have been spoken of as an annoyance . . . . The Shakers learned the hard way that a church must have children in order to survive!

In effect, what they had at St. George's was two churches—one left over from the previous rector, who had been there for thirty years and still resides in the area, and the one composed of people who came into the parish since the arrival of Charles Sydnor as rector in 1976. That the authors of the two opposing statements are still members of the congregation shows that something of a miracle has occurred at St. George's.

## UNDERSTANDING THE STORY

When Robert Baker, a retired reporter and editor for the *Washington Post* and *The Free Lance-Star*, joined St. George's in 1976, the parish was "a traditional old Fredericksburg church. Old families gave the money and they called the tune."[14]

It was, however, becoming harder and harder for the old families. They had lived through the changes of the Civil Rights era, their beloved city was being inundated by new residents, many of them young and bright, who were not content to fit in and conform to the established ways of old Virginia families.

Nor was the change confined to the city of Fredericksburg. Change had also intruded into the Church in the form of a new Prayer Book, more Eucharists, fewer services of Morning Prayer, a new hymnal, and guitars to accompany unfamiliar hymns. This group was feeling embattled and even embittered, since all the structures and assumptions of their lives were changing. The ground beneath them was shifting both in the world around them and in the Church. In the words of the Rev. Charles Sydnor, the rector, "We had people in pain. People felt left out, unlistened to, unheard, not part of the action."[15]

Two and a half years ago, forty-eight of the members wrote a letter to the rector citing a long litany of complaints. They noted the tide of overwhelming change—Prayer Book, hymnal, new people in Fredericksburg, new people in church—and they invited the rector and the vestry to a meeting. They were asked merely to listen, neither to argue, defend, or rebut any of the criticisms. Fortunately, Sydnor agreed to the meeting and, odd though it may seem, it became the first step in the transformation of St. George's. The "Gang of 48" brought the issues to a head, and the congregation has not been the same since.

Many meetings followed in which issues were brought to further focus and clarification. Particularly significant was a vestry retreat led by the Rev. Robert Hansel, director of program for the Roslyn Center in the Diocese of Virginia. Hansel acknowledges that both the rector and the vestry members were in a state of low morale. But what they discovered, according to Hansel, was

> ... a way to work together as a team—ordained and lay—as partners in every aspect of ministry. It isn't "Father, you take care of the spiritual side." It's that division that spells death in the Church.[16]

Vestry members and the rector began to "recognize the spiritual dimension in practical matters, and the practical dimension in spiritual matters."[17] Hansel explains:

> At the retreat they discovered a structure by which the leadership and involvement and participation could be broadened. That is the key to all parish renewal and vitality. People need to have a sense of ownership and accountability.[18]

With his help, the parish shifted to a system of commissions—Service; Capital Planning and Historic Preservation; Worship and Music; Education; Evangelism, Faith and Friendship; Pastoral Care; and Stewardship. Each commission has a chair, who is not a vestry member, and each has a liaison, who is a part of both the vestry and the particular commission. This commission system vastly increased the numbers of persons who share leadership in the congregation—to about one hundred. Each commission now sets yearly goals along with the vestry.

This opening up of the parish's leadership has released energies and identified a wealth of new talent. There are opportunities for involvement that are on a small enough scale to yield practical results as well as personal satisfaction. These "chewable bites," as Hansel calls them, allow the busy Washington commuters to participate in the life and structure of the congregation without feeling overburdened. It also affords scope to those members who have more time to take "bigger bites."

"We're still in for some growing pains. It's not quite as comfortable for some as it was before," according to John Pearce, the registrar (i.e., clerk) of the parish. But, according to Robert Hansel, "The turn-around has been nothing short of dramatic."[19]

In retrospect, there was much good that had been occurring in the parish even before the blowup precipitated by the "Gang of 48" and the restructuring of the parish. It had its long tradition of service to the community. It had been the first white church in the area to become integrated. In the 1980s alone, the parish initiated a shelter for the homeless and a hospice. There has been an active Education for Mission (EFM) group for eight years. EFM is an intensive four-year course for the laity in the Bible, theology, and church history. There is the tradition of excellent music and church school programs. The difference, according to David Adams, the district health administrator and senior warden, is that " . . . there is now a spiritual quality of relationships."

And what do members of the congregation look forward to in the future?

The rector would like members of the congregation to continue to identify and attempt to address the needs in the community that remain unmet.

> Let's look at the needs that are not getting attended to, get it [projects, services, etc.] going, and let it go. The parishioners will get involved as they are so inclined.[20]

Among the unmet needs he is particularly concerned about are those of teenagers. As the city of Fredericksburg's representative on the youth commission of the area planning district, he would like to see the parish address the needs of young people who are at loose ends, with no place to hang out after school and in the evenings. He would like to start a teen center that would be a gathering place for parties, pool and other games, and the like, but also offer counseling services.

David Adams points out that "we're the fastest-growing area of the state and St. George's is right at the center of the growth." Because of this, he would like the parish to make the most of its geographical position. "We're primed. We're getting set to grow."

## DISTINCTIVE FEATURES

Undoubtedly the most important factor in the changes of the past decade is the restructuring of the parish. The issues that came to a head in the confrontation with the disaffected members, and the constructive manner in which they were handled, produced a change, after which everything else seemed to fall into place.

Within the circle of harmony thus created, many things have contributed to St. George's success:

- **Central Location and Public Role:** This church is situated in a central and visible location in the community, and its members see the congregation as taking a public role in the community. The congregation takes full advantage of its place. As John Pearce explains,

> The building is the focus of lots of other interests in the community and our plain physical location at the center of the old town means that we are unavoidably part of almost anything that is going on here, and this is a plus.[21]

And Charles Sydnor continues,

> It's nice to "own" that role. In June, three successive chamber music series with nationally known artists will be held here—partly because the acoustics are magnificent and partly because the church is in the center of town. These events bring people downtown who otherwise might not come. I sometimes grow sick of "Tiffany window, Tiffany window," but these windows and these concerts bring folks in.[22]

- **Service in the Community:** The Church discerns the real needs of the community and marshals the broad-based support to meet those needs, drawing in others who may not be members but who nonethless share a desire to help. That this public role has brought in members is evidenced by Tim Melton and Linda Grigsby, who came to the parish through community housing projects.

- **News, Not Publicity:** The activities of the church are frequently in the news, not because of publicity (paid advertisements and the like) but rather in reports of humanitarian services and projects that get started at St. George's. Edward Jones, *The Free Lance-Star* editor, says,

> I have an interesting problem in terms of telling our story to the community. It's a sort of conflict because, as managing editor, I have to almost bend over backward to make sure we're not giving our church favored treatment. But the church just keeps making the news all the time.[23]

Because it is constantly in the local newspaper, many people know about St. George's, and it is thus a natural place for the general public to turn when they need or want a church,

- ***Saint George's Is a Place Where People Embody the Message:*** The congregation is a family in which members are free to be themselves, where members give and receive from each other and enjoy each other's company. The rector is a giver and receiver of ministry, but all the ministry of the congregation does not revolve around him. As John Pearce explains:

> Before I came here I had been going to a church in Washington where the rector is wonderful, but there my relationship to the Church was largely through the wonderful rector and a wonderful assistant. Here it's through a wonderful rector but it is *also* through this larger circle.[24]

Participation in the life of this congregation frees people to know each other, to serve Christ in each other, and to talk about their experiences of faith. Bob Baker talked about himself:

> For myself, for a long time I was a "closet Christian." I attended church as an escort. First I escorted my mother when I was a child, then I

> escorted my wife. Then I covered Civil Rights for the *Washington Post*. I was there when "Ol' Miss" [i.e. the University of Mississippi, a center in the Civil Rights struggle] blew up. I was in Birmingham. I was at Dynamite Hill. I was there when the Sunday school kids were blown up right there in the church.
>
> I covered the story of the guy who had just returned from Vietnam who was shot and killed the same day as the Sunday school kids. I attended his funeral at Good Hope Baptist Church. Everyone there was black except me. During the service the young man's mother got up and screamed, "O God, why do they hate us so?"[25]

Bob wondered too. Why is there such violent hate? These experiences, culminating at the funeral at the black Baptist church, brought Christianity alive for him. It has also inspired his work, both in the Church and in the community, for the elimination of racism.

David Adams appreciates the Church's role as family. He acknowledges that ours is not an age of extended families. We no longer live within easy reach of parents and siblings, aunts and uncles, cousins and grandmothers—all those who formed a natural support system.

> Here you have the need both to support people and to be supported. We have something here that society lacks. That is an extended support group. There are people in the Church that I would not hesitate to call on for 'most anything, and I have called on them. And I'm sure they feel the same way about me.[26]

Edward Jones believes that,

> ... the kinds of relationships built here help us go out and do things in the community more responsibly. Here we see the many different facets of the same issues and people. We have mission projects. We have our work. We have the educational opportunities to help us reflect upon the spirituality of it all.

You also have Episcopalians for Fun! Sure, Episcopalians for Fun! We do some wine-tasting, and that's yet another different facet. You put this all together, and it adds up to a full-blooded connection you have with people, and because of it I think it's a lot easier to relate to people outside the parish too.

It's like I know this guy; he's in a Sunday school class with me. I know this guy; I work with him at the shelter. I know this guy; I work with him at the paper. I've tasted some wine with him. I know him well.[27]

- ***Professional Consultation:*** Three years ago, members of the parish recognized that the old ways were no longer working. They were not too proud to face the facts. They realized that there had been many changes in both the Church and the city of Fredericksburg—changes that they needed to understand and take into account as they charted the future course of the parish's ministry. They were then wise enough to obtain the services of a professional consultant, the Rev. Robert Hansel, who at the time was director of program for the Diocese of Virginia. Hansel assisted both the rector and the vestry members to discern the issues and make appropriate changes.
- ***Shared Leadership Responsibilities:*** With the restructuring of the parish and the shift to a system of commissions, leadership became more widely shared. Many more members now have made a personal investment in the ministry and have a stake in the future of St. George's.
- ***A Sense of Balance:*** The Rev. Abigail Hamilton, a member of the visiting team from the Diocese of Newark, noted the following:

> I am struck by the sense of balance apparent in the activities of both the church as a whole and . . . of individuals. Care for the surrounding community is balanced well with care for the faith community.
> 
> One obviously effective way to ensure that is to expand the core of people active in all areas of the church's life. I think St. George's willingness to have its commissions chaired by other

than vestry members is particularly laudable . . . . Not only does a greater diversity of talent become available but issues of authority are less apt to interfere and no one gets worn out.[28]

- **The Rector:** The rector's preaching and teaching help members of the congregation make the connections between their faith and the rest of their lives. Innumerable people reported that "he connects with me," "he relates with me," "he speaks to me in my situation."

    Undoubtedly one of the reasons Charles is such an effective teacher is that he teaches on the basis of real knowledge and understanding of the community of Fredericksburg. He himself takes a full part in the environment that shapes the people, and so he is able to interpret theologically what is going on there and in the lives of the people. He makes the connections himself; he thus helps others to make connections.

    Charles Sydnor is not an extrovert. Nonetheless he appears very secure in his personal identity and in his role as parish priest. He is obviously a strong and respected leader who also thrives on the strength and vitality of others. Susan Onderdonk, the parish's director of music, says, "Charles has the ability to hold on by letting go."

## *An Issue Raised by This Visit: Ministry in Daily Life Is a Necessity*

Susan Onderdonk said that when she quit her job in Washington, it added three hours to her day. Before that, when she returned home at night she had no desire to rush off to a church meeting—or any meeting, for that matter. There are many Susans in Fredericksburg.

If a congregation does not want to add further to the commuters' burdens, it will need to help its members see the natural opportunities for ministry in their regular jobs, so that without ever darkening the doors of the parish on a weekday evening, they will know themselves engaged in ministry.

## RESOURCES

Education for Mission and Ministry Unit of the Episcopal Church Center. "Guide for Congregational Self-Evaluation." Popularly known by the acronym SWEEP (service, worship, evangelism, education, and pastoral care) this is a way for a congregation to evaluate the effectiveness of its mission and discern new ways of responding to human needs. St. George's restructured itself along the lines of the SWEEP model.

Hansel, Robert R. "The Church of Jesus Christ—Its Foundation and Ours." Mimeographed material. This is a 10-session course of readings and a discussion guide for adults based on the book *Salty Christians* by Hans-Ruedi Weber. It is a straightforward and helpful plan to open up the issues of ministry in everyday life. For information, please contact the Rev. Robert R. Hansel, Roslyn Center, 8727 River Road, Richmond, VA 23229.

## NOTES

[1] G. Scott Thomas, *The Rating Guides to Life in America's Small Cities,* April, 1990, as reported by Scott Rafshoon in *The Free Lance-Star,* Fredericksburg, VA. April 17, 1990, p. 1. The book's author examined 219 "micropolitan" areas with populations between 15,000 and 50,000. The best two cities are San Luis Obispo, California, and Corvallis, Oregon.

[2] "Growth: The Region's Future Can Be Shaped by Better Planning, Stronger Will," *The Free Lance-Star,* Monday, April 16, 1990, p. 1.

[3] Housing Data Reports of Washington," *Ibid.,* p. 14.

[4] Fritz Leedy, interview in Fredericksburg, April 26, 1990.

[5] Tim Melton, interview in Fredericksburg, April 26, 1990.

[6] Chip Willis, interview in Fredericksburg, April 26, 1990.

[7] *Ibid.*

[8] Janet King, interview in Fredericksburg, April 26, 1990.

[9] Chip Willis, interview.

[10] Edward Jones, telephone interview, May 2, 1990.

[11] Linda Grigsby, interview in Fredericksburg, April 26, 1990.

[12] Catherine Hicks, interview in Fredericksburg, April 26, 1990.

[13] *Ibid.*

[14] Robert Baker, interview in Fredericksburg, April 27, 1990.

[15] Charles Sydnor, interview in Fredericksburg, April 27, 1990.

[16] Robert R. Hansel, telephone interview, May 1, 1990.

[17] *Ibid.*

[18] *Ibid.*
[19] *Ibid.*
[20] Charles Sydnor, interview in Fredericksburg, April 27, 1990.
[21] John Pearce, interview in Fredericksburg, April 27, 1990.
[22] Charles Sydnor, interview, April 27, 1990.
[23] Edward Jones, interview, April 27, 1990.
[24] John Pearce, interview.
[25] Robert Baker, interview, April 27, 1990.
[26] David Adams, interview, April 27, 1990.
[27] Edward Jones, interview, April 27, 1990.
[28] Abigail Hamilton, correspondence, May 2, 1990.

*Visiting Team:* The Rev. Edwin Gulick and the Rev. Abigail Hamilton
*Date of Visit:* April 26-27, 1990

> *Jesus told them a parable, "The Kindgom of heaven is like this: a mustard seed is sown in the field. It is the smallest of all seeds, but when it grows up, it is the biggest of all plants. It becomes a tree, so that birds come and make their nests in its branches."*
> —Matthew 13:31-32

─────────── CHAPTER 3 ───────────

# Intimacy and Small Groups
## STORY OF A CATECHUMENAL PROCESS
### SAINT LUKE'S CHURCH
### MADISON, WISCONSIN

## *THE CONTEXT OF MISSION DISCERNMENT: MADISON, WISCONSIN*

Madison was only a dot on the map when it was selected as the capital of Wisconsin Territory in 1836. By 1838 there was one inn and a general store. With Wisconsin's attainment of statehood and the establishment of the University of Wisconsin in 1848, the city began to assume some of its present character.

Madison is home to some 170,000 people, many of whom work for the city's four largest employers: the State of Wisconsin; the University of Wisconsin; "Oscars," that is, Oscar

Meyer Foods (hot dogs and other prepared meats); and American Family Insurance, the city's largest private-sector employer.

The German and Scandinavian descent of the majority of Madison's residents is clearly evident, from the supermarkets, with their rows of "brats" (that is, bratwurst) to the street corners, with their Lutheran churches. One of them, Bethel, with a membership of 7,000, is nationally known for its Bethel Bible Series. Madison is an excellent city for beer, Scandinavian pastry, and cheese—Wisconsin prides itself on being the Dairy State.

Members of other ethnic and cultural groups also call Madison their home: Poles, African-Americans, Latinos, Native Americans. Ethnic festivals abound. Once a year at "A Taste of Madison," according to St. Luke's deacon, Judi Cirves, "You can eat yourself sick in 3,000 languages."

This city, built between five lakes, is a study in contrasts. Early in the 20th century it was the home of Robert La Follette and the Progressives, and a more recent mayor, Paul Soglin, was a 1960s political radical. Those of conservative persuasions are equally at home in Madison.

Until very recently, Madison had been considered a city with a small-town atmosphere, a family place hospitable to a wide variety of politics, cultures, viewpoints, and religious denominations. And the mixture worked well. But Madison is changing. It is a "welfare magnet," it is kind to people of low and no income, who gravitate there from other upper Midwest cities. Drugs are coming in as well as big-city problems. Recently three children burned to death in a subsidized housing development ten minutes from St. Luke's. This gave some pause. It raised a few questions about the quality of housing the poor endure. Racial struggles are increasing. Fighting recently broke out at a local west side high school, whose students are drawn from both upper-middle-class white and low-income minority neighborhoods. Teenage gangs are also becoming more common.

Life goes on in Madison, but somehow things don't feel quite as comfortable as they once did.

## *SAINT LUKE'S TODAY: SOMETHING SPECIAL*

The red-and-white bumper stickers decorated with trumpets declare that St. Luke's is "something special." That same "something special" logo adorns the T-shirts and coffee mugs of each member of the congregation, and it is placed at the top of the monthly newsletter. The members want to get the message out loud and clear: St. Luke's is something special, and the members want to talk about it. And most especially they want to talk about Jesus Christ.

The parish's mission statement, adopted in 1985, states that "The purpose of St. Luke's Parish is to know the love of Christ and share it with others so that they may know it too."

St. Luke's is located in a residential neighborhood on the east side of the city, close to the Madison-Monona line. Because it is on the edge of town, the members consider it a suburban parish. One hundred and fifty people worship on an average Sunday, up from 120 just a few years back.

To use Arlin Rothauge's terminology, it's a "program-sized" congregation with a full "program-sized" range of activities. Recently a parish member counted up the choice of activities available and named sixty-six, from altar guild to Cursillo, from a Kerygma Bible study group to Dramatis Personae (the chancel drama group). Members can join Foyers, a short-term group of about six to eight people that meets six times over a six-month period in each others' homes with no agenda except that of getting to know each other and practicing Christian hospitality. Or they can make a long-term commitment to Kerygma, an intensive two-year Bible-study program.

The congregation has a warm, friendly, and welcoming feel to it. On Sundays the coffee pot is plugged in before the 8 o'clock service. By the time that service is over, the coffee is ready, and the members of the 9:30 congregation have begun to trickle in. Members of both congregations mingle with each other over coffee, and the pot stays there until the conclusion of the later service. This creates a relaxed and inviting atmosphere, particularly in good weather, when the pot is placed outside on the church's back terrace—a natural gathering place. All the members wear name tags, and newcomers and visitors are conspicuous by their lack of tags. Members are always on the lookout for them. But they are only newcomers once, for everyone coming for the first time is taken in tow by the "Shepherd of the Day."

About seventy-five of the members of the congregation have been to Cursillo. The parish has gone through the SWEEP process, as well as two Faith Alive weekends. The traditional inquirers' class has been replaced by a twenty-four-session catechumenal process. The process is open to parish members who want to learn about faith in Jesus Christ and about the Episcopal Church. It's used as a preparation for adults seeking baptism, confirmation, or reaffirmation of baptismal vows.

St. Luke's members clearly enjoy each other's company, and they have plenty of opportunities to get to know and care for each other. "Care and share" groups—the generic term for all of St. Luke's groups—involve most of the members of the congregation. In addition the whole parish spends one weekend a year together at Camp Webb, the diocesan camp.

St. Luke's members have brought the lunch break to a fine art. During the working day, many of them, including the rector, use the lunch hour, taken in local restaurants, in an intentional way, sharing friendship, discussing matters of concern, or engaging in informal counseling.

The parish Marys and Marthas—also known as "M and Ms"—provide meals and receptions after funerals and for members of the parish who are ill, as well as for the community food program. The parish also has a much-used prayer chain.

The congregation is outward-looking. One of the members, Bud Buehner, obtained the donation of property for the building of a Habitat for Humanity house. Members take turns delivering meals to elderly and shut-in Madisonites. They volunteer at the homeless shelter, and once a week at least one parish member donates blood to the blood bank.

The members go to great lengths to support each other in hard times. A young woman—Janet, we'll call her—the daughter of one of the members, was featured on the nightly news, but she was no media star. Drug addicted, she has been convicted of an armed robbery in which two persons were injured. Before the sentencing Janet was incarcerated in the Dane County jail for seven months. According to her mother:

> People were wonderful. Gloria Waite and the rector visited her in jail. This parish literally prayed her back to health. On the day of her sentencing [for a possible 45 years] the courtroom was overflowing with members of St. Luke's. They took work time off for her. They were there for her. People loved her back to wholeness.[1]

Fully expecting a lengthy sentence, the youthful offender walked out of the courtroom that day with probation, a fine, and the requirement that she do community service, but no further incarceration. Was the judge swayed by the room full of St. Luke's members? Was he moved by their prayers? At any rate, Janet is now drug-free. She is a pre-med student at the University of Wisconsin, her tuition paid for by a member of St. Luke's. Janet's mother concluded the story of her daughter by suggesting that "the world is not made up of Walton families, but we're still a family."[2] She should know!

Members of the congregation talk easily and naturally about their faith, and they are not shy about expressing it in the workplace and through their work. They really do understand that the world is the arena for the exercise of their faith. Bud Buehner, a retired attorney who was an executive in a savings and loan business, has had thirty "adopted sons," members of the University of Wisconsin athletic teams, for whom he and his wife, Kay, have provided a "home away from home." Bud has gotten the student-athletes summer jobs and has helped them get into graduate school. He goes to their weddings and is godparent to several of their children. A whole wall of the Buehner family room is filled with photographs of "my boys."

Sharon Vanderzyl, a psychotherapist, opened a center for Christian counseling in Madison in 1981, when she realized that the city had no counseling center where the therapist had a Christian perspective. Sharon decided to open the center because so many people, knowing of her professional background, sought her out.

> People knew I was a Christian. They told me they needed to go to a therapist who would not tell them that their faith was a problem. So three of us got together and started a service.[3]

The center is doing well, and Sharon says "I get paid for my time but not my love."[4]

Bill Schweers acknowledges that "I don't consider myself a deeply religious person." Nonetheless, a year ago, he resigned his position as senior vice-president—and "the token liberal"—of a large Wisconsin health insurance company for ethical reasons. He supervised a staff of 2,500, he had ". . . good money, car, all the perks." But Bill had became concerned about the self-serving nature of the health insurance industry, whose purpose, or so he had understood it, was to serve others.

> Their prices are too high. The industry is motivated by greed. I tried to show them how to cut costs and improve service, but they didn't want to do anything. So I said "Good-bye."[5]

Schweers explained:

> In Wisconsin most doctors want to do what's right, but they're getting just like any other business. We've lost touch with the moral issues. Insurance people have forgotten they're in the *insurance* business.[6]

Now Bill is helping clients cut costs by eliminating intermediaries and introducing alternative—and more just—systems of finance. According to Schweers, "Heaven is full of people who go out of their way to help others. Good deeds, action, helping people is what it's all about."[7]

Judi Cirves, St. Luke's deacon, works as a budget analyst for the State of Wisconsin, with special responsibilities for welfare programs. Other members of the congregation include Brother Bernie La Reau, a member of the Brotherhood of St. Gregory, who works as a special needs teacher in a tough Madison public school. Carol Dietmeyer is also a teacher. Roy Johnson recently retired from supervising sixty Midwest convenience stores; Jan Decker, parish coordinator for the diocesan catechumenal process, is a retired professor of occupational therapy. Diane May, head of the parish's "Shepherd Program," is a nurse. John Schroeder is an oncologist who was a conscientious objector during World War II. He prays for his patients, but is distressed by the lack of belief in many who he feels would be comforted by Jesus Christ. Sue Rohan is a teacher by training who is a member of the Wisconsin State Legislature. She is a single parent with children aged seven and ten. She admits that holding job and family together is stressful, but her faith helps her.

> When I look at the issues, my faith enters in. I have had to come to grips with the separation of Church and State, and yet I have learned to see a Christian perspective in other beliefs.[8]

One of the issues Sue has struggled with is abortion. Just beginning to gear up for her fourth election campaign, she says,

> Initially I ran as a pro-life candidate, which was difficult to pull off in a pro-choice county.[9]

While Sue is still pro-life, she has begun to question whether or not she can impose her personal beliefs on others. She admits that her ambivalence may cost her votes. But considering this and other matters she must legislate, she is always looking at what is underlying. She considers the root causes. Her faith encourages her to get behind and under the issues in an effort to determine what is really going on, and thus what are the best courses of action. Abortion, child abuse, overcrowded prisons and the cry for more correctional facilities—why? What is underneath?

> I apply the process of faith to some of the problems we see working in society. Why not put money into prevention? Why not help parents? The tax code militates against single parents, single parents who are more likely than anyone else to be financially hard-pressed in the first case. Worrying constantly about finances only makes them more frantic.[10]

So Sue initiated legislation for "Healthy Start"—a program like Head Start but designed for younger children and their parents. She is now working on making the tax code more equitable.

These are just a few examples of how the many members of the congregation make connections between faith and the rest of their lives. Of the parish members as a whole, Sharon Vanderzyl says,

> People are genuinely doing things. There are many ministries. People are doing things because they love each other. And they're really out there too—the food pantry, Habitat, the blood donor program . . . .
>
> It's real. People are allowed to be real here and still be loved and accepted.[11]

# UNDERSTANDING THE STORY

St. Luke's began in 1946 in a Quonset hut, a mission of Grace Church in downtown Madison. People had started moving into the east side of town, and subdivisions were springing up all over, so the location was an excellent one for a new congregation. But when Roy Johnson first saw it, St. Luke's didn't seem like any Episcopal church he'd ever seen before. "This is an Episcopal church!? . . . this Quonset hut?"[12]

> But it was a friendly parish. There was a small core of members and there was a lot of vision. It took a lot of vision to go from mission to self-supporting.[13]

No endowments and sheer hard work were "coordinating factors," according to Jan Decker:

> We worked on the old rectory. We didn't hire out work unless absolutely necessary. People here painted, mowed the grass, washed windows . . . . They still do. It's like caring for a family.[14]

The parish hall was built in 1951, and the present church building—an award-winning architectural design—in the early 1970s. The mortgage—for $35,000 at 6 percent—was burned during the Eucharist on Good Shepherd Sunday during the visit of the Mission Discernment Project team. St. Luke's had become self-supporting in 1951.

Apparently the congregation moved from "family size" to "pastoral size" while still maintaining the feel and intimacy of a family-sized congregation (50-100 members). The present rector, the Rev. Lynde E. May IV, known affectionately as "Ted," "Father," and "Father May, and his wife, Diane, arrived in 1983. According to Bill Schweers, "They fit in and were well-loved in the parish community almost immediately."[15] At the time of his arrival, May recalled, "This congregation was a group of people at the starting gate ready to go."[16]

Shortly after the arrival of the Mays, the whole congregation went off to Camp Webb, where the members could get to know each other even better and incorporate the newly arrived clergy family. It was a relaxed setting. There were games,

Bible studies, recreation, and informal services. They had such a good time, the Camp Webb weekend has now become an eagerly anticipated annual event.

About the same time the parish participated in the SWEEP survey. Father May conducted it himself rather than engage the assistance of an outside consultant, in order to learn more about St. Luke's.

The congregation's first Faith Alive weekend occurred in the fall of 1983. Ninety members of the parish participated. It was a huge success. According to Judi Cirves, "It was like Cursillo with the whole parish."[17]

But Cursillo had had a mixed effect on the parish. As the Faith Alive weekend was being planned, some of the members had the impression that, as Carol Dietmeyer recalls, "The Cursillo people are making us do this." As it evolved, however, even those who at first had been skeptical acknowledged the overwhelmingly positive effect of the weekend. Dietmeyer went on to explain, "It was a totally different style of doing things. It was talking about religion in an affective, feeling way."[18]

The key to the success of the weekend was the follow-up. The Faith Alive Follow-up Committee soon became the Spiritual Life Committee. Regularly scheduled services of Morning Prayer came out of the weekend and, in Dietmeyer's words, "the grouping of the parish."

> These groups became a place where you could talk about the real issues of your life.[19]

It is these "care and share" groups that, as Father May expresses it, were "bridging the intimacy gap."[20] And for the next two years the parish grouped itself: Prayer groups, the lunch groups, Foyers groups, groups of members who went on Cursillo weekends and met together for follow-up. A chancel drama group was started, as were the Shepherd Program to welcome and integrate newcomers into the parish, the M and Ms, a group for short Bible studies, Kerygma, and Journey in Faith.

A word about Journey in Faith, now a diocesan catechumenal program that is receiving national attention: The Rev. A. Wayne Schwab, Coordinator of Evangelism Ministries for the Episcopal Church, said, "Here's a concept—see what you can develop."

Can Christian commitment mean being a conscious agent of the reign of God in one's daily places—work, home, community, citizenship, leisure and church? Can a congregation find a way to lead its people beyond nominal membership? The Diocese of Milwaukee, Dr. Louis Weil, and the Evangelism Ministries Office of the Episcopal Church Center found the first year of their joint pilot project answered "yes."[21]

Father May explains that Journey in Faith (also known as "The Milwaukee Catechumenal Process," and "Living our Baptismal Covenant") is the difference between *information* and *formation*.

Unfortunately the reason why so many education programs fail is because we pass on *information*. But information does not form faith.[22]

Parish coordinators of Journey in Faith—always lay—are trained for three days at the diocesan conference center. The Journey in Faith process itself begins on Advent Sunday and ends in the late spring. The average size of the group is fourteen, plus the five team leaders. The curriculum consists of Scripture study, listening to faith stories, the development of personal spirituality, an exploration of ministry in daily life, and support in carrying out these ministries. Irene Gonzalez, a member of St. Luke's who is now the diocesan coordinator of Journey in Faith, says, "The basic premise of the catechumenate is not to give facts, but . . . to expose them to thinking and discovering. It's formation, forming."[23]

Currently in the Diocese of Milwaukee, three more parishes are preparing to begin the catechumenal process, and their lay coordinators are being trained; eight other parishes are fully participating. The process is overseen by a six-member Diocesan Commission of the Catechumenate, which includes the Bishop of Milwaukee. Their goal is to have the process fully implemented throughout the diocese by 1995.

After spending a whole weekend experiencing the process and seeing its results, Dr. Charles Huttar, a member of this Mission Discernment Project's visiting team, commented:

What the catechumenal process is doing to move

the Church from the model in which it's the priest's responsibility and prerogative to prepare people for confirmation, for he's [or she's] the one who's theologically trained and so on . . . . From that to a system in which the people, as a part of their Christian witness, take on the responsibility of the discipling of others.[24]

In short, this process works! Almost half of the active members of St. Luke's have been through it, and they are—almost to a person—ready and eager to talk about their faith in Jesus Christ. They easily make the connections between the faith expressed on Sunday and the faith lived out every other day of the week.

Looking ahead, the Rev. Susan Clark, another member of the Mission Discernment Project's visiting team, suggested that, "I see the next step as an easy move into evangelism . . . evangelism in a way in which we're comfortable."[25]

## *DISTINCTIVE FEATURES*

It is simple to understand why St. Luke's is successful. Not that they have ever compared themselves to any standard checklist, but if they had, they would notice that they were doing almost everything right. Taking just two indicators of healthy congregations—Kennon Callahan's and the models developed by the United Methodist Church—St. Luke's is almost a perfect fit.

St. Luke's is strong in eleven of Callahan's twelve characteristics of an effective church. As described in the book *Twelve Keys to an Effective Church,* they include: specific and concrete mission objectives; pastoral and lay visitation; dynamic worship; significant relational groups; strong leadership resources; participatory decision-making; several competent programs and activities; open accessibility; high visibility; adequate parking; and adequate space facilities.[26] As for the twelfth key—"solid financial resources"—St. Luke's is only just there. Its finances are not a serious problem, but they could be better. Other than that, St. Luke's meets the criteria of a strong congregation and has a few extras as well.

St. Luke's style of ministry is also very much in keeping with the recent literature on "baby boomers," and the findings of *Reaching for the Baby Boomers,* a national project sponsored by the Education Section of the United Methodist Church. As part of it, Tex Semple cited the need of churches to plan *with* people, have quality programs, be emotionally expressive, build relationships, provide lots of options, be with who is there, look at the community, connect faith with life, include people, seek God's spirit.[27]

Specifically, the following features of St. Luke's contribute to its success:

- **New Members Are Welcomed:** Roy Johnson said,

    I can tell if a parish has a newcomers' program the first time I walk in the door of a new church.

    When I visited my daughter's church no one came up to talk to me or my wife. There was obviously no program to greet new people. The members only talked among themselves, conducted their business, you know . . . .

    I think a newcomers' program is the easiest vehicle in the world to bring people into the parish. I think it's a prerequisite.[28]

    St. Luke's has the Shepherd Program, which consists of a group of laity trained to be involved with newcomers from the time they first walk in the door until they are full members of the parish family. Members of the Shepherd Program have read the research that stresses the importance of a lay person's making contact within three days of the newcomer's first visit to the church. Visitors are generally more impressed if that first follow-up visit or contact is done by a lay person because they feel—generally correctly—that the laity volunteer whereas the clergy are paid, and it's their job. Lay visits are more likely to yield returns. The Shepherd Program is carefully structured. It has identified thirty things a newcomer to St. Luke's may want to have information about, from "Where's the restroom?" to "What is a bishop and what does he do?" The key to the program is the matching of the shepherds with the newcomers. Each Sunday morning during the announcement time, "The Shepherd of the Day" is introduced. Afterwards a match is made between a shepherd who might be congenial to the particular newcomer.

- **Practical Evangelism:** St. Luke's attractive red-and-white

"Something Special" bumper stickers can be seen all over Madison and the county, wherever St. Luke's members take their cars. Members wear their St. Luke's T-shirts. They readily talk about faith in Jesus Christ and what it does for them. They talk about the congregation that nurtures their faith.

- *An Open Environment for Developing and Nurturing Faith:* Participation in a Cursillo weekend is encouraged but not pushed. There have been two Faith Alive weekends. There is careful follow-up to both these experiences. That follow-up counters the we-they atmosphere that resulted from the early Cursillo experiences of some at St. Luke's. Parish members spend one weekend a year together at the diocesan camp. In the words of the Rev. Susan Clark, "If mission can be defined as including mission to the individual's interior life, then this parish exhibits a great sense of mission.[29]
- *Ample Opportunities for Study:* Kerygma, the Tuesday Bible study group, and Journey in Faith, already exist, and the congregation is open to any other opportunities that may develop.
- *Small Groups and Intimacy:* The most distinctive aspect of this congregation is its small groups. Virtually everyone in the parish is involved in one—from the Foyers Program, where there is no agenda save friendship, to "doing lunch" at local restaurants, from a group to study mysticism to Journey in Faith and Journey in Faith follow-up groups, Cursillo groups, a men's group, groups formed for one or two meetings only to discuss a specific topic. Groups, groups, groups. Through them the "intimacy gap" is bridged; through them members of the congregation know each other and are known; they value others while at the same time they feel valued themselves.
- *Shared Style of Ministry:* The rector has a genuinely collegial style of ministry. He is not running everything, and he will even let a program fail if necessary rather than take over the reins. He does not run in with the rescue net. Members of the congregation take real responsibility, and not just responsibility for the less important aspects of the congregation's life. Irene Gonzalez, in reviewing the congregations where Journey in Faith has taken hold, said the process has the greatest impact in locations where it is authentically lay led. The parishes in which the clergy have had too strong a hand in developing the process have had fewer results. This was true even at St. Luke's: When the congregation went through the process for the first

time, Father May took a leading part in its organization and leadership, and many said that that first year was Journey in Faith's least successful!

From a practical viewpoint, St. Luke's has so much going on that it would be impossible for the rector to lead it all.

- **Making the Connections between Fatih and Everyday Life:** This is a congregation in which members encourage each other to make the important connections in their lives.
- **Openness to New Ideas:** The Visiting Team was on hand to experience several examples of St. Luke's openness. Bill Schweers faulted the Episcopal Church generally:

> The Church has to stand up and say what it believes—about drugs, about having babies, abortion. Where is the Church on practical matters? I think we should talk about some of these political things—Central America . . . . If the Church stands for the good, you have to debate what's good. Maybe that's healthy. Maybe that's healthy to have a good, hot debate. Maybe if the Church believes [this or that social or political issue] it should say so! It should say, "Here's where the Church stands!"[30]

The rector walked into the middle of this conversation, and in short order, he and Bill were talking about the possibility of arranging parish forums and discussions. They began thinking about inviting speakers who would present several sides of issues and stimulate discussion and the formation of intelligent opinions.

At the final meeting of this season's Journey in Faith, it was acknowledged that several members are children of alcoholics. Thus they began to talk about starting a parish group for adult children of alcoholics.

- **Fun:** The atmosphere of St. Luke's is contagious. Clearly this is a congregation in which members enjoy each other. They laugh. They laugh at themselves. They are quick to share an amusing story. While it is also true that they are with each other at serious moments, they do not take themselves too seriously. They have a light touch. They are refreshing.

# *WEAKNESSES*

No congregation is perfect; otherwise it would not be real. There are two weaknesses, and both deal with education. One weakness—the issue of Christ and culture—is shared by probably at least 95 percent of Episcopal churches (thus, in this respect, St. Luke's is not exceptional). Since the site visit of the Mission Discernment Project team, there has been substantial attention given to areas cited here as being weak.

- *Church School for Children:* Although there are plenty of children in the congregation, the church school program has not been as successful as other aspects of this parish's life, and members of the Christian Education Task Force are looking for alternatives. According to Carol Dietmeyer, "I will not apply Band-Aid solutions to a problem that needs major surgery. We need to pull it all apart and start from the beginning."[31]

In March the Education Task Force visited St. Luke's Church in Kalamazoo, a parish whose Christian education program is geared to the Worship Center Model as described in *Young Children and Worship,* by Sonja M. Stewart and Jerome W. Berryman.[32]

> It goes back to the old tradition of storytelling—
> Bible stories—and I know, for me, that my life has
> been changed by stories.[33]

Note: Since the visit of the Mission Discernment Project Visiting Team, the status of the Christian education program at St. Luke's has changed dramatically. In August, Carol Dietmeyer joined St. Luke's staff half time as Christian education director. She visited the Worship Center at Western Theological Seminary (Reformed Church of America) at Hope College in Holland, Michigan, to learn more about implementing the ideas of the Worship Center. This fall St. Luke's established two Worship Centers, one for three- to seven-year-olds, the other for children in grades two to five. As Carol describes this beginning:

> This has involved a lot of change, yet the Worship Center has been very well received by children and parents alike. We work not as teachers but as facilitators and enablers. Our main function is to enable children to encounter God. Instead of tell-

ing children *about God,* we set the stage for the children to *encounter* God and to do their own theology. It's mind-blowing, and it works![34]

- **Christ and Culture:** While St. Luke's members are nothing short of impressive in the manner in which they talk about their faith, they do not readily discuss the relationship between faith in Jesus Christ and the transformation of society, nor Christian responsibility for social renewal, in working to implement the reign of God in the wide structures of our world. Bill Schweers gets close. This issue of Christ and culture is also the most difficult part of the Milwaukee Catechumenal Process to implement. While the diocesan guidelines call for involvement in both social service and social change, members of the congregation fall short in actual implementation.

    Another note: Following the visit of the Mission Discernment Project Team to St. Luke's, parish members began considering this issue. Should St. Luke's institute means for considering the issues of Christ and society? The membership was polled to determine what topics they would like to discuss. As it evolved, the members were strongly in favor of instituting a new program, which they called All Things Considered. The idea is that *all things* that are of concern to members will be aired and considered: issues of what it means to live as responsible and informed citizens in society, and other matters of concern as well. The topics initially suggested by the members were environmental issues, suicide, AIDS, the Middle East (understanding Islam), family issues (marriage, "blended families," raising children in the United States today, interracial families, multigenerational families, aging parents, etc.), and "What goes on in Dane County?" The program has just started, but to date forums have been held on business ethics, politics and religion, and AIDS. The latest parish newsletter reported that "attendance and participation in 'All Things Considered,' the adult forum, has been great!"[35] To the question, Do you want to hear more on the subject (the subject of the forum), the overwhelming response recorded on the evaluations was an overwhelming yes!

## RESOURCES

Ball, Peter. *Adult Believing.* New York: Paulist Press, 1988.

Diocese of Milwaukee. *The Right Rev. Roger White Presents "Living Our Baptismal Covenant": Our Experience in the Diocese of Milwaukee as the Pilot Project in the Catechumenate for the Epsicopal Church.* Produced by seminarians connected with the Nashotah House Media Center, no date. Video.

Fenhagen, James C. *Mutual Ministry.* San Francisco: Harper and Row, 1986. Originally published by Seabury Press in 1977.

Stewart, Sonja, and Berryman, Jerome W. *The Worship Center: Young Childen and Worship.* Louisville, KY: Westminster/John Knox Press, 1989.

Walter, James A. *Kerygma.* Pittsburgh: The Creative Edge, 1984. Kerygma study resources are distributed by the Kerygma Program, 300 Mt. Lebanon Blvd., Suite 205, Pittsburgh, PA 15234.

Wolf, Barbara and Frederick. *Journey in Faith.* New York: Seabury Press, 1960. A 10-week course which includes a leaders' guide and two other small books. Now out of print.

## NOTES

[1] Mother of Janet, interview in Madison, May 6, 1990.
[2] *Ibid.*
[3] Sharon Vanderzyl, interview in Madison, May 5, 1990.
[4] *Ibid.*
[5] Bill Schweers, interview in Madison, May 5, 1990.
[6] *Ibid.*
[7] *Ibid.*
[8] Sue Rohan, interview in Madison, May 6, 1990.
[9] *Ibid.*
[10] *Ibid.*
[11] Sharon Vanderzyl, interview.
[12] Roy Johnson, interview in Madison, May 5, 1990.
[13] *Ibid.*
[14] Jan Decker, interview in Madison, May 5, 1990.
[15] Bill Schweers, *Something Special,* St. Luke's newsletter, March 1990, p. 6.
[16] Ted May, interview in Madison, May 5, 1990.
[17] Judi Cirves, interview in Madison, May 5, 1990.
[18] Carol Dietmeyer, interview in Madison, May 5, 1990.
[19] *Ibid.*

[20] Ted May, interview in Madison, May 5, 1990.
[21] A. Wayne Schwab, "Changed Lives," paper, August 12, 1987, p. 1.
[22] Ted May, interview.
[23] Irene Gonzalez, interview in Madison, May 5, 1990.
[24] Charles Huttar, conversation in Madison, May 7, 1990.
[25] Susan Clark, conversation, May 7, 1990.
[26] Kennon L. Callahan, *Twelve Keys to an Effective Church: Strategic Planning for Mission* (San Francisco: Harper and Row Publishers, 1983).
[27] Tex Semple, "Ways to Plan for Being Inclusive," in *Reaching for the Baby Boomers Workbook,* by Kirk McNeill and Robert Paul (Nashville: General Board of Discipleship of the United Methodist Church, 1989), pp. 41-42.
[28] Roy Johnson, May 7, 1990.
[29] Susan M. Clark, Site Visitor Report.
[30] Bill Schweers, May 6, 1990.
[31] Carol Dietmeyer, May 6, 1990.
[32] Sonja M. Stewart and Jerome W. Berryman, *Young Children and Worship* (Louisville: Westminster, 1989).
[33] Carol Dietmeyer, May 6, 1990.
[34] Carol Dietmeyer, telephone interview, November 7, 1990.
[35] "All Things Considered," *Something Special,* November, 1990.

*Visiting Team:* The Rev. Susan Clark and Dr. Charles Huttar
*Date of Visit:* May 5-7, 1990

> *I was hungry and you fed me, thirsty and you gave me a drink; I was a stranger and you received me in your homes, naked and you clothed me; I was sick and you took care of me.*
> —Matthew 25: 35-36

## CHAPTER 4

# HOOSIER HOSPITALITY

## STORY OF WAGE EARNERS IN COMMUNITY SERVICE

### SAINT MARK'S CHURCH
### PLAINFIELD, INDIANA

### *THE CONTEXT OF MISSION DISCERNMENT: PLAINFIELD, INDIANA*

When Jeannie and Charles Campbell moved to Plainfield in 1951, it was indeed a plain field, a Quaker town with a population of 2,500. Located between US 40 and Interstate 70, Plainfield is about fifteen miles west of downtown Indianapolis. Though no one knows the exact meaning of *Hoosier* or where the nickname originated, *Hoosier* has come to connote all that is typically American and down-home—and Plainfield fits all that Hoosier tradition to a T. It has its commercial strip on the edge of town. Hardees is there, along with Wendy's, McDonald's, Dairy Queen, Taco Bell, Kentucky Fried Chicken, and Wal-Mart. Plainfield had a wide main street—called Main Street—in the center of town. But Main Street has a "seen better days" look to it.

Most of Plainfield's 15,350 residents have moved to the newer, more prosperous neighborhoods that have sprouted up in fields that were once farms, and they shop in suburban malls where corn used to grow and cattle graze. And as subdivisions have edged their way into corn and hog farms, so have their inhabitants changed not only the landscape but also the character of the town—from a quiet haven, where generations of families knew and cared for each other, to an Indianapolis bedroom community, where people come and go as industries move in or out of Indianapolis. Yet Hoosier down-home friendliness has been maintained, and neighbors are still important to each other. Change has been steady, but only dramatic to those who have paused to notice, like the Campbells. Of course, not everything was perfect back in the fifties. The Quakers had always controlled the town, and they intended to continue doing so. "The Catholics couldn't even get a lot to build their church on in Plainfield until the president of Public Service Indiana moved in. He *was* a Catholic. He changed things. They got their church."[1] And so, in time, did the Baptists, the Methodists, the Disciples of Christ, the Presbyterians, the Assembly of God, the Congregationalists, and the Episcopalians.

Some of the townships in the Plainfield area are still unincorporated, but that is likely to change.

The transition began in 1951 when PSI (Public Service Indiana) moved into town. PSI now employs 1,000, but it has been joined by other industries: a pallet manufacturer, a commercial printer, a metal moldings company. There are also a beer distributor, a manufacturer of movie speakers, a company that makes model cars and airplane accessories. But most of Plainfield's residents earn their livelihood in Indianapolis. One of the attractions of Plainfield is that it is located on the side of Indianapolis where a family can still buy a suburban home at an affordable price. Charles Campbell explains:

> North, east and south of the City [Indianapolis] have built up. This is the only place you can go where youngsters can still afford to buy a house.[2]

According to Irma Lee White, a member of St. Mark's congregation who hosts "Viewpoint," a local radio talk show on WSYW (AM/FM), people come to Plainfield because:

They want to be out of the city. They don't want industry. They don't want economic development. They moved here to get away from all that.[3]

Irma continues,

> I've been hosting "Viewpoint" for three years. I've been in radio for twenty-seven years. I've seen a lot of changes. For seven years I did a two-hour talk show, "Saturday Morning Live"—get it, from "Saturday Night Live"?!—I did it in the corner booth at Cindy's, a restaurant on the edge of town. I interviewed the customers. Anyone who wanted to could talk on the show. We got a lot of laughs. They weren't shy. They spoke up about anything that was on their minds. They still do, even though we now do the show from the studio.[4]

Washington Township, where many of St. Mark's members live, is one of the fastest-growing townships in the state. The trouble is, Irma explained, big-time Indianapolis problems have come to Plainfield like an express train. "They are here now. There is homelessness, drugs, satanism and [the] occult."[5] The issues callers to the show most want to talk about right now are abortion and the proposed county airport.

> The pilots' group wants an airport here. Five areas have been proposed for it, and residents in all five areas are protesting! These protesting groups always call themselves "Concerned Citizens Against...." Always concerned. Always against. Never concerned *for* something. I've had 'em all on my show.[6]

Doug VanDemark concluded the discussion about the town by suggesting that:

> Plainfield is 95 percent Republican, even if they are working people. You can hardly find a Democrat in the county. 1936 was the last time a Democrat got in as County Clerk and that was only sliding in on the coattails of Franklin D. Roosevelt.[7]

# SAINT MARK'S TODAY: HOME OF HOOSIER HOSPITALITY

Doug VanDemark, who works at the air traffic control center at the Indianapolis Airport, expalined how St. Mark's is making a difference to the town of Plainfield:

> You say, "I'm from St. Mark's," and they'll invariably say, "O yeah, that's the church that does all those good things."[8]

The most distinctive "good thing" St. Mark's does is its shelter ministry. St. Mark's shelter is the only one in the whole county, and literally hundreds of people have come through its doors since it started six years ago. People get stranded hitchhiking, they get in a wreck on Interstate 70, they come up from the South for a job that never materializes, their trailer catches fire and burns to the ground on December 23rd—the coldest night of the year. They turn up on the doorstep from all over the country and beyond. A husband and wife walked all the way from Elkhart. The police called one night to see if the shelter would help a young German who had been robbed on the Interstate. Bob Brown, an electrical engineer who is chair of the Shelter Committee, said, "He was reluctant to come because he was Jewish, but when they got him over here he could see that we were friendly."[9]

They have sheltered runaway children who have gotten stranded and persuaded them to contact their parents. When a family was burned out of their home at Christmas, St. Mark's people took them in and bought new gifts for the children.

The shelter is unusual in that it is housed in the downstairs rooms of the parish hall and residents are free to use the church's kitchen. It has no paid staff. The facilities include a large room arranged with beds and a television for a family. They will also set up as many cots as are needed in the other rooms, including the church school rooms. Irma White said,

> You'd be surprised. Homelessness is a bigger problem than people realize. It just seems that people want to look the other way. We tried to get the other churches in town involved in this ministry, but they're not interested. Many people I know have said things to me like "How can you trust *those people* in your church?" I tell 'em they're just

like you 'n' me and nothing bad ever happened
'cept a $60 phone bill we got stuck with once.[10]

As the Rev. Jackie Means, rector of St. Mark's, says,

> If it's a club they want, we've got the Elks, the
> Moose, and Eagles. *This is a church.* When the
> Church stops helping people, we might as well
> forget it.[11]

St. Mark's is the twelfth largest parish in the Diocese
of Indianapolis, with 240 baptized members. It has as its rector
the Rev. Jacqueline Means, referred to universally as "Jackie,"
the first officially ordained woman priest in the Episcopal Church
USA. When she came in 1984, she worked on Sunday and one
other day. Now she works in the parish four days plus Sunday.
At the time of her arrival, St. Mark's was known as a "priest
killer," and the people were depressed.

The congregation's membership mirrors the community. When the Mission Discernment Project was planning locations for site visits, St. Mark's had been described as a parish
that was "blue collar and proud." Although many members are
indeed what might be considered blue-collar workers, during the
visit many questioned that designation. Bob Brown explained:

> St. Mark's is not a blue-collar church. We all work
> for a living. We are not business owners. We are
> a church made up of people who do not control
> their own time, who do not control their own
> destiny. We are wage earners.[12]

"Doc" Soughers is a veterinarian, Mark Pickett is a
pipefitter in a General Motors factory. His wife, Judy, works as
a junior high school guidance counselor at the poorest school in
Indianapolis. Bill Shadwick is a lineman for Indianapolis Power
and Light. He climbs utility poles in blistering heat and in chilling ice storms. Even though there hasn't been an accident in two
years, Bill's wife, Julie, worries about him. Dave Reddick has a
Ph.D. in American Studies but works for the State of Indiana
Department of Insurance. His wife, Becky, who serves as St.
Mark's treasurer, is manager of facilities at Methodist Hospital
in Indianapolis, where she supervises a crew of 128 workers.

I started out in the construction business. When

I got out of high school, I tried to be a secretary, but I just couldn't sit behind a desk. I didn't go to college. I'm self-taught, you might say. I worked with my father. I've got a contractor's license. The hospital [largest in the state] has to have a licensed contractor in its staff. There is one other woman in the country who has a position like mine. There are a lot of women engineers, but this is a lot more "hands on" than engineering.[13]

Dinah Farrington is chief lobbyist for Planned Parenthood of Indiana. Bill Imel is the retired chairman of labor relations for the United Transportation Union, a union whose membership is composed of railroad firemen, conductors, brakemen, and yardmen. "I spent the first twenty-five years working as a brakeman on the New York Central."[14] Margaret Stockwell is also retired. She worked for thirty-three years with an electric utility company. Byron Stockwell sells Sherwin Williams paint. "I work central Indiana. I'm always on the road calling on painting contractors."[15] John Brown works as a technician for Rolls-Royce and fixes cars on the side; Hope, his wife of just two weeks, is a home health aide. LeRoy Anderson is a "meathead" (his word) at the I.G.A. grocery, and his wife, Mickey, takes care of her grandchildren every day. Ellen Scott also works at home taking care of nine-month-old Andrew. Her husband, Doug, is a computer programmer with Electronic Data Systems. Kathy McDaniel is president of the Auxiliary of the Eagles, a service club with a local chapter in Plainfield. She is pleased that statewide the Eagles raised $85,000 for seven charities and honored that she has been selected as the Plainfield Eagles' "Mother of the Year." This tribute has special significance, since Kathy is a young widow without any children of her own.

Ten members of the congregation form a clown troupe. They have been trained in an intensive 40-hour course, in which they studied the history of Christian clowning, developed their characters, and learned to dress for their acts and apply makeup. In the troupe are tramps, bag ladies, agustes (funny, uncoordinated ladies), and whitefaces, who are the tragicomedy elite. Steve Johnson, who in reality is orderly and neat to a fault, is "Farquar," a tramp. In his clown character he trips over himself, falls, drops things, and struggles to keep up with his bag-lady partner,

"Esmeralde." "Clowning," according to Steve, "gives me permission to be everything I'm not in real life. It gives me permission to try out a new persona."[15]

Jackie Means, describing the process, says

> There is a prayer we use while we are putting on the makeup. The whiteface signifies death, and we don't speak while we are putting on the whiteface. Then we bring in the colors—they signify the resurrection.[17]

In actuality, Jackie is an extrovert, but not as a clown:

> The amazing thing about clowning is that when I clown I don't talk to anybody. I had wanted to be a whiteface. I'm tired of being a second-class person. I wanted for once in my life to be a Cadillac. But I ended up being an auguste, which is a klutz.[18]

Jackie continues:

> Steve, the professor, is a wonderful tramp. Byron is a good clown, too. Dick Copeland is real quiet, just like Mark Pickett, but when he puts his clown character on, he just talks and talks. He won't shut up.
>
> His wife, Mary Ellen, "Esmeralde," is a stroke victim. She loves clowning. She's Steve's partner and she just can't get off the stage. So that is part of the skit—getting "Esmeralde" off the stage. You never know what she'll do![19]

What does St. Mark's ministry do for its members? Most say it is home, it is family with a big heart. Dinah Farrington explains,

> We all love and respect each other. We are a family. We don't always agree . . . but we have that love. I don't have a family close by. I am not married. I am an only child and an only grandchild. I'm here with people who love me in spite of my politics [pro-choice in a predominantly pro-life area]. For me St. Mark's is a touchstone.[20]

This sense of family is the reason most often mentioned why new people come to St. Mark's, and the reason older people have stayed.

For Margaret Stockwell, "We came looking for a church that had some heart in it. We came once and were at home."[21] The Scotts found a home at St. Mark's because St. Mark's is home to those with no place to go, and that seems intuitively to them what the Church is all about. Bob Brown agrees, "For me half the fun of the shelter is meeting people."[22] For Bill Drake, St. Mark's is a church that responds quickly. Bill first visited the church in desperate circumstances. The Drake family had just moved to Plainfield from Chicago, having had to leave their two-pound premature infant to be cared for in a Chicago hospital:

> I met [the late] Millie Tomlin, who wrote the church newsletter. She was a lovely person. I saw the Episcopal Church sign outside and decided to stop in. It was on Friday and I spilled the whole story to Millie. I came back on Sunday and I was amazed to see William's name on the prayer list. Imagine that—from Friday to Sunday. They responded that fast. Also the word had gotten out to the congregation that we were the family that was having all the difficulties. People came up to me at the coffee hour and asked if I was the father of the kid with all the problems. They really cared.[23]

Members come to give and receive support from each other. Colleen Gibson said, in describing Kathy, the Eagles' Mother of the Year:

> Kathy is just like a mother to me. I lost my mother and she helped me through it. I had depression. She kept me busy. My mother left me her wedding ring, but I gave it to Kathy because Kathy is like a mother to me.[24]

St. Mark's rector, the Rev. Jacqueline Means, is another reason people come to St. Mark's and stay. In Doug VanDemark's words, "Whether or not it's good, it's a reality," and as Dave Reddick said:

> Jackie is an attraction, and people love her. She is very religious and very down to earth. She has a special relationship with everyone. She is always calling me at work about something. She has a knack for drawing out your particular strengths. She capitalizes on everything.[25]

Abby VanDemark explained:

> To me, Jackie's a minister that does things that other ministers would like to do but are too pious, too self-righteous to do. And she's a clown, of course. She's a draw. She's a catalyst. She can make you feel comfortable. I would say she's a blue-collar priest. She's a "diamond in the rough." She was a truck driver's wife. She doesn't have refinements. She's just a nice down-to-earth person that you can talk to about anything.[26]

St. Mark's members are active in the wider community. Bob Brown is president of the Plainfield Church Federation, composed of laity and clergy from thirteen faith communities. Dick Soughers, Bill Drake, and Charlie White are among the 25 percent of the congregation who volunteer at Dayspring, a diocesan-sponsored shelter for the homeless and feeding program at All Saints Episcopal Church in Indianapolis. When St. Mark's had 80 members, as many as 25 volunteered and provided leadership at the shelter. Big-city churches gave money, but often could get just a few volunteers. They often marveled at this small church's having so many people willing to serve.

When the Diocese of Indianapolis concluded its companionship relationship with the Diocese of Haiti, St. Mark's continued it on an informal basis. Under the leadership of one member of the congregation, Dick Soughers, St. Mark's collects money and supplies and Dick visits Haiti once a year. Now St. Mark's members are talking about forming a parish-to-parish relationship with a congregation in Appalachia.

Twenty percent of the congregation have participated in Cursillo. They use the inclusive-language liturgical texts on Wednesday evenings.

St. Mark's—from "priest killer" to Hoosier hospitality—a congregation with a big heart and a welcome hand for all.

# UNDERSTANDING THE STORY

In 1951 there were seven families in Plainfield who identified themselves as Episcopalian, and three became founding members of St. Mark's. Charles Campbell was responsible for building the town's high school and elementary school and was also a builder of Plainfield's first Episcopal church.

In those early days these few Episcopalians drove into Indianapolis to be a part of the cathedral congregation, but they lived in Plainfield and they wanted a church in their hometown. In 1953, with Mr. Campbell as warden, this handful of families became a small Episcopal congregation in Plainfield. They met in the basement of the town library, and the children congregated in the Campbell home for church school.

From this modest beginning the congregation grew rapidly. In 1955, with the help of the diocese and the bishop they bought a church building from the Christian Church (Disciples of Christ). So appreciative were they of Bishop John Craine's help and personal interest in the project that the members named their fledging congregation St. Mark's in honor of Bishop Craine, whose birthday coincided with St. Mark's feast day.

The early days were good ones, and members of the congregation took particular pride in the annual vacation Bible school. It involved 125 children and eight teachers, and by all accounts was enjoyed by all. "In this small town," according to Charles Campbell, "you'd better have a vacation church school. That's how you get taken seriously as a church. That's how you compete."[27]

Members of the church were occupied with other activities as well. According to Bill Drake,

> Doug and Abby VanDemark assisted in bringing the Episcopal Cursillo movement to the Diocese of Indiana. There was ecumenical Cursillo but no exclusively Episcopal Cursillo. So Doug and Abby went to Evansville, Kentucky, for Cursillo weekends there. About 1981 the Diocese of Indianapolis held its first Cursillo weekend—staffed half with people from Kentucky and half with people from Indianapolis.[28]

There were other diocesan projects and the companionship with the Diocese of Haiti but, for one reason or another, for twenty years or so prior to Jackie's coming, they were not able to sustain any growth. Some members attribute their problems to ineffective leadership by the clergy. There was some ministry going on at St. Mark's but, as Campbell remembers, "Before we got Jackie and we were not doing well."[29]

Jacqueline Means became rector of St. Mark's in August, 1984. It was a part-time position—Sunday and one other day a week. At that time the average Sunday attendance was fifty-six. By 1986, Jackie was in the parish for four days a week, and the attendance had almost doubled. Attendance increased so much that the congregation was bursting the seams of its modest church building. Everything was too small: the church itself was not adequate, nor was there sufficient space for the church school or fellowship following the services.

The members of the congregation considered their options. Some years ago the diocese had purchased ten acres of land on the edge of town. St. Mark's could build a more spacious building there. After all, the Roman Catholics, mainline Baptists, Presbyterians, Lutherans, and Methodists had all moved to Plainfield's more prosperous residential areas. Perhaps the Episcopalians ought to follow suit. That was one possibility. Another was to add on to their present building, and they got architectural plans drawn up to help them consider this choice. Another possibility was to do nothing.

Considering their possible solutions, the members decided to stay in town. They had started a tradition of service in the downtown area, and they felt called to continue it. Besides, since virtually all the other denominations had departed from the town's center, many of St. Mark's members felt that they might be turning their backs on downtown people with serious needs if they too joined the exodus. So after much discussion, the decision was made to stay in town. However, the size of the church building remained a problem.

Miraculously perhaps, at this point the Baptists—seeking to expand—approached the diocese with a proposal to purchase the suburban ten acres. If a deal could be made, they could build a new church on the newly acquired property, and they would have an old one to sell. So, as Bill Drake recalls, "The light went on collectively over a lot of people's heads."[30]

St. Mark's members saw the Baptist church, liked it,

and bought it. It was in excellent condition and as a bonus, the property also came with two houses. During the visit of the Mission Discernment Project, St. Mark's made the last payment on the property. The church itself is a very attractive building, and the parish hall is just right. The houses bring in $700 in monthly rents while they tickle the imagination of St. Mark's members as they consider their future uses: day care for infants and adults, a more ample shelter, a community center . . . .

St. Mark's is a parish on the move, and its members are making plans for the Decade of Evangelism. They say they want to change the way the Episcopal Church has done evangelism in the past. Byron Stockwell commented that traditionally the Episcopal Church takes the fish tank down to the lakeside and expects the fish to jump in. "And the Methodists have fish frys." But, as Doug VanDemark, chair of the newly formed Evangelism Committee, says, "We don't want to fry the fish. We want to catch them. We're not going to expect them to just jump in. We're going to go for them."[31] Vestry members are going to start loosening things up by talking about their faith and the meaning of St. Mark's in their lives. They expect these conversations to go on in other parish groups. Getting into the practice and habit of talking about their faith with each other, they reason, congregation members will be able to talk to visitors and their fellow Plainfield residents. When they come to church, according to Jackie,

> It would be nice to have a sign in the parking lot for guests—because you can't get a parking space on a Sunday morning . . . . Have a sign that says "For our guests." That would make them feel important.[32]

The apple and cherry trees are in bloom in Plainfield. The corn is knee-high. Grass is growing green and lush in the town's neighborhoods and parks. Plainfield is blossoming, and so is St. Mark's.

## DISTINCTIVE FEATURES

- ***Hoosier Hospitality Is Gospel Hospitality:*** When Rita Scholes arrived at St. Mark's with her small son, Brandon, she was accompanied by her sister, Dena, and Dena's son, Danny, her brother, Jim; and her mother, Janet. The family had little more than the clothes on their backs. They had been trying to get into a trailer park and get jobs, but everything had proved unsuccessful. "Without the church," Rita explained, "the welfare would have taken our kids away."[33] That was six weeks ago. Now Rita has a job that the church helped her get, the family has an apartment they are planning to move into just two blocks from the church, and members of the congregation are busy accumulating furniture, crockery, and clothing to help the family get set up. The little boys were baptized at the Easter Vigil, and members of the Shelter Committee became their godparents. "Jackie is God-sent," Rita maintains, "and so are all the other members here."[34] She continued:

> I hadn't been to church in four years. But now we feel comfortable going to this church. If we didn't go on a Sunday, we'd feel we were missing something.
>
> Both boys got baptized at the Easter Vigil. We was [sic] wanting them to get baptized, and they was really interested in it. And we thought Jackie should be the one to baptize them. Every day they see Jackie they just run up to her and give her a kiss and a hug.[35]

And Janet Scholes added,

> I have never been to a church where I felt more at ease. I've never had this feeling before.[36]

Hoosier hospitality, Gospel hospitality: the hungry, the stranger, the naked, the outcast—St. Mark's takes them all in and makes friends of strangers. St. Mark's is Matthew 25 in action. Such radical hospitality is the main factor in St. Mark's success. In Rose Brown's words, "If you don't take people in, if you don't treat *everybody* just the same, you're just a club."[37]

St. Mark's is no club. Other factors include:

- ***A Congregation That Responds Quickly:*** Bill Drake stopped by the church on Friday; by Sunday his hospitalized infant was on the parish prayer list.

A group of residents at a group home for the

developmentally disabled attend St. Mark's on Sundays. They greatly enjoy both the service and the coffee hour afterwards. During the week before Mother's Day they had cleaned their house from top to bottom and made ready for a party to honor their mothers on Mother's Day. With pride and expectation they issued the invitations. But none of the mothers was able to accept. When Andrea Collins, a parish member who also works at the home, got the word out to St. Mark's members, the group home residents had guests from the church to look forward to along with clowns to entertain them.

St. Mark's responds quickly to human need.

- **Continuity between Saying and Acting, Being and Doing:** Observing the members of St. Mark's in action, one is reminded of Dorothy Day's criticism of the Episcopal Church of her day:

> Children look at things very directly and simply. [As a child at church] I did not see anyone taking off his coat and giving it to the poor. I didn't see anyone having a banquet and calling in the lame, the halt and the blind .... [38]

Perhaps Dorothy Day would have remained an Episcopalian had she experienced a St. Mark's, Plainfield, in her day.

- **The Decision to Stay in Town:** St. Mark's members made a bold decision to stay in town and minister to the people there. The conscious decision not to follow other churches as they relocated to the comfortable areas of Plainfield has borne fruit by attracting new members and serving downtown needs.
- **High Visibility:** St. Mark's is very conspicuous in town. It serves as a community gathering place: for AA, ALANON, ACOA, Cub Scouts, aerobics, a support group for battered women, and other groups. It sponsors public forums. Recent forum topics have been AIDS awareness and the occult. There was a celebration following the prison release of Nelson Mandela. When people show up at the Plainfield Police Station or the police station of a neighboring town or the sheriff's office, when they are found wandering with no place to go, when they have had an accident on the highway and the police wonder what to do with them, St. Mark's is invariably contacted. Likewise, the clowns—who take their skits to schools,

nursing homes, and prisons—have received considerable press publicity, and thus increased St. Mark's visibility.

- **The Person of the Priest:** Rita Scholes said, "Jackie is God-sent." Jackie has been described as a "diamond in the rough," with the stress on *diamond*. She is a priest with a big heart, an infectious, generous spirit, and an expansive personality. Jackie has an authenticity about her. "She is very real," as many members of the congregation stated in various ways.

  The success of Jackie—the person of Jackie the priest—raises significant issues about who the priests of the Episcopal Church are, where and how they are recruited, how they are trained, how they maintain their vitality. Also, how do high-energy clergy avoid burnout? How are congregations prepared when such priests eventually leave, since they all must one day depart?

- **Partnership between Priest and Congregation:** The fit, the chemistry, between the priest and congregation, is electric. Jackie has a knack for bringing out the strengths of those around her. The members of the congregation respond with affirmation; that affirmation feeds into and extends her creativity. But it's not a love feast, in which priest and people merely care for each other. It is not a fuzzy cocoon. It is a circle of energy and imagination that is expressed in concrete action, action that radiates outward to be ever-inclusive of others. What you have at St. Mark's is a fit between priest and members that benefits both, and an extended family of Christian inclusiveness that is continually extending its outer limits. St. Mark's has an effective priest, yes—and she would probably be effective in many locations. The magic—if you will—of the St. Mark's story is the partnership between congregation *and* priest. As Marcy S. Walsh, a member of the Site Visiting Team, expressed it,

  > A big factor in the success of this congregation is a cycle of affirmation that enhances total ministry: she affirms and encourages and calls forth the laity to DO things, and they affirm her creativity and energy with responsiveness and willingness to work together.[39]

- **Willingness to Look Forward:** Appropriate uses of the church's two houses, the Decade of Evangelism, a parish-to-parish companionship relationship, planning for increased membership, extending the clown ministry .... What needs are not being met in Plainfield? St. Mark's members enjoy dreaming of what they would like to do in the future. They get excited about new opportunities. Tomorrow is more important to them than yesterday. They are pregnant with the possibilities of what they yet will do.

## RESOURCES

St. Mark's members invite teams from other congregations to experience their life. Contact St. Mark's Episcopal Church, 301 South Center Street (P.O. Box 25), Plainfield, IN 46168; telephone: (317) 839-6730.

## NOTES

[1] Charles Campbell, interview in Plainfield, May 12, 1990.
[2] *Ibid.*
[3] Irma Lee White, interview in Plainfield, May 12, 1990.
[4] *Ibid.*
[5] *Ibid.*
[6] *Ibid.*
[7] Doug VanDemark, interview in Plainfield, May 12, 1990.
[8] *Ibid.*
[9] Bob Brown, interview in Plainfield, May 12, 1990.
[10] Irma Lee White, interview.
[11] Jacqueline Means, interview in Plainfield, May 12, 1990.
[12] Bob Brown, interview.
[13] Becky Reddick, interview in Plainfield, May 13, 1990.
[14] Bill Imel, interview in Plainfield, May 13, 1990.
[15] Byron Stockwell, interview in Plainfield, May 12, 1990.
[16] Steve Johnson, interview in Plainfield, May 12, 1990.
[17] Jacqueline Means, interview.
[18] *Ibid.*
[19] *Ibid.*
[20] Dinah Farrington, interview in Plainfield, May 13, 1990.
[21] Margaret Stockwell, interview in Plainfield, May 12, 1990.
[22] Bob Brown, interview.
[23] Bill Drake, telephone interview, May 14, 1990.
[24] Colleen Gibson, interview in Plainfield, May 13, 1990.
[25] David Reddick, interview in Plainfield, May 12, 1990.

[26] Abby VanDemark, interview in Plainfield, May 12, 1990.
[27] Charles Campbell, interview.
[28] Bill Drake, telephone interview, May 14, 1990.
[29] Charles Campbell, interview.
[30] Bill Drake, telephone interview.
[31] Doug VanDemark, interview.
[32] Jacqueline Means, interview.
[33] Rita Scholes, interview in Plainfield, May 13, 1990.
[34] *Ibid.*
[35] *Ibid.*
[36] Janet Scholes, interview in Plainfield, May 13, 1990.
[37] Rose Brown, interview in Plainfield, May 12, 1990.
[38] Dorothy Day, *The Long Loneliness: The Autobiography of Dorothy Day* (New York: Harper and Row, 1952), pp. 39 and 42.
[39] Marcy S. Walsh, Site Visitor Report, May, 1990.

*Visiting Team:* Susie Casto and Marcy S. Walsh
*Date of Visit:* May 12-13, 1990

> *Your people will rebuild what has long been in ruins, building again on the old foundations. You will be known as the people who rebuild the walls, who restore the ruined houses.*
>
> —Isaiah 58:12

## CHAPTER 5

# CREATING A VILLAGE

## STORY OF THE TRANSFORMATION OF AN INNER-CITY COMMUNITY
### CHURCH OF THE MESSIAH
### DETROIT

### *THE CONTEXT OF MISSION DISCERNMENT: DETROIT'S EAST SIDE*

In the shadow of Detroit's mighty Renaissance Center, its new convention center, and glittering, expensive, high-rise hotels lies another Detroit—one that in mind and spirit could be 3,000 miles away. This other Detroit, also on the East Side, is called the Island View neighborhood. It is a 123-block area that includes 1,100 empty lots, which once held the gracious residences of Detroit's elite fronting wide, tree-shaded avenues and boulevards. Between 1970 and 1980, Island View lost 3,000 housing units. Some of the inhabitants vacated their homes by choice, others by decree or circumstances. When blacks came in, whites moved a few blocks east to Grosse Pointe and other suburbs, which form a tight white ring around Detroit's center. When a new Cadillac plant moved in, it displaced the entire population of Pole Town. Chrysler closed down a plant last year. These are the realities of metropolitan Detroit, and their consequences affect far more people than Island View residents. But closer to home, a parking lot displaced an apartment building; a corner grocery store was broken into one more time than its owners could take, so they fled, and now their little store is a crack house.

A house falls into disrepair; the city pulls it down. The landlord can no longer maintain his urban rental properties; the buildings mysteriously catch fire and burn to the ground in the night. It's a familiar and continuously repeating cycle in street after street, in block after block.

The population of Detroit, which was just over one million in 1980, has steadily declined. It's the same exodus that is occurring in virtually all urban centers, but in Detroit the population shift is exacerbated by shifts in the automobile industry. Ford, Chrylser, General Motors—they're all in Detroit and they've all been in trouble. According to Charles Turner, Mission Discernment Project Site Visitor and a native of Detroit, "Cars move Detroit, and when cars aren't moving, neither is Detroit. Detroiters need jobs, but automobile labor is cheaper in Mexico."[1]

Detroit's unemployment rate of 9.5 percent is high, but for inner-city blacks it is 20 percent, and for black teenagers it rises to 51 percent. Fewer jobs, declining population, reduced tax base, racism: these have led to half-empty classrooms and poorly supported schools. Detroit planned to close ten elementary schools in September, 1990. The Roman Catholic Church likewise planned to close several parochial schools. This after having already closed the doors of thirty-five churches within the previous eighteen months. According to the Rev. Dean Cole, who was associate rector of the Church of the Messiah:

> People fled the city and left their problems behind . . . . Every kind of hurt is here . . . . Every kind of problem is clustered here.[2]

The corner grocery store has gone the way of the Model

T, and supermarkets and department stores have joined the exodus to the suburbs. According to Pat Mentzer, director of the Church of the Messiah's food pantry:

> Target is the only mall in the city. At Lafayette Park there was an A & P. The store was dirty and wasn't near anything. Makes you wonder if they deliberately let it get that way so no one will want to shop there. So then they can say, "Well sorry, not enough people are shopping at the store." So they let it run down and that justifies closing it down and opening up another store in the suburbs. Sears had one store in Highland Park, but it wasn't convenient. Our people want to go to K-Mart. They want to go to Toys R Us. Should they have to travel outside the city to shop?[3]

Boarded-up buildings, fire-damaged houses, empty lots where once there were stores—this is urban desertification. It's eerie. Block after block after block. But if whites, jobs, supermarkets, and shopping malls have moved out of Detroit, crack cocaine has moved in. One of the worst drug corners in the city of Detroit is within three blocks of the Church of the Messiah. Here in this city, where the high school dropout rate is 70 percent, the beeper (worn, like doctors' beepers, on belts for ease in making drug connections and drug deals) is a more enduring status symbol that the high school diploma. Phil MacVean, a Church of the Messiah member, who is supervisor for the East Side of Detroit for Children's Protective Services of the Wayne County Department of Social Services, says of crack:

> Look at it . . . crack is so cheap, so addictive, it's created a whole new scene. Parents on crack are trying to raise their kids. Look at that blue house [pointing down the street]. We're dealing with twenty-two people living in there. People beating up on kids. They don't want to live like that. They don't want to abuse their kids, but crack makes them crazy.
>
> So that affects us. We can't get people into our profession. It's too draining. Crack is too

untreatable. Social workers now ask themselves, why should we work with these crazy people?"[4]

So social workers join the exodus.

Beverly Loudon, Messiah's teen youth director, expresses the distress of many who try to comprehend what Detroit's morass of problems is doing to the youth:

> I see their giftedness. I see their talent. These kids have been through so much they don't have a vision for themselves. We don't yet have a kid in youth ministry that has graduated from high school. Here the whole welfare mentality is internalized.[5]

In this urban desert, this wilderness of so much human suffering, confusion, and anguish, the Church of the Messiah stands as an oasis. In this environment, according to the Church of the Messiah's rector, the Rev. Ronald Spann, "We are always trying to integrate . . . . What is faith? What does the Gospel have to offer here?"[6]

## *THE CHURCH OF THE MESSIAH TODAY IS CREATING A GLOBAL VILLAGE*

Detroit provided much of the inspiration for the 1988 General Convention's resolution, "Taking Action for Economic Justice." In fact, a member of the Church of the Messiah, James Perkinson, wrote the theological statement for the resolution. In it he also captures the theological undergirding of the Church of the Messiah:

> At issue is not only our willingness to reach out and help the disadvantaged but, even more critically, the development of the capacity to *receive* from them . . . . [In Jesus' time, in first-century Palestine] it was a question of *reception*. The challenge to the Twelve in their servant role as co-leaders of the poor masses with Jesus was to become vulnerable to them to the point of genuine interdependence. The masses were to become for the Twelve a primary sacramental reality (Mt.

25:31-46) and a significant human community (Mk. 4:31-35) .... At the heart, then, of the Biblical vision of the People of God is the idea of a historical community living the eschatological *reversal.* "Church" is that human geography in which they own and live out their need for the poor and the poor discover and live out their gifts for the rich in the name of Jesus Christ.[7]

The Church of the Messiah's core members live out that idea of eschatological reversal so intensively that through it their lives, livelihoods, and lifestyles are being transformed. They see their lives and their futures as bound up with the life and future of the neighborhood.

The Church of the Messiah is located on East Grand Boulevard, known locally simply as "The Boulevard." It was once *the* grand promenade of the city of Detroit and continues south directly to Belle Isle Park, a delightful island park in the Detroit River.

Structurally, the Church of the Messiah's leadership consists of 1) a pastoral team which is composed of the rector, a lay associate, and two elders who are called by the congregation; 2) ministry directors for children, teens, adults (including the residents of the various adult foster care homes located close to the church in the Boulevard's once-grand homes), Girl Scouts, housing, and the food pantry; 3) the vestry; and 4) office assistants. The great majority of the members of the congregation walk to church, though a few members drive in from other areas.

The members are organized under the explicit assumption that "the redemptive power of Jesus Christ can work through a local church to change individual lives and transform a neighborhood."[8] Thus the main focuses of Messiah's ministries are housing, serving the nutritional needs of the elderly, and training and developing youth.

The Church of the Messiah is a founding member of the Christian Community Development Association (CCDA), a coalition of church-related ministries whose goal is to mobilize spiritual and economic resources in ways that are holistic and redemptive. According to CCDA's John Perkins:

> Someone must take responsibility for redeeming America's ghettos and fostering leadership in our

apathetic youth . . . . We are rolling up our sleeves and doing it ourselves. Together . . . we can take the whole Gospel on a whole mission to the whole world.[9]

In 1978 the Church of the Messiah established the Messiah Housing Corporation, whose primary purpose is to buy and renovate multiunit residential properties and make them available to low-income individuals and families. Currently two housing projects have been completed and two more—a thirty-unit building and a seventy-eight-unit building—are being developed. New housing, providing some 200 units, is in the planning stage. In addition, forty-one homes were repaired in 1989.

Through the food pantry, 100 area seniors are provided with staple food products as well as fresh fruit and vegetables. Food is delivered by volunteers to those who are unable to come to the church.

Through the training and development of youth, the leaders of the Teen Ministry are attempting to offer a viable alternative with a stronger appeal than the prevailing ethos of the streets. These programs consist of Bible study, tutoring, group meetings, recreation, summer camping, and field trips. Messiah's church school enrollment increased by 100 percent in 1989. New plans include programs of enrichment in the arts called "Super Saturdays."

Dozens of the once-grand mansions of East Grand Boulevard are now group homes for people with special needs. They provide a sheltered environment for the elderly, for those released from psychiatric hospitals, for sexually abused children and adults, for drug addicts, for alcoholics, and for those who are developmentally disabled (mentally retarded). Serving these residents has been one of the Church of the Messiah's ministries.

Each Sunday morning, Dave Beer and Liz Rogers, who are responsible for this ministry, pick up the residents at their homes and bring them to the church, where they enjoy morning coffee, doughnuts, and fellowship and participate in Bible reading, prayer, and singing. Many of them remain at the church for the main liturgy of the day.

With group-home members scattered throughout the congregation, the most conspicuous feature of Messiah's Sunday liturgies is the makeup of the congregation. Here truly is an eclectic mix, a "Rainbow Coalition," which includes all sorts and conditions of people—black and white, people dressed in everything from blazers to blue jeans. Psychotics and social workers sit side by side. Schoolteachers and waiters and welfare moms, doctors and down-and-outs—they're all here. And children are everywhere.

The worship itself is just as eclectic—traditional Book of Common Prayer, with a variety of voices reading Scripture and prayers; Hymnal 1982 and Gospel music, piano and guitar and percussion instruments. The Church of the Messiah gets as close to lay presidency of the Eucharist as the Discernment Team members have ever experienced. Presidency is shared by the clergy and the elders of the congregation. Visually, too, the altar has been moved right out of the sanctuary and placed at the crossing, with the pews in a semicircular formation around it. The focus is on God's action at the table and God's action among the people of God.

The worship leaders sit among the worshipers. Modest, understated vestments are worn only by the clergy. Robes are worn neither by choir members nor eucharistic ministers. Visually, through the arrangements of worship, a unity is conveyed. It is symbolic of the unity also expressed in members' living and serving beyond the church doors, where members of the congregation see themselves as partners in ministry.

Several of Messiah's members of longest standing contend that community building, if it is to be authentic and enduring, is a twenty-year process. Trust-building, relationship-building, networking, do not happen overnight. As Jackie Spann says, "We had to *earn* a place of trust."[10]

Much of Messiah's ministry developed through trial and error, as the community's leaders readily admit, "through many mistakes." There have been losses and disappointments. Some members have left, but others have come. New growth is coming from the neighborhood; people were living in the vicinity and discovered the church, whereas members who came in the 1970s and early 80s came first to discover a Christian community, then stayed to discover God's call in the neighborhood. In the course of it all, Pastoral Associate Nancy Cannon said that:

> Our motivation always needs to be purified and abandoned to the one who goes before us, Jesus

Christ. He leads us and calls us. There are some check points that are important. Whatever we do we must ask ourselves if it is loving, if it is giving, and if it is just.[11]

## *UNDERSTANDING THE STORY*

The Church of the Messiah was built—as St. Paul's Church—in 1851 on Congress Avenue. It is the third oldest church building in the city of Detroit and has official historic designation. In 1906 the building was moved to its present location and renamed the Church of the Messiah. According to Charles Turner:

> Messiah was *the* proper East Side church. There were two other Episcopal churches on the East Side, but Messiah was *the church* of the East Side.[12]

But in the 1960s the white East Siders left for the surburbs. For a while some of them commuted in on Sunday mornings. As the neighborhood changed, a few members were concerned that the Church of the Messiah do something to reach out to its new neighbors. Sister Hilda Mason, the first black woman commissioned in the Church Army, came to the church as an outreach worker. With Sylvia Peabody and Deloris Colman, she started a day-care center for children in the neighborhood.

In spite of these efforts, there was a gap between those who occupied the church during the week and those who drove in on Sunday mornings. And the Sunday morning suburban membership was declining fast. By 1971, with the parish on the verge of collapse, Archdeacon (later Suffragan Bishop) Irving Mayson, who was responsibile for the Wayne District where Messiah is located, was ready to consider almost anything to revitalize the church. The Church of the Epiphany, close to Messiah, was in similar straits (and actually closed down in 1974). In these circumstances, the Diocese of Michigan decided to link these two marginal parishes together in a team pastorate and call a black rector and a white associate to serve as a team. While in the background of the story during the following years, the diocese continues its commitment to the Church of the Messiah and has made significant investment in the congregation by grants and other means.

The European-American priest was easier to find than the African-American, so the Rev. Dean Cole arrived first. Ronald Spann, a recent seminary graduate, was one of twelve clergy to be interviewed for the position and recalls now that he "only interviewed for the experience of interviewing." Spann, who came in November, 1971, was made rector and priest—in that order—within a year. Indeed Spann and Cole were, by appearances, quite the odd couple: Cole white, slight of build with red hair, and Spann tall and black. Cole had been a priest for fifteen years, Spann less than a year. Nonetheless they were a good match and an effective team.

Ronald Spann had been formed for the ministry in interesting ways. He explains:

> As a black pastor whose formal theological training began at the end of the sixties, I was deeply affected by the revolution of awareness that swept African America in that era. The quest for freedom, justice, and a new consolidation of our peoplehood were central to the movement, and their ideals led to a renewed self-image and historical self-awareness in my own life.
>
> Toward the end of that period, my own journey included an encounter with Agnes Sanford, a pioneer and mentor in the sacramental healing ministry. Through her gentle and articulate witness I was introduced to the dimension of personal renewal as it was burgeoning in the charismatic renewal among the mainline denominations. A freshly articulated sense of the indwelling Holy Spirit soon involved me in a total reframing of my understanding of spirituality as life in the Spirit, in the Spirit of Christ and the prophets.
>
> This new impulse of faith soon led me to explore the vision of the Church's corporate renewal, particularly as it was lived in Houston's Church of the Redeemer. Through appointment to my present cure, that church's renewal as a

> ministering community would greatly influence our development in Detroit. So I found myself doubly preoccupied throughout the last two decades with the vision of justice and community as the keys to human destiny.[13]

Spann felt he might be able to do something with Messiah. "I wanted to bring charismatic renewal to the parish, but I didn't know how that would happen."[14] In addition to Sanford, the Rev. Graham Pulkingham, who had passed through Detroit in May of 1971, became an important figure to Spann. Hearing Pulkingham in Detroit, Spann felt that perhaps what he was doing in Houston could have some application at the Church of the Messiah. Thus the following August, Spann and Dean Cole spent a long weekend at the Church of the Messiah where Pulkingham was then serving.

> Graham had a vision of the Church I'd not encountered before. Sure, as I looked around at the Houston church, I didn't see many blacks or Hispanics. While I didn't see the ethnic diversity which was important to me, the obvious reality of their vital community was an unavoidable fact for me to process.[15]

At the invitation of Messiah, in February, 1972, the Church of the Redeemer dispatched two members, Jerry and Esther Barker, to come to Detroit to help them get started. With Ron they moved into the Epiphany parish, and later to Deloris Coleman's home and other sties over the next fifteen months. The Barkers stayed for over a year. Jerry helped Spann and Cole adapt the Redeemer model to East Side Detroit, and they began to gather their congregation. As Phil MacVean recalls it:

> In the college town I grew up in, the Episcopal Church was always an upper-crust institution. It was eye-opening to come to Detroit and be enticed to come to a prayer meeting at Messiah and find such an interesting situation. Nancy Cannon [now part of the Pastoral Team] invited me down to a prayer meeting. I work in social services. I was running into road blocks all the time. I saw how

poorly we do it. At Messiah I was excited with what I was seeing.[16]

He went on to explain how a holistic approach to persons was often lacking in city social services. At Messiah,

> They were excited about the Gospel, excited about Jesus. On an intellectual level it was exciting but I could see it was more than that. Here people were putting their lives on the line.[17]

As MacVean and Spann concede now, many of the people who came to Messiah in the early days of the present ministry were white, middle-class young adults who were psychologically and spiritually very needy. The nation was, after all, just emerging from the torments of the Vietnam War. Flower children and hippies, dissatisfied with traditional models, were searching for alternatives. Many intentional communities were formed as a response. While those who discovered the Church of the Messiah weren't exactly hippies and flower children, they were searchers. They had heard about what was going on at Messiah, and they wanted to be a part of it. They bought and shared houses close to the church and, like early ecclesial communities, they shared all things in common. They pooled incomes and assets; they shared cars; they helped each other. Months passed, and years. According to Ron Spann,

> During the initial five years we were involved with our neighbors through the day care center, the school, summer programs and vacation Bible school as well as overnight hospitality to "street people"—some of them right out of the area—but our efforts were not strategically systemic.[18]

Nonetheless, by late 1976 the members of Messiah's households had become increasingly aware of the gap between the community of the church and the neighborhood community. Although Messiah members were living in the community, they began to feel that they were not of the community. They began to ask themselves if, even though they lived on the Boulevard, they were really engaged in the neighborhood, or were they in fact more engaged with their own church community's perceived needs.

As certain realizations were beginning to dawn, the twenty-four-unit apartment building across the street from Messiah was heavily damaged by fire. Through sheltering and feeding the displaced residents in the fire's aftermath, the Messiah members were confronted with the prospect that this building right on the church's doorstep might become an empty shell, a lifeless skeleton, just like so many other buildings on Detroit's East Side. They asked themselves what would become of those who would be dislocated, and were themselves challenged to seek a solution. As James Perkinson recalls now:

> The gap between "church" and "neighborhood"—between "community households" set up on nearby streets, and ordinary households of disadvantaged neighbors who were trapped there by poverty and racial discrimination—had revealed itself as a spiritual and sociological gap the size of the Grand Canyon. The leadership core of the parish began to face this reality. Gospel wholeness either redeemed across racial and class lines or it wasn't "gospel."
>
> Consequently, a new step of faith was contemplated by the leadership on this late winter evening in 1977. Community leaders had shown themselves willing to be vulnerable to each other's needs and gifts, and in so doing, had created a liberated zone for Gospel values that flies in the face of mainstream culture.
>
> But . . . the real test was yet to come. Would the church so trust the Gospel imperatives and promises that it would willingly offer itself in vulnerable relationship to the disadvantaged and marginalized of our culture, even at the risk of its own modest comfort and well-being?
>
> . . . The advocacy of Jesus for the poor of his day was based upon community *with* the poor and a beginning liberation and salvation of the poor. The advocacy of the church on behalf of poor neighbors needed some structure of mutual vulnerability and community *with* the neighborhood and some process of social and

spiritual liberation *of* the neighborhood. So, talk that night in 1977 centered not only on purchase of a building to provide decent affordable housing for those with low income, but even more upon the initiation of caring friendships with tenants by the handful of church members who would move in.[19]

Messiah bought the building in April, 1978, and all the residents of its extended households moved in with the neighborhood residents. They called this building, appropriately, The Mustard Tree. It was the seed, a first step, in reclaiming the neighborhood.

But any naive thoughts the Messiah members—who made up about 10 percent of the Mustard Tree's residents at that time—might have had, were quickly dispelled. As long as the Church of the Messiah was landlord and held the keys of ownership, they held the keys of power; and that created a built-in adversarial relationship. The Messiah members' efforts to form a tenants' association failed, but perhaps the failure was fortunate since the neighborhood tenants themselves formed their own association with their own controls. Hard though it was for the good-willed Messiah residents, the experience supplied the impetus for the maturing of the Messiah Housing Corporation (1978) and the adoption of a formal cooperative model for ownership. Thus as events developed, in 1984 the Mustard Tree was acquired by its residents and became an autonomous, self-managed cooperative with *all residents* sharing equal ownership and responsibilities.

In 1987 the Church of the Messiah purchased St. Paul Manor, a fifty-unit apartment complex, and converted it to thirty-six units (to accommodate more families with children).

With two more large apartment units in the process of being rehabilitated and plans for new construction, the Church of the Messiah Housing Corporation is making a dent in the renovation of the neighborhood. It is lending hope in an environment that was once an unrelieved urban wasteland. Is it a coincidence that gardens are springing to life in vacant lots? That straight rows of beans, lettuce, and zucchini are rising out of the ashes of burned-out homes? There is a long way to go, but these scattered plots suggest new life appearing.

A street artist has taken over several blocks of nearby Heidelberg Street, where he is using junk to make art forms with serious and humorous themes. There is a doghouse with a television in it. There are park benches with shoes lined up on the seats. Colorful clutter covers whole sides of abandoned houses. The artist has been discovered by the *Detroit Free Press* and the Detroit Institute of Arts, and he serves as a symbol and a reminder that art, beauty, and vitality can arise from the wasteland.

As art emerges, as flowering plants appear, as ordinary buildings are saved from the junk pile by becoming cooperatives, so also is the Church of the Messiah flowering as its many ministries are maturing and stabilizing.

Looking back on it now, it appears that with the reclamation of the Mustard Tree and the shift in focus from the internal community needs of Messiah's members to following the call of Christ to serve the whole neighborhood, the tensions between the pastoral role of the church community and its prophetic voice became clear. It is not that the needs of the members were being ignored; rather, the church members' lives and hopes were seen in relationship to the destiny of the wider neighborhood. It became clear that those who simply came to Messiah because of the pastoral community were not having their needs met, and they drifted away. Nancy Cannon explains:

> We had to ask ourselves whether we were going to be foreigners in our neighborhood. We had been almost like a cloistered community, closed in on ourselves. There had been an almost subconscious transition to becoming a neighborhood church, where the neighborhood altered what happened.
>
> We've had important touch points along the way. There's been the Sojourners Community in Washington. The influence of John Perkins [founder of the Christian Community Development Association] was very great. He could be described as a modern-day apostle coming out of a southern black church experience. He speaks of the three Rs:—reconciliation, relocation and redistribution—as strategies for community development.[20]

It became clear that the earlier ministries and priorities

had run their course: The day-care center closed. A small school the church had established (up to third grade) also closed, since members wanted better schools for their children than their own parish community was able to provide. The economic sharing among Messiah members ended in 1987. Members of the church community who had been working for small salaries wanted to work in the neighborhood and beyond. Since the Mustard Seed experience, in short, the church community was opening up. As Nancy Cannon expressed it:

> The school and the day-care center closed, but then the youth ministry and the housing corporation expanded. It's like the energy shifted. We channel our energies into youth ministry. We're in relationship with a lot more kids now than we were before. The energy has shifted. These earlier ministries didn't just close down.
> 
> Jackie's brother's in jail for murder. Behind the alley some kids broke in and stole money. We're clearly fighting for souls with these drugs. Some kids are coming to church with their beepers on. We know we're dealing with several drug dealers right now. Their business pays a little more than ours [i.e., the church], but we're working on finding these kids summer jobs.[21]

The Mustard Tree was what Richard Cannon, director of the Church of Messiah Housing Corporation, called a "bonding event." Another bonding event was the murder (still unsolved) of a much-loved member of the Messiah community.

On April 7, 1988, Michelle Marie Rougeau was stabbed to death in St. Paul Manor, and Messiah members are still dealing with the significance of her death. Murders are commonplace in the Boulevard area. Five-year-old Justin Cannon, an otherwise sensitive and fragile youngster, talked in an almost matter-of-fact manner of three people he knew of who had been killed in house fires. But Michelle's death was different. A number of Messiah's members talked about it in chilling detail, as if it had occurred yesterday. In Nancy Cannon's words, "From that day our lifes have never been the same." Messiah's children deal with it by frequently taking flowers to Michelle's grave, which is very close to the church. For their parents, acceptance is more difficult.

Michelle had come to the community about 1980. A neurological nurse, she was young, talented—a folk dancer—and beautiful. She had a big heart and was held in great affection. Discussing her violent death, John Trombley reflected:

> The effect is interesting. A lot of people left. They felt that this was more than anyone could ask of them and their families. Michelle was mourned throughout the city. She was always doing something for someone else. She'd been in Africa. She was involved in Wayne State dance groups and international dance.
>
> At her death we realized just how many lives she had touched. She'd written letters that spoke to many.[22]

Trombley went on to explain that before Michelle's death,

> We'd had some illusions about God's call in our lives. We all had kind of this false sense of, well, if God called us here there was nothing that could happen to us. It really jarred us, in the sense that this is *not* what God says and it is not what the promise is.
>
> It's tragic to think that it might be God's doing to weed out the flock and bind us together. I think that's what happened, because we're always learning things in terms of our faith. We're always being pushed to the limits.[23]

And Nancy Cannon says:

> As we reflected on the meaning of Michelle's death two things came to mind: 1) We formed a "blood bond" with the neighborhood, and 2) We finally put to death any illusions that God would somehow protect our bodies from harm since we had embraced the danger of this lifestyle. We had to accept the fact that living in the ghetto meant no guarantee for us any more than for our neighbors.[24]

Indeed, illusions won't last, and there are no guarantees that anyone will be prevented from physical harm. The Church of the Messiah members are being "pushed to the limits" as John Trombley expresses it. But as they are being pushed they are also learning the extent of Jesus' reign over all of life. Theirs is a life of radical discipleship. They are often troubled, but not crushed; in doubt at times, rarely in despair. They are hurt at times, but not destroyed. They carry in their bodies the death of Jesus, and Jesus' life is plainly seen in them. And through it all they illustrate that supreme power belongs to God (2 Cor 4:7-11).

## *DISTINCTIVE FEATURES*

According to the rector of the Church of the Messiah, Ronald Spann:

> God uses the fruit of our faithfulness to achieve something bigger than all of us together. What I need is a burst of hope to give energy to my faithfulness.[25]

That "burst of hope" can be something as small as a phone call from a youth member in jail (which directly prompted that comment of Spann's) or as big as the Mustard Tree, the Church of the Messiah's first multiunit cooperative housing project. But it is clearly hope and faith that have pushed the Church of the Messiah members to their limits and sustained their ministries. There is no "cheap grace" here but a deep and abiding hope. Specifically a number of factors contribute to the success of the Church of the Messiah, but the main one is the fusion of prophetic vision, true justice, and pastoral vocation.

- ***An Integration of Prophetic Vision and Social Justice with Spirituality and Pastoral Care:*** Ronald Spann explains:

> Many prophetic renewal leaders seem unable to extend the prophetic vision into an integration of the Church's pastoral vocation. They have a preoccupation with the rights and wrongs of the Church and world that ironically turns prophetic activism into a ministry of law, to which Paul speaks urgently: "God . . . has made us . . . ministers of a new covenant, not in a written code, but in the Spirit;

for the written code kills, but the Spirit gives life" (2 Cor 3:5-6).

In too many parishes and dioceses distinguished by extraordinary prophetic leadership I hear of declining membership, inability to keep program commitments, polarization. An overwhelming burden is laid on the flock without the corresponding help needed to bear it. At this point two authentic movements of the Holy Spirit in the Church [prophetic activism and spiritual renewal] beg to come together.

The renewal of spirit and of conscience are inseparably linked precepts in the biblical evangel . . . . Consider Jesus' words from the Sermon on the Mount; "Seek first God's kingdom and God's righteousness [justice], and all these things shall be yours as well . . . ."

The Kingdom of God orders human experience first in the *spiritual reality;* second, a *moral reality;* and third, a *socioeconomic reality.* Authentic renewal must take a path through all three aspects, regardless of which may be the point of departure. The supreme religious question is the triumph of life over death, which is the heart of the vision of the Kingdom. The supreme moral question is the vision of God's justice, beginning with the law and the prophets and culminating in Jesus Christ. They are meant to be embodied in a living community, provisionally in the Church, ultimately in the Kingdom.[26]

- **Willingness to Risk Something New:** In 1971 the Church of the Messiah was down to fifty members and on its last legs. Willingness to experiment, to try something new, even something not very traditional, opened the doors of Messiah to the possibility of new life.
- **Flexibility and Freedom to Allow the Community to Change:** Many intentional communities (i.e., communities drawn together by idealism and a strong desire to live an alternate lifestyle) have "bitten the dust, because of doctrinaire adherence to expectations and ideals long after their usefulness

has ended. Athol Gill, in a *Sojourners* article, "Unity at the Center: Lessons of Diversity in Community,"[27] talks about the pitfalls of many intentional communities. Messiah's community has avoided most of them through its flexibility.

Through the years circumstances have changed: members have married, have become parents, have seen their children through various stages of growth. Members have gone from working in the parish community to outside employment. They have sought better schooling for their children, sometimes by working with the Detroit public schools. They have modified the economic sharing among community members: some of Messiah's members live in shared households, others live as nuclear families in their own homes and apartments. Some live in Messiah's co-ops. Others commute in to Messiah. There are all levels of psychic involvement also. This loosening up is probably what has both enabled the community to remain a community that has kept pace with current realities and has opened the door to more genuine neighborhood participation. The main growth now is from the community of people who were living in the vicinity of the Church of the Messiah anyway, not from those who come to Messiah specifically seeking an intentional community (although some of this still occurs also).

- ***Patience for the Long Haul:*** Generally speaking, deep change only occurs after deep trust has been established. It evolves slowly over an extended time period. Why should the neighborhood folks have immediately jumped to the tune of a ragtag band of youthful idealists led by an "odd couple" of priests? Wouldn't they be gone when the next fad came marching down the Boulevard? As Jackie Spann said, "We had to *earn* a place of trust." And it has taken this long—almost twenty years—for it was not until two to three years ago that the Church of the Messiah began to get significant numbers of new members from the neighborhood.

- ***Shared Leadership:*** Richard Cannon said, "Leadership has to be a function of the community. Leadership comes up out of the community."[28] It's a very Pauline idea, and has been given contemporary expression by Roland Allen and Latin American liberation theologians. The principle of leadership's coming from the community is evidenced by the makeup of the pastoral team, expressed and celebrated in the liturgy.

In particular, as far as clerical leadership is concerned, Ronald Spann's leadership has been collegial from the start. It has been a ministry of long duration that, although shaped by definite ideas, has also been determined by the realities of the situation.

- **Contextual Analysis:** Messiah members really wrestle with the meaning of the Gospel in their place and time. How are the issues of the neighborhood to be related to the heart of the biblical vision of God's justice for all people? What does radical discipleship mean? What does it cost? How is the idea of eschatological reversal to be understood and acted upon right here, right now? What is the meaning of death? Is life really stronger than death? What is the meaning of community? The members of the Church of the Messiah do not shrink from asking the big theological questions of our day. And they are formed by the exploration and the actions that result.
- *A Story to Be Shared:* The Church of the Messiah's housing ministry gave birth to The Michigan Plan, which became Taking Action for Economic Justice, a plan for the whole Church. Modestly, the Rev. Ronald Spann, says "They [Episcopal Church USA] would have done something on economic justice anyway, but the co-op image came out of here. Of course they got their other reasons after that. We live by sharing. Everybody lives by sharing. When we see ourselves being imitated . . . that's our hope."[29]

## AN ISSUE RAISED BY THE VISIT TO THE CHURCH OF THE MESSIAH

What is evident on the East Side of Detroit—in the 123-block Island View Association Neighborhood—is, in an exaggerated form, just what is going on in every urban area of the United States. Homelessness, drugs, the disintegration of the family, the scrambling for jobs, abuse of all kinds, alcoholism, suicide, and murder. It goes on in every town and suburb too, but in urban centers the issues are not hidden by money and pretense.

Surely the health of a society and the quality of its justice can be measured by the quality of its inner cities and the quality of justice its urban dwellers enjoy.

## RESOURCES

Jackson, Meta and David. *Coming Together: All Those Communities and What They're Up To.* Minneapolis: Bethany Books, 1979.

*Life in the Spirit Seminars,* Team manual. Ann Arbor: Servant Books, 1973, 1979. Tapes also available.

Perkins, John. *A Quiet Revolution.* Ventura, CA: Regal Books, 1978.

Perkins, John. *With Justice for All.* Ventura, CA: Regal Books, 1982.

Perkinson, James W. "Havens of Trust in Detroit: A Parish Bridges the Gap between 'Church' and 'Neighborhood.'" *The Living Church,* July 10, 1988, pp. 8-9.

Schillebeeckx, Edward. *Ministry: Leadership in the Community of Jesus Christ.* New York: Crossroad, 1984.

Spann, Ronald. "Justice and Community: A Renewal Perspective," *Liturgy,* Ethics and Justice Issue, Vol. 7, Spring, 1989, pp. 8-15.

Vanier, Jean. *Community and Growth.* New York: Paulist Press, 1979.

Wallis, Jim. *An Agenda for Biblical People.* New York: Harper and Row, 1976.

Wallis, Jim. *Call to Conversion: An Agenda for Biblical People.* New York: Harper and Row, 1981.

**For Consultation:**

Christian Community Development Association, 3848 W. Ogden Avenue, Chicago, IL 60623.

PRH—Personality and Human Relations, Box 721, Winnipeg, Manitoba, Canada R3C 2K3.

John Perkins Foundation for Reconciliation and Growth, 1582 Navarro Street, Pasadena, CA 91103.

## NOTES

[1] Charles Turner, interview in Detroit, June 1, 1990.
[2] Dean Cole, as quoted in "Messiah Neighborhood House, All People Welcome," *New Covenent,* p. 19. No other publication details.
[3] Pat Mentzer, interview in Detroit, June 2, 1990.
[4] Phil MacVean, interview in Detroit, June 2, 1990.
[5] Beverly Loudon, interview in Detroit, June 3, 1990.
[6] Ronald Spann, interview in Detroit, June 3, 1990.

[7] James Perkinson, "Taking Action for Economic Justice: A Theological Assessment," Episcopal General Convention, Detroit, 1988, pp. 11 and 12 *passim*.
[8] Church of the Messiah brochure.
[9] John Perkins, as quoted in Church of the Messiah, "Annual Report of 1989 Ministries," p.1.
[10] Jacqueline Spann, interview in Detroit, June 2, 1990.
[11] Nancy Cannon, interview in Detroit, June 3, 1990.
[12] Charles Turner, interview.
[13] Ronald Spann, "Justice and Community," *Liturgy*, Ethics and Justice Issue, Vol. 7, Spring, 1989, p. 9.
[14] Ronald Spann, as quoted in "Messiah Neighborhood House," by Mary Ann Jahr, p. 21. No other publication details.
[15] Ronald Spann, interview in Detroit, June 2, 1990.
[16] Phil MacVean, interview in Detroit, June 1, 1990.
[17] *Ibid.*
[18] Ronald Spann, manuscript correction, August 7, 1990.
[19] James W. Perkinson, "Havens of Trust in Detroit: A Parish Bridges the Gap between 'Church' and 'Neighborhood,' " *The Living Church*, July 10, 1988, pp. 8-9.
[20] Nancy Cannon, interview.
[21] *Ibid.*
[22] John Trombley, interview in Detroit, June 1, 1990.
[23] *Ibid.*
[24] Nancy Cannon, correspondence, June 5, 1990.
[25] Ronald Spann, interview in Detroit, June 3, 1990.
[26] Ronald Spann, "Church Renewal: Seek First the Kingdom," *Episcopalian*, Professional Pages, November, 1989, p. G.
[27] Athol Gill, "Unity at the Center: Lessons on Diversity in Community," *Sojourners*, Vol. 19, June, 1990, pp. 21-23.
[28] Richard Cannon, interview in Detroit, June 2, 1990.
[29] Ronald Spann, interview in Detroit, June 3, 1990.

*Site Visitor:* Charles Turner
*Date of Visit:* June 1-3, 1990

*The tension between self-reliant competitive enterprise and a sense of public solidarity has been the most important unresolved problem in American history. Is it possible that we could become citizens again and together seek the common good?*

—Robert N. Bellah,
Habits of the Heart

## CHAPTER 6

# A PUBLIC CHURCH

## STORY OF A CORPORATION-SIZED CONGREGATION

### SAINT LUKE'S CHURCH
### ATLANTA

### *THE CONTEXT OF MISSION DISCERNMENT: ATLANTA*

"Atlanta is a city of newcomers," according to Joe Martin, president of Atlanta Progress. "We've attracted a lot of well-trained, well-prepared people."[1] To Myrtle Davis, a member of Atlanta's City Council, "Atlanta is still a small city with big-city attitudes."[2]

Atlanta, capital of Georgia, is representative of the New South. The cityscape of the commercial, industrial, and financial giant is lined with steel and glass fingers, crisscrossed by traffic-filled expressways. Atlanta is a booming manufacturing and business center. Some 1,800 industrial plants manufacture more than 3,500 different commodities—aircraft, textiles, chemicals, automobiles, food products, paper, iron and steel, to name a few. Coca-Cola was introduced to the world in Atlanta in 1886, and still maintains its corporate headquarters here, as do 400 other Fortune-500 companies.

Atlanta is the birthplace of Dr. Martin Luther King, Jr., and the current home of former U.S. President Jimmy Carter.

In 1837, Atlanta was little more than a railroad surveyor's stake in a pine clearing named Terminus. It grew rapidly to become an important railroad and manufacturing center. It became a Confederate arsenal during the Civil War. In 1864 the city was leveled by Sherman's occupying forces, but with ingenuity and carpetbagger money, the city was booming again by the turn of the century.

Then, as now, people came to Atlanta, according to Joe Martin, "To seek fame and fortune. Atlanta attracts the most highly educated and talented and the least educated and talented."[3] In Atlanta wealth and poverty sit side by side, for in the shadows of Atlanta's glittering skyscrapers hover the homeless and outcasts who shuffle about waiting for handouts and helping hands.

There are, in effect, two Atlantas—the Atlanta of the well-educated and upwardly mobile who have found the fame and fortune Joe Martin speaks of, who work in Atlanta's bold office buildings and skyscrapers, and the other Atlanta of those who linger at their doorways. Of the twenty-five largest urban areas in the U.S.A., Atlanta has the smallest urban core.[4] To this small downtown area are drawn those seeking better health care, better homes, better schools, better opportunity. Atlanta has become a welfare magnet, and yet it cannot keep up with the influx of people with serious needs who keep pouring in. Economic development and code enforcement have caused the loss of 8,000 housing units since 1980. Yet people keep coming. They come in from the rural South to blend their voices to the 40 different native tongues heard in Atlanta's public schools.

Georgia is third in the nation in high school dropout rates and, according to the Rev. Tim MacDonald, head of Atlanta's Concerned Black Clergy, the city has between 8,000 and 10,000 homeless people—men, women, and children—who clamor to get in the city's fifty shelters. The United Way of Metropolitan Atlanta calculated that in 1989 the fastest-growing segment of Atlanta's homeless population was children under the age of six, with 38 percent of Atlanta's homeless composed of families with children.[5]

In order to understand St. Luke's, it helps to understand the two Atlantas, for St. Luke's is a public church with a mission and ministry in Atlanta. Thus the way Atlanta goes, so goes St. Luke's. Studs Terkel describes the widening gap between the haves and have-nots as "the great divide," and wrote a book about it, called *The Great Divide*. The great divide is evident in every American urban center, but perhaps it is more evident in Atlanta, owing to Atlanta's extremes of wealth and poverty, and the smallness of the downtown area where they are crushed together. Kevin P. Phillips, a political analyst, has also written about the gap, but does not believe Americans have yet comprehended its significance.

> The 1980s were the triumph of upper America—an ostentatious celebration of wealth, the political ascendancy of the rich and a glorification of capitalism, free markets and finance. Not only did the concentration of wealth quietly intensify, but the sums involved took a megaleap. The definition of rich—and who's no longer rich—changed as radically during the Reagan era as it did during the nouveaux riches eras of the late 19th century and the 1920s . . . . But while money, greed and luxury became the stuff of popular culture, few people asked why such great wealth had concentrated at the top and whether this was the result of public policy. Political thinkers, even those who professed to care about the armies of homeless sleeping on grates and other sad evidence of a polarized economy, had little to say . . . .[6]

The 1970s were years of confidence, years when Americans felt certain the answers to social problems were within their reach. There was optimism. There still is, but Atlanta, just like every other U.S. city, has been through the 1980s, and the cracks are starting to show and solutions are not so easily come by. The same can be said of St. Luke's. There was optimism, there still is, but the times are more difficult now as the gap between wealth and poverty widens, as more and more people are falling over the edge into poverty. As Atlanta stretches itself to accommodate its two populations, so St. Luke's holds within itself the two Atlantas, while it is at the same time challenged by the needs and problems of Atlanta's shadow side.

St. Luke's Episcopal Church is at the crossroads between the two Atlantas. As Joe Martin (incidentally, not a member of St. Luke's) reflected on St. Luke's ministry and its contribution to the City of Atlanta, he said,

> St. Luke's Episcopal Church has been right in the middle of all this social ferment. St. Luke's got started trying to alleviate the homeless problem in our city before most of us knew there was a homeless problem. And members of St. Luke's have individually in their own right been actively involved in Atlanta's community affairs.[7]

## *SAINT LUKE'S TODAY: A PUBLIC CHURCH*

St. Luke's is a public church, a characterization that is borne out in profiles of several of its members. Ann Cramer, for instance. Ann Cramer, St. Luke's junior warden, is director of I.B.M.'s Community and Government Relations Office for Atlanta and board chair of Leadership Atlanta. In 1990 the *Atlanta Constitution* (the well-known daily newspaper) bestowed on her its Public Service Award for her contributions to the public life of Atlanta. Ann walks easily through Atlanta's City Hall, greeting many friends and associates as she does so. Atlantans know and respect Ann. She makes a difference to the public life of Atlanta. She is just as much at ease among the milling crowds of homeless waiting for a ticket to get into St. Luke's Community Soup Kitchen for a noonday meal.

Neil Shorthouse, a vestry member and chair of St. Luke's Christian Education Committee, is the founder and executive director of Exodus, also known as the Street Academy, for children who are not doing well in Atlanta's traditional educational settings. Shorthouse started with seven teenagers in 1974 in space lent by St. Luke's. With a current budget of $1.2 million—including $562,000 from Atlanta's Board of Education and $13,000 from St. Luke's—the program is now operated in six locations.[8] When asked what preparation he had for the Street Academy, Shorthouse commented only that "I grew up in a country club and graduated in poli. sci. at the University of Pittsburgh!"[9] But he went on to say,

> I became converted to Christianity. My first conversion, if you will, was "I'm all right, I'm O.K." The second and deeper conversion was basically "It's all wrong." It was that "all wrong" conversion that motivated and pushed me into doing something to break kids' cycle of failure.[10]

Another vestry member, Bruce Gunter, who is chair of St. Luke's Community Outreach, is vice-president of the Social Responsibility Investment Group, an investment firm he and a partner founded in 1985. Gunter believes that we "should be aware of how one makes one's money."[11]

> For me this goes back twelve years when I determined to make Christianity a part of my life. I got politically involved and determined to make faith a part of everything I did.[12]
> ... These days more investors are recognizing that all investments have an ethical dimension. Consequently many individual and institutional investors are now investing their assets in companies that promise both financial, as well as social, benefits. Indeed, investors are discovering that the economic and social judgments of any business decision incurring great risks cannot be separated without incurring great risks now or in the future ....[13]

Gunter's firm handles the portfolios of individuals and institutions and specializes in investments dealing with environmental, human rights, and peace issues.

St. Luke's member Dr. Richard Groepper is director of client development for a private health-care management company and convenor of La Solidaridad, a group of St. Luke's members who are concerned about global economic justice and human rights, particularly as they pertain to Latin America. Groepper is also president of the neighborhood association where he lives. His wife, Betty, is a full-time lobbyist for Atlanta's League of Women Voters. Al Caproni, an attorney, is also president of his neighborhood association.

These are but a few of the many members who contribute to making St. Luke's "a public church." In Bruce Gunter's words, "We can reach anyone in the city with one telephone call."[14]

The term *public church* was coined by the theologian Martin Marty to describe churches whose members see their congregations as contributing to and shaping the public issues of the communities in which they are located. A Candler School of Theology group (Rollins Center for Church Ministries) at Emory University in Atlanta chose St. Luke's as an example of public church for their study, directed by Thomas E. Frank and James Fowler, *Research Project on the Faith and Practice of the Congregation.* Frank and Fowler cite seven characteristics of a public church, and St. Luke's is strong in all of them.[15]

According to Frank and Fowler, a public church:

1. Fosters a clear sense of Christian identity and commitment;
2. Manifests a diversity of membership;
3. Consciously prepares and supports members for vocation and witness in a pluralistic society;
4. Balances nurture and group solidarity within the church, and formation and accountability in work and public life beyond the wall of the church;
5. Has a pattern of authority and governance that keeps pastoral and lay leadership initiatives in a fruitful balance;
6. Offers its witness in publicly visible and publicly intelligible ways;
7. Is shaping a pattern of *paideia* for children, youth, and adults which works toward combining Christian commitment with vocation in public.[16]

St. Luke's is ideally placed to be a public church. Some say that "it's blocking downtown development" by its location, by the appearance of people who loiter on the grass in front of the church and on its steps, or rest in a line a block and a half long to wait for the Soup Kitchen to open its doors. But that depends upon what kind of "development" one has in mind. Bruce Gunter says, "We're uniquely positioned to be a bridge.

We're at the transportation, the wealth, and the cultural crossroads of the city."[17] Robert Fowler, a St. Luke's member for three years, agrees:

> As we strive to bring an international flavor to the city, we have to solve problems at our back door. Getting the Olympics here in 1996 won't solve poverty and crime. We wrestle with this because the mission of the city church is to bridge the gap between the ideology and the realism of the community, or the myth of the community. Through our building of bridges we can articulate the glory of God and be proud of it.[18]

Through its wide variety of ministries, St. Luke's is a public church that attempts to bridge the gaps.

Although St. Luke's is known mainly for its ministries in and to the wider Atlanta community—ministries that give it the image of a public church—St. Luke's does a great deal to nurture and enhance the lives of its own members. Of the 2,484 members on the parish rolls, on Sunday morning some 700 members attend one of the four services, including a service in Spanish for St. Luke's Latino members. Many are attracted to the Folk Mass, a popular setting of the liturgy written by Herbert Draesel, which has a very participatory flavor to it. Many are attracted by St. Luke's outstanding Christian Education Program, particularly for children. John Beane, senor warden, first came to St. Luke's in 1981 for its Christian education program. His family was attending another Atlanta parish, but his daughter Kathryn, then three years old, was unhappy. She explained to her father, "I love God, but not his church."[19] At St. Luke's Kathryn discovered that she could love God *and* God's church. St. Luke's church school has between 120 and 200 children in Sunday school, second only to the First Baptist Church. The Christian education director, Judy Jones, sees the church school as a prime vehicle for attracting new members to the congregation.

> Any church that is having an attendance problem should look at what they're doing for children, the preschool children in particular.[20]

St. Luke's has a lively youth group for high school students, led by an engaging young man, Eric Phelps, who also plays the guitar. In the summer he organizes Summer Youth Adventures. In 1989 the group went to Navajoland, where the youth group members taught Bible school and learned about the faith in a Native American context. In 1990 they went to Puerto Rico to work in a Diocese of Puerto Rico economic development project, planting coffee bushes and citrus trees.

St. Luke's has adult classes, Bible studies, special Lenten series. There is a new, year-long, Latin American curriculum, *Latin America—The Christian Reality and Promise,* which is organized by La Solidaridad. Guest speakers, many of them nationally known in church and public life, are often part of St. Luke's education programs.

There are small groups. Loaves and Fishes, for example, meets in members' homes for dinner, fellowship, and discussion led by a visiting speaker. There is a singles' group, study groups, and even neighborhood "zip groups," informal fellowship meetings for St. Luke's members who share the same ZIP code.

Among St. Luke's large staff and lay leaders there is a family atmosphere. Many of those now working on the staff are St. Luke's members who started as volunteers in parish programs. It was just one such St. Luke's family member, Jenny Pierson, who started the Community Soup Kitchen in 1974. She began by handing out sandwiches to people who were hanging around the church's back parking lot with no place to go and nothing to eat. In fact, many of Atlanta's most visible community services got their beginning at St. Luke's.

The Community Soup Kitchen has grown to a feeding ministry at which 540 guests have lunch daily, served by volunteers from two synagogues, three Roman Catholic churches, and seven Protestant denominations. There is access for the handicapped, a health clinic run by nurses from the Georgia Nurses Foundation, counseling services, and alcohol counseling meetings. There is MOPO—a mobile post office—which opened in 1988 to give people who live on the streets of Atlanta an address to receive their mail. Today MOPO is the home address for over 2,000, and the U.S. Postal Service has asked St. Luke's how they do it, since it might follow suit.

Montgomery Rocque, who used to live on Atlanta's streets, talked about the Community Soup Kitchen and its related ministries:

> I came here out of a basic need to get something, I was at level zero. I worked in labor pools. Now I'm trying to get a business started, but about a year ago I was nowhere. I was nothing. I came in from California. I heard about St. Luke's by word of mouth. When you're down and out you gather with other down-and-outs. You know there aren't many places for us to go. Now I come down here to economize and socialize. Most people I know are here. It gives me motivation. Maybe someday I can cut the strings totally.[21]

Out of the recognition that it's jobs that get people off the soup lines, SLEDCO (St. Luke's Economic Development Corporation) was established in 1982 as a separate corporation located at the church to identify jobs and to provide job placement and counseling services. In 1989, according to Richard Vaden, SLEDCO's director, 2,058 people were placed, of whom 102 have been successful in holding their jobs.

The Atlanta Food Bank, founded in 1979, channels surplus food that would otherwise be discarded from such sources as grocery stores, packinghouses, restaurants, and caterers to 400 soup kitchens, food pantries, halfway houses, orphanages, and the like. Bill Bolding, director of the Atlanta Food Bank, acknowleges St. Luke's help:

> In a very real sense, it started with the people of St. Luke's Episcopal Church. They gave us the emotional and moral strength that was to become our foundation. But they also gave us something tangible as well: our first home in the basement of the church.[22]

Bruce Gunter said, "The wonderful thing about St. Luke's is that it—whatever that it may be—can happen here."[23] Many of the members who have come to St. Luke's since the late 1970s will say that they came because of St. Luke's community ministries. Most of them have driven past one or two other Episcopal churches to get to St. Luke's, and many who get involved in the life of the congregation would concur with Nancy Burnett, a vestry member who says, "Most of our best friends are those we go to church with."[24]

Parish members, particularly the younger ones, feel that they are shaping St. Luke's ministry of service and its public face. They are not just recipients of ministry. For example, a group that was concerned about the deepening crisis in many Latin American countries visited Nicaragua, Peru, and Costa Rica "to increase our understanding of the Church's role in Latin America and our relationship with our southern neighbors."[25] Learning about global injustice which favors the North (particularly the U.S.A.) at the expense of the South, strolling through barrios, experiencing ecclesial base communities, hearing accounts of peasants who had disappeared for the "crime" of insisting on workers' rights—this led to the formation of La Solidaridad when the study group returned to Atlanta. When six Jesuits and their helpers were murdered in El Salvador on November 16, 1989, La Solidaridad sought and gained the approval of the vestry to erect crosses on the front lawn of St. Luke's. The crosses would stand, according to the words of the vestry's resolution, as a

> . . . silent witness to all who pass by of our deeply felt grief over the tragedy of violence—in El Salvador, in Lebanon and other countries around the world, and in the housing projects and streets of Atlanta, where children fall victim of drug users' bullets and the homeless die unnamed and unmourned.[26]

But the public character of St. Luke's is shaped by considerable dialogue and the direction provided by prayer. The vestry's response to the killing of the Jesuits is a good example: Dick Groepper remarked that prior to the vestry decision just quoted, members at first had "the immediate reaction that we're making a political statement by our actions and this is inappropriate."[27] La Solidaridad also wanted the vestry to endorse a letter it had drafted, addressed to President Bush, demanding an immediate investigation of the murders. This the vestry refused to go along with.

As the social situation in downtown Atlanta rapidly deteriorates, some parish members wonder if the needs on the streets will psychically overwhelm the members' ability to provide for them. The Community Outreach Ministries' Annual Report hints at some of the strain members feel:

> 1989 could be characterized as a "holding on" period in the face of mounting pressure, caused by the swelling increase of homelessness and substance abuse in our community.[28]

Some are asking whether perhaps the time has come for St. Luke's members to get more involved in looking at the root causes of poverty. Dan Todd, community relations director of the United Way, said,

> Churches haven't seen themselves in the role of advocacy. But people are now beginning to talk about lobbying the General Assembly, so perhaps it's coming.[29]

But there are others at St. Luke's who are beginning to question, not whether or not the parish should take on more of an advocacy role, but whether the parish should be so involved in community service using its own buildings. Wouldn't St. Luke's better serve the economic interests of downtown Atlanta if it were to move the Community Soup Kitchen farther out to the edge of the city? According to Tad Zelski, who owns Atlanta Hearing Aid Service, just a few doors down the street from St. Luke's,

> My business fronts Peachtree Street. As long as St. Luke's takes it [the soup kitchen ministry] on, it doesn't give others the opportunity. They [the street people] pee on my wall, they sleep in the back, they sleep in cars. They look in the windows. It scares my customers.[30]

And Al Caproni continued, "We're going to have to change. We're going to have to do whatever it takes to find out why they [the street people] are here and get them off."[31] As St. Luke's members consider how to handle the parish's public role in the future, and particularly in light of Atlanta's mounting social problems right outside the church doors, Dick Groepper says,

> We haven't talked enough to the business community. We need to say to them, "Come down here and talk with us. You need to come to the party too." And we need to face the government.[32]

Summing up, Ann Cramer concluded that "our greatest gifts are our clout and access to power and resources."[33]

## UNDERSTANDING THE STORY

Becky Zelski, who came to St. Luke's with her family in 1973, said, "The church was basically dying when I came."[34] Indeed, on April 18, 1974, *The Atlanta Constitution* came out with a story on St. Luke's entitled, "Rebirth of a Church: Gimme That New Time Religion."

*Rebirth* was the right word, because St. Luke's, just like so many other inner-city churches, had suffered from the ravages of the 1960s—white flight to the suburbs and the inability to refocus its ministry to the racial and ethnic groups that were moving into urban centers. In the *Atlanta Constitution* article, the Rev. Thomas Bowers, St. Luke's newly arrived rector, was quoted as saying, "A church must have a commitment beyond itself . . . . We must reach out into the community and be vital in many different ways."[35]

The year 1971 can be seen as the dividing line between the old St. Luke's and the new St. Luke's and also the dividing line between the way "public church" was understood by the old and new St. Luke's.

The old St. Luke's membership was composed of public leaders of Atlanta, and they came from "old families" and "old money" of the Old South It used to be said that social status in Atlanta could be measured by "a pew at St. Luke's and membership in the Piedmont Driving Club."[36] These old St. Luke's members, with their inherited wealth and social position, lived in what were then gracious houses surrounding the parish in what is now Midtown. As a history of the parish recounts:

> Atlanta society practiced deference to order and to one's place within it. While this was most evident in legal segregation of the races, it was also apparent in the respectful hierarchy of elected office and business leadership. The newspapers attended to the words of influential citizens. The rector of St. Luke's was often among them, providing a weekly sermon or column for publication.[37]

Although pew rents went out in 1921, and the growth

of the parish through the 1930s and 1940s kept pace with Atlanta's expansion, St. Luke's was not yet a "downtown church"; it was rather considered a family parish with a ministry to its own members. But the idea of a congregation as an extension of family and class could not be maintained in a newly emerging, more pluralistic Atlanta. The social upheavals of the 1960s changed Atlanta and forced upon St. Luke's members the task of rethinking the congregation's place and mission in Atlanta.

One cannot look at a refocused St. Luke's—the parish of "newtime religion"—without looking at what was going on in the larger milieu of Atlanta. As several authorities have pointed out:

> By the 1960s and '70s a much more cosmopolitan public was coming into force .... A place in Atlanta's circles of power was as likely to come by professional competence as by inheritance, by achievement as by ascription, or authority imputed by reason of birth. Atlanta was experiencing an influx of younger, well-educated professionals .... This new population valued social mobility, diversity, participation, and inclusiveness. They tended to be impatient with inherited authority, elected officials, and traditional institutions.[38]

A new St. Luke's emerged in the 1970s—one that would be shaped by the needs, imagination, and possibilities of new Atlantans. On the heels of Woodstock, hippies, flower children, and the relaxed social customs of the 1960s, St. Luke's new Folk Mass, introduced in 1972, spoke in the musical idiom of its day. It was participatory, fun, informal; it suggested *making* worship and *doing* liturgy, rather than being passive observers conforming to old molds that no longer fit the day.

St. Luke's television ministry began in 1972 and brought the Sunday service live to 20,000 viewers each week. The Community Soup Kitchen opened its doors in 1974, as did the Street Academy. A training and counseling center was added; the Atlanta Food Bank got started. New ministries seemed to be springing up everywhere. As one member expressed it, "St. Luke's was like a bumper car arena at an amusement park, with varied groups roving around and sometimes colliding."[39]

Such a proliferation of interests mirrored Atlanta's "yuppie" expansion. St. Luke's acquired a reputation as an open space where people with innovative ideas could find support and give them a try. This was a parish that valued what the new public valued: participation, inclusiveness, diversity, and commitment to a workable "urban lifestyle."[40]

While old St. Luke's members remained—those who had not fled to suburban parishes, that is—new St. Luke's members, more diverse, more representative of the new Atlanta, shaped a different image of a public church. The rector, the Rev. Thomas Bowers, had brought with him a great deal of energy, and he was a good match for the energies and talents of St. Luke's members. The Rev. Daniel P. Matthews, who arrived as rector in 1980, was also a popular leader. During his tenure at St. Luke's, urban social programs were strengthened. Dr. Matthews added a woman priest to the staff—at the time one of the few ordained women in Atlanta. He invited the Rev. Reynell (known as "Rey") Parkins, a native of Panama, to join the staff. Parkins started the St. Luke's Economic Development Corporation (SLEDCO). Parkins recruited the Rev. Isaias Rodriguez, a Spanish-born former Roman Catholic who had been ordained in that Church, to develop St. Luke's Hispanic Ministry Program.

New players, new ministries, new life—St. Luke's was clearly an exciting congregation to be part of. In an article commemorating the ministry of Reynell Parkins, John Fleming wrote the following:

> Many people turning on their televisions and seeing white priests, a black priest, and a Hispanic priest functioning as a team say to themselves "That is where I belong."[41]

The Rev. Charles E. Bennison, Jr., became rector of St. Luke's in May, 1988. His tasks and those of the congregation are clearly more difficult than those of his two popular predecessors. The heady days of the 1970s are long since gone. In the wider public, both in Atlanta and in the nation as a whole, many of the social programs established in the 1970s were dismantled in the 1980s. There are limits to growth and few illusions—both in the Church and in society. Members of St. Luke's are expressing the tensions of the times, and so is the city of Atlanta. According to the "Rollins Report":

> Atlanta is graduating toward a social and economic pattern that mirrors third-world cities. Glittering towers of glass and granite overlook scenes of desolation and abandonment. Atlanta is the second poorest city in the U.S.A., with one of the highest homicide rates in the country. Education and job training fights uphill against the giants of cocaine and crack.[42]

While St. Luke's members struggle to comprehend what is happening around them in city and Church, there is an emerging consensus that what is needed now is a reshaping and a reappropriation of the ministries the congregation developed in the past two decades. There is the need to reach a new understanding of what it means to be a public church in the 1990s. The senior warden in 1989, Margot Graettinger, said it succinctly:

> Now we face the key question, "Where do we go from here?" As a parish we have been richly blessed. Those who have gone before us have left us with an excellent location, a degree of financial stability, a heritage of service to the greater community, and a great deal of self-confidence. We have had as leaders people with deep spiritual commitment and vision. We are a congregation of bright, enthusiastic people who are not afraid to question either tradition or change, who share a deep love for St. Luke's and her possibilities.[43]

To answer that question, Where do we go from here?, a strategic planning process has been initiated. It is also a means for the new rector and the parish members to get to know each other, so that together—re-formed and reshaped—they may faithfully minister to each other and to the city of Atlanta in appropriate ways in the 1990s.

The process so far has included a parish survey, with 600 responses, and "focus groups" (small groups) to discern where God is leading the congregation. In February, 1990, the vestry adopted a new Mission Statement, which declares in part:

> Building on our heritage, our crossroads location, and our growing diversity, we respond to God's call to be faithful stewards by becoming a center of renewal, worship, service, and education, and a community which affirms the precious nature of all in Christian love.[44]

And finally, two imperatives underscore their resolve:

> We must nurture the faith and spirituality among members while empowering them for Christian vocation in the challenges of life . . . . We must apply the resources of the people within our Church to address the systemic causes of brokenness in our society and to become a catalyst for change; deepen our commitment to model programs; influence public policy; and to concentrate our resources to make a difference in an identifiable way . . . .[45]

## *DISTINCTIVE FEATURES*

- ***Public Church:*** Bruce Gunter pointed with some pride to the fact that "you can reach anyone in the city with one phone call." St. Luke's members, many of them personally involved in the public life of Atlanta, care about their city, and they want to be a part of a church that helps the city work.
- ***Meeting Social Needs:*** Even those members who are not part of St. Luke's outreach ministries are pleased that their church is doing its fair share to meet human need.
- ***Church School:*** Many members are attracted to St. Luke's because of the church's excellent Christian education programs for all ages, particularly for children.
- ***Lively Worship:*** The Folk Mass, the parish songbook, the participatory nature of the worship—these are compelling features of St. Luke's.
- ***Meeting Personal Needs:*** The "Rollins Report" observed that:

> When asked to state the primary task of their church, respondents overwhelmingly put first the ministry to members, their individual growth and spiritual needs.[46]

St. Luke's does this through a wide variety of small groups—Loaves and Fishes, "zip groups," Bible study groups, "focus groups," special interest groups of all kinds, and pastoral counseling.

- **Lay Initiative:** The Community Soup Kitchen began as the result of the initiative of one member. So did the Street Academy. Although strong, creative clergy have had, and continue to have, an important role in shaping the ministry of St. Luke's, there is the powerful sense at St. Luke's that *the ministry of God's Church belongs to all members.*
- **Keeping Current While Keeping Faithful:** It would be wrong to say that St. Luke's merely responds to fads or that it is a trendy parish, but it is a congregation that in a serious way sees itself in its wider context and allows and encourages its ministry and mission to be shaped by the changing realities of Atlanta. At the present moment the congregation is in one such reshaping.
- **Talent Nurturing More Talent:** St. Luke's is full of talented members. Its lay leaders are confident achievers. St. Luke's clergy and other professional staff are similarly talented. It is a case of talent breeding talent and talent used to good effect.

## *ISSUES RAISED BY THE VISIT TO SAINT LUKE'S, ATLANTA*

The complex issues raised by St. Luke's, Atlanta, as it seeks to be faithful to its wider context while still nurturing and supporting the ministries of its individual members apply to all churches located in all U.S. urban centers. Many of our urban congregations, as is painfully evident, have not kept faith with the cities in which they are located. They have not ministered to those who are there at their doorsteps. They have retreated into themselves. They have lost membership. St. Luke's, too, could become overwhelmed by the two Atlantas outside its doors and retreat.

In the light of this, the Mission Discernment Project Site Visitors ask, What is the glue that holds such a diverse congregation together? How do the staff maintain the energy to keep such a complex operation going without burnout?

St. Luke's Mission Statement and Mission Imperatives

have been written. Specific goals, objectives, and action statements are yet to come. As the congregation continues the tasks of reshaping itself, it is hoped that it will be successful in developing a style of ministry that will enable the church to continue to engage and shape the public life of Atlanta, while at the same time continuing to nurture the lives of its members. The "Rollins Report" declares:

> The question is more poignant than ever: Which people, or what institutions will be bold enough to stand in the middle of this maelstrom and be a sign of redemption and hope?[47]

The way St. Luke's evolves its public role for the 1990s will have significance beyond Atlanta. St. Luke's could become a bellwether. It could suggest ways forward to other U.S. Episcopal churches in other urban centers.

---

## RESOURCES

Bellah, Robert N., et al. *Habits of the Heart: Individualism and Commitment in American Life.* Berkeley: University of California Press, 1985.

Frank, Thomas E., and Fowler, James W. "Research Project on the Faith and Practice of the Congregation," Report to St. Luke's Episcopal Church. Rollins Center for Church Ministries, Candler School of Theology, Emory University, Atlanta, GA, December 15, 1989.

Galley, Howard E. *The Ceremonies of the Eucharist.* Cambridge, MA: Cowley Publications, 1989.

Hatchett, Marion J. *A Manual of Ceremonial for the New Prayer Book.* Sewanee, TN: School of Theology, University of the South. An occasional publication of the *St. Luke's Journal of Theology.* Paperback, no date.

Stuhlman, Byron D. *The Prayer Book Rubrics Expanded.* New York: Church Hymnal Corporation, 1987.

Terkel, Studs. *The Great Divide: Second Thoughts on the American Dream.* New York: Avon Books, 1989.

Vogelsang, John. *Scriptural Community: Conversations with Sacred Texts.* Unpublished manuscript, December, 1989.

# NOTES

[1] Joe Martin, interview in Atlanta, June 6, 1990.
[2] Myrtle Davis, interview at Atlanta City Hall, June 6, 1990.
[3] Joe Martin, interview.
[4] Myrtle Davis, interview.
[5] United Way of Metropolitan Atlanta, *Annual Report—1989*, p. 6.
[6] Kevin P. Phillips, "Reagan's America: A Capital Offense," *New York Times Magazine*, June 17, 1990, p. 26. See also Phillips's book, *The Politics of Rich and Poor: Wealth and the American Electorate* (New York: Random House, 1990).
[7] Joe Martin, interview.
[8] Tracy Thompson, "A Unique Partnership: Exodus Inc. and the St. Luke's Street Academy," *St. Luke's Magazine*, June, 1986, p. 13.
[9] Neil Shorthouse, interview in Atlanta, June 6, 1990.
[10] *Ibid.*
[11] Bruce C. Gunter, interview in Atlanta, June 6, 1990.
[12] *Ibid.*
[13] "Social Responsibility Investment Group, Inc.," Atlanta, Georgia, flier.
[14] Bruce Gunter, interview.
[15] See Thomas E. Frank and James W. Fowler, "Research Project on the Faith and Practice of the Congregation," Rollins Center for Church Ministries, Candler School of Theology, Atlanta, Georgia, December 15, 1989. Here after referred as the "Rollins Report."
[16] *Ibid.*
[17] Bruce Gunter, interview.
[18] Robert Fowler, interview in Atlanta, June 6, 1990.
[19] Kathryn Beane, as reported by John Beane, in Atlanta, June 6, 1990.
[20] Judy Jones, interview in Atlanta, June 8, 1990.
[21] Montgomery Rocque, interview in Atlanta, June 7, 1990.
[22] Bill Bolding, "Annual report—Atlanta Food Bank, " 1989, p. 1.
[23] Bruce Gunter, interview.
[24] Nancy Burnett, interview in Atlanta, June 6, 1990.
[25] Charles E. Bennison, Jr., "Learning to Travel: Some Thoughts on St. Luke's Latin American Study Tour," *St. Luke's Magazine*, Vol. 5, Winter, 1990, p. 18.

[26] St. Luke's Vestry Resolution as reported in *St. Luke's Magazine,* Vol. 5, Winter, 1990, p. 21.
[27] Richard Groepper, interview in Atlanta, June 7, 1990.
[28] "Community Outreach Ministries" insert in the *1989 Annual Report,* p. 1.
[29] Dan Todd, interview in Atlanta, June 6, 1990.
[30] Tad Zelski, interview in Atlanta, June 7, 1990.
[31] Al Caproni, interview in Atlanta, June 6, 1990.
[32] Dick Groepper, interview.
[33] Ann Cramer, interview in Atlanta, June 7, 1990.
[34] Becky Zelski, interview in Atlanta, June 7, 1990.
[35] Thomas Bowers, as quoted in *The Atlanta Constitution,* April 18, 1974. Quoted in the "Rollins Report."
[36] "Rollins Report, " p. 3.
[37] *Ibid.*
[38] *Ibid.* See also Floyd Hunter, *Community Power Succession: Atlanta's Policy-Makers Revisited* (Chapel Hill: University of North Carolina, 1980).
[39] "Rollins Report," p. 4.
[40] *Ibid.,* p. 5.
[41] John Fleming, "A Tribute to the Ministries of the Rev. Dr. Reynell M. Parkins and the Rev. Dr. Gene Ruyle," July 30, 1989, p. 9.
[42] "Rollins Report," p. 5.
[43] Margot Graettinger, *St. Luke's Magazine,* Vol. 5, Winter, 1990, p. 34.
[44] Preamble to St. Luke's Mission Statement, February 19, 1990.
[45] *Ibid.*
[46] "Rollins Report," p. 11.
[47] "Rollins Report," p. 5.

*Site Visitor:* Alan George
*Date of Visit:* June 6-7, 1990

*The desert will rejoice, and flowers will bloom in the wastelands. The desert will sing and shout for joy.*

—Isaiah 35:1-2a

---

CHAPTER 7

---

# GUMBO STEW
## STORY OF COMMUNITY SERVICE
### BASKERVILL MINISTRIES
### PAWLEYS ISLAND, SOUTH CAROLINA

## *THE CONTEXT OF MISSION DISCERNMENT: PAWLEYS ISLAND, SOUTH CAROLINA*

The Gospel of Jesus Christ speaks to us of wholeness in the face of division. It speaks of unity where people see separation. It speaks of God's justice. Most important, it declares that unity and justice are not distant and merely hoped-for events. With struggle, people of diverse economic, racial, and social backgrounds can work together towards a more just community. Such is the case now in Camp Baskervill at Pawleys Island.

Pawleys Island lies just south of the midpoint of the sixty-mile-long swathe of white sand beach known as the Grand Strand. To the northeast is Myrtle Beach, a resort in the style of Coney Island or Miami Beach, complete with boardwalk, cotton candy, nighttime hangouts, miniature golf, and serious golf (there are some fifty golf courses to choose from). To the southwest is historic Georgetown, where rice and indigo planters arrived in the early eighteenth century to make their fortunes. And make them they did: by 1840, Georgetown County (of which Pawleys Island is a part) was producing nearly half the total rice crop of the United States. The fruits of this wealth were an aristocratic way of life and opulent mansions straight out of *Gone with the Wind*.

Indians were the original inhabitants of Waccamaw Neck, where Baskervill Ministries in Pawleys Island is located. In 1526 the Spanish established a small settlement at Waccamaw—the first by Europeans in North America—but were driven out by Indians and disease.

After the Civil War, Waccamaw Neck was left to nature and freed slaves, known as Gullahs. The Gullahs' culture was based on hunting, fishing, and small farming. Henry Smith, a retired dockworker and bearer of local culture, explains the Gullah language:

> The Gullah language comes from Africa. The slaves didn't know how to speak in the American way so they mixed African, English, and maybe a little French. I can speak it, you know. I can lapse into it. My parents and my grandparents spoke it.[1]

With the Atlantic Ocean on one side and the Waccamaw River (which forms part of the Intracoastal Waterway) on the other, Waccamaw Neck was isolated from the mainstream of modern life. As Luther Dennison, who at the age of sixty-six has lived all his life on Pawleys Island, recalls:

> Route 17 was a dirt road. Chickens, hogs and cows ran freely. We clipped the ears of the hogs and cows, and with these simple brands we just let them roam. Everyone did. We just let the animals go. And they came home with calves and piglets. We grew peas, corn, sweet potatoes and peanuts. I went fishing and crabbing and I used to hunt. There were plenty of deer.[2]

Staple foods were delivered by boat, and indeed many found employment working on the docks loading and unloading the boats. Henry Smith was among them.

My regular occupation was on the waterfront loading wood for the International Paper Company, steel from Georgetown Steel Company and general cargo.³

In a song Smith wrote about his days on the river, he sang:

> We were in our early teens.
> Steamships, schooners, tugboat,
>   plied these waters
>     in numbers large.
>     We toted the barge
>   and lift' the bale.
>     It was hard work and it ain't no tale.
> Tide comes in and the tide goes out,
> you don't know what it's all about,
>   but there's one thing I do know.
> It was all hard work,
>   and ain't no show.
> The sun goes up and then goes down.
> The only work that can be foun'—
>   unload cargo from ship to shore
>   to buy the groceries in the store.
> It was in the nineteen twenties . . .
>   river men worked and sang their songs,
>   river men toiled all day long.⁴

People relied on their family and friends in their closely knit communities for all things, including medical care. Children were born at home. According to Luther Dennison:

> All my children came through a midwife at home. She lived in the neighborhood. We had Miss Worth, Miss Reya, Miss Charlotte. And the lady that "caught" me was Sue Richardson.⁵

But such a way of life was not to continue. A bridge connecting Waccamaw Neck to Georgetown was built in the 1920s. In the late 1940s the dirt road—the Broadway of Waccamaw Neck—was paved over to become U.S. Highway 17. Now, according to Luther Dennison,

> Where deer used to run they have houses here, houses there, houses everywhere. Jack Nicklaus

came down here and built a golf course, and then came houses, houses, houses . . . .[6]

The Gullah people, who once quietly conducted their lives and meandered freely over Waccamaw Neck, have now become the victims of white people's nostalgia and unbridled conspicuous consumption. The black people of Pawleys Island are trapped between super rich white Americans' demand for the best in golf and the most luxurious homes and their attempts to revive an illusion of old southern plantation life.

Real estate developers—mostly from the North—have often obtained the land of the black inhabitants by dubious means.[7] They invite the rich and the prosperous to discover "the real South." Real estate developments, called "plantations" and "retreats," promise old sourthern charm along with world-class golf. Take the Litchfield Plantation, for instance:

> Enduring elegance since 1750—the Litchfield Plantation stands proud. A modern-day monument to eighteenth century life, Litchfield welcomes you through our live oak avenue into a most rare collection of beautiful amenities.
> Our Pawleys Island Beach Clubhouse offers the best in casual oceanfront enjoyment . . . . Golf on 3 grand courses. You'll agree this rare chance for ownership in the most prestigious of plantations cannot be missed. Distinctive residences from $175,000 to $500,000, homesites from $85,000 to $200,000.[8]

Or the Heritage Plantation for

> A unique opportunity at Pawleys Island to inherit a legacy of true Southern Coastal plantation living.
> Nestled among giant oaks and fragrant magnolias, the dramtic Plantation overlooks historic rice fields and a magnificent golf course. The Heritage Plantation is a meticulously planned and *carefully controlled* residential community with planned amenities. Immerse yourself in the renowned golf experience of the Heritage Golf Club, Ltd.[9] (Emphasis added.)

In an effort to ascertain just how "carefully controlled" a plantation was, two members of the Mission Discernment Project Visiting Team (both white and well-dressed—a laywoman and a priest in his clerical collar) attempted to visit the Pawleys Plantation and Golf Club, "a private country club community featuring a superb new Jack Nicklaus golf course, Charleston style villas, swimming, tennis and an expansive clubhouse to enhance a lifestyle rich with elegance and charm."[10] They were turned away at the gatehouse. As the result of blatant land grabs, legal but morally questionable, the black residents whose land these "plantations" and "retreats" occupy have been "carefully controlled." They have been pushed into the interior of Pawleys Island. They have lost the land they had always thought was theirs. They have also lost free access to the ocean and rivers. It's a contemporary rerun of the Native American story of a century ago, when Indians had their land grabbed and were relegated to areas not of their choosing.

A lush green golf course now stands where once there were woods, and a chain link fence covered with heavy black plastic divides the world of the white rich from that of the rural black poor. According to the Rev. Antoine (Tony) L. Campbell, director of Baskervill Ministries, the resident of one of the houses directly behind the golf course said,

> First I lost my lovely woods and the deer I used to hunt—but at least I could see the pretty green grass of the golf course. Then they put up the black tarp. Now all I think about is the Berlin Wall.[11]

One plantation's developer built a modern sewage and septic system for his property, but placed the collection units outside the walls in a black residential area. So the longtime Pawleys Island people literally found the dunghill of their new white neighbors in their backyard. To be sure, development has created some jobs, but middle management comes from elsewhere. The regular Pawleys Island folk are employed in the lowest-level jobs on local plantations. Others work in Myrtle Beach's restaurants and hotels.

Pawleys Island is as sharp a study of contrasts as can be found anywhere in the United States. Not just whites, but wealthy—millionaire and billionaire—whites, moving in on rural people of color. Ramshackle trailers, shacks, stray dogs and cats, unpaved roads, and rusty cars lie in pockets surrounded by private property signs, keep-out warnings, guard houses, walls, and access-controlled, electronic fences and gates. This study of contrasts is the context for Baskervill Ministries. Here, according to Tony Campbell, "We're bridge builders."

## *BASKERVILL MINISTRIES TODAY: GUMBO STEW*

Camp Baskervill's annual Gumbo Stew Festival is described as "seasonings for life and spiritual renewal," and that would describe all the ministries of Camp Baskervill and its center, Holy Cross-Faith Memorial Church. Camp Baskervill is a holistic community, with education programs, programs for the elderly, home building projects, a medical clinic, art—in short, all manner of ministries to nurture the material and spiritual well-being of the people. A strong thread of evangelism runs through all of Baskervill's ministries. A recent video of Camp Baskervill describes it as "an umbrella religious institution with Holy Cross-Faith Memorial Church at its center."[12] According to Tony Campbell,

> This historic role and mission of Camp Baskervill has been a commitment to witness to Jesus Christ through service. This commitment began in the life of Holy Cross-Faith Memorial Episcopal Church and Faith Memorial School . . . . Baskervill has worked to become incarnational in the life of the community in order to be a vehicle of hope.
>
> Being the body of Christ in the community grows out of an awareness that—for many people—the level of despair and hopelessness is so great that the Church must combine work, deed and sacrament in order for the Gospel to be heard . . . .
>
> It is this hope, provided through medical care, education, housing programs, respite care, crisis ministries, and through the Church, which is the basis for the realization of God's love for God's people.
>
> It is this hope—in the midst of

hopelessness—which is the basis for the discovery of Jesus Christ and the power for new life in His incarnation, crucifixion, and resurrection . . . . Camp Baskervill provides this witness to Christ through its various ministries in the community. It is our belief that service rendered with love, Christian reflection and devotion provides the medium by which the love of God in Christ may be felt by all people regardless of their cirumstances in life.[13]

Every Camp Baskervill program is interlocked with the life of the Holy Cross-Faith Memorial congregation. Christian education, prayer, and Christian reflection are part of every program. "If you don't offer the Gospel," according to Tony Campbell, "you don't offer the best the church has to offer."[14] He says:

We have discovered for ourselves two basic truths: 1) Sociologically, if you don't invest in the community, the community won't invest in you. And the converse, if you invest in the community, the community will invest in you, and 2) The Gospel is true. It is in giving that we receive.[15]

Camp Baskervill's care for people individually and as a community is amply expressed through all its ministries and programs.

Camp Baskervill stretches and nurtures the minds of children: The school, Faith Memorial Episcopal School, serves children from kindergarten through the fourth grade. Its principal, Mrs. Ruby M. Forsythe, known by all simply as "Miss Ruby," is a devoted teacher who has received national acclaim. She was included in *I Dream a World* (1989), a book of photographs and interviews of influential American black women. She has been featured as one of the nation's unsung heros in *Newsweek*. Her story has been aired on "Sixty Minutes" and "NBC Nightly News." All these accolades have come as a result of Miss Ruby's pioneering work with the children of the school. Her loving and strong Christian influence has enriched the lives of scores of Pawleys Islanders. Miss Ruby believes in kids:

Education is more than reading or just setting

something out in a book. Education is a process of teaching people how to help themselves. Teach them how to help themselves and they will be able to help others, how to respect themselves and they will be able to help others respect themselves. [Education is about] how to live with people so they will be able to live with themselves.[16]

Miss Ruby is assisted by a staff of volunteers and friends.

Camp Baskervill has another educational ministry called "Summer Step." Summer Step is a program for some 150 to 180 South Carolina children who are at risk—those who have failed academically and socially in their regular schools, those who have been physically and sexually abused. At Summer Step, middle school children receive a "step ahead" in language arts and math skills, a "step out" into recreational activities, a "step into" community life, and a "step forward" in spiritual growth.[17] Summer Step teachers use biblical themes to help the children reflect on each day's activities. Last year, during the course of the three- to four-week camp there was a 40-percent improvement in language arts, a 16-percent improvement in reading, and a 24-percent rise in mathematics scores. Summer Step also includes vocational courses in auto mechanics, golf course technology, computer programming, culinary arts, and hotel and motel management. As Father Campbell recounts, "One youngster came last summer who had been failing in everything and discovered he was really gifted in auto mechanics."[18]

Camp Baskervill cares for the health of the community: A Baskervill Medical Clinic operated by an entirely voluntary staff of five doctors and a dozen nurses provides medical care for people who cannot otherwise afford it. Dr. Cathcart Smith, a retired physician who "still had some useful talents" to give to the community, borrowed $7,500 to buy a used office trailer where he opened a clinic. When the general public learned about it, donations came streaming in, and the loan was paid off in three months. The clinic is open from nine to eleven on weekdays and offers all basic medical services.

In close proximity to the clinic is the Adult Day Care program, where elderly people are brought together for healthful meals, medical supervision, recreation, education, and life-skill programs in a comfortable, caring environment. James Patrick, the director, said, "We've become a family, and we really love one another."[19]

The Baskervill community is building housing for the elderly on its property. Again, another retired Pawleys Island resident offered his assistance. Bill Clark had moved from Connecticut in 1982, ". . . determined I was not just going to put my feet up."[20] Clark's energies led to the formation of the Baskervill Housing Development Corporation and the construction of forty-eight low-cost housing units for the elderly and handicapped. Construction, all funded with public monies, is now in progress. According to Bill Clark:

> I think we should do sensible things like this that will help more older people live in dignity and comfort here on Waccamaw Neck. It will help [keep] our community from becoming affordable only to the affluent.[21]

Clark acknowledged that the needs of the poor often go unrecognized and unmet. He explained:

> Baskervill is the only thing I know about on Waccamaw Neck that really goes after the problem. We have 21 directors—11 black and 10 white. I have never seen anything around here that has got so much enthusiasm from the persons involved. We had 100 percent acceptance from people asked to be on the board . . . . It's a damned good kind of venture for whites and blacks to be working on. The more you work together with people, the less hostility there is and the more problems you solve, whether in education, housing or anything else.[22]

Another housing program is Salkehatchie Summer, run in cooperation with the South Carolina United Methodist Church. Teenagers and adults pay $125 per week to come to Camp Baskervill to rebuild the houses of local residents, working with the people whose homes are being repaired. Every evening there is an opportunity for the participants to reflect upon the activities of the day. Jim Hunter, assistant director of Salkehatchie, said of the participants:

> They come to worship and make friends. The older

people teach the youngsters building skills and do the driving. Both young and old learn a great deal from this setting.[23]

At the end of the week all the volunteers bring to the church something from the sites they worked at. These gifts are laid at the cross at the final Eucharist, and during the shared sermon anyone who wishes to can take his or her gift and use it to reflect upon what the experience has meant personally. By all accounts, these closing Eucharists are powerful events, both emotionally and spiritually.

In the five years of Salkehatchie Summer Service, about fifty homes have been rehabilitated. In the summer of 1991 an Episcopal group was scheduled to come to build houses.

Inadequate housing is a serious problem throughout the rural South, but it is particularly conspicuous alongside the opulent "plantation" housing of Pawleys Island. With this in mind, Camp Baskervill began a program called "Thanksgiving House." During the Thanksgiving season, the Camp Baskervill community expresses its thanks to the Lord by building new homes for persons whose houses are beyond repair. Labor and most of the materials are donated by members of local churches. Volunteers have built eight homes in four years. Practice has made them fast. The first house took six months to complete, but recently four houses were built in four days.

> An inspirational community service kicks off the first day of the house raising which is usually on the Wednesday before the Thanksgiving holiday weekend. Then work begins. Volunteers and families pause for Thanksgiving Day dinner at Camp Baskervill, then resume building. The blessing of the house ceremonies follow, with scriptural readings, sprinkling of holy water in each room, praying and recitation of the Lord's Prayer. The old house is torn down, its wood given to the community for firewood.[24]

As part of the house blessing, the residents of the new house are given a new Bible signed by all its builders. An account of one of these house raisings was reported as follows in the local press:

> When his wife died he moved into the shadows

of life. He dressed shabbily. He was nearly blind. His neglected tiny frame house gradually fell apart; the floor rotted, the windows simply disappeared.

The house was beyond repair but not his life.... Camp Baskervill gathered the community of conscience. Time, skill, and materials were volunteered, and a new house was built. At 78 he had been brought back into the community.

Tony Campbell blessed the house, joined by a goodly company of new friends and neighbors. There were tears of happiness.[25]

Thanksgiving Houses are blessings to those who build them and those who dwell in them. Consider the story of Verdell Carr, who had been living with her four children in a trailer attached to an old wooden house with eight other family members. The house leaked every time it rained. At the house blessing of this new Thanksgiving House, Ms. Carr said, "I would like to thank my Lord and Savior Jesus Christ who has made it possible and blessed us with a new home. It's a miracle."[26] Danny Chamblee, one of the workers on the Carr home, said,

We started Wednesday morning with bare ground. Here it is Sunday, and we have people moving into a new house. To me it's just incredible. It was just a bunch of people who reached out in the name of God. Nobody is down here thinking we can make it on our own.[27]

With such a record of community service, people naturally turned to Camp Baskervill for help when Hurricane Hugo came roaring into town on September 22, 1989. Within hours of the storm's striking, Camp Baskervill staff and volunteers were at work serving meals. Each day, 2,000 people were fed from a kitchen that is only of regular house size. It is a contemporary loaves-and-fishes story, for without even asking, food, volunteers, and money poured in. Before long, Camp Baskervill was serving the four-county area, taking food out to those who couldn't come get it. At one point a very wealthy white woman was observed in the kitchen, cooking over a hot stove and laughing with a black grandmother. Seeing them so happily enjoying each other's company, Tony Campbell called the scenario "a little piece of God's grace."

Government officials asked Camp Baskervill to function as an official county relief center, for which it received federal and state emergency funds. So "I CARE" was created. In this program over 500 houses were rebuilt. So many supplies were sent in that a warehouse in Georgetown had to be rented to hold them all. People, too, came to help. Becki Brantley, now head of Hugo Relief, had taught vocational education at a technical school. She came to Pawleys Island from Columbia, South Carolina, for a weekend to offer her services. In Becki's words:

> I came to volunteer for a weekend. I stayed. I couldn't walk away from it. There was such a tremendous need here. There still is. As I got involved in Camp Baskervill, I realized it was a place I could put my energies. So I became a part of this great family. When you experience the family of Camp Baskervill, it's contagious.[28]

Camp Baskervill nurtures the artistic spirit of the people through its arts ministry. The Gumbo Stew Festival, one of the arts programs, began in an unusual way. There was a meeting held at Camp Baskervill to discuss the incorporation of Litchfield Beach, a community of wealthy plantation houses, as a separate town. Black people sat on one side of the room, whites on the other, for what turned out to be an exceedingly tense encounter. It was explained to the Mission Discernment Project visitors that in Pawleys Island blacks and whites come together over business, politics, and conflict. That was the case on this particular evening. In its aftermath several of the participants expressed dismay at the hostility in the room. The result was the Gumbo Stew Festival, designed to appeal to blacks and whites alike through art, music, and fun. Gumbo Stew's purpose is to stimulate and foster the appreciation of local arts and crafts. There are demonstrations of Gullah basket making. There is folk and Gospel music, and local food—hush puppies, smoked fish, blackberry dumplings, and, of course, gumbo stew.

The first Gumbo Stew Festival was held four years ago, with 400 in attendance. In 1990, about 2,000 came. Blacks and whites, young and old, rich and poor, shared in the preparations and worked together to provide an enjoyable occasion for the whole community.

The year-round arts ministry, which has received funding from the South Carolina Arts Commission, sponsors artists in residence—dancers, playwrights, painters, and poets. Beulah White, a poet who heads Baskervill's arts ministry, says that

> The goal of the arts ministry is twofold—to provide a service to the community and to use art as a means of bringing the community together.[29]

As area residents are introduced to the pleasures of art, and appreciation develops, the community, in turn, is strengthened.

To illustrate how serious Camp Baskervill is about proclaiming the Gospel through every aspect of its ministry, staff and volunteers emphasize that no new project, however small, is started without seeking the guidance of Christ through prayer, nor ended without thanksgiving. Tuesday staff meetings always include a reflection on Scripture and a discussion of the meaning of each activity to the staff members both personally and corporately. Staff members readily point out that the church is the first building one sees when coming into Camp Baskervill and the last building passed upon leaving.

> The Church is fully integrated in all of Camp Baskervill's programs and stands as the Body of Christ. It is a witness of hope and good news to all that God's hand is at work in the community, living evidence that no problem is so big that it cannot be solved by God.[30]

## *UNDERSTANDING THE STORY*

In 1985 Holy Cross-Faith Memorial Church could only attract five members on a Sunday morning. The community was so depressed that it was easier to interest people in coming to a funeral than in attending a Sunday service. Camp Baskervill's budget was $50,000, and the staff consisted of one person.

Church members Nathan Brown and Elaine Blake acknowledge that today, in 1990, the change has been startling. Thirty-five regular members—not including the seasonal students and workers at Camp Baskervill—now attend every Sunday. They feel hopeful and expectant. According to Mr. Brown, "The Church caused the community to move into the mainstream of life.[31] Today, in addition to modest church growth, Camp Baskervill has grown to sixteen full-time staff members—and forty in the summer—with a $1.3 million budget.

Though Camp Baskervill may have fallen on hard times in the late 1970s and early 1980s, its tradition of service is deeply rooted in Pawleys Island.

The ministry grew up around the church and the school. The school was organized in 1903 for black children. From 1927 until 1974, the Rev. William Essex Forsythe served as vicar of the church and principal of the school. His wife, Miss Ruby, carries on Father Forsythe's work in the school, which remains central to the life and ministry of Camp Baskervill.

In the 1930s, the Bishop of South Carolina, the Rt. Rev. Albert S. Thomas, had had the idea of developing a center "for colored churchmen" on the 25-acre grounds of Holy Cross-Faith Memorial Episcopal Church. The idea grew and took shape with Archdeacon Erasmus L. Baskervill, whose son, Lewis Baskervill, also a priest, was secretary of the Archdeaconry for Colored Churchmen. In the summer of 1939, the first Camp Baskervill building was erected under the direction of the Rev. Lewis Baskervill. Through the years, other buildings were added to what was essentially a diocesan summer camp for black Episcopalians. Shortly after the death of Erasmus Baskervill, the camp was named in his honor.

The school has continued steadily, but the camp has had its ups and downs, and was even closed for a period in the early 1960s. It was revived again in 1965, when the Rev. Canon Henry L. Grant reopened Camp Baskervill for disadvantaged junior high school boys. Under Grant's leadership, the camp facilities were completely rebuilt.

Operation Compenso—now called Summer Step—was begun in 1968. An adult day-care center, then basically a meals program, for the elderly was initiated in 1975. So there was new life, but it was difficult to maintain Camp Baskervill on a day-to-day basis, since Father Grant supervised its operations from Charleston.

In 1985, fresh out of seminary and not yet a deacon, the Rev. Antoine L. Campbell was appointed executive director of Camp Baskervill and vicar of Holy Cross-Faith Memorial Church and St. Cyprian's in Georgetown. "I came here as a member of the first order of ministry."[32] Though young and inexperienced in the operation of congregations, Father Campbell had qualities that made him right for the job. During his seminary years he had done a study of Camp Baskervill with recommendations about what direction its ministry should take. A U.S. Naval Academy graduate and a former Marine, he had excellent organizational skills. An athelete and track star of Olympic rank (qualifying for the 1976 Olympic trials in hurdles), he'd been a Yale track coach. He brought to Baskervill both energy and discipline. Most especially, he brought the determination to do everything possible to make the ministry succeed and flourish.

His wife, Julie Campbell, was also added to the staff as administrative assistant, as was Sara Carroll, the bookkeeper. This trio of workers set about meeting the actual needs of the people of Pawleys Island. A summer camp and summer school were fine as far as they went, but wasn't there something more Camp Baskervill should be doing? According to Tony:

> I interviewed the movers and shakers in the community. I interviewed the politicans. I visited the churches. Too often vestries try to inflict something on the community. There's no discernment as to what's really needed in the community. I could plainly see that what this whole community needed was the empowerment of the Gospel. It's more than doing social programs. It's acting the Gospel imperative.[33]

As Campbell listened to community leaders, as he visited the homes of Pawleys Island's black residents in the areas immediately behind Camp Baskervill, it became clear to him that substandard housing was a major issue. So housing programs were developed.

In 1986 the Salkehatchie Summer Service came to Camp Baskervill. In 1987, Baskervill Housing Development became incorporated and the idea of Thanksgiving House emerged. In the summer of 1991, the Episcopal Diocese of South Carolina was scheduled to send its first group to build houses.

Other churches and community groups have caught the vision. There is now a Georgetown County Housing Authority and Habitat for Humanity. All Saints Church—the other Episcopal church at Waccamaw Neck—has a line item in its parish budget for housing this year. All Saints members are volunteering in

Camp Baskervill's housing projects. Bill Clark, the chair of Baskervill Housing Development Corporation, is an All Saints member.

The Adult Day Care Center has vastly extended its programs, and a medical clinic has been established—all these express in concrete ways Camp Baskervill's holistic approach to ministry.

Camp Baskervill was recognized as a Jubilee Center by the Executive Council of the Episcopal Church in 1987. This designation was an important recognition of Baskervill's ministries, and it has stimulated more extensive local funding.

Camp Baskervill staff and volunteers have demonstrated their ability to act quickly and effectively. After Hurricane Hugo struck, *Jubilate Deo* reported:

> Coordinating relief along this coastline is a ministry centered at Camp Baskervill in Pawleys Island . . . . As many as 900 hot lunches and 500 takeout dinners were cooked in the camp kitchen by volunteers in a single day, trucks from Baskervill or other churches daily bring food and canned goods to such centers as Hemingway, Oatland, Dunbar, Lanes' Creek, Plantsville, Santee, Potato Bed, Big Dam and Sampit, as well as McClellanville . . . . Camp Baskervill stepped up its regular program to provide for the increased needs of the community. Twenty homes were worked on in the first week after the hurricane; the medical clinic provided emergency care; the elderly gathered for the usual meals and fellowship. Baskervill is an impressive example of the way in which a well-organized program geared to meeting community needs can expand effectively at a time of disaster.[34]

The Baskervill staff attribute the rapid growth of their ministry to their reliance of God. According to Father Campbell,

> We place radical trust in God and in God's strength. It's God's ministry, not ours, and we can step out into the water trusting that God, who called us to this, will be faithful. It's God's work

through and through. It's trusting that God will send a person, that God will open a door.

Take Gumbo Stew. We needed help with it, so God sent Beulah White. Same with Salkehatchie. God dropped it in our lap. Bill Clark came along who had the skills to organize the elderly housing.

It's a result of a real commitment to the Gospel. It takes trust in God so that every program we design speaks and breathes the Gospel.

This is a service ministry to the poor and broken-hearted. We live with people who live in hopeless situations. I'm convinced that if we're going to proclaim the Gospel of hope for people who live in hopeless situations that the peace and hope and joy of the Gospel has to reside within you and flow from your life to your work.[35]

## *DISTINCTIVE FEATURES*

Odd as it may seem, Ray Baake's book, *The Urban Christian: Effective Ministry in Today's Urban World,*[36] could have been written with Camp Baskervill in mind. Baake's strategies include getting to know the real needs of the community; networking; cooperating with other churches, community, and civic organizations; biblical reflection; having the ministry team live in the community where it serves; and other features. Camp Baskervill leaders have done them all and demonstrated that perhaps there are basic principles of effective ministry that have applications in many settings, and that a strategy we may think of as applying in an urban center may be just as effective in a rural one.

- ***Determining and Meeting Real Needs:*** Camp Baskervill is successful because, quite simply, it meets the needs of people in all kinds of ways. Camp Baskervill meets spiritual needs, educational needs, material needs, health needs. It feeds and nourishes the spirit with creative arts, and it feeds the soul with the Gospel. Specifically, many features of this many-faceted ministry contribute to its effectiveness.

  Before a new ministry was started at Camp Baskervill, the community was surveyed, leaders interviewed, conditions and needs assessed. The programs were then designed in the light of the results. As Mission Discernment Project Site Visitor the Rev. Canon Jervis O. Burns, Jr., expressed it:

> Tony said [that] upon his arrival at Holy Cross Church, he met initially with the matriarchs and patriarchs of the congregation as customary, but then went on to visit the movers and shakers of the community at large—the politicians and such. He did a lot of networking to discover the problems that needed to be addressed in the community and to identify resources available to meet these needs. He and the church leaders were then able to plan from a broader perspective than their own.[37]

- ***Gospel Centeredness and Gospel Values:*** At Camp Baskervill, the Gospel is proclaimed through every program, through deeds and words. Projects begin with prayer, reflection, and formal liturgies. They end in prayer and the Eucharist. In Jervis Burns' words:

    > The most important learning about the community was that its most pressing needs was hope—a commodity in great supply in the Church and in the Gospel. The discovery that Holy Cross-Faith Memorial and the community were interdependent—one couldn't survive without the other—led to a long-range plan with a radical focus *on* the poor and *in* the Gospel. Tony stated, "We won't do a program unless we can figure out a way to proclaim the Gospel in the midst of it." Every activity at Camp Baskervill begins and ends in worship—a clear and constant reminder to all that they are about God's work and are empowered by God. I'm sure this accounts in a significant way for the high level of both energy and enthusiasm displayed by the ministry workers. This, in turn, helps explain the remarkable success in attracting new workers from throughout the Pawleys Island area and beyond to ministry.[38]

- ***Matching Needs and Skills:*** The Camp Baskervill staff is skilled at matching people who have needs—whether physical, educational, artistic, or spiritual—with those who are able to meet those needs.

- **Serving and Being Served:** While the college student who comes to Camp Baskervill for a week to build a house for a poor family might be considered the one doing the serving, he or she invariably discovers that in the act of reaching out he or she is also being served and touched by Christ. All serve at the same time that they are being served.
- **Personal Affirmation:** Members of the Camp Baskervill family help people feel good about themselves. Staff and volunteers alike frequently express confidence in the people they serve, and this starts with the children. Expressing confidence and care helps them have confidence in themselves. Miss Ruby said, "Education is a process of teaching people how to help themselves and they will help others; to respect themselves and they will be able to respect others; how to live with people, and they will be able to live with themselves."[39] Canon Burns agrees:

> The tremendous success of this so obviously Christian ministry has given hope and a sense of personal worth to a segment of the community that has lacked both for a long time.[40]

Furthermore, Camp Baskervill's encouragement of the arts, both fine art and folk art, strengthens the spirit, the imagination, and the creativity of the people while at the same time preserving folk art traditions.

- **The Right People at the Right Time:** Those with talents and skills to offer have come at times when their gifts were most urgently needed. They are still coming. Becki Brantley wandered in to help for a weekend after Hurricane Hugo. She now runs Hugo Relief for the area. Bill Clark and Cathcart Smith were retirees with energies and imagination who wanted to be useful. Clark is now chair of the Baskervill Housing Development Corporation and is supervising the construction of elderly housing units at Camp Baskervill. Dr. Smith set up a clinic and supervises it. Beulah White came when the Baskervill staff needed help with the Gumbo Stew Festival and stayed to coordinate the arts program. John Trump, a Lutheran pastor who is also a New York playwright, came to be an artist in residence one summer and returned to help with Hugo Relief.

Sometimes help comes down the telephone lines. Four weeks after the hurricane, when the staff was bone-tired and becoming discouraged at how much still needed to be done, a call came from the governor of South Carolina. According to Tony Campbell, "He just told me how grateful he was about how we were responding to Hugo. That call came just when I needed it."[41]

- *A Sense of Family:* Staff and volunteers enjoy working together, and many have described Camp Baskervill as "one big family."
- *Quick Response:* In the wake of Hurricane Hugo, Camp Baskervill reacted quickly. The immediate response, in turn, has enhanced respect for Camp Baskervill in the Pawleys Island area.
- *Organization and Administration:* Camp Baskervill is well organized and efficiently run.
- *Leadership Team as Models of Wholeness:* Tony and Julie Campbell—husband and wife, Camp Baskervill director and Summer Step director, respectively—are models of the Gospel wholeness they proclaim. They are clearly in this ministry together; they are warm, accepting, helpful, and supportive to each other, and they pass on warmth, acceptance, help, and support to those among whom they work.

    They are strongly identified with their ministry setting. When they first went to Pawleys Island, they rented a house several miles away from Camp Baskervill. As time went on they felt the need to identify more fully and completely with the people they serve, so they now live with their children in a house they bought on a pleasant but rather poor street right behind Camp Baskervill. The Campbells are what they proclaim; they live what they say.
- *Success Breeding Success:* Camp Baskervill illustrates that to those whom much has been given, and have used it in accordance with Gospel values, more will be added. People want to come to Camp Baskervill; they want to get involved; they want to donate money and buy building materials. They want to lend their skills. They want to be a part of the good thing God is doing in their midst.
- *Breaking Down Barriers and Building Bridges:* Before the first Gumbo Stew Festival, blacks and whites met together only over business, conflict, politics, and problems. Meetings were often characterized by acrimony and ill-will. Indeed, racism

is alive and well in Pawleys Island, and blacks have more than ample cause for anger as they experience the downside of the clash between wealth and poverty. Though Camp Baskervill has done nothing directly to alleviate economic inequities between the races, it has been successful in getting blacks and whites to cooperate in joint projects. It has created opportunities for the races to talk with each other, and perhaps lay the foundations of some mutual trust and respect. Lives are being rebuilt. Homes are being rebuilt. Bridges between black and white are being constructed. Tony and Julie Campbell, an interracial couple, are themselves examples of the bridges being built and the restoration of the wholeness God intends for all humanity. Observing them and their work, along with the whole Camp Baskervill community, is like seeing Isaiah 58 coming true: "Your ancient ruins shall be rebuilt; you shall raise up the foundations of many generations; you shall be called the repairer of the breach, the restorer of streets to dwell in."(Isaiah 58:12; RSV)

## NOTES

[1] Henry Smith, interview at Pawleys Island, June 9, 1990.
[2] Luther Dennison, interview at Pawleys Island, June 9, 1990.
[3] Henry Smith, interview.
[4] Henry Smith, "Workin' on the Sampit River."
[5] Luther Dennison, interview.
[6] *Ibid.*
[7] Real estate developers obtain property by combing through municipal records in search of land parcels whose titles are not recorded. This legal but suspect practice puts the natural occupiers of the land in a difficult position. Those whose families have lived on the land for generations, who informally have had it passed on to them by their parents, are forced to prove ownership through official titles and deeds, which is often impossible. Land is also obtained by legal but dubious tax schemes in which, unbeknownst to the occupiers of a property, developers pay taxes on it and then, after seven years, claim the land and evict the people who thought they owned it. To the best of available knowledge, neither the diocese nor the congregation has challenged this practice to date. The same issue arose after Hurricane Hugo in 1990 devastated much private property. Insurance companies refused to pay claims if the claimants could not prove

ownership. At this point, the diocese intervened on behalf of the claimants with positive result for the claimants.

[8] "Georgetown County, South Carolina, Visitor's Guide."
[9] *Ibid.*
[10] *Ibid.*
[11] Pawleys Island resident, quoted by Antoine L. Campbell, June 10, 1990.
[12] "Good News of Camp Baskervill," video, 1990.
[13] Antoine L. Campbell, "Camp Baskervill: A Ministry of Service," p. 1, no date.
[14] Tony Campbell, interview at Pawleys Island, June 8, 1990.
[15] *Ibid.*
[16] Ruby M. Forsythe, quoted in "Good News of Camp Baskervill," video, 1990.
[17] "Camp Baskervill: A Ministry of Service," p. 5.
[18] Tony Campbell, interview.
[19] "Good News of Camp Baskervill."
[20] Lu Hook, "Bill Clark Knew He Wasn't Ready to Put His Feet Up," *Coastal Observer*, July 16, 1987.
[21] William J. Clark, quoted in "Camp Baskervill: A Ministry of Service," p. 9.
[22] Hook, "Bill Clark Knew He Wasn't Ready to Put His Feet Up."
[23] Jim Hunter, interview at Pawleys Island, June 10, 1990.
[24] "Camp Baskervill: A Ministry of Service," p. 9.
[25] "Jubilee at Baskervill," *Coastal Observer*, no date, no page.
[26] Verdell Carr, quoted in "Community Reaches Out to Build Sisters' New Home," *Coastal Observer*, no date, no page.
[27] Danny Chamblee, quoted in *ibid.*
[28] Becki Brantley, interview at Pawleys Island, June 9, 1990.
[29] Beulah White, "Good News of Camp Baskervill," video, 1990.
[30] "Camp Baskervill: A Ministry of Service," p. 4.
[31] *Ibid.*
[32] Tony Campbell, interview at Pawleys Island, June 9, 1990.
[33] *Ibid.*
[34] "Days After That . . . Redemption Begins," *Jubilate Deo*, no date, [Fall, 1989] no page.
[35] Tony Campbell, interview at Pawleys Island, June 10, 1990.
[36] Ray Baake, *The Urban Christian: Effective Ministry in Today's Urban World* (Downers Grove, IL: InterVarsity Press, 1987).
[37] Jervis O. Burns, Jr., Site Visitor Report.
[38] *Ibid.*

[39]"Good News of Camp Baskervill," video, 1990.
[40]Jervis O. Burns, Jr., Site Visitor Report.
[41]Tony Campbell, interview, June 9, 1990.

*Visiting Team:* The Rev. Canon Jervis Burns and Bryant Hudson
*Date of Visit:* June 8-10, 1990

> *In the borderlands between the U.S.A and Mexico, peoples who had never really met before are today meeting one another, intermingling, and becoming a new and united people. Differences are not being destroyed, but they are being transcended and celebrated as together we usher in the beginning of the new race of humanity. We are on the way, that all might truly be a united human family on the planet earth.*
>
> —Virgil Elizondo,
> The Future Is Mestizo

## CHAPTER 8

# GRAPEFRUIT AND GOOD NEWS

## STORY OF A HISPANIC JUBILEE MINISTRY
### SANTA FE EPISCOPAL CHURCH
### SAN ANTONIO, TEXAS

### THE CONTEXT OF MISSION DISCERNMENT: THE SOUTH SIDE OF SAN ANTONIO

"The only people who are not of *La Raza* who come here are the police and social workers," according to Pat Castillo, a member of Santa Fe (Holy Faith) Episcopal Church on the South Side of San Antonio. "Here," she continues, "It's 150 percent Mexican!"[1] On San Antonio's South Side there's no need for store signs to assure customers, "Se habla Español," since it's obvious that this is Little Mexico. There are Spanish names on corner grocery stores, on restaurants, on billboards. Churches' names are in Spanish. A stroll through the supermarket is a delight to the senses. There are corn tortillas, flour tortillas, corn chips, and tostados. The smell of spices wafts through the air. Here is an array of chili peppers from red-hot to mild, there mounds of grassy green cilantro, and a rainbow assortment of beans—beans in cans, small and large, beans in bags of every size and shape. The supermarkets are full of beans and tortillas and chilies and most especially people—mostly women—mothers and grandmothers and lots of children.

Here on the South Side, color, life, and vitality abound, from the aisles of the supermarket to the city streets, where the music that floats from open car windows has a distinctly Latin beat to it. Virgil Elizondo, the author of *The Future Is Mestizo*, whose home is San Antonio, remarks that

> Walking through the streets of San Antonio, you can easily recognize the native faces of the present-day descendants of the Apache, Comanche, Chichimeca, and other pre-Columbian inhabitants of this land. They are not extinct or living on reservations. They form part of the complex organic mosaic that makes up this city on the great frontier between the United States and Latin America.[2]

The Hispanic presence in the area around San Antonio began 300 years ago, when the Spaniards moved in on a Coahuiltecan Indian village in 1691. Between 1718 and 1731 they built five missions in the area. One of them—San Antonio de Valero—would be remembered simply as the Alamo. Until 1836 San Antonio was the scene of constant struggles—struggles for national sovereignty and identity, struggles amongst cultures and people. Texas itself was an independent nation for almost ten years, and the flavor of that independent spirit is still alive amid the mix of cultures.

With a population of 843,000, San Antonio is still both a military center (with five military bases within or just outside the city limits) and a city of Hispanic life and culture. English and German cultures have also left their mark on San Antonio, but people of Northern European descent and others still only account for 30 percent of San Antonio's population. African-Americans make up about 10 percent.

Euro-Americans, however, have made their presence felt beyond what their numbers would suggest. Priscilla Murguia, who supervises Jubilee interns and training for the Episcopal Church's Volunteers for Mission at the Good Samaritan Center, close to Santa Fe, said,

> As soon as we got to first grade we got the message that we were second-class citizens. In the 1950s and 1960s I was not allowed to speak Spanish. If I slipped I had to stay after school and write repeatedly "I will not speak Spanish. I will not speak Spanish." After several warnings, children who persisted in speaking Spanish were suspended [for three days]. To re-enroll the parents had to bring the children in to school, taking a day off from work to do so. But look what happened. The parents couldn't speak English so they couldn't talk to the teacher, and they sometimes lost their jobs because of taking the time off.
>
> So kids weren't regularly in school. As soon as you hit first grade, you'd be tested in English. You didn't understand so you failed. My sister flunked first grade![3]

In an environment where the language, the culture, the value system are not affirmed, many children still fail. The Rev. Carmen Guerrero adds:

> Being Mexican and an American was like it must have been being black in the South. I have been refused entrance to restaurants. I know discrimination. I know lack of affirmation.[4]

Understandably, children of the barrio have a high dropout rate. For those who stay to high school, college is not encouraged. Priscilla continues. "You get the message. And you deny. You deny yourself. In my case, I grew up and got out of the barrio."[5]

Some of the earliest government-built housing is located

on the southwest side of San Antonio and is occupied by Mexican-Americans. The Rev. Carmen Guerrero grew up in "the projects." A sign of doing something better for one's children, just as Priscilla Murguia suggested, was to get out and move to a single-family house. The two census tracts where Santa Fe concentrates its ministry are an area which is that step up out of the projects. It is the barrio, it is heavily Mexican-American, but it is not the projects. According to Carmen Guerrero:

> People got an education, and they moved to the South Side. People moved up here from the projects. They could get a house for $15,000, and this was a big step up. Unfortunately one of the things we see now is that they had good enough jobs to buy their homes, but the jobs . . . didn't include pensions. So that when they retired they did not have the money to keep their houses up.[6]

There are 16,000 people living in the barrio surrounding Santa Fe Episcopal Church. Incomes here average $5,000 a year. It is an area that the local media have described as a "dusty, shabby, south San Antonio neighborhood." But according to the Rev. Carmen Guerrero,

> We happen to see it as the vineyard of the Lord— a place where we can be of service through outreach ministries, leadership development, and evangelistic worship services as we intentionally spread the Gospel to people in need within our community.[7]

In this "vineyard of the Lord," Santa Fe is a sign of God's love, of God's holy community, of God's hope, and God's transforming action.

## SANTA FE EPISCOPAL CHURCH TODAY

Santa Fe Episcopal Church is a place where, according to Rosa Elia Mejia, "One day you can be the sweeper and the next day you'll be at the altar, and you have just as much value either place."[8] It's where, as Jerry Escarzaga, says, "People help you find the answers you have within you."[9] Santa Fe is full of members who express that sense of radical equality and personal affirmation, and invariably they will say that it is the vicar, the Rev. Carmen B. Guerrero, who first unlocked the answers within and opened up doors and lives to the power of the Gospel. Reducinda Davila, a senior citizen who comes every Wednesday morning for Bible study, says, "I call Carmen the woman who makes grass grow overnight."[10]

Members and friends of the Santa Fe Church readily introduce themselves and describe why they're there. Guadalupe Arauza is a Roman Catholic who is not a member of Santa Fe but comes to help with the food bank. He also cuts the grass and does any other jobs as needed. "I like to be here because here people are happy. I feel good coming."[11] Lupe, as he is called, explains how he gives and receives from Santa Fe:

> I make $700 a month from disability. That's all. Sometimes I can't manage, so I say, "Carmen, give me rice, give me bread." Sometimes I need to ask because I can't pay rent, phone. I have three kids still at home. So Carmen says, "Take anything you need." In return I tell her, "I'll help you." So I sort the food and get the bags ready.[12]

Socorro Flores and Jacoba Garcia also help with the food bank, and they cook meals for thirteen neighborhood shut-ins twice a week. They started coming to the church in the grapefruit season two and a half years ago. According to Mrs. Garcia:

> I came for Bible study. Now I'm going to get confirmed. I like to help the people. I'm a diabetic. I can't work, but I am a good cook: I see God in the people. I feel God in front of the altar.[13]

Esther Reynosa, a single parent of three children who is a founding member of the church, teaches emotionally disturbed children in the San Antonio school system, and runs a summer recreation program at the Wesley Community Center. Every day in the summer she sends the church extra lunches that aren't claimed by the children in the program. Santa Fe makes them available in the neighborhood. Jerry Escarzaga helps in a similar way. A couple of times a week a local supermarket gives Jerry its extra bread for the animals at his 28-acre farm just outside of the city. Law prohibits the store from giving bread to people, but animals are different. The bread is perfectly good and fresh, only slightly dated. Jerry turns it over to Santa Fe. Now the church is able to provide bread for almost the entire neighborhood.

Jerry admits that it is "not cool" for a Hispanic male to be active in church affairs, but:

> Christ kept calling. I went to Cursillo eleven years ago. I had the need and the desire. I came to Santa Fe just before Carmen came. In our everyday life there is much discrimination. A lot of us have been divorced and have gone through the hurt of a divorce. We have to own that hurt.
>
> If I need to talk to someone I call them up at night. We can talk frankly and discern what the problem is. We all have problems and we have to talk to someone.
>
> What does the truth look like? At one time I was having trouble with my son, Tony. I was trying to help him, and I shared it with Ruth Asher [the senior warden]. In Ruth I got a listening ear. Here we all share. There's no special cliques here. Christ has brought about healing and a lot of love.[14]

Susie Bruni, the parish secretary, says,

> I began by coming to Bible studies. I needed my own [Mexican-American] people who understood where I was coming from. You have a void, and you have to fill it. I had lived in a "Leave It to Beaver" world. I had never even been on a trip before. Then I went to North Dakota and San Francisco for Women in Mission and Ministry meetings. These meetings gave me confidence. I learned to stand by my convictions.[15]

Ruth Asher first started coming to Santa Fe when she was five, but she has been away during times when there was very little going on at Santa Fe. Recently Ruth moved to be closer to the church, and she's serious when she says "I had to pick an apartment that would be big enough for my EFM group."[16]

Cynthia Reyes, the mother of three children, has experienced affirmation at Santa Fe. She said the first time she came to Santa Fe:

> I was hugged by everybody. I liked it! When I first came, I couldn't wait to come back and be hugged again. Neya [one of the matriarchs of the congregation] spoke on an even level. She didn't speak down to me.[17]

Nora Mejia, an eleven-year-old, says "They trust you like a grown-up. It's very special. And they always treat you like an equal. I love this church."[18]

Pat Castillo had no church, nor was she looking for one, but she discovered Santa Fe through her employment. As program coordinator of MATCH (Mothers and Their Children, a program of the Bexar County Detention Center), Pat got to know Carmen through the weekly Bible studies Carmen leads at the jail. Pat was impressed but not ready to attend church until some of the women, upon their release, said, "We want to go to Reverend Carmen's church. Will you take us?" Pat felt she could not refuse them:

> I learned about Santa Fe from Carmen coming into prison and working with the women. Carmen made the words cf Scripture come to life for me. When I came, everybody had smiles for me. You get introduced [during the service] to the congregation. They clap. You feel like it's OK to be here. The leaders are not an elite group . . . . Here I feel like I've got ten moms and all the kids are like my little sisters. We're all concerned about the kids and want them to get on well. I'm a single woman, and the warmth of this place has made me want to take on the responsibility to help these kids. Here the kids are acknowledged and given rights. We have one little boy in a wheelchair. He just zooms up and down. We have a little girl with a deformed leg. She just crawls right up to the altar. And Bianca [a healthy four-year-old] just crawls with her.
>
> I think these children symbolize this parish. If all you can do is crawl, there will be

someone who will be willing to crawl with you, even if you can walk.[19]

Faye Davis, Bianca's mother, said:

> What's kept me here is family. I've been involved in a lot of things. This togetherness, this family. I'm part of a family. I come from a large family, and this is my extended family. I can always count on someone being here for me. Always, always, always. It keeps my eyes focused on who I am serving.[20]

The most distinctive feature of Santa Fe Episcopal Church is Bible study. Every ministry of this congregation flows out of Bible study. The Bible shapes the direction of all the congregation's ministries; the Bible sustains and nurtures them. Every member of the church is involved in the mission of the Church, and there are many who are not members but who come to help with the congregation's many programs. Some who are not members also come for Bible study. Carmen Guerrero says:

> Life came to Holy Faith Episcopal Church when they began, as a congregation, to study the Scriptures in small groups. And one could find them studying in their homes, and studying in the church, and studying in the parish hall, and they did this at all hours. Sometimes they would do it in the evenings, and sometimes they would do it in the mornings, and sometimes during the week. Why, they even began to look at the Scriptures in the local county jail. And not only this, they also didn't seem to have any limits about who could be a part of the study groups. There were groups of four-year-olds, and there were groups of senior citizens, and then one day the priest and vestry noticed that they didn't have enough room. There just wasn't enough room for all the ministry that was happening at Holy Faith Church.
> 
> . . . What happened to the Church of the Holy Faith? They had become a scriptural community. They had entered into dialogue. They had entered into conversation with Scripture. And as

a result of being in conversation with God's written word, they began to give a different meaning to the people and the things in their lives . . . .

. . . It's a conversation that may be risky because it might mean that we will change. We are being called to live into the promise that God has made to his people. And this is what began to happen to this community, it dared to believe that as a people God was calling them to something . . . . They began to see the connectedness between each other so that they began to see that there was a communal character to conversation. That God is speaking to a community and a community is responding to God's call.[21]

Bible study forms the center of a whole list of ministries that flow from Santa Fe Church. The church is like a community center—a holy community center. People of all ages pop in and out all day long, every day. They come to prepare food bags and cook meals; they come to pick up food; they come for Bible study; they come for high school equivalency training. Children come for music lessons. They come for services and fiestas. And there are fiestas for everything—weddings, baptisms, episcopal visitations, fiestas for quinceañeras (coming-out parties for girls of fifteen). According to Ruth Asher:

We have a dance for everything. Whenever we want to have a party, we have it! We have a New Year's Eve party at the church. At midnight we pass the peace and wish everybody "Happy New Year." Everybody dances. Men, women, children, they dance together. You don't have to have a partner.[22]

They come to listen to the music of mariachi bands; they come to donate clothes to the thrift store in the old vicarage; they come to buy clothes at the thrift store; they come for craft classes; they come to help out. They come just to be around the church. Children of migrant workers, ages four to six, come for a head start program geared especially to their needs. Children come after school for the "latchkey" program, where they are taken care of by grandmothers until their parents finish work. They come for support groups, to participate in seminars to explore the connections between their faith and their action in the community. They come for Cursillo follow-up meetings. They come for Alcoholics Anonymous and Al-Anon. They come for adult literacy classes, citizenship classes, English as a second language classes. They come to apply for scholarship help at local colleges; they come to request funds for Mexican-American Legal Defense Training. When they run short of money, they come for assistance in paying their utility bills. When they need a car loan countersigned, they come. They come to develop their listening skills by participating in LEAD (Leadership, Education, and Development). They come for EFM (Education for Ministry), they come for IAF (Industrial Areas Foundation, a program of training for community organizing). They come to strategize about political issues of the neighborhood. They participate in "Project Rebuild," in which the community is organized and working together with the church to repair, paint, and clean homes and yards in the area. At election time the women in the church organize voter registration drives.

About 200 families are provided with food from the food bank, and virtually the whole neighborhood is kept in bread through the efforts of Jerry Escarzaga.

Through the one-year Legalization and Amnesty Program of the U.S. government, 5,000 people gained temporary residency, which put them into the process for later becoming American citizens. Jobs were provided for two Santa Fe members, and the church made $25,000. People were only charged $75 for the service—a modest fee when one considers that other churches engaged in the program often charged as much as $1,000. According to Carmen Guerrero:

> I have seen the look on people's faces when they received that first official card that legally authorizes them to be employed. It is the first step toward becoming a real human being in this country; it is being free for the first time in their life; it means no more hiding and denying I exist. It means the beginning of dignity.[23]

All Santa Fe's ministries, programs and services are run by volunteers and just four paid staff; the vicar and three lay people.

Most of the members come from Roman Catholic roots, and most of them were first attracted to the church through Bible study or one of the service programs. There are quite a large number who regularly attend Bible study, and supervise the preparation of the Tuesday morning food bank who are regular members of the Roman Catholic Church, like Lupe Arauza, Jacoba Garcia, and Socorro Flores. Although there is no pressure put on them to join Santa Fe, many will, in time, find their way into membership.

Sunday services are lively celebrations, which can last as long as two and a half hours. The music is led by a very able musician, Ramiro Rodriquez, who also supervises the outreach ministries and participates in the jail ministry with Carmen. There are four guitars on a Sunday morning as well as occasional organ music. There is a list of children waiting to be old enough to be acolytes. Visitors are newcomers only once, for they are introduced during the service and warmly welcomed by the congregation, who make every effort to make them feel at home quickly. A number of members described Sunday worship as "happy."

"Something has caught on with the people," according to Carmen Guerrero. "They're excited and full of life."[24] And the community around them has, almost overnight, become the "vineyard of the Lord," a vineyard yielding rich and delicious fruits.

## *GRAPEFRUIT AND GOOD NEWS: UNDERSTANDING THE STORY*

It was a Sunday morning in January. The priest opened the door to the church and turned on the heat. Fifteen minutes later he began the service with the congregation of six—each one sitting in a different pew. He announced the processional hymn (in English) and, along with the Hispanic woman priest who had just come to help on Sundays, started down the aisle. Halfway down, he observed that no one was singing. He muttered under his breath that "trying to sing is a total waste of time," closed the hymnal, and continued to process in silence. Thirty minutes later, the service ended, the heater was turned off, the front gates were locked, and the church was closed up until the next Sunday, when the same process would be repeated.

That was Santa Fe Episcopal Church in January, 1987:

a congregation of six people (who couldn't or wouldn't sing), served by a part-time priest with a budget of $8,000 and a church building that was open for only one hour each week. Carmen Guerrero was the woman priest. It was her first Sunday. She was shocked. "I just couldn't believe it. We're a people of music. We should be able to sing."[25]

Three years later Santa Fe is a vital congregation, with a hundred people worshiping every week. They have to come early if they want to be assured of getting a seat. The church building is open and full of activity seven days a week. It is a Jubilee Center with a budget of $180,000, half of which goes for outreach. What happened? It's a story of grapefruit and Good News.

Carmen Guerrero had arrived back home in San Antonio after spending the previous two years in Honduras. The Bishop of West Texas, the Rt. Rev. John MacNaughton, gave her the job of doing a study to determine if there was a place for the Episcopal Church among Hispanics in the Diocese of West Texas. Carmen sometimes thinks it was just a nice gesture on his part, something to keep her busy for a few months.

There were only two Hispanic congregations in the diocese of almost a hundred parishes, and one of them—Santa Fe—was failing badly. Closing Santa Fe was a real possibility. With such a diminished ministry there would be, after all, very little to lose if the church did close. So Carmen was hired for two hours a week to "try anything."

Carmen went over to the church on a Wednesday morning and, to her amazement, found a long line of people waiting in front of the church. She couldn't figure it out. Only six people come on a Sunday morning, and a whole crowd on Wednesday? "That's when I found out about the grapefruit," Carmen said. Every Wednesday morning during the grapefruit season (November to March) a truck full of grapefruit would arrive in front of Santa Fe, and the driver would distribute them to anyone who wanted them. There are similar "grapefruit stops" at other churches in the area. After the grapefruit is distributed, the truck drives away until the following Wednesday. Carmen recalls:

> I began to think. There's something missing here. This many people would gather to pick up grapefruit and yet it was a good, good, Sunday

morning when they had fifteen people in church. Something's not right, something's not connecting here. So I decided that the next Wednesday when they came, I would turn on the heat, get some cookies, make some coffee and invite the people to wait inside the parish hall where it would be warm. I did that. And when they came in, we began to talk. I found that there was hardly anybody who had not, in one way or another, been touched by some kind of ministry from this church. And I said, "If you could see this place come alive again, what would you like to see happen?"[26]

Carmen listened to the people, who indicated that they would like to meet for Bible study before the grapefruit truck arrived. This they did. The number of people who came to study the Bible rose to forty in some weeks, and even to fifty. Bible study became more important than grapefruit. When the grapefruit harvest was over, the people still wanted to meet, so they came for Bible study and a potluck lunch. A Tuesday night Bible study was added to accommodate all the people who wanted to participate in what was rapidly becoming "the miracle of Santa Fe."

The people started coming on Sunday mornings, but there was no one to help with the music. "I prayed for a guitar player," Carmen recalls. "Then a little girl who was working with the Mennonites came by. She was looking for a place to do ministry. She started a song book. She was with us for a year. She really got us singing . . . . Then Ramiro [Rodriquez] came for grapefruit. He said he could play. I asked if he could come back on Sunday morning."[27]

Ramiro is now a paid worker on Santa Fe's staff, with a wide variety of ministries, and the church is overflowing with music. Three pianos have been given to the church, and the children are having music lessons at the church.

Needless to say, Carmen spent a good deal more than two hours a week at Santa Fe. The bishop was quickly persuaded that there was indeed a place for the Episcopal Church in the Hispanic community, at least at Santa Fe, and Carmen was made vicar on March 2, 1987.

That was to be a full year, when all sorts of ministries were started, when Santa Fe became a Jubilee Center. Towards the year's end, Carmen wrote a Christmas letter to the members:

> What does feeding the hungry in our city have to do with the Gospel? All I can say to this is what I have read in the Gospel of Matthew: "in as much as you have done it unto the least of these, you have done it unto me." Thank you for what you are providing.
>
> However, providing food for the hungry is not the only thing happening at Santa Fe. I have been here since March 2, 1987, and sometimes I feel like asking God to take a break!!! Thus far we have had 14 baptisms, 4 weddings, and will be preparing about 16 people for confirmation/reception for our next visit by the bishop. The leadership of the church is emerging and exercising their gifts . . . .
>
> . . . We are called to "Lift up the Lord Jesus Christ and He will draw others unto Him," and this is what is happening at Santa Fe. Just as it looked like the end, God raised up a remnant, and has brought us new life in Him.[28]

The congregation revitalized by "Sister Grapefruit," as Carmen has aptly been called, had begun as a mixed congregation of Anglos, blacks, and Hispanics in 1945 and was called Todos Los Santos (All Saints). In 1947, parish records indicate that seven people were confirmed with sixty members present. In 1949 the name was changed to Santa Fe Mission, and in 1951, Melchor Saucedo (later bishop) arrived from Mexico to become priest-in-charge of the mission. The church was quite active during those years. A parish van picked people up at their homes for services. A clinic was started; there were parish suppers and rummage sales every weekend. Saucedo left in 1961, and parish records bleakly describe the years until 1965 as "years of searching for leadership. Desert." Things looked up when a San Antonio native, Clifford Waller, came. Waller had been a youth worker at the Good Samaritan Center, a community center that deserves note for its distinguished tradition of service—still continuing—in the barrio. With Waller's departure in the late 1970s, membership started to drop, and a series of clergy came and went. The years 1980 to 1985 were described as "bilingual and bi-cultural," but that's probably more as a result of city programs than parish projects, since by that time the city was renting most of Santa Fe's space for various community projects.

In early 1986 the diocese commissioned a professional consulting firm to conduct a study of Santa Fe "for those engaged in planning the future of the Santa Fe Mission Church."[29] One of the real alternatives suggested was closing the church; another was relocating "to an area with a more balanced Hispanic/Anglo population mix, or move to a location that is more readily accessible to commuting communicants."[30] The other alternative was to keep the church in its present location for " . . . outreach to bring Hispanics into the Episcopal faith. [Should this alternative be chosen], the neighborhood in which it is located is close to ideal."[31]

How fortunate for all that the final alternative was selected! The seed of the grapefruit has grown into a whole tree, offering food for the body, nurture for the soul, empowerment, affirmation of Hispanic life and culture. Grass has grown green overnight in a South San Antonio barrio. In the words of Carmen Guerrero,

> . . . when one choses to address essential issues in a society or in the church, one . . . becomes intimately involved with those in need of transformation and with their condition . . . one connects more with the empowering of people as well as the providing of programs to help them. One comes in contact with the truth. One comes in contact with God.[32]

## *DISTINCTIVE FEATURES*

Santa Fe is a story of life coming back into dry bones. It is living proof that a body that is almost dead can become vital and life-giving in a short time. Dry bones can live. A number of factors contribute to the success of Santa Fe: the right people, the right timing, the right use of opportunities, the right circumstances, the right response to human need, the righteousness of God.

- ***Scriptural Community:*** The revival of Santa Fe came about when people began reading Scripture, believed that the Gospel is true, and acted on it. In the Rev. Carmen Guerrero's words:

    > They had become a scriptural community. They had entered into dialogue. They had entered into conversation with Scripture. And as a result . . . they began to give a different meaning to the people and the things in their lives.[33]

- ***A Community Meeting Needs:*** The Rev. Paul Worley, Mission Discernment Project Site Visitor, observed that:

    > Santa Fe is a place to get needs met. Sometimes the needs are physical, such as food, clothing. Sometimes the need is for education. It's a place where the spiritual hunger is fed through study and worship. At Santa Fe one is made to feel wanted, needed (lots of volunteer work is available) and most of all loved.[34]

- ***A Community of Love:*** Virginia Ramos, a grandmother who has ". . . so many grandchildren I have lost count," has been a member of Santa Fe for thirty-four years. Mrs. Ramos says of Santa Fe, "It's little but it's full of love."[35]

    Love is expressed by members of the community helping each other, supporting each other, being there for each other, even in the middle of the night—like Jerry Escarzaga calling Ruth Asher for advice in handling his teenage son. Love is taken out into the community in the form of the meals that Socorro Flores and Jacoba Garcia prepare and that Mario Bruni and Mr. Mejia deliver to the homebound. Love is taken to the county jail. Love is expressed in daily bread for the entire neighborhood. Love walks in the clothes sold or given away at the thirft store.

- ***Family:*** Faye Davis, Virginia Ramos's daughter, said, "I'm part of a family, this togetherness, this family."[36] Or as Pat Castillo said, "Here I feel like I've got ten moms and the kids are like my little sisters."[37] This is a family in which everyone is included, newcomers and old-timers, the young, old, everybody. Nobody is left out of the family. Nobody is made to feel unimportant. "Family," Paul Worley said; "perhaps this is the strongest message of all."

- **Development of Lay Leadership:** Ruth Asher reflected on how life had come back to Santa Fe: "We discovered different ministries we weren't even aware of. We've learned to see special gifts we didn't know we had."[38] Esther Reynosa agrees: "The awareness of the importance of lay people is [the] key to our ministry. We have discovered in ourselves our own ministries. It's as if we were given back *ourselves* as a free gift."[39]

All agree that it is Carmen who has been responsible for helping members see their own strengths and ministries. Carmen will readily point to the responsible jobs many of the members of the congregation—and expecially the women—have in the community. She will stress the important place they have in their households, many of them single parents both holding down jobs and raising families. And yet she has also seen the lack of confidence the women have in themselves and their capabilities. She points to the schools and to the dominant society, in which Hispanic culture has not been affirmed. Carmen says,

> You know there's that image of the macho Hispanic male. Well I think that Hispanic culture is very matriarchal. The women really run it. I tell the women in this congregation that they're really *las Amazonas*. They have this legend in the Amazon about super women, very strong women. Well, that's what we have here— *las Amazonas*— but at first the women didn't believe it. They didn't feel empowered. But once people understand, they are liberated, they are free. They can never go back. That's what's happened here.[40]

At Santa Fe, gifts for ministry are discovered, and leaders are identified and receive formal training to enhance their natural abilities. They are encouraged to participate in diocesan and national Church activities.

- **Fun:** Can the health of any community be evaluated on how much laughter is shared? On how much the members want to spend time together and enjoy each other? On how much they sing, dance, share jokes? On how genuinely easy they are with one another? Santa Fe is in no way a frivolous community; nonetheless, no occasion is too small for a fiesta. Fiestas and fun surely contribute to the health and strength of this congregation.

- ***Clerical Leadership:*** All agree that Carmen can take a great deal of credit for initiating a process of empowerment at Santa Fe. Ruth Asher says, "She is one of us. She understands. She has overcome. We can too."[41] There are many reasons for Carmen's success, but Ruth emphasized the particular appropriateness of a Hispanic woman priest in a Hispanic congregation: "It's the mother figure. The mother is always honored, obeyed, and revered in our culture. When you extend that to the congregation, it makes sense."[42]

Carmen Guerrero grew up in the Alazan-Apache Courts, one of the earliest government-built public housing projects. It is within a few miles of Santa Fe. It was a tough neighborhood full of gangs. It still is. One had to be smart to survive there with one's self-image intact while all around were the forces in society that were giving the message, "You're no good. You're Mexican." Carmen's mother was an Aztec, and she thanks her for instilling—by word and example—a positive attitude toward life. "My mother taught us never to accept 'I can't.' She would say to us, 'It is better to admit "I won't" rather than use the excuse "I can't." ' "

Carmen's intellect, determination, and "street smarts" must have been evident early on, as well as her sincere desire to help her friends develop survival techniques. Carmen explained that the Mexican children in the projects didn't know how to speak English. Because they were afraid of their teachers, they were afraid to use Spanish even to make so basic a request as, "May I go to the bathroom?" If they asked in Spanish, they would be punished. Unless they could ask in English, they would sit there and wet their pants. "So when I was six years old I opened a little school in my neighborhood. I charged 10 cents a week for expenses. I taught the kids how to get along. I taught them how to ask to go to the bathroom in English."[43]

Carmen was married at seventeen and adopted a son, Danny, who is now twenty-two. She didn't start college until she was twenty-six. When she graduated, she went back to the projects where she had grown up, to coordinate guidance programs for black and Mexican youth who were in trouble with the law. Although Roman Catholic by birth, Carmen had joined the Evangelical Free Church and was active in many of its programs. At the time of her divorce, after eighteen years of marriage, she met some Episcopalians, who invited her to a Bible study group at Christ Church in San Antonio.

> I knew a little more about the Bible than the people in that group knew, and they knew a whole lot more about the love of God than I was experiencing at the time. The connection was just perfect! I remember saying that if I had known the Episcopal Church was that alive, I would have been there years ago. That group literally loved me into the Episcopal Church.[44]

She and Danny were both confirmed in the Episcopal Church and became active. In time Carmen went to seminary and then to Honduras, where she establsihed a theological educational program for the purpose of raising a Honduran priesthood. She was ordained a priest there and later took charge of two small Honduran parishes.

> The [Honduran] people taught me a whole lot about the cross. One of the things that kept going through my mind is "How am I going to convince these people that they are not abandoned, that God is in their midst?" And the truth is, they already *knew* it.[45]

With what the Honduran people taught Carmen, she came back to serve her own people. She had been liberated and made able to affirm her Hispanic culture and the faith that is in her. In doing so, she is a powerful agent for the liberation of others. "I have a passion for justice," Carmen says. And she has a great deal of love to go with it. "If I have a concern for my life, it is that I might sell out."[46] It doesn't seem likely that she will.

Soon "Sister Grapefruit" will move to the Diocese of Los Angeles, where she will coordinate Hispanic ministry. She will understandably be greatly missed at Santa Fe. Yet as Herlinda Trevino says,

> Carmen has tuaght us enough. With the help of the Lord we'll make grow the seed Carmen planted here. All of us. We can do it. She's gotten us in gear.[47]

# ISSUE RAISED BY THE VISIT TO SANTA FE CHURCH

The Episcopal Church needs to see the connection between its need for numbers and new life and the natural gifts people of Hispanic culture have to offer the whole Church. They have a warmth and *joie de vivre* that are infectious. Their authenticity shines through all they do. Their worship is heartfelt and passionate. They are a devout people with a lively spirituality, which they readily apply to all of life.

Already one in four Americans defines himself or herself as Hispanic or nonwhite. Between 1980 and 1988, the number of Hispanics increased by one third (owing to higher birth rates than Euro-Americans and immigration). By the year 2020, U.S. residents who are Hispanic or nonwhite will have increased to 115 million, while the white population will not have increased at all.[48]

The area covered by the Diocese of West Texas is at least 50 percent Hispanic, yet only two of its nearly one hundred congregations is Hispanic. And that is the case in diocese after diocese after diocese of the Episcopal Church—USA.

This is a unique opportunity. There is everything to be gained by taking it very seriously and acting on it. It is more than numbers that the Episcopal Church needs: it is the Hispanics' passionate and lively faith; it is their wholesome outlook on life. The dominant culture, whose representatives make up the major membership of the Episcopal Church, badly needs what Hispanic people are more than willing to offer. In the words of the Rev. José R. Vilar:

> Hispanics have a great and distinct contribution to make to the church and the church must facilitate this ministry.... Anglicanism has always been open to the Spirit and receptive to all the people of God and their gifts. Hispanics tend to be charismatic and spontaneous rather than planners and programmers; they are oriented to family and friends rather than to institutions; a smile takes you closer to Jesus than a sermon. Hispanics need to make themselves felt as who they are, with their gifts, music, language, folklore, history and journeys.[49]

# RESOURCES

The Rev. Carmen Guerrero stressed that the Bible is the single most important source used in the development and maintenance of the congregation.

Cabestero, Teofilo, ed. *Conversations with Contemporary Theologians*. Maryknoll, NY: Orbis Books, 1981.

Elizondo, Virgil. *The Future Is Mestizo: Life Where Cultures Meet*. Bloomington, IN: Meyer-Stone Books, 1988.

Rowthorn, Anne. *The Liberation of the Laity*. Wilton, CT: Morehouse-Barlow, 1986.

School of Theology, The University of the South. *Education for Ministry* workbooks.

Aorilla, Hugo. *Estudio y Interpretación de la Bíblia*. Costa Rica: Seminaro Bíblico Latinamericano.

# NOTES

[1] Patricia Castillo, interview in San Antonio, July 9, 1990.
[2] Virgil Elizondo, *The Future Is Mestizo: Life Where Cultures Meet* (Bloomington, IN: Meyer Stone Books, 1988), p. 1.
[3] Priscilla Murguia, interview in San Antonio, July 10, 1990.
[4] Carmen B. Guerrero, interview in San Antonio, July 19, 1990.
[5] Priscilla Murguia, interview.
[6] Carmen B. Guerrero, interview in San Antonio, July 9, 1990.
[7] Carmen B. Guerrero, printed paper, undated.
[8] Rosa Elia Mejia, interview in San Antonio, July 10, 1990.
[9] Jerry Escarzaga, interview in San Antonio, July 10, 1990.
[10] Reducinda Davila, interview in San Antonio, July 10, 1990.
[11] Guadalupe Arauza, interview in San Antonio, July 10, 1990.
[12] *Ibid*.
[13] Jacoba Garcia, interview in San Antonio, July 9, 1990.
[14] Jerry Escarzaga, interview.
[15] Susie Bruni, interview in San Antonio, July 10, 1990.
[16] Ruth Asher, interview in San Antonio, July 10, 1990.
[17] Cynthia Reyes, interview in San Antonio, July 10, 1990.
[18] Nora Mejia, interview in San Antonio, July 10, 1990.
[19] Patricia Castillo, interview in San Antonio, July 10, 1990.
[20] Faye Davis, interview in San Antonio, July 10, 1990.
[21] Carmen B. Guerrero, presentation made on Scriptural Communities in Province VII with John Vogelsang in 1989.
[22] Ruth Asher, interview.

[23] Carmen B. Guerrero, quoted in "PFE Legalization/Amnesty Program Short on Funding," by Jean E. Abney; source of article unknown.
[24] Carmen B. Guerrero, quoted by Steve Schlather in "Preacher Sees Church Revive," *San Antonio Light*, no other information available.
[25] Carmen B. Guerrero, interview in San Antonio, July 10, 1990.
[26] Carmen B. Guerrero, typewritten material, no other reference.
[27] Carmen B. Guerrero, interview, July 9, 1990.
[28] Carmen B. Guerrero, letter to the parish, December 15, 1990.
[29] Becker and Associates, "Santa Fe Mission Church: Neighborhood Profile," March, 1986.
[30] *Ibid.*
[31] *Ibid.*
[32] Carmen B. Guerrero, printed notes, undated.
[33] Carmen B. Guerrero, transcript of a conversation.
[34] Paul Worley, Site Visit Notes, July 11, 1990.
[35] Virginia Ramos, interview in San Antonio, July 10, 1990.
[36] Faye Davis, interview.
[37] Patricia Castillo, interview, July 10, 1990.
[38] Ruth Asher, interview.
[39] Esther Reynosa, interview in San Antonio, July 10, 1990.
[40] Carmen G. Guerrero, interview, July 12, 1990.
[41] Ruth Asher, interview.
[42] *Ibid.*
[43] Carmen B. Guerrero, interview in San Antonio, July 11, 1990.
[44] Carmen B. Guerrero, quoted in printed notes, no title, no date.
[45] *Ibid.*
[46] Carmen B. Guerrero, interview, July 11, 1990.
[47] Herlinda Trevino, interview in San Antonio, July 10, 1990.
[48] William A. Henry, III, "Beyond the Melting Pot," *Time*, Vol. 135, April 9, 1990, pp. 28 and 30.
[49] José E. Vilar, "Hispanic Ministry," *Ministry Development Journal*, No. 15, 1988, p. 26.

*Visiting Team:* Bryant Hudson and the Rev. Paul Worley
*Date of Visit:* July 10-12, 1990

*Within the traditions and customs of the American Indian people are the guidelines for [humankind's] future. . . . The lands wait for those who can discern their rhythm. . . . The future of [humankind] lies waiting for those who will come to understand their lives and take up their responsibilities to all living things.*

—Vine Deloria, Jr.,
God Is Red

## CHAPTER 9

# MITAKUYE OYASIN

## PARTNERS ON THE PRAIRIE STORY OF A NATIVE AMERICAN LUTHERAN-EPISCOPAL MINISTRY

### PINE RIDGE INDIAN RESERVATION
### PINE RIDGE, SOUTH DAKOTA

### *THE CONTEXT OF MISSION DISCERNMENT: PINE RIDGE INDIAN RESERVATION*

Shadows are gathering between the buttes and hillocks of South Dakota's rolling prairie, and the setting sun rests on the herd of wild horses clustered at the water hole. Beyond them graze black Angus cattle, lazily chewing the dinner they have taken from the wavy golden grain of the prairie floor. It is a Friday evening in midsummer on the Pine Ridge Indian Reservation.

Raymond Pipe On Head at Loneman, a reservation community of five households, is preparing to "take a sweat."

In front of Raymond's sweat lodge, the rocks are heating up in the fire. When they are ready he will carry them in with a pitchfork and place on them a handful of sage. He'll then cover the door of the sweat lodge and pour water over the hot rocks and sage. The steam created will clean his body while it refreshes his mind. A sweat lodge is more than an Indian version of a Finnish sauna, for it has a spiritual and psychological function of healing and purification.

> My alcoholism was healed in the sweat lodge. On August 2nd I was dry for a year. The calluses on my feet healed up after two sweats. It eases the pain in my joints. I take a sweat in here in preparation for the sun dance.[1]

Pipe on Head's sweat lodge is a small tipi-like structure covered with blankets, with a hole dug in the middle for the hot rocks and a place to sit facing the door. He points to a brown and white Indian pony grazing in the draw below it. "That's my war horse," he says with a chuckle. "The snowplow doesn't come up here in the winter, so I need my horse to get me to the store. I go straight over the hills there into town."[2]

The town of Pine Ridge is a few miles away from Loneman. Tonight it's busier than usual because the Oglala Nation's annual powwow is in full swing. A few blocks from the town center, hundreds of people are camped at the fairgrounds in tents, trailers, and tipis. Their camps are arranged around the shade, a circular frame structure covered with richly scented pine boughs. Here Indians in brightly colored dancing costumes, crafted from skins and decorated with beads, porcupine quills, feathers, fur, bones, and bells, dance to the rhythmic beat of drums and the haunting chants of the singers. Others, many also in costume, drift through the crowd, meeting up with old friends and family members. They patronize concession stands, which are mostly sponsored by civic, community, and church organizations. Everyone—dancers and guests alike—is in a festive mode. According to Harold D. Salway, president of the Oglala Sioux Tribe, the powwow

> ... is a time we all look forward to, a time when our members who live off the reservation, in other states and urban areas, look forward to coming home, to join together for celebration and unity.

It is a time when we set aside our differences, rekindle old friendships, celebrate our customs and traditions as our ancestors did, and give thanks for the survival of the Oglala Indian Nation.[3]

Amid the great beauty of the rolling plains and big sky at Raymond Pipe On Head's house and the colorful good times of the powwow, it is almost impossible to comprehend that Shannon County, which covers two-thirds of the Pine Ridge Indian Reservation, is the poorest county in the United States. It's hard to believe the unemployment figure of 73 percent. Statistics provided by the Wounded Knee District School state that on the reservation the suicide rate is three times the national average, that 57 percent of all households are below the poverty level, and that Native Americans on the reservation have the lowest life expectancy of any group in the U.S.A.[4] Nonetheless, there is great pride in what the people are accomplishing. In announcing plans for a new playground, Wounded Knee District School Board members stated that:

> Our role is to promote the overall welfare of our children in the home, school and community. And we strive to develop programs that will benefit the people of this district. Only by accomplishing these goals will we ever be able to improve the quality of life in the school and community. Our isolated location, the lack of a stable economy, plus many other factors have contributed to these dismal statistics [stated above. We seek to] build a spirit of sharing and establish an enduring vision of cooperation and hope for the future.[5]

The Rev. Benjamin R. Tyon, the Episcopal priest in charge of the Western Christian Unity (the name for the Episcopal ministry in the western area of the reservation), says, "We want to emphasize our success stories. We want to emphasize our progress and the good things we do."[6] Tyon, along with many others, believes that a disservice was done by the NBC special report, "Tragedy at Pine Ridge." It is Tyon's view that the report, which appeared on national television in 1989, did little but emphasize the negative, and only serves to reinforce old prejudices and stereotypes. According to the Revs. Barbara Wangsness and Natanael Lizarazo, the Lutheran pastors in the Lutheran-Episcopal joint ministry on the Pine Ridge Reservation,

> Yes, the alcoholism rate is high and so is unemployment. Yes, there is violence, physical abuse, poverty, many health problems, and other undesirable realities going on in Pine Ridge. But there is also hope, courage, energies, and committed Native Americans who are doing their very best to turn this situation around, and who are gradually succeeding. The very fact that Native Americans have never given up; that they are trying so hard with such limited resources; that despite all the injustices and oppression they have historically suffered, they continue to survive; all these are the most reassuring signs of hope! Native Americans indeed call us all to rethink our priorities in life, to question our uncritical allegiance to our government and human institutions, to discover them as brothers and sisters rather than as enemies and obstacles to our unbalanced sense of "modern progress."[7]

The Pine Ridge Indian Reservation, an area of 2.5 million acres, is situated in the southwest corner of the state of South Dakota. The Badlands (spectacular low hills, clay cliffs, and irregular ravines) begin their gradual rise from the prairie at the reservation town of Manderson. The Black Hills lie to the northwest. This combination of rolling prairie, rising Badlands, buttes and draws, and occasional glimpses of the Black Hills appearing at the northwestern end of the reservation makes the Pine Ridge Reservation one of the outstanding locations of austere natural beauty in the country. But the historical clashes between Native American and Euro-American cultures, and the hardships of present-day realities on the reservation, present a far more mixed picture than is suggested by nature's artistry and the extreme beauty of the area.

After the Battle of the Little Bighorn and the murder of the great warrior Crazy Horse, the Sioux were assigned to reservations. The Pine Ridge Reservation was established in 1878, and the mighty Sioux were forced to settle there and on eight other

Indian reservations, which make up the present state of South Dakota. At the same time the reservations were established, the buffalo herds were wiped out. This meant the end of the Indians' traditional means of livlihood as well as an important avenue for achievement, prestige, and honor.

U.S. government agents attempted to introduce farming to Indian lands, but to the strong warriors, accustomed to the unfettered life of the plains, such a suggestion was considered demeaning. Presbyterian, Roman Catholic, and Episcopal churches were appointed by the government to "civilize" the Indians. Indians who were cooperative and accepting of white people's ways were regarded as "the friendlies." Those who persisted in their traditional beliefs and practices were dismissed as "the hostiles." Such harmful distinctions led to the breakup of the *tiopaye* (extended family). Since the extended family was the primary means through which the Lakota learned and followed traditional ways, this breakup of the family also broke the hearts of the proud people.

Indian efforts to restore the sense of family, to increase the buffalo, and drive out the white man took the form of the ghost dance. According to Avis Little Eagle,

> The federal government was threatened by the ghost dance, their main fear being that the Indians from different reservations would join forces and revolt.... In 1882, the federal government issued the "Code of Indian Offences," targeting the Sun dance, ghost dance, war dance and other religious ceremonies. The ban was enforced through political pressure from Indian agents and the newly established Indian police forces.[8]

Despite the prohibitions, traditional practices continued. The ghost dance movement reached its culmination in the massacre of Chief Big Foot's band at Wounded Knee (a village on the Pine Ridge Reservation) on December 29, 1890. In all, 146 Indians, including 44 women and 18 children, were killed. Thirty soldiers also died. The Indian dead were buried in a mass grave on a hill overlooking Wounded Knee. The memory of the tragedy is still very much alive today among Indians, particularly in view of the centennial of the Battle of Wounded Knee.

Wounded Knee has remained a potent symbol of Indian pride and has served as a catalyst for Indian political activity. It is the location of what is referred to as the Second Battle of Wounded Knee, a skirmish in 1973 between militant Indians and nonmilitant tribal members. The U.S. government, in the person of FBI agents, federal marshals, and other personnel, was also involved in the conflict, in which several people were killed. AIM (the American Indian Movement), which was at the center of the struggle, still has its adherents on the Pine Ridge Indian Reservation, but now some of AIM's leaders are talking in terms of reconciliation.

This theme of reconciliation—first introduced by Tim Giago, editor of the *Lakota Times*—has been taken up by the governor of South Dakota, George Mickelson, as well as tribal and church leaders. The Bishop of South Dakota, the Rt. Rev. Craig B. Anderson, is a member of the Governor's Council for the Year of Reconciliation. The idea was to use the year 1990—the centennial of the Battle of Wounded Knee—as an occasion to:

> ... identify issues, attitudes and historical experiences that have contributed to the need for reconciliation and to implement strategies for change, utilizing education, governmental policy review and cultural awareness activities with the goal of better understanding and respect for one another.[9]

While not denying the difficulties that exist on the Pine Ridge Reservation, there are many signs of encouragement and hope welling up in a variety of places.

The town of Pine Ridge, with a population of about 4,000, is the administrative center of the reservation. The Pine Ridge School, of which the Rev. Benjamin R. Tyon was once superintendent, has about eight hundred students in grades kindergarten through twelve. There is a hospital and the administrative offices of the Bureau of Indian Affairs and the Oglala Sioux Tribe; there is the Sioux Nation Super Store, a new housing complex for the elderly, and various small businesses. The newest business is Big Bat's Conoco—a gas station, restaurant, and convenience store combined—situated at the central intersection in Pine Ridge. "Big Bat" Pourier and his wife, Patty, opened their business on May 14. Big Bat's Conoco is the only business establishment of its kind in Pine Ridge. It is attractive and inviting in appearance and an impressive example of Indians taking initiatives for themselves. According to Pourier,

> Things are going good. We are pleased with the business, and people have received us well.... We think people here deserve a place that is as nice and looks just as good as any place in Rapid City or Denver. We didn't want this place to look like a jail or correctional facility with bars on its windows [like the Sioux Nation Super Store, for instance].... People take pride in this business. It's because it's their business.... We want to become a positive role model for others learning to do business.... We want them to learn that this is a viable business place.[10]

By all appearances, business is booming at Big Bat's, which employs an almost entirely Indian staff twenty-four hours a day.

Other signs of hope include an FM radio station, KILI, owned and operated by Native Americans. KILI has some programming in the Lakota language. It often features Indian music, as well as news and discussions of Indian concerns. Another successful and highly influential enterprise is the *Lakota Times*, founded by Tim Giago, a Lakota from Pine Ridge. In Manderson, a town of 150 a few miles north of Pine Ridge, is Pinky's, a convenience store owned and operated by Pinky White Plume Clifford, which is also doing well.

These are but a few signs of hope and empowerment on the Pine Ridge Indian Reservation. They are important. According to Ben Tyon:

> The reason I dwell so much on the positive is because when you feel good about yourself you do positive things. You feel good about yourself, you feel good about your environment. Your spiritual life is dovetailed and included in that. You stop and say, "Hey, it all fits together."[11]

Father Tyon continues:

> There's something our people have. It's common sense. It is like all are related. It's what we say in

Lakota: *mitakuye oyasin.* It means all my relatives, all my loved ones, all my brothers and sisters. We say it as a beginning and an ending. It is a greeting and a parting. Its underlying meaning is that we're all in relationship with each other—with all our relatives, with our past, with our present and especially with God.[12]

The "Big Three" churches (Episcopal, Roman Catholic, and Presbyterian) are all present in Pine Ridge, as are others including the Lutherans. The conjunction of Lutherans and Episcopalians is informally called the "Lutepisc" Ministry.

Churches and their clergy are important on the reservation. The high regard in which the clergy are held in the community is illustrated by the fact that the four judges for the powwow's parade down the main street of Pine Ridge were clergy representing the Big Three. That they were selected for such a role by the community says something about the respected place of the Church and its leaders on the Pine Ridge Reservation.

In such circumstances of respect, of *mitakuye oyasin,* of mutual cooperation and trust, Episcopalians and Lutherans have become partners on the prairie and signs of reconciliation between cultures and denominations, between peoples and worldviews.

## *THE LUTHERAN-EPISCOPAL MINISTRY ON THE PINE RIDGE RESERVATION TODAY*

This ministry is like a marriage of convenience, a marriage arranged by the parents, in which the partners are adapting to each other's ways and even falling in love!

The Evangelical Lutheran Church in America (ELCA) in South Dakota is the largest denomination in the state in terms of numbers and financial resources. Yet because of the historical arrangements of denominations in the state, it does not have buildings or long-established ministries in Indian lands. The Episcopal Diocese of South Dakota, on the other hand, is rich in land and buildings, with a long and well-established presence on the reservations, yet it is poor in personnel and financial resources. With these factors in mind a joint "Lutepisc" ministry has been established on the Pine Ridge Indian Reservation by the two denominations.

For a little over a week each month, the co-pastors of Trinity Lutheran Church in Edgemont, South Dakota, the Rev. Barbara Wangsness and her husband, the Rev. Natanael Lizarazo, join the Episcopal priest, the Rev. Benjamin Tyon, and two Episcopal deacons, in joint ministry on the western third of the Pine Ridge Reservation. The Edgemont church, a small non-Indian congregation in western South Dakota, 95 miles from Pine Ridge, is a half-time job for the Lutheran pastors. They spend 40 percent of their time in the joint ministry with the Episcopal Church, and 10 percent in interpretive work (that is, speaking and sharing insights with other Episcopal and Lutheran congregations both on and off the reservation'.

Together the Lutepiscs share services, participate in Bible studies, host summer work projects, run vacation Bible schools, and work towards addressing the needs for adequate education, employment, health, and equal justice. Together they work at building trust for what will, they hope, eventually be a full and equally shared ministry. The purposes of the joint ministry are, in part:

> 1) To provide opportunity for ministry centered on the Gospel of Jesus Christ;
>
> 2) To build upon cordial relationships already established between Native Americans and non-Native Americans, and between Episcopal and Lutheran people;
>
> 3) To utilize the resources of the South Dakota Synod, ELCA, along with the Episcopal Diocese, to work toward addressing the needs of adequate education, employment, health, and the rights of equal justice under the law; and
>
> 4) To provide educational resources to congregations of the Synod concerning Lakota history, culture and ministry needs.[13]

The Lutepisc ministry, unique in the state of South Dakota, is supervised by a coordinating council that represents Trinity Lutheran Church in Edgemont, the Pine Ridge Deanery, and the Bear Butte Conference of the ELCA.

The ministry team itself displays some of the cultural diversity and unity of spirit that the ministry points to. The Rev. Benjamin Tyon and Deacons Fred Mesteth and Leo American Horse are Native Americans. The Rev. Barbara Wangsness is a Euro-American of Scandinavian heritage, and the Rev. Natanael Lizarazo is from Colombia, South America. All team members, in their own ways, have lived with material poverty—the poverty of a South American barrio, the poverty of the reservation, the leanness of an Iowa farm. In fact, Lizarazo thinks the Pine Ridge Reservation is almost luxury compared with the way his family lives in Colombia!

The Episcopalians are delighted with the partnership. They need the help, since Father Tyon is the only full-time and paid staff member, and he is responsible for five churches. (The deacons are unpaid and have regular jobs.) They are also invigorated by the challenges of working together. Fred Mesteth respects the Lutherans' style of cooperation:

> Sects come in, and they just take our people. They do not work in a cooperative way. The Lutherans, when they came in, they wanted to serve cooperatively with the Episcopal Church . . . . And people are beginning to accept them. Sometimes I think they are making more friends than we are!
> They are helping with youth projects. Lutheran youth groups have come from Minnesota. A Lutheran group came last summer from Germany.[14]

All the members of the team agree that there appear to be far more obstacles between the Indian churches on the reservation and non-Indian churches off the reservation of the same denomination than between Lutherans and Episcopalians on the reservation. Indian congregations attempt to make links with non-Indian churches off the reservation, but they are not making much headway. According to Pastor Barbara Wangsness:

> It's racism. One of the biggest issues before the Christian faith is combating racism. I don't mean just in South Dakota but everywhere.
> Until the Church addresses it, the Church will always be hindered. Until the Church

addresses it, we will never be able to do evangelism and stewardship effectively . . . . All programs are affected by racism, and until we address it the Church will be hindered.[15]

Taking this issue of racism seriously makes them strong supporters of South Dakota's Year of Reconciliation. According to Fred Mesteth:

> The Indian people want to make this a *decade* of reconciliation, since there's too much to do in a year. If it's going to be real reconciliation we're going to discuss *everything,* the Black Hills [land sacred to the Sioux, which was grabbed from them], the Bradley Bill [regarding giving the Black Hills back to the Indians], everything.[16]

Mesteth goes on to say that reconciliation is necessary among Indians themselves. He explains that AIM's (American Indian Movement) emphasis on traditional Indian values meant repudiating the white oppressor along with the "white man's church," which was harshly imposed on them.

> That's why we have a void of youth and young adults in our church. When I was a young guy we had a lot more native ordained clergy than we have now. After these guys got old, retired and died, the young people weren't there to fill the gap. The young Indians were going for traditionalism.[17]

Thus, many look towards a Decade of Reconciliation with ardent hope for concrete changes within and between cultures, changes that will issue in concrete results. The members of the Lutepisc team feel that they are ahead of the state in working towards reconciliation and that reconciliation is already being realized in their sharing and ever-deepening mutual respect.

The Mission Discernment Project Visiting Team questioned why ecumenical cooperation is so much more evident on the reservation than it is in other areas of South Dakota. For example, wakes and funerals are community events on the reservation, and by custom, representatives of all churches are expected to attend. There is a good deal of informal sharing among denominations. Father Joseph Sheehan, a Jesuit priest working at St. Agnes Roman Catholic Church in Manderson, explains:

> It's because out here we all are humbled about what we're doing. We realize that basically we must look towards each other. We've got to come together to overcome our smallness.
>
> Some of the obstacles that keep churches apart are not present on the reservation. I think when you're in an area where the Church is humble you're not showing off. With that put aside, other things draw you together. It's from a position of poverty and simplicity that you realize that what might keep us apart isn't very important. Here we can love and respect one another more simply.[18]

Sheehan discusses what ministry among the Lakota people has come to mean to him in his eleven years of service and what he feels is an appropriate role for church leaders like himself, who are non-Indians:

> I have felt it a great privilege to be here because I have learned a lot from the Indian people. I think it is the cross. I think the Indian people are on the cross. Theirs is a poverty of voice and opportunity. They are looked down upon. That's why they leave the reservation but so quickly return. Here the Indians can't say, "This is my country," because they don't feel respected and loved off the reservation. And the white people who live closest to the reservation are the harshest of all.
>
> Wherever Indians are trying to get their rights they get tremendous resistance. The Black Hills is a case in point. The Indians believe if they don't have land they have nothing. But the salvation of the social situation has to come from Indians. They can and they will rekindle self-confidence in themselves. AIM started in the right direction, but for many it was too violent.
>
> What I think is that an Indian will come forth who will lead the people. Anything the white

man has done has failed. They won't accept it. They don't trust white people at all. They have been so terribly hurt by them.

An Indian leader [like an Indian Martin Luther King] will emerge. But until then we have a role. I think my place is to be here—at the foot of the cross—watching.[19]

## *UNDERSTANDING THE STORY*

The Diocese of South Dakota is predominantly an Indian diocese, since two-thirds of the state's baptized Episcopalians are Indian people, and 75 of its 110 Episcopal churches are located on Indian reservations.

The Episcopal, the Presbyterian, and the Roman Catholic churches make up the "Big Three"—also called "The Big Three D" (for denominations)—and became established on South Dakota Indian reservations as a result of President Ulysses S. Grant's "Peace Policy," enacted on April 10, 1869. This policy provided, in part, that the Indians

> . . . be taught as fast as possible the arts of agriculture and civilization through the aid of Christian organizations . . . and that through the instrument of Church organizations the Indian might be taught a better way of life and . . . be trained to be citizens of this great country.[20]

Thus, according to Virginia Driving Hawk Sneve, a Dakota Indian author and historian, "The Dakotas' acceptance of Christianity was at first an acceptance of the God of their conquerors."[21]

But if Christianity on the reservation once was an agent for hastening the demise of Indian culture, it may now become an agent for preserving traditional beliefs and practices. In this effort the Episcopal Church has a new partner on the Pine Ridge Reservation in the South Dakota branch of the Evangelical Lutheran Church in America.

Although the Evangelical Lutheran Church is the largest denomination in South Dakota—with 270 congregations—it was not apportioned a place on the reservations when the "Big Three" were making their arrangements with the U.S. government. But official developments in the partnership between Lutherans and Episcopalians have now laid the foundation for cooperation between the two denominations. A common resolution was passed in 1982 by the General Convention of the Episcopal Church and the Lutheran churches that now make up the Evangelical Lutheran Church in America. It stated that Lutheran and Episcopal churches would:

> Encourage the development of common Christian life throughout the respective churches by such means as . . .
> a) Mutual prayer and mutual support, including parochial/congregational and diocesan/synodical covenants and agreements,
> b) Common study of the Holy Scriptures, the histories and traditions of each church . . .,
> c) Joint programs for religious education, theological discussion, mission, evengelism, and social action, and
> d) Joint use of facilities.[22]

Guidelines for "common, joint celebration of the Eucharist" were also established.[23]

The development of the Lutheran-Episcopal partnership on the Pine Ridge Indian Reservation is a marriage arranged by Lutheran and Episcopal parents (that is, the national legislative bodies of the respective denominations). It is also an authentic love story of two Lutheran pastors. To this add the right people at the right time and in the right place. These ingredients have been stirred up, molded, and shaped by intelligent and sensitive planning and leadership.

Barbara Wangsness, a seminary student, who had formerly been a teacher at St. Francis School on the Rosebud Reservation, wished to return to South Dakota reservation lands for her seminary internship year. She looked into a number of possibilities, and the seminary was successful in working out an arrangement whereby she would serve three-quarters of her time in an Anglo congregation in Edgemont, and work one-quarter of her time with the Indian Episcopal churches on the western third of the Pine Ridge Reservation (known appropriately as Western Christian Unity).

She and the Rev. Robert Two Bulls, who was then the

Episcopal priest at Pine Ridge, struck up a good working relationship. During the course of their time together, Two Bulls asked her to see if she could obtain the necessary funding to buy a secondhand chain saw to cut wood for the wood-burning stove in one of the reservation chapels. That would enable the people to keep the chapel open and warm in the winter. Through an ELCA pastors' fund and ELCA congregations and friends in northeast Iowa, $1,300 was raised—far more than the amount required for the saw. Two Bulls and seminarian Wangsness asked Reginald Cedar Face, a health service educator, to suggest possible uses of the excess funds.

Cedar Face suggested repairing the pump on Raymond Pipe On Head's well in Loneman, a remote community nestled between buttes and approachable only by dirt road. The water in Loneman is good, unlike that of much of the reservation, which is too alkaline to drink, and Pipe On Head's well serves five surrounding households. But good water is of little use without a pump to reach it. After a visit by Two Bulls, Wangsness, and the Rev. Larry Peterson of the ELCA's Indian Relations Commission in South Dakota, the well was selected for repair.

A picture of a little child getting the first drink of water from the well was picked up by a national news bureau. Its appearance in newspapers across the nation elicited donations for building and restoring more wells. To continue the project, Reginald Cedar Face obtained a $600,000 grant from Christian Relief Services in Washington, D.C., which was ultimately used to restore 68 wells in 1987.

Ironically, Pipe On Head's well is broken again, but the fresh waters of friendship between Lutherans and Episcopalians have continued to flow (and it is hoped that the well will soon be repaired).

Barbara Wangsness returned to Wartburg Seminary (Dubuque, Iowa) and met the Rev. Natanael Lizarazo, a student who had arrived from Colombia for graduate work. They were married in May, 1988, and in September the two pastors returned to the Edgemont congregation and the Pine Ridge Reservation. On September 18, 1988, the Rev. Benjamin Tyon was installed as priest at Pine Ridge, replacing Father Two Bulls. The Episcopal celebration of his new ministry included an official recognition of the partnership between the Lutepiscs. At the service, Wangsness and Lizarazo were presented with Niobrara crosses (given to all South Dakota Episcopalians at their baptism) as a symbol of the friendship and partnership between the two denominations, which were just beginning a new relationship of joint ministry in the Pine Ridge area.

Father Tyon is well-known and respected in Pine Ridge. He had already had a track record of service to the people as school superintendent. Natanael Lizarazo has risen quickly to the challenges of the reservation, bringing with him many insights gained from his formative years in Colombia. He raises, in a holistic Lutheran approach, challenges brought forth by Latin American liberation theology, especially its social-justice aspects. Barbara Wangsness had proved she could get along with the Indian people and accomplish concrete results in her work as a schoolteacher on the Rosebud Reservation and during her intern year. Bishop Anderson feels that Barbara, being an effective woman pastor, has helped pave the way for South Dakota Episcopalians to accept women priests, still new in the diocese.

Wangsness and Lizarazo's interest in serving in Pine Ridge evolved just as Bishop Anderson was looking for specific ways Lutherans and Episcopalians could cooperate in joint ministry. He has thus been very supportive of the relationship, as has ELCA's South Dakota District Bishop Norman Eitrheim.

While the Lutepiscs are still in the very early stages of their partnership, they have gotten behind several important projects on the reservation. These include encouragement and financial contributions to KILI, the Indian radio station. They have also supported the Lakota Community Store, a new cooperative venture in Manderson that sells used furniture, appliances, bicycles, and household goods at affordable prices while also beginning to provide much needed employment for a limited number of teenagers and adults.

Looking ahead, Bishop Anderson would like to see Lutheran clergy actually celebrating the Eucharist in Episcopal churches, as well as the introduction of more Indian cultural symbols and practices into services. However, he would not impose his views, since he also feels that it is up to the parties concerned to move at a pace that feels right for them.

Trust is an important key—if not *the* important key—to the development of this Lutepisc ministry. In a December, 1989, report, looking back over a year of partnership, Lizarazo and Wangsness said the following of the shared ministry:

> . . . this Lutheran-Episcopal joint ministry is like a new day in the long overdue ministry between Anglo-Lutheran congregations and Native Americans here in South Dakota. Thanks be to God, the desired journey has already started. Both blessings as well as challenges are characterizing our traveling together the new roads of mission. . . . We are thankful for the growing sense of friendship, trust, openness and togetherness which has been part of this joint ministry.[24]

Father Tyon agrees:

> This Lutepisc ministry is one of the best things that's happened to me, and maybe someday you'll invite us to the national offices of the Episcopal Church in New York. We'd like to sit down and talk. We want to share our story and our ministry.[25]

## *DISTINCTIVE FEATURES*

The Lutepisc ministry is different from the other stories described in this project in that, although it concerns a congregation in Pine Ridge, it is not strictly a congregational story, since it involves ministry in five distinct congregations, led by clergy of two denominations. Nor did the laity and clergy of Holy Cross Church in Pine Ridge discern their mission in the ways other congregations have done, as described in this project. Nonetheless, a sense of mission has been discerned by Lutheran and Episcopal planners and leaders as well as by the members of the joint clergy team. While it is still in its infancy, a number of factors contribute to what looks like an effective partnership:

- ***The Stage Was Set:*** In 1982 the General Convention of the Episcopal Church and the Lutheran churches that make up the Evangelical Lutheran Church in America passed the common resolution that laid the framework for denominational sharing.
- ***People and Buildings:*** The Episcopalians have the buildings on the reservation but lack funds and sufficient personnel. The Lutherans have few buildings on reservations, yet are better equipped with funds and clergy. Thus the partnership at Pine Ridge is a meeting of needs and assets.

- **Need and Purpose:** The Lutheran pastors, supported by their district bishop, were looking for a site where they could perform a cross-cultural, cross-denominational ministry on an Indian reservation. The Episcopal bishop of South Dakota and the clergy of the Western Christian Unity responded. According to Susie Casto, Site Visitor from West Virginia:

    > The special commitment of the ELCA and the excellent gifts of pastors Barbara and Natanael come at a particularly open time for the Episcopal Church with the leadership of Bishop Anderson.[26]

- **Quality and Stature of the Clergy:** Each member of the clergy team is a leader in his or her own right. The Native American Episcopalians in the partnership are or have been teachers, coaches, and administrators in the Pine Ridge School. They are natural leaders and hold the respect of the people. The Lutherans, of course, have not held such positions on the reservation. However, they are both strong and intelligent leaders. The leadership and organizational abilities of Barbara Wangsness became apparent during her internship year, as the chain saw and well projects illustrate. Pastor Natanael, newer to the South Dakota venue, brought his own distinct gifts and strengths—organizational skills, a sturdy character, and particularly his passion for justice.

- **Cooperation, Not Competition:** Susie Casto was impressed with the "sharing of the richness of a truly cooperative, ecumenical model of ministry."[27] Site Visitor Dawn Conley, from Connecticut, also noted the cooperative character of the relationship:

    > Their success they attribute to their approach. As Fred Mesteth states, "Other denominations came to the reservation in a competitive way, but the Lutherans came in really wanting to work with Episcopalians."[28]

- **Planning, Goals, and Objectives:** According to the Rev. A. Wayne Schwab, evangelism coordinator of the Episcopal Church and project director of the Mission Discernment Project, who also visited the Lutepisc ministry:

    > A clear contract, a clear setting of goals and ob-

jectives and a clear evaluation of achievement at various stages have probably helped the Lutepisc collaboration.[29]

- *A Sense of Trust:* A sense of mutual trust is very evident in this shared ministry. It is trust coupled with patience. All partners are willing to let trust evolve naturally and deepen over time. One or the other of the partners might like to move faster in various aspects of the ministry, but hold back in order to allow the trust to build. Their attitude of developing trust is an important cornerstone on which to build. This ministry has yet to reach its full potential, but much more will be possible, since there is already a sturdy foundation based on trust.

At this stage, it looks as if something very special and very wonderful will be accomplished on the Pine Ridge Indian Reservation, through a partnership that, if replicated, could have great significance for both Lutherans and Episcopalians alike.

## *AN ISSUE RAISED BY THE VISIT*

The issue of the Church's affirmation of Indian culture has been raised. In many ways, the Episcopal churches on the reservation could just as well be Episcopal churches anywhere. Unlike many of the newer buildings built by the tribe, which are often in the shape of a circle—so important in Indian culture—the churches are typically white, wooden structures more in keeping with the European-American heritage of the early missionaries than with Indian tradition. Inside, one is struck by the general absence of Lakota artwork and indigenous crafts. Mission Discernment Project Visitors missed the visible signs and symbols of affirmation and support of Indian culture.

Depending on the style of the particular priest, the Eucharist may be celebrated all in Lakota, all in English, or in both languages (this latter is the practice of Father Tyon). A new Lakota Prayer Book will be ready for use soon. There is a Lakota hymnal, but the haunting rhythms of Indian drumbeats and singing of the style found at powwows is missing from the churches.

The new Prayer Book will certainly help, but these

Site Visitors found the liturgy they attended quite distant from the rich and colorful Lakota culture they had seen elsewhere.

According to Bishop Anderson, the Lakota clergy vary greatly in how much Indian culture they feel would be an appropriate part of the liturgy. It is understandable that there is some reluctance on the part of Native American clergy, since many of them have been affected by the vestiges of the old Episcopal Church, where their parents learned their lessons only too well, that Indian culture, with the exception of the language, was not to be tolerated—much less celebrated. So to unlearn lessons of respected elders is something that will take time and perhaps even mean a shift of consciousness.

Nonetheless, some change is beginning to occur. The Rev. Joe Bad Moccasin said,

> The Episcopal Church is now asking Indian clergy to integrate [aspects of Lakota culture and spirituality] into its theology, its Christology. Maybe someday we can take the sacred pipe into the Church and work with that as a sacred element, just like Holy Communion, the wine and the bread. The pipe, the eagle feathers, the sage, the sweet grass, the cedar—these are symbols to the Indian, just like the Bible, the cross, the candles, the vestments are to Christians.[30]

Bishop Anderson cites the distinction between Lakota spirituality accommodating certain aspects of Christianity (Lakota medicine men and holy men incorporating certain forms of Christianity into their traditional rites), on the one hand, and Christianity accommodating Lakota spirituality on the other. "Chrisitanity accommodating Lakota spirituality," according to Bishop Anderson,

> ... is my commitment. My own personal sense is that we need to in some way find opportunities to bring Lakota spirituality back because it's something the Lakota people need. Others are more cautious. They say, "Let's not get carried away with this stuff." But I think it also offers great potential for the non-Indian churches in terms of the kind of cultural conversion that

is desperately needed. I think that some of the Lakota rites as well as some of the understandings coming out of Lakota culture have much to do with helping us understand incarnation in new ways. Also what we mean by theology as ecology. I think an understanding of *tiopaye* [extended family] could help us with an understanding of ecclesiology which is less institutional and more relational in terms of family.[31]

Bishop Anderson said that about half of the twenty-two Lakota clergy in the Diocese of South Dakota incorporate some aspects of Indian culture into liturgical celebrations—use of sweet grass, the inclusion of the Lakota naming ceremony into the Confirmation service, some use of the eagle feather and prayer wheel, to name a few. But while he personally might like more Indian culture represented in the liturgy, he is sensitive to the fact that the shape of Episcopal Lakota liturgy must be left to the initiative and sensibilities of the Indian people.

## *AFTERWORD*

Is it an overstatement to suggest that perhaps the keys to the survival of God's creation may lie imbeded in Native American culture? The first Americans have a great gift to share with all Americans, if we of the dominant culture will but listen carefully and learn.

After one short weekend in the Land of the Lakota, Susie Casto reflected:

> One only has to visit and experience the beauty and wisdom of the Indians to be assured that they indeed are on their way to recapturing the basic strengths of their culture and are a great witness to the rest of the world, with much to teach.[32]

Native American understandings of *mitakuye oyasin* (relationships), of *tiopaye* (extended family), of the sacredness of the land and all living creatures, of sharing—if these, and so much else in Indian culture that is rich and wholesome, can be learned by all Americans, humankind just might be held back from walking across the threshold to ecocide. As Vine Deloria, Jr., a Dakota

Indian and leading Native American scholar and spokesman, expressed it:

> ... within the traditions and customs of the American Indian people are the guidelines for mankind's future .... The lands wait for those who can discern their rhythm .... The future of mankind lies waiting for those who will come to understand their lives and take up their responsibilities to *all* living things.[33]

And he furthermore stated that

> Christianity itself may find the strength to survive if it honestly faces the necessity to surrender its narrow interpretation of history and embark on a determined search for the true meaning of man[kind]'s life on this planet.[34]

So may it be . . . .

## RESOURCES

Bowden, Henry Warner. *American Indians and Christian Missions: Studies in Cultural Conflict.* Chicago: University of Chicago Press, 1981.

Brown, Joseph Epes. *The Spiritual Legacy of the American Indian.* New York: Crossroad Publishing Co., 1982.

Neihardt, John G. *Black Elk Speaks.* Lincoln: University of Nebraska Press, 1982.

Stolzman, William. *The Pipe and Christ: A Christian-Sioux Dialogue.* Chamberlain, SD: St. Joseph's Indian School, 1986.

Zeilinger, Ron. *Lakota Life.* Chamberlain, SD: St. Joseph's Indian School, 1986.

Zeilinger, Ron. *Sacred Ground: Reflections on Lakota Spirituality and the Gospel.* Chamberlain, SD: Tipi Press, no date.

## NOTES

[1] Raymond Pipe On Head, conversation in Loneman, South Dakota, August 5, 1990.

[2] *Ibid.*

[3] Harold D. Salway, *Lakota Times,* July 31, 1990, Supplement, p. 1.

[4] Wounded Knee District School, "The Playground Is Coming," flier.
[5] *Ibid.*
[6] Benjamin R. Tyon, interview in Pine Ridge, August 4, 1990.
[7] Barbara Wangsness and Natanael Lizarazo, "A Report Letter," December, 1989.
[8] Avis Little Eagle, "Survival and Pride at the Heart of a Pow Wow," *Lakota Times,* July 31, 1990, Supplement, p. 1.
[9] Mission statement for the Year of Reconciliation," quoted by Craig B. Anderson, in "Reconciliation Is a Time to Remember, Repent, Resolve," *Argus Leader* (Sioux Falls), date and page unknown (some time in late spring, 1990).
[10] Bat Pourier, quoted in "Big Bat's Conoco: Leading the Charge for Change," *Lakota Times,* July 31, 1990, Supplement, p. 4.
[11] Benjamin Tyon, telephone interview, August 9, 1990.
[12] *Ibid.*
[13] "They Call Them 'Lutepiscs' as Lutherans, Episcopalians Share Ministry," *The Lutheran,* South Dakota, December 14, 1988, p. 26A.
[14] Fred Mesteth, interview in Pine Ridge, August 4, 1990.
[15] Barbara Wangsness, interview in Pine Ridge, August 4, 1990.
[16] Fred Mesteth, interview.
[17] *Ibid.*
[18] Joseph Sheehan, interview in Manderson, South Dakota, August 4, 1990.
[19] *Ibid.*
[20] "Grant's Peace Policy of April 10, 1869," as quoted by Virginia Driving Hawk Sneve, in *That They May Have Life: The Episcopal Church in South Dakota, 1859-1976* (New York: Seabury Press, 1977), p. 5.
[21] Virginia Driving Hawk Sneve, *That They May Have Life,* p. 4.
[22] Resolution A-37a; Resolution A-44a, *Journal of the General Convention—1982,* pp. C-47 and C-53.
[23] *Ibid.*
[24] Betty Schultes, Barbara Wangsness, and Natanael Lizarazo, "A Report Letter," December, 1989.
[25] Benjamin Tyon, telephone interview.
[26] Susie Casto, Site Visitor Report, August 10, 1990.
[27] *Ibid.*
[28] Dawn Conley, Site Visitor Report, August 10, 1990.

[29] A. Wayne Schwab, Site Visitor Report, August 10, 1990, p.3.
[30] Joe Bad Moccasin, quoted in *Sacred Winds,* Video, Episcopal Diocese of South Dakota, 1988.
[31] Craig B. Anderson, interview in Sioux Falls, August 6, 1990.
[32] Susie Casto, Site Visitor Report.
[33] Vine Deloria, Jr., *God Is Red,* Delta paperback (New York: Dell Publishing, 1973), pp. 300-301.
[34] *Ibid.,* p. 287.

*Visiting Team:* Susie Casto, Dawn E. Conley, and the Rev. A. Wayne Schwab
*Date of Visit:* August 17-19, 1990

*I will pour out my Spirit upon all flesh. Your sons and daughters will proclaim my message; your young will see visions, and your elders will have dreams.*

—Acts 2:17

CHAPTER 10

# JOYFULLY SERVING GOD AND COUNTRY
## STORY OF A CHARISMATIC/ EVANGELICAL CONGREGATION
### SAINT STEPHEN'S CHURCH
### OAK HARBOR, WASHINGTON

## *THE CONTEXT OF MISSION DISCERNMENT: OAK HARBOR*

Whidbey Island, where Oak Harbor is the largest of six island communities, has been called "the enchanted wonderland of the Pacific Northwest." It is situated in northern Puget Sound, not far from the southern tip of Vancouver Island. On a clear day in Oak Harbor one can see both the verdant Cascades to the east and the spectacular jagged mountains of the Olympic Peninsula to the west, rising like giants straight up from the sea.

But today is not a clear day. And the emotional atmosphere is as cloudy, in the wake of the Iraqi takeover of Kuwait and its effects on Oak Harbor. Wednesday's *Whidbey News-Times* informed readers:

> Half the staff at Oak Harbor Naval Hospital has joined a nation-wide military exodus responding to the Middle East crisis, forcing the hospital to suspend outpatient services for retirees and their families.
>
> In an unexpected second call for more medical staff, the hospital has lost at least half of its 178-member staff as thousands of American military forces converge on the Middle East.[1]

Captain Frederic Jackson, commanding officer of the hospital, said, "Everyone in the hospital is shuffling around to take on extra duties."[2]

The Naval Air Station at Oak Harbor is the largest naval installation in the Northwest. It is home of thirteen of the Navy's electronic warfare squadrons, composed of A6 Intruder bombers and EA-6B Prowlers, the newest generation of carrier-based radar-jamming aircraft. Five squadrons—about 1,200 men—had already left for the Middle East, and more were on alert to leave at any time.

Eighty percent of St. Stephen's membership consists of active-duty Navy personnel and their families, civilian naval employees, and those retired from military service. They were directly affected by this largest U.S. military mobilization since the Vietnam War. Vestry member Tom Giesecke, who is a doctor at the Naval Hospital, is among those working extra hours. The same is true of Dallas Viall, a nurse practitioner, who is a civilian employee of the hospital. Mike Patterson, a naval doctor, thought his military term had ended. He and his wife, Angie, had been looking forward to re-entering civilian life, but now Mike has been ordered to remain at Oak Harbor until further notice.

Every week the parish prays "for families separated by USN deployment, or work-ups, or by work away from home." But this week the prayer contained in the parish newsletter had a special poignancy:

> Please pray especially for the families whose husbands and fathers are presently in the Middle

East. Pray, too, for all the Navy families you know who are involved in the current crisis, whether ship's crew or airborne.[3]

Before 1941, when the U.S. Navy decided to build a seaplane base on the farmland at the western side of town, Oak Harbor was a quiet country community. There wasn't even a bridge to the island until 1935.

This "Paradise of Puget Sound" was Indian territory (Swinomish) until it was discovered by three adventurers (from Switzerland, New England, and Norway), who staked claims where the city now lies. The Irish arrived in the 1850s. Forty years later the island took on a Dutch character when Hollanders came to Whidbey Island. They established schools, Dutch Reformed churches, banks, and places of business.

"It's still a Dutch town," according to Berry Meaux, a St. Stephen's member.

> They ran everything. Why, there wasn't even a fast-food place here until the late 1970s. Kentucky Fried Chicken arrived in about 1974, but that was about it. They were protecting their businesses. They liked things quiet. I'll tell you, it's still a Dutch town.[4]

Indeed, the local telephone book lists twelve Zylstras and a whole page of Van and Van ders, from Van Alten to Van Zytveldt.

But Oak Harbor is even more a military town. Two-thirds of its population of 14,790 are military or military-related. The U.S. government pours some $273 million into Oak Harbor payrolls every year, money that finds its way into the local economy. And "it has big-city problems, too," according to Sid Parker, a St. Stephen's vestry member who recently retired as principal of Oak Harbor High School.

> Half the students are Navy dependents. The men are away for six to nine months. The wives have some problems. Lots of problems are caused by absentee dads. We see them show up with the kids in the schools.
>
> Oak Harbor is a small town, but people have been all over the world. This isn't a group of hicks gathered on a rock. All the problems you

find in a big city—drugs, booze, teenage pregnancy—it's all right here. Still, all that not withstanding, Oak Harbor is a wonderful place to raise a family. It's a town you can get involved in.[5]

Washington, according to the Rev. Jack M. Tench, rector of St. Stephen's, is the most unchurched state in the nation, with 70 percent of its population not members of any church or synagogue. Yet Oak Harbor is a community of churchgoers who attend some thirty churches in the town. Most of them work together ecumenically on a wide array of service projects. In this community of church communities, St. Stephen's takes a leading role. According to Roger Edwards, one of the newer members, "There's no other parish like this anywhere."[6]

## SAINT STEPHEN'S CHURCH TODAY: JOYFULLY SERVING GOD AND COUNTRY

Roger Edwards, an employee of the Island County Road Department, was a newly recovering alcoholic close to suicide when he came to St. Stephen's twenty months ago. Now he is neither, and he attributes his recovery to the ministry of St. Stephen's. "A lot of people come here in trouble and find the Lord. I became a Spirit-filled Christian at St. Stephen's."[7] Mike Fitzgerald added:

> I came here destitute eight years ago—spiritually destitute and financially destitute, and our marriage was "on the rocks." A parishioner of St. Stephen's saw us, grabbed us. The congregation paid for our electric bills, our phone bills. We received money orders anonymously to the tune of several hundred dollars. Food was delivered to our house.
>
> We are here because people took the Gospel and moved it into our lives. They picked us up, washed us. We were literally picked up through the love of other Christians.
>
> Here they take you by the hand. They give you a hug. They are not afraid to get involved and to touch one another.[8]

Another member, Carol Teays, says:

> We had a life on a merry-go-round with two kids on drugs. Through our friends here we learned that Christ is with us and helps us get through. This is one of the ways this beautiful family of St. Stephen's makes Jesus Christ real in our lives. Without this family here we would have failed the test. We would have been bitter and unhappy.[9]

Mignon Zylstra and her husband, Bob, the administrator of Whidbey General Hospital, are members of the First Reformed Church in Oak Harbor. Their son, Scott, was ill with AIDS. AIDS had not yet arrived in town and even now there are only three confirmed cases on all of Whidbey Island. The Zylstras' own church dealt with the issue by rejecting Scott. Nor was the family supported by the Church until much later in the course of Scott's illness. Mignon tells their story:

> In September 1987 the superintendent of Scott's apartment building in L.A. called. Scott was ill. It was diagnosed as AIDS. I went down to Los Angeles to bring him home, and when we got back, members of St. Stephen's were already there waiting at the house. He arrived back home in Oak Harbor suicidal and completely lacking in self-esteem.
>
> AIDS had not really visited Oak Harbor before, so our community had to face it with a real live person whom they knew. The first problem was finding a doctor. Scott said he'd like Dr. Teays [Carol's husband] to take care of him. Dr. Teays, a member of St. Stephen's, agreed. Scott explained the choice to us. "I know he's a Christian and he'll look after you when I'm gone." Both John and Carol Teays visited Scott regularly.
>
> It is unbelievable how weak AIDS patients get. It was exhausting for Scott to go anywhere. But the church got a wheelchair and brought Scott to church. He sat through and cried through the whole service. The music was beautiful. We all felt so at home. All the choir

members hugged him as they filed past. Scott felt their warmth. Through them he felt God's understanding love.

Father Tench visited weekly. He was very important to Scott. Scott was so spiritual at that time. Church was always such a precious time of prayers, and singing—always singing. This church is filled with the Holy Spirit. The people did everything. A member of St. Stephen's took care of Scott so we could visit our daughter in Japan.

Sometimes when Scott was too weak to receive visitors, people just called and talked on the phone. In eleven months Scott was hospitalized eighteen times. As he grew weaker he grew in faith. He talked about wanting to belong. He was confirmed in this church. It was such a happy day. From that day on Scott referred to St. Stephen's as "my church." He felt so peaceful when lay people brought Communion to him on Sunday.

As he got sicker, Dr. Teays understood that Scott needed to talk about his fears of dying. Scott said he wanted a man from the church. Dr. Teays sent Howard Patrick [a retired judge] who had known Scott ever since he was nine. Judge Patrick came at 12:30 sharp every day. This was their special time.

Every day Judge Patrick read Scripture and *Forward Day by Day* with Scott and prayed with him. This was a very bonding time for Judge Patrick as it was for Scott.

Scott had a difficult time. He didn't want to die. One night I just said to him, "Scott, if there's anything you don't feel forgiven about, you're forgiven. We forgive you." He died twenty minutes later.[10]

The newcomer information packet which introduces the parish says: "St. Stephen's is a church in renewal, and our life and worship centers on Jesus Christ as Lord and Saviour."[11] The theme for the parish's last vestry retreat had a similar renewal flavor: "Jesus is Lord! Take courage! Don't be afraid to step out in faith."

This congregation "steps out in faith" through a wide variety of ministries to its own members and to the wider community. Most of the community ministries are lay-led, and all of them are done in cooperation with people from other denominations.

Outreach ministries include support of and active involvement in the ecumenical Crisis Pregnancy Center, a food bank, and a prison ministry.

The Crisis Pregnancy Center was established in 1986 by Christians to offer real alternatives to abortion and concrete help to women. "This Crisis Pregnancy Center takes seriously the challenge of Matthew 25:31-46, to reach out to those in distress with acts of mercy and compassion. It brings the resources of the local church and the community to bear upon the problems facing pregnant women."[12]

The center provides volunteer counselors and "shepherding homes," where pregnant women who have been turned out of their own homes can stay with families through the delivery of their babies. The center helps with clothing, layettes, and equipment for the babies and their parents. To date 2,000 women have come in for pregnancy counseling and 4,000 for clothing and supplies.

St. Stephen's was the first congregation to make a regular commitment to HELP House, the community food bank. In providing food, St. Stephen's members manifest the conviction that they are serving none other than Christ.

> What would you buy if it were something that you had to put directly into the hand of Jesus? And look Him in the eye as you did so? Chances are it wouldn't just be any item off the kitchen shelf you don't need any more. Jesus really wasn't fooling when He said that whatever you give to the poor and needy you give to Him.[13]

Quite a few members of St. Stephen's participate in Kairos, an international nondenominational Christian ministry in prisons, which began in 1986. Kairos, like Cursillo, is a three-day short course in Christianity, but in a correctional institution. Sherman and Bee Black have involved their fellow Episcopalians at St. Stephen's in the ministry, along with members of Oak Harbor's Roman Catholic, Lutheran, Presbyterian, Assemblies of God, Foursquare Gospel, and Christian Reformed churches. The ministry is twofold: there are teams who commit themselves to the weekend plus a once-a-month meeting at the prison for one year, and the local support community, which bakes cookies, participates in prayer vigils, etc., and performs other services. Each weekend requires 6,000 dozen homebaked cookies. Inmates who have been through Kairos already serve as team members. Kairos weekends have been held at Washington State Reformatory in Monroe, a men's prison, and at the Women's Correctional Center in Purdy. For the initial participants in the weekend, leaders in the cellblocks are selected, people who have gained the respect of their peers, in the hope that they will have an impact on the general prison population following the weekend. Regularly scheduled reunion weekends provide support to inmates who are attempting to Christianize their prison environments.

Leaders of Kairos claim that whereas the recidivism rate is typically somewhere between 30 and 70 percent, it may be reduced to as low as 10 percent among those who have been through a Kairos process.[14] But statistics aside, St. Stephen's members know what a weekend leading a Kairos experience does for them. In Bee Black's words,

> These women say to me when I go back "Oh, Bee, it's wonderful to see you." Then they put their arms around me and make me feel terrific. Some people say, "Why do you bother?" But I say, "Because we feel Christ is with them."[15]

There are many small groups at St. Stephen's. A Loss of Spouse Group has been started recently. A Men's Bible Study Group meets every week at a local restaurant, Mitzel's American Kitchen. There are several house churches, which meet regularly in members' homes for worship and discussion. There is a healing ministry and prayer and praise meetings.

St. Stephen's members place a high value on being informed about the faith and about the Episcopal Church. There is a rapidly growing library with a wide variety of books, cassettes, and tapes. It includes fiction, books for children, and theology. Almost every week a newly acquired book is reviewed in *The Scroll,* the parish newsletter.

*The Scroll,* delivered to the homes of members weekly, may well be the congregation's most regular vehicle for shaping its members' consciousness. Week in and week out, it sets a style of engagement with persons, the immediate community, and the world. It is only two sides of a ledger-sized page, but it is packed with book reviews, announcements, addresses of Navy personnel abroad who would like to receive mail, a short teaching by the rector, notations for daily Scripture reading, and a prayer list. Every day of the week, issues and people are listed to be prayed for under the following headings: parish, healing, community, outreach, ministry, and world. The "world" category is particularly impressive. It includes prayers for everything from the national debt to the Islamic community in Iran, from meetings of the Washington State Legislature to the elimination of apartheid in South Africa, for Palestinians on the West Bank and in Gaza. Along with the usual prayers for parishes of the diocese, the Presiding Bishop and the staff of the Episcopal Church Center are listed to be prayed for every day. At the time of the visit, as the conflict in the Middle East intensified, all Middle Eastern countries and their leaders were prayed for by name.

The Adult Sunday School offers three classes each Sunday in the winter: a Discovery Class for newcomers, those preparing for confirmation, and anyone else who is looking for a refresher course on the Episcopal Church; a Bible study course; and a third class, which offers short-term forums on a variety of topics with a Christian emphasis—usually current affairs and issues in the community or the wider Church.

Annually, Life in the Spirit Seminars are held. Sessions follow a prescribed curriculum leading to a deepened understanding of baptism and the application of Christian values to daily life. Most members of the congregation have participated in a program developed by the Fuller Institute for Church Growth which focuses on the discernment of spiritual gifts for ministry.

This strong educational emphasis is important, Father Tench believes, and he feels that Episcopalians need to be clear about what they believe and able to communicate their faith. There is a strong current of New Age religion on Whidbey Island. According to Jack Tench:

> The Chinook Learning Center is located at the south of the island. This is a major New Age train-

ing center. They have a lot of conferences and weekend training sessions. We have a major channeler who lives close by. She is nationally known. There is an organized community of four hundred witches on one of the islands close to here. There's another one just across the water into British Columbia. You see New Age everywhere. Even ordinary bookstores now have New Age sections with a full range of books. And, of course, there's the whole hook-up with the West Coast, California . . . . It's all very real.

Up here in the Northwest you also have some of that Neo-Nazi fringe. About a year ago the Aryan Nation had an event here. They're the ones who want the whole Northwest to be an independent white nation. They want to get rid of all the Jews and blacks. So we have that fringe too.[16]

Christians strong in the faith, well taught and grounded in Jesus Christ, are the best defense in countering both fringes, in Father Tench's opinion.

St. Stephen's and other churches in Oak Harbor cooperate on many projects. Father Tench has twice been president of the local ministerial association, a group that includes most of Oak Harbor's clergy. He is also a member of Interfaith, a coalition of charismatic and Pentecostal pastors. St. Stephen's members have a particularly close relationship with the American Baptist Church down the street. They share services and joint educational programs. They attend and are mutually supportive of each other's events. Summing up his feelings about St. Stephen's ministry, the Rev. Clint Webb, First Baptist Church's pastor, remarked:

> Looking at the congregation . . . . they're not out there just playing church. They are real human beings who really love the Lord. They go through the liturgy from their hearts. Looking at some of the people and how they minister to the community, to see this church really rally around a young man who had AIDS. These people are really humble in their ministry. I appreciate Jack [Tench]. He

too is a very genuine person who loves the Lord.[17]

St. Stephen's, with a baptized membership of 400, is a parish full of members who are excited about faith in Jesus Christ and keen to share it. They talk very readily to others about what Jesus means to them and how their lives have changed since belief has been awakened in them. In this, Cursillo has probably helped, since between eighty and eighty-five parish members have attended Cursillo weekends. LaDonna Wind, a Mission Discernment Site Visitor from Alabama, remarked that:

> I was most impressed with the well-developed understanding of the ministry of *all* baptized persons. Every lay person we talked with understood his/her call to ministry, not only within the life of the parish, but perhaps more importantly in the greater community. There was no hesitation on the part of anyone to talk about one's faith and how faith is lived out in their work, their families, their community involvement or their places of leisure. This was illustrated in a myriad of ways.[18]

In April, 1990, the parish was given a new opportunity to share the faith. "God has given us in his family of St. Stephen's, an open door to proclaim His Word over the radio. Station KJTT in Oak Harbor has offered us 30 minutes of free air time each week."[19] So now a radio ministry has started. Called "The Heart of God," the show includes a varied program of Bible teaching, interviews with Christians—mostly laity—who talk about their ministries, and music.

The parish sponsors a booth at the annual Island County Fair in August, the only church on Whidbey Island to do so. St. Stephenites offer free ice water along with various booklets, tracts, and copies of John's Gospel.

The congregation's life finds its focus in Sunday worship at the two main services of the day. Between forty and fifty people attend the 8 a.m. service, which is a Rite I Eucharist on three Sundays and Holy Communion from the 1928 Book of Common Prayer (with the bishop's permission) on the fourth. Most of those who attend the early service are sixty years old and up, although several younger members also attend.

The main Sunday service is attended by members of all ages. It is a Rite II service, with music from both *Hymnal 1982* and various songbooks. It is a physically expressive service, with hands held and raised at various points throughout. It is lively, and the effect does not seem particularly stylized, nor is everybody expressive to the same degree. The atmosphere is upbeat, yet at the same time prayerful. Visitors are welcomed and prayed for. Those who are about to depart—for trips, vacation, relocation, military deployment—are sent off with prayers. Intercessions, readily entered into by many members of the congregation, are extensive, and their content ranges from personal matters to global political problems. It is a service where everyone appears to feel valued and included, where members sincerely seem to understand that they are seeking and serving Christ in each other, just as they are empowered by the Holy Spirit to seek and serve Christ in the community the other six days of the week.

Considering all these ministries, Junior Warden Shirley Viall expresses the sentiments of many: "The Holy Spirit has done it."

## UNDERSTANDING THE STORY

The idea to form an Episcopal congregation in Oak Harbor dates back to an evening in September, 1952, when several Navy couples were socializing together.

It transpired that these friends were all Episcopalians who were missing their familiar form of worship. So they started organizing right away.

> Maxine D'Vincent volunteered to have a tea at her home, publicize our meeting to organize an Episcopal congregation here, contact the Bishop of the Diocese and go from that point.... Our work went on from there. Mae Louise Koch and Stella Cox searched out Episcopalians and called them. Chet Thomas and Mrs. T. negotiated for a meeting place, others organized church school, materials and services. Dick Koch, a licensed lay reader, planned services....[20]

Events moved quickly. Donations were received,

church school materials supplied, the Odd Fellows' Hall in town was rented, and the first service was held on December 21, 1952.

From the start, the congregation was an enthusiastic one. According to Trudy Christy, one of the founding members, "We loved it and we loved each other, and each newcomer was greeted with that same love and enthusiasm."[21]

And they worked hard. They organized parish suppers and all manner of money-making projects and work parties. For several days each week they received the able help of the Rev. Charles Forbes, who came down from Everett. By Christmas, 1953—one year after the first service in the rented hall—the congregation held its inaugural service in its own building, a tiny A-frame church largely built by the members themselves.

> Many prayers of thanksgiving went up that night. The women kept the church clean, and the men kept it repaired. We worked on the landscaping, taught the children and did all the loving things St. Stephen's people are still doing.[22]

A series of part-time, but apparently able, clergy came and went. The congregation was officially designated a mission of the Diocese of Olympia in January, 1954. It soon outgrew the A-frame. And again members rallied to build a bigger church. They held their first service in it on Easter Day, 1960. That building is now the parish hall.

In 1976 the congregation burned the mortgage and became a parish in its own right—fitting ways for a patriotic parish of military families to celebrate the birthday of the nation.

A big boost also came with the Tent Revival, planned by an interdenominational group of Christians at the Oak Harbor Air Naval Base. The idea was to celebrate the 1976 Bicentennial with a festival of renewed religious commitment. The Navy sent out publicity and took on most of the organizational responsibility. But as it happened, the American Civil Liberties Union protested this mixing of religion and state, and so forced the celebration off the base. The town ministerial association took over the planning, and the revival proved to be a huge success. Big-time preachers came into town to lead the revival, which involved hundreds of people from all over Whidbey Island.

At about the same time, several members of the congregation read the book *Nine O'Clock in the Morning* by Dennis

Bennett. Bennett, rector of St. Luke's Church in Seattle, is the person most responsible for bringing the charismatic renewal movement to the Episcopal Church in the 1960s. He had built up the small Seattle church from mission to thriving parish with his unique (to the Episcopal Church) style of ministry: a lively and personal interpretation of Scripture, being "baptized in the Spirit," speaking in tongues, and the like. Actually, the Rev. Hugh (Jacob Hubert) Miller, who served the parish during this time (1970 to 1980) was not charismatic. Nonetheless, he seems to have gone along with the way the parish was evolving. According to Berry Meaux:

> Hugh Miller had a heart of gold. I don't think he ever had a bad word to say about anybody. He had a charming personality and was very active in the community and in Navy affairs. But he was not charismatic.[23]

In the late 1970s the congregation had grown so much that meeting space again began to be a problem, and once again members busied themselves with plans for building their third church structure. Hugh Miller retired during the process, content that St. Stephen's members were again breaking new ground and increasing in numbers.

Jack Tench, the current rector, came in 1981. He had been a missionary in Guatemala and Honduras, and he too proved himself a popular, spirited, and intelligent leader. His skills and interests reflected the evolving charismatic style of the parish. As Berry Meaux recalls:

> Jack believed in reading the Bible and making Scripture the basis for everything. He was one of several Episcopal priests in the Diocese of Olympia that made a Roman Catholic Cursillo together, in order to form a core of clergy to be a part of Cursillo teams. Even now he does one Cursillo a year as spiritual director. Jack and Hugh's styles were very different. Jack likes to play the guitar . . . , and this attracted more people.[24]

Building the new church absorbed a lot of energies. The church could not obtain a loan, but they managed to fund it through money-making projects and their own "sweat equity."

They designed and made the stained-glass windows themselves, and the structure has a light and inviting feel to it. The first service in church building number three was held on Pentecost, 1982.

Dennis Bennett, now retired, came to St. Stephen's twice in the 1980s to lead the congregation in Healing of the Whole Person Seminars. These have been important events. They added to the laity's already growing sense of empowerment.

Now, across the board, one observes that laity have taken charge of their ministries. They naturally reach out to each other and to the community, and they find a great deal of pleasure in their ministries. According to Barbara Hunt-Petitt:

> One of the things Jack has been encouraging us to do ever since he first came was to understand that the ministry of the Church is not limited to the ordained minister. He has encouraged all of the lay people to use their training and gifts to minister. So I think some of us have just fallen into the habit [of] doing a lot of ministry with people. It's become so much a part of us that we don't isolate it. It's like being a mother . . . you don't say, "Well what kind of skills and what kind of mothering do you do?" You just do it. So as we try to be Christian and walk the Christian way, we become aware of our strengths. There's a lot of encouraging that happens among ourselves as we're ministering to each other and to people who are oustide of our Church most of the time. I think it would be hard to sit any of us down and say, "Well, how many minutes a week, or how many hours, or whose lives have you touched?" because it's become so interwoven into everything. In prayers, for example. Often we'll either stop right there and pray for somebody, or if it's not appropriate to do it out loud, we go along praying for the person or situation as we walk away. It's like eating, drinking, sleeping, walking. You just do it. So ministry just becomes part of life.[25]

Indeed, among members of St. Stephen's, Oak Harbor, ministry has "just become part of life."

# DISTINCTIVE FEATURES

Judith Conley, president of the Union of Black Episcopalians, who was a member of the Mission Discernment Project's Visiting Team, commented that "St. Stephen's is probably the 'top of the line' of congregations of this type."[26] It is a charismatic congregation that has managed to avoid most of the pitfalls that sometimes go along with this style of ministry. Perhaps one could say that theirs is a *settled* charismatic ministry. It has been going long enough for the members to be able to articulate their understanding of the faith confidently and straightforwardly. They are not defensive or critical of other churches or expressions of the faith that are less enthusiastic than theirs. They do not talk in a jargon that can be understood only by other charismatics, nor do they implicitly force on others the affective style of behavior most of them feel comfortable with. In fact they are the most *un*doctrinaire and open charismatic congregation this writer has ever experienced. While most of the eight o'clockers are older and could be considered "more traditional," they appear to be well integrated into the congregation. The Visiting Team noticed that after the early service, they did not rush off but lingered and talked to those who were arriving for the later service. The rector, the Rev. Jack M. Tench, appears genuinely pleased to provide a monthly service from the 1928 Book of Common Prayer. While a personal interpretation and expression of the faith are obviously valued, this congregation's prayers are probably the most global we have run into throughout this Mission Discernment Project. They don't just pray "for the peace of the world" and leave it at that. They are global in specific ways by identifying particular issues, international problems, and international leaders about which to pray.

This parish has not discerned its mission as a result of any particular plans or goals, but rather its mission has evolved and been clarified and tested as its members have reached out in concrete ways in the community. This congregation has *listened* to the pulse of the community and to the persons and causes that have presented themselves to the congregation, and it has *responded* and *acted*. So, in this case, we look back to see a pattern of how mission has been discerned (and thus how it will, no doubt, continue to be discerned). On the other hand, the congregation has been very definite and directed in dealing with individual and group growth in the development and nurture of faith. It has also been very intentional in pursuing its church construction projects.

A number of factors contribute to the effective ministry of this congregation:

- ***A Common Employer and a Working Population with Common Goals:*** This congregation is distinctive in that the U.S. Navy provides a unifying force, in the town and in the church. According to Father Tench: "There's an attitude of serving in the military. This sense of serving helps in creating an atmosphere of unity throughout the whole town."[27] And the habits and skills learned in the military—discipline, organization, delegation of responsibilities, responding to duty—are used to good effect in the congregation.

  Are military personnel more churchgoing than others? They are probably more patriotic than any other section of society. By the very fact of choosing a military career when there is not a mandatory draft, they have already pledged their allegiance to something other than themselves. Does this spill over into also "pledging one's allegiance" to God? Serving God and serving the country both spring from the same basic human desire to spend oneself in behalf of something greater than self. Both find focus at St. Stephen's.

- ***Reaching Out:*** In terms of individuals' extending themselves to help members in need as well as those who just turn up, and in terms of official parish outreach ministries, St. Stephen's is an outward-looking, outward-reaching, and outward-serving congregation. They have shown themselves willing to step in in instances where others have held back, as in the case of Scott Zylstra, the person with AIDS who was shunned by his own congregation.

- ***Backing Up Convictions with Action:*** St. Stephen's support of the Crisis Pregnancy Center is an example of members' not merely saying they do not believe abortion to be right, but actively and in concrete ways supporting workable alternatives.

- ***Ecumenical Cooperation:*** Duplication of services is avoided by joining forces and reaching out ecumenically. None of St. Stephen's outreach ministries are specifically Episcopal in nature. Such cooperation results in effective, unified outreach while at the same time eliminating the stress of being solely responsible for outreach programs.

- ***Welcoming Newcomers:*** St. Stephen's members go out of their way to welcome newcomers. Newcomers are identified and welcomed before the liturgy begins. There is an attractively designed newcomers' information packet, which succinctly describes and summarizes the parish's services, programs, and ministries.
- ***Evangelistic Focus:*** Members of the congregation are not at all shy about going public about their faith in Jesus Christ. When the opportunity for a free half hour on the local radio station came up, St. Stephen's members jumped at it. They also actively seek opportunities, both individually and as a congregation, to spread the faith. Taking a booth at the county fair is one such an example, weekly Bible study at a local restaurant is another. As LaDonna Wind reflected:

  > The visibility of the community through their booth at the county fair was illustrative of not only commitment on the part of the people in the parish, but a creative way to make St. Stephen's and the Episcopal Church known through a non-threatening way of proclaiming their faith and Church.[28]

- ***Affirmation of One Another's Ministries:*** Established members help and support each other and assist new members to identify their own distinctive ministries. They do this in formal ways, such as in Life in the Spirit Seminars, and in discussion groups planned specifically for the identification of gifts for ministry.
- ***A Sense of Family:*** St. Stephen's is like any well-functioning extended family in which most of the needs of the individual members are met. The members feel needed and valued. They are patient with each other. There is a lot of touching and verbal expression of warmth and inclusion. And just as a family marshals its resources to help a member in particular need, so St. Stephen's members go out of their way to help its members—and often strangers—who are in special need.
- ***Fun, Food, and Fellowship:*** One wonders whether one barometer of the health of a congregation could be how much they sing, how much they come together for food and fellowship, how much they laugh and have fun. St. Stephenites do all three very well. They get together often. They obvious-

ly know each other well, and they exhibit the sense of humor and the casual joking that goes with this ease and familiarity. Aside from all the gatherings at the church, the spring and summer of 1990 saw an annual parish picnic, joining a diocesan party for a Boston Red Sox-Seattle Mariners baseball game, participation in the bishop's golf tournament, and a white-water adventure for youth. A committee plans receptions following weddings and memorial services, and they have a party every spring for all the graduates.

- **Clerical Leadership:** The clerical leadership of St. Stephen's is strong, settled, sensible, and secure. According to Berry Meaux: "The ability Jack Tench has is the ability to pick people. He's able to bring out the best in people. And he says, 'Go ahead.' So we have a real involved laity."[29]

## *ISSUES RAISED BY THE VISIT*

St. Stephen's Episcopal Church is unquestionably a strong parish in all the areas just listed. It illustrates many of the positive factors that are evident in other strong parishes, as well as some of the issues that confront them. One of the issues raised by the Visiting Team has come up in other congregations visited throughout the course of the Mission Discernment Project. It is the area we have informally labeled Christ and Culture. The other issue applies not only to St. Stephen's but to all congregations that are located close to military bases and installations, congregations filled with Pentagon or Central Intelligence Agency workers and the like, congregations in places where nuclear weapons and nuclear submarines are produced and assembled. Congregations, in other words, that are located in areas where what is produced or promoted may raise moral or ethical questions. The question is, What happens when allegiance to the country comes into conflict with allegiance to God?

- **Christ and Culture:** St. Stephen's members are exemplary in meeting human need. Judith Conley observed that "they deal effectively with short-term responses to issues, i.e., support for a person with AIDS, support for single and divorced people in the congregation and the community. A.A. meets in the building, the parish is active in a feeding program, and they're strong supporters of a crisis pregnancy counseling center. [But] the parish is not addressing systemic causes for the problems identified in the parish and community."[30]

What is there in the socioeconomic system that contributes to hunger and homelessness? Why aren't we scandalized by the fact of so many hungry people in our society? What are the underlying causes of teenage pregnancies? Why has the teenager been thrown out on the street when her family learned that she was pregnant? What has caused the breakdown and disintegration of families? Why are jails overcrowded? When the Gospel tells us that we are to be our brothers' and sisters' keepers, why have we turned into our brothers' and sisters' jail keepers?

Through St. Stephen's ministries, many people in need are being saved *from the culture,* but why do we fall short in understanding that God is *transforming culture itself?* How can Christian congregations move from a stance of treating the symptoms of dis-ease to a position of rooting out the factors that caused the dis-ease in the first place? If it is believed that the earth is of God and "that it is good," that Jesus Christ finally intends nothing short of the transformation of society and of the whole earth, then that ought to have implications for the extent and depth of service we are being called to. Of course, Christ is for the transformation of the individual, and St. Stephen's members excel in being agents for the transformation of individual lives, but how are congregations also to be moved beyond the individual in need to the transformation of the social order?

That St. Stephen's falls short here is not to be interpreted as a particular failing of St. Stephen's. Probably most of our congregations also fall short!

- **God and Country:** The particular circumstances of St. Stephen's, a congregation started and maintained by military-related families, raise some critical issues.

    Berry Meaux commented that "Military people are church people." That is undoubtedly true. Otherwise what else would explain thirty churches in a town of 14,000? And, as mentioned, the disciplines, skills, and administrative abilities Navy personnel bring with them are distinct assets to the congregation.

    The question, though, arises: What if allegiance to the country conflicts with allegiance to God? Can a Christian say, "My country right or wrong?" The question was raised, "What if someone at the Naval Air Station wanted to explore conscientious objector status, how would he or she be received in the church? What would happen if the person began to question the weapons being stored at the base, weapons whose only purpose is that of killing? If these matters were becoming a dilemma for someone, how would parish members deal with it?" Jack Tench is a thoughtful pastor, and his honest response points to some of the dilemmas of parishes and clergy in such situations. He reflects:

> That has never come up. A "CO" . . . , I'm not sure. If someone was actively an activist, standing at the base with signs and all that stuff and attended the church, that would be real interesting. I don't have the impression that even the military would find that a big deal. I think if there were *ten people* like that . . . it could be a different story.
>
> Oddly enough the controversy here is kind of on the other side. And that is that air flight crews practice south of here [on an OLF, or outlying field, shaped like the landing deck of an aircraft carrier]. It is noisy and it has become really divisive.[31]

Dallas Viall adds:

> We live in the noise zone, just a mile from that OLF strip. We don't belong to WISE [the activist group attempting to stop the practice landings], and we don't subscribe to their methods. Their last letter was very bad. It was all about the dangers of airplanes crashing into your house and this sort of thing. That really got a lot of people upset.[32]

Father Tench continues:

> Theirs is a legitimate concern, but even at that it's still kind of divisive. All of a sudden you can't quite talk to them [WISE members] quite freely anymore because they're so hot on this issue. You know the military is the major economy here, so you're dealing with . . . . Well, very few churches would have full-time pastors . . . . I mean if you're starting to get down to it, a lot of people

would go out of business if the Navy ever left, so this "pushes all the buttons."

There was an anti-nuclear group here formed by one of the local doctors and one of the retailers in town. He [the retailer] was part of it, and that's surprising because he was so passive.

But that kind of stuff just doesn't exist. I think it doesn't exist because there's just so little involvement in anything here that isn't related to the military. Here someone wouldn't want to be a CO, you know what I mean? Everyone here is either with the Navy or retired military. And the retailers and service people in the community are here essentially for the military. There is very little other industry.

But again, nobody is threatening unless there's a lot of them. One person and you can take it. If there were a whole lot of people in our church that were getting identified with anti-military, I think it could be very divisive.

To the south of the island it's different. It's a different attitude entirely, a whole different ball game. There you could have parades. They wanted to have a parade against El Salvador involvement here, and it was like "No, thank you."

If I was with Greenpeace and went down there and picketed every month, there'd be a high level of discomfort in this congregation.[33]

And Dallas Viall interjected, in good humor, "Yeah, he'd be out of here in a month!"[34]

---

## *RESOURCES*
### Books
Foster, Richard. *Celebration of Discipline.* New York: Harper and Row, 1978.

Foster, Richard. *Freedom of Simplicity.* New York: Harper and Row, 1981.

Word of God Ministries. *The Life in the Spirit Seminars Team Manual.* Rev. ed. Ann Arbor: Servant Books, 1979.

Wagner, C. Peter, ed. *Wagner Modified Houts Questionnaire for Discovering Your Spiritual Gifts.* Pasadena, CA: Fuller Evangelistic Associates, 1985.

### Newsletters and Journals

*Equipping the Saints.* Vineyard Ministries International. P.O. Box 65004, Anaheim, CA 92815.

*CRI Journal.* Christian Research Institute. P.O. Box 500, San Juan Capistrano, CA 92693-0500.

*Focus on the Family.* P.O. Box 500, Pomona, CA 91769.

### Consulting Services

Episcopal Renewal Ministries. 2942 Highway 74, Suite 205, Evergreen, CO 80439.

Trinity Episcopal School for Ministry. 311 11th Street, Ambridge, PA 15003.

Fuller Theological Seminary. 135 North Oakland Avenue, Pasadena, CA 91101.

---

## NOTES

[1] Gretchen Young, "NAS Whidbey Hospital Down to Half Staff; Services Cut," *Whidbey News-Times,* August 15, 1990, p. 1.

[2] Frederic Jackson, quoted in Young, "NAS Whidbey Hospital...."

[3] *The Scroll,* St. Stephen's newsletter, week of August 19-25, 1990, p. 1.

[4] Berry Meaux, interview in Oak Harbor, August 18, 1990.

[5] Sid Parker, interview in Oak Harbor, August 18, 1990.

[6] Roger Edwards, interview in Oak Harbor, August 17, 1990.

[7] Roger Edwards, interview in Oak Harbor, August 19, 1990.

[8] Mike Fitzgerald, interview in Oak Harbor, August 17, 1990.

[9] Carol Teays, interview in Oak Harbor, August 18, 1990.

[10] Mignon Zylstra, interview in Oak Harbor, August 18, 1990.

[11] St. Stephen's Parish, information packet.

[12] "Providing Alternatives for Life," brochure, p. 2.

[13] "And Speaking of Giving," *The Scroll,* parish newsletter, week of June 3-9, p. 3.

[14] "God's Special Time," Kairos brochure, p. 5.

[15] Bee Black, interview in Oak Harbor, August 17, 1990.

[16] Jack Tench, interview in Oak Harbor, August 18, 1990.

[17] Clint Webb, interview in Oak Harbor, August 18, 1990.

[18] LaDonna M. Wind, Site Visitor Report.

[19]*The Scroll,* April 1-7, 1990, p. 3.
[20]Trudy Christy, "An Historical Sketch," November 6, 1977, mimeographed paper, p. 1.
[21]*Ibid.*
[22]*Ibid.*
[23]Berry Meaux, interview.
[24]*Ibid.*
[25]Barbara Hunt-Petitt, interview in Oak Harbor August 19, 1990.
[26]Judith Conley, conversation between Oak Harbor and Seattle, August 19, 1990.
[27]Jack Tench, interview in Oak Harbor, August 19, 1990.
[28]LaDonna M. Wind, Site Visitor Report.
[29]Berry Meaux, interview.
[30]Judith Conley, Site Visitor Report.
[31]Jack Tench, interview, August 18, 1990.
[32]Dallas Viall, interview in Oak Harbor, August 18, 1990.
[33]Jack Tench, interview, August 18, 1990.
[34]Dallas Viall, interview.

*Visiting Team:* Judith G. Conley and LaDonna M. Wind
*Date of Visit:* August 17-19, 1990

*God's House: Build it up. Who's going to help us build it up? Bring us a hammer. Build it up. Bring us a saw. Build it up....*
—Children's Song

CHAPTER 11

# GOD'S HOUSE: BUILD IT UP

## STORY OF A PROGRAM-SIZED CONGREGATION IN NEW ENGLAND

### CHURCH OF THE NATIVITY
### NORTHBOROUGH, MASSACHUSETTS

## *THE CONTEXT OF MISSION DISCERNMENT: NORTHBOROUGH, MASSACHUSETTS*

By all appearances, Northborough is a quiet, pastoral New England town. White clapboard houses with pots of autumn chrysanthemums adorning their front doorsteps are nestled amid sensible Cape Cod-style houses, and the occasional, spectacular glass-sided contemporary. The lush green of the maples that line the town's streets is just beginning to give way to their fiery fall fashion of colors.

Downtown Northborough is a crossroads with several gas stations, a garage, a CVS pharmacy, a bank or two, and a convenience store. Around the corner is the typical stately white Congregational church, except in this case it houses a Unitarian-Universalist congregation. Only the lack of a town green prevents Northborough from fitting anyone's image of a "classic New England colonial town."

Today Northborough has a population of 11,900, more than double that of 1960, when the Church of the Nativity was organized. But even back then, farms and fields were beginning to sprout a crop of suburban subdivisions as high-tech industries spilled over from Boston-Cambridge, Harvard and M.I.T. to Route 128 and, later on, Interstate 495. In this "Silicon Valley of the East," Northborough was well-placed to become a bedroom community for workers in the high-tech industries. Nestled in a rectangle between the Massachusetts Turnpike and Interstates 290, 90, and 495 (which becomes I-190), it's an easy trip east to 128 and Boston and west to Worcester.

Northborough, along with Hudson and Marlborough, is part of a three-town regional area (Region 3, using the United Way classification). These communities are all north of Route 9, which forms a social-economic barrier. South of Route 9 is Worcester, the second largest city in Massachusetts, with all the problems of any urban center. North of the road things are more prosperous. Region 3 has a population of 65,500 (Marlborough, 36,000; Hudson, 18,500; and Northborough, 11,900), and this is the area from which most of the Church of the Nativity's members come. It's an area where almost everyone commutes a half hour to an hour to work, where people work an average of sixty hours a week, and families have yearly incomes—with both partners working—between $55,000 and $60,000. Most residents are white and middle-class and have had at least one or two years of college. They are engineers, office managers, troubleshooters. Many have worked themselves up in the computer industry. Digital, GTE, Raytheon, and Hewlett-Packard are major employers. Michael Foust is a computer systems analyst. Ken Bishop works with the commercial telephone division of GTE, installing and servicing telephones on commercial airliners. "On your average coast-to-coast flight, seventy to eighty phone calls will be made. Faxes are coming next,"[1] according to Ken. Bill Gagnon is a computer repairman for IBM who admits to being "short-fused" and a "workaholic" who is on the job seven days a week. The rector of the Church of the Nativity, the Rev. Fred Goodwin, says, "Bill works real hard as a computer troubleshooter here in New England. The only time he's not called to work is when he's on his vacation. He works sixty hours, and that's not counting the side job [woodworking and carpentry] he does with Charlie."[2] Wayne Deslauriers is an electrical engineer at Digital. Sally Ann Duffy also works for Digital, as manager of the job resource center. Alan Fraser is a software programs manager for Raytheon. Gail Goudreau is an office manager for a machine shop that makes tools for GTE and Digital. Cindy Loverin is a systems interface supervisor in the GTE accounting office.

But not all of Nativity's members work in the high-tech field. Brad Nutting is a history professor at Framingham State. Dawn Chaput is a self-employed dance instructor. Bob Kimball is a lawyer. Barbara Robinson works for United Way. Her husband, Rob, repairs power tools and sells mechanical fasteners. Nancy Gove is the office manager for the Division of Neurosurgery at the University of Massachusetts Medical Center in Worcester. Rocco Longo is the administrator of the Town of Northborough. Fraser Glenn is a lieutenant colonel in the U.S. Army, where he works for the Research Institute of Environmental Medicine. Jane Plante is a receptionist in the same Northborough pediatrician's office where Lindy Baker is a nurse-practitioner. While many of Nativity's members have jobs like these, most would agree that the basic economy of the community is driven by the computer chip. Lindy Baker's husband, Jim, is in the computer business. He says, "I'm an example of one of the high-tech people in this area."[3] He is also a member of the Northborough School Board, and is thus in a position to see some of the side effects of highly competitive lifestyles:

> The people here expect a great deal from public education. They put heavy expectations on public employees, who are expected to give little Johnny and Susie the very best. So one of our biggest problems is kids' trying to overachieve, kids pushed beyond their native abilities.[4]

Parents are achievers, and so they want their children to achieve. But that is made more difficult by the well-known and well-publicized downward slide of the Massachusetts economy where people are working harder but no longer really getting ahead, where they are running faster to stay in place, where two incomes are essential to make their monthly payments. These realities have created an unprecedented need for more day care and child care. Maintaining mortgage payments and keeping homes in good repair are also problems. This is the state in which home foreclosures have doubled every year since 1987, where one realtor admits that "I used to do home closings. Now I do foreclosures."[5]

Barbara Robinson, a Church of the Nativity member who works for United Way, shared the results of that agency's survey assessing community needs. The report points to some of the pressures that are affecting the people. Residents of the three towns served by the Church of the Nativity cited the following issues (out of a list of sixty-three) of major concern to them: finding child care; not having enough money for basic needs such as rent, mortgage, and food; housing in poor condition and in need of repair; anxiety, stress, or depression; and behavioral and emotional problems among children.[6] According to the report:

> The demand for child care in Massachusetts has increased dramatically during the past ten years and is expected to increase another 23% by 1995.[7]

It goes on to explain that economic changes are leading to stress:

> Many familiar jobs in the workplace are disappearing to be replaced by jobs that require higher levels of training. [Furthermore,] employees today are feeling stress due to work/home conflicts and 41% of employees who are parents want their employers to take a role in reducing the stress.[8]

Thus Northborough is not quite the perfect New England colonial village where Dick and Jane live. Dick and Jane have grown up to be anxious and stressed. They demand high performance of themselves and of the schools that educate their children. They want to succeed, and they want their children to succeed, yet they are worried about their children's care. They are worried about their jobs and the quality of their lives. Nonetheless 85 percent of the residents of Northborough, Marlborough, and Hudson still say their neighborhoods are good to excellent places to live, and about half of them also feel that they have opportunities to affect how things happen in their towns.⁹

## THE CHURCH OF THE NATIVITY TODAY: BUILDING GOD'S HOUSE

The high-pitched hum of the electric saw, the ring of hammer taps reverberating through the shell of the half-finished parish hall, the flow of easy conversation and laughter—this is Saturday morning, and the Church of the Nativity's members are hard at work building their new, two-story parish building. They serve as their own contractors and builders, and will bring this $1.2 million building in for an actual cost of $400,000, because of untold hours in parishioners' "sweat equity." Pausing for a moment to reflect, Bill Gagnon, the computer troubleshooter who is also this project's building coordinator, reflects:

> It's a miracle. We get them every day. The Holy Spirit resides here. It's fantastic. I think we surprise ourselves at what we can do when we get together. You start a project like this, and we put it up a board at a time. If you can count—one board, one hammer, one nail. That's it, one board at a time, and off we go. And we've had a lot of fun.¹⁰

Charlie Dexter, another member of the "Black Nail Society" (what the construction crew have called themselves ever since Alan Fraser accidentally whacked his finger rather than a nail!), adds, "Bill and I gave up a week of vacation to work on the building. I just think it's my commitment to be here."¹¹ It's a commitment shared by many, and people have just happened to appear when they were needed. Ken Bishop started coming to the church two years ago, but only got really involved through working on the construction project. "I was new to the area. I'd never before settled in any place. But this place was very open, very warm. They welcome you. You just come."¹² Rob Robinson, who was celebrating his fiftieth birthday by working this Saturday, agreed: "When my wife, Barbara, and I come on Sunday, Fred and the Greeters welcome us. Here you don't have to go six months to have people talk to you."¹³

Wayne Deslauriers, an electrical engineer, is also hard at work. He is doing the wiring, along with Ken Hidenfelter, who installs alarm systems as his regular work. So the workers have skills and expertise, but there is not a professional builder among them. What they have, as Charlie Dexter mentioned, is commitment. And they gain a good deal of fun and personal satisfaction besides.

But a parish hall is not all that the Church of the Nativity is building. Members like to consider that they are building up Christian lives as they build up Christian community. Church members describe their congregation as:

> ... a family of caring people from several communities. We take great joy in this diversity and cherish each participant for their unique gifts. Our goal is to reach each member at their particular level of Christian growth and offer spiritual food through continuing education and spiritual awakening.
> ... In Jesus Christ we find great comfort and love. We know that the Holy Spirit is working powerfully through the Church of the Nativity, and we invite you to experience this marvelous renewal.[14]

The building up of the congregation takes place through a wide variety of programs: small groups, adult education, pastoral care (prayer groups, prayer chain, fellowship groups), a variety of Bible study opportunities, youth programs (both junior and senior high school), church school. There are almost as many youngsters in the church school as there are adult members of the parish. The congregation is building Christian lives through mission outreach—23 percent of Nativity's budget is given away. They are building through financial stewardship—the Church of the Nativity is number one in the diocese in terms of pledging. The average amount pledged weekly for 1990 was $29.03. This, added to the average pledge of $25 for the building fund, means that Nativity's members are giving an average of $54 every week to the church. By contrast, the average pledge of parishes in the Diocese of Western Massachusetts was $10.48 for 1990.

A new nursery school opened its doors in the fall of 1989. It is a Christian preschool for 44 children and operates Monday through Friday with state-qualified teachers who are all members of the Church of the Nativity.

In 1990, the Evangelism Committee was organized, with a new emphasis for the Decade of Evangelism. One of its initial activities was to sponsor a Living Nativity. Expanding on the familiar idea of building a crèche in front of the church at Christmas, members decided to create a Nativity scene with real people, real goats and sheep, and Mary and Joseph riding in on a donkey. There were singing and refreshments and media coverage of what turned out to be a real community event, and one to be repeated annually.

Fairs—the Strawberry Festival and the Novemberfest—are seen more as fellowship and evangelistic events than as ways of raising revenue. The very engaging young couple Ron and Angie Trombley, who coordinate the senior high youth group, first came to the church through one of its fairs.

The congregation is being built up through the following programs, ministries, and projects:

- **Building through the Bible:** Bible study is built into just about every program at the Church of the Nativity.

    Sixty members are, or have been, a part of Bible-study groups using the Serendipity format (specially designed Bibles with study guides built in). Serendipity Groups meet in homes and include participants from other denominations.

    While the Mission Discernment Project Team was visiting, the senior high youth group was using two passages in Matthew as the basis for answering the question, Who is this Jesus anyway? The format they were following was from a *Group Magazine* study guide. According to Nancy Gove, whenever the young people deal with an issue, "If there is a way of biblically illustrating it, they will show it."[15] Bible study is also a part of Crossroads, an ecumenical youth program.

    Bible study forms a large part of the Christian Foundation Program (CFP), the certificate program developed by Trinity School for Ministry in Ambridge, Pennsylvania. According to Lois Hummers, CFP coordinator:

    > Now in its third year, CFP continues to be a significant vehicle for adult Christian education at Nativity.... CFP offers seminary-level

courses directed toward mature Christians who wish to deepen their faith and enrich their gifts and ministries. Courses cover the Scriptures, theology, history and last for twelve weeks each. Students prepare one lesson per week, requiring three to five hours of study and homework, and then meet in a weekly two-hour class with their seminary-trained tutor for review, discussion, fellowship and worship.[16]

Eight members of the parish have been trained at Trinity to serve as tutors in the program, and thirty parish members have participated.

- **Building Youth:** One hundred children were registered in the church school in 1990. Many young parents say they came to Nativity because of its Sunday school. Jane Glenn, one of the newer members, said of the Church of the Nativity:

> It is growing because so many kids are here. Once we had children we wanted to go to a church that was good for them. We liked the curriculum, we liked the music, we liked the worship service they have for the kids.[17]

Doug Cole and his wife, Diane, were also looking for a church that would be good for their children. Doug, a native of Northborough, had been a member of the local Baptist church for thirty-five years.

> There was a growing separation between parents and children. The congregation was growing older, and we were losing five to seven people a year, and these were not being replaced by young people. I was teaching Sunday school to seventh graders, and I wanted the minister to come down and talk to the class. He refused. He didn't think it was important. That was it for me! It was the end of the school year anyway, so I didn't just leave the kids stranded. But I didn't go back. I realized the pastor didn't really care about the kids. I wanted something better for my children. My neighbors said why didn't we go over to Nativity. They're a family-

oriented church. So we came over here. Brad Nutting and Fred [Goodwin, the rector] greeted us at the door. About eight people talked to us at the coffee hour. They all said, "Welcome! How are you? It's great to have you!" After the next Sunday, Fred came over that afternoon. He joined us for lunch and stayed two hours. Now Diane's teaching first grade in the Sunday school, and the kids love it.[18]

The senior high youth group has been mentioned, and there is an equally lively junior high youth group. Seventh- and eighth-graders meet Sunday afternoons for swimming, volleyball, hiking, bowling, and other activities, interspersed with discussions of Christian values and perspectives. The afternoon the Mission Discernment Project Team members were visiting, both youth groups were going to Camp Bement, the diocesan camp, to mark the conclusion of Doug Wilcox's summer hike around the Diocese of Western Massachusetts parishes. Wilcox spent forty days, often joined by other walkers including some from the Church of the Nativity, walking 650 miles to all the parishes as part of a diocesan program to highlight the evangelistic thrust of the Church as we begin this Decade of Evangelism.

- ***Building through Service:*** Church of the Nativity members support a wide variety of service projects through funding and some voluntary participation. They are one of the twelve area churches that sponsor Our Father's Table, a feeding program in Marlborough. They are a major sponsor of a Volunteer for Mission volunteer in Zaire, and they contribute to the support of children in the Philippines and Oklahoma. They organize a cookout and a Christmas party at the Westborough State Hospital, as well as bingo and fellowship nights at a local nursing home. Some of the members are making quilts for AIDS babies. Individually, members are involved in a number of projects. Jim Baker is a member of the local school board. John and Ann Klump have a clown ministry in several Worcester nursing homes. Olive Moroney and others do hospital visitations.

One of the needs cited by the United Way report is housing repairs. When the members finish building the parish hall they would like to offer their skills to the community to help fix the homes of those who need the help—mostly the elderly. In fact, there is a strong feeling among members that when the parish hall is completed it will afford opportunities to use the space to meet community needs. They are dreaming of a feeding program, like Our Father's Table, and they are talking about a program for elders who are often isolated in their homes.

- ***Building through Worship:*** Sunday worship at the Church of the Nativity is upbeat and personal, with music from both *Hymnal 1982* and praise books. A multitalented senior choir led by Ann Silvernail—who also directs the junior choir—leads a variety of music from classic to contemporary, traditional to Gospel. On the Sunday of the Mission Discernment Team's visit, they used the communion setting developed by the Fisherfolk Community. A digital piano purchased in 1990 has been added to the Allen digital organ bought in 1987. With occasional guitar accompaniment, or violin and trumpet, the music offered is diverse enough to appeal to a wide variety of tastes. Preaching is direct and straightforward. When the Team was there, the sermon included an exercise that invited the congregation members to share with each other in the pews. The children came in during the Eucharist, after having had their own liturgy in the parish hall. There is a "Praise Eucharist" every Thursday evening.

> Our community life is centered around the Eucharist. We gather around the Lord's table as a family to be nourished, refreshed, united and strengthened by the power of the Holy Spirit to go out with the peace of the Lord to serve in His name.[19]

- ***Building through Welcoming:*** Members and visitors are greeted as they arrive for worship on Sunday mornings. Members are used to looking out for new faces, whether or not they are official greeters for the day. Commending their church has a high priority. Members want visitors to return, and take care to make them feel wanted and needed. Follow-up contact is usually made within twenty-four hours of the newcomers' first visit to the church, usually by a lay member, and it has proved to be effective. Recently the Evangelism Committee developed a very attractive information packet for newcomers with details of all church programs, services, and ministries. A newcomer class is offered every month for those new in the parish family.

The Church of the Nativity's members run the gamut from old-time "traditional Episcopalians," who have been members of the Church all their lives, to those whose desire for a lively church mattered more than choosing the Episcopal Church. Some would describe themselves as charismatics who are seeking a "Spirit-filled" church, and some are Anglo-Catholics. The great majority of members are young couples, but there are divorced people, single parents with school-age children, and members whose children are off in college or the service. There are a few elderly people. One of them, Victoria Karagosian, is an Eastern European lady, almost blind, who is dearly loved by everyone in the congregation, young and old. She especially loves the young people. She hugs them and makes them feel special. According to Barbara Dexter: "Vicki is an inspiration to all of us. She shows her love to everyone. [Although she is almost blind,] her gift to the congregation is her wonderful cooking. Her pastries are delicious. She uses a jeweler's magnifying glass to set the temperature control on her oven."[20] The parish had a ninetieth birthday party for the congregation's "Matron Emerita," Letitia Howe, who has been a member for twenty-five years. She told the Visiting Team, "I've seen the additions put on. The church is a great comfort to me. They are my family. They are the joy of my life."[21] Sharon Foust, a second-grade teacher in Marlborough, probably speaks for many as she reflects on the ministries of the Church of the Nativity:

> Throughout the past twenty-two years the Church of the Nativity has been a loving constant in my life. The Church as an institution and I in my personal life have experienced many changes during these years. We have known times of great joy and celebration and times of intense sadness and internal turmoil. We have grown in compassion and love. In spite of the weaknesses of individuals and sometimes, perhaps, because of them, this church has re-

mained a constant reflection of the love of Christ for all people.[22]

## *UNDERSTANDING THE STORY*

"By the time we finished the ninth window, everyone became a believer. The windows were a sign of the go-ahead to build the building,"[23] according to the Rev. Fred Goodwin, the rector of the Church of the Nativity. And in Sharon Foust's words, "Everyone worked together on them. We could do it. When we accepted that, we felt we could build the addition."[24]

The background was this: after the simple A-frame mission church was completed in 1963, no funds remained for stained-glass windows, and the members put aside any hopes for colorful windows and went on to develop their life and ministry together as a congregation. But they never forgot the dream of one day replacing the clear glass with stained glass.

After several hard years in the mid-1980s, the members were at last liberated to dream again. By this time, the Rev. Fred Goodwin had arrived as rector, and hope was being restored among the members.

The cost of professionally executed stained-glass windows (seven panels of three windows each) proved prohibitive. But Colleen Longo, a member of the congregation who had done a little stained-glass work as a hobby, came forward. Using resources in a specially designated memorial fund, she directed the project and taught others the craft. About sixty people spent nights and weekends cutting glass, preparing the lead, and fitting together the pieces. All went smoothly until Colleen, who was expecting a baby, was no longer able to supervise the work. But the church members who had learned the craft continued, and as they did so they began to see something of great beauty emerge. They marveled at what was happening before their eyes. At the same time they were growing in confidence at the wonderful artistry that could flow through their hands.

Nativity's numbers began to increase rapidly, and children began to overflow the three small Sunday school classrooms. More space was badly needed. A new and much larger parish hall was clearly the answer. But how would it be built? Who would build it? Where would the money come from?

Once again the members looked to themselves and most especially to Jesus, who had led them thus far. According to Marge Carlson, "If we could make windows, why not build a whole building?"[25]

So according to Bill Gagnon:

> On April 29, 1989, we broke ground for the new expansion. By Memorial Day excavation work had been done and the floor had been laid. During the following weeks walls were erected, roof trusses were raised, and parishioners pitched in to put on the new roof .... In August of 1989 vinyl siding was started and window installation began .... The floors were poured .... In early January, 1990, with help from the Senior High Youth Group, the upstairs hall and kitchen ceilings were insulated, and a wall separating the kitchen and main hall was built.[26]

Most of Nativity's members have worked on the project, either in the actual construction or by cooking for the Saturday work crews. A few of the members coordinated the fundraising campaign. The original target goal for the pledges was $300,000, but $310,000 was actually raised. Cindy Loverin was out of a job for a time, so while unemployed she volunteered her services every day to work on the building.

As Sharon Foust and Letitia Howe have suggested, there have been many changes in the Church of the Nativity's life as a congregation. According to the late Mildred Swift, who wrote a brief history of the parish:

> It all began in the late 1950s. At that time the Town of Northborough was a quiet little suburban town with a population of approximately 4,000 to 5,000 people. A vast growth potential was already becoming evident, the influx was gradual, but all the signs were pointing to a population explosion, but there was no Episcopal Church ....
>
> In 1959 the inevitable questions arose. Would it be possible to establish an Episcopal Church in Northborough? Were there enough

Episcopalians residing in the town to support a church? How did one go about all this?[27]

Those interested in forming a congregation worked fast. Sixty signatures were obtained on a petition to the Diocese of Western Massachusetts to start a mission, and $10,000 was raised. Arrangements were made to use the town's Grange Hall for services. The first service was held in the hall in January, 1960.

The diocese purchased a seven-acre farm just a little back from the center of town. In June, 1960, a vicarage was built where the old farmhouse had been, while the members went on holding services in the Grange Hall and working hard at fund-raising.

> The time spent in the Grange Hall was a period of solid togetherness. Seldom has a group been so united, overcome so many obstacles and inconveniences, or worked so diligently toward the goal of a church building. There were bazaars, food sales, clothing sales, auctions, carnivals, suppers, theatrical productions. Name it! If it could raise funds, it was done.[28]

The building was finished at the end of 1963, and a series of vicars came and went, usually for short time spans. Some of them were helpful in contributing to the development of the congregation, others less so. The laity, who had been so instrumental in getting the Church of the Nativity established in the first place, have been what has kept it going throughout its short history. In 1973 the fourth priest to serve the parish, the Rev. J. Edward Putnam, said,

> A parish or mission cannot afford to rely solely upon its priest for its leadership and direction. It must seek out its laity who have been blessed with the skills and insights to lead as the Holy Spirit inspired them.[29]

Several leaders, including Sharon and Michael Foust and Marge Carlson, have learned the value of lay leadership as well as the difficulties encountered when there is not sufficient lay responsibility. As Sharon stated, "I've been here long enough to see several sinking periods. But each time the church rebounded."[30] Her husband, Michael, continues:

> One of the reasons the church has rebounded is the strength of the people. The people who have stayed have learned that *it is the people who are the Church* and it really shouldn't matter who the priest is because it's the people who make the Church.[31]

Nonetheless, the people have been severely tried. During a period without a priest in 1980 Nancy Kimball recalls that,

> Marge Carlson [the senior warden] took over when we didn't have a rector. She took us through a difficult emotional and spiritual time. And Elizabeth Rixham stood up at an annual meeting and said that we'd just have to stay together and build things up ourselves. She encouraged us to do it.[32]

When a rector did come, it was not a successful match, and in spite of the strength of the lay leadership, numbers decreased and morale sank to a low ebb. All agree that it was through the energies of a very talented interim priest that the congregation gained in strength and cohesiveness. As Marge Carlson recalls:

> Bob Ginn, the interim priest, would say continually what wonderful people we were. He told us we were wonderful at a time when we weren't feeling good about ourselves. We began to see that maybe we had to be at rock bottom to accept that it is the Lord who is in charge. Bob told us we were worthy so often that we became worthy of his good opinion of us. He helped us regain the confidence in one another which we'd lost. I think he was the catalyst. So when we chose Fred [the current rector] both the Calling Committee and the Vestry were of one mind [the first time ever that members were unanimously in agreement over the calling of a particular priest to serve the parish].[33]

This time the fit between priest and parish has been excellent. The members feel that they are on the right track. The congregation is growing at the rate of 15 to 20 percent a year. They have moved quickly from being a pastoral church to a program church. There are plenty of programs, activities, and ministries to suit all ages, interests, and levels of spiritual development. There are plenty of small groups.

One of the organizational actions that has helped has been the restructuring of the vestry. Now each vestry member chairs a significant area of ministry, planning and accomplishing tasks and ministries with his or her own committee members. For example, Norma Dragon is responsible for pastoral care. It is an area that includes the Assistance Committee, memorial funds, the prayer chain, healing ministry, lay ministry training, marriage preparation, the men's breakfast, the women's breakfast, and the coffee hour. Evangelism, mission outreach, adult education, worship, and youth programs are similarly structured each with its committee and subcommittees. Each of these committees has its area of responsibility and makes its own decisions and controls its own budget. The advantage of this format is that significant responsibilities are now much more widely distributed. More people are involved and have a greater stake in decision-making. There is a greater sense of ownership. Now vestry meetings are devoted to issues of policy, broad directions of ministry, and the like. Another change is the holding of a vestry Day of Discernment. Any member of the parish who feels called to serve in any leadership capacity is invited to attend this session, where he or she can discuss the calling and discern where and how he or she should serve. In this way, people are encouraged to serve where their real strengths and interest can be used most appropriately in the parish community.

Naturally the Church of the Nativity members are thrilled and delighted with their progress, yet they constantly remind themselves that it is God's work, and not their own to take credit for. As they seek to remain faithful and continue to build up God's house, Ed Church, the chair of the Evangelism Committee, cautions,

> As long as people see Church as merely a place to come, then the Church won't have a vibrancy. People need to sense that the Church is there and that they are members of the body. But we need to be clear that the call is first and foremost to the

Body of Christ—not to the Episcopal Church, not to the Church of the Nativity.[34]

## *DISTINCTIVE FEATURES*

This is a congregation that wants to "make a difference" through worship, outreach and care in the name of Christ. It is a congregation blessed with a visionary and active priest, and a fortunate geographical location. Newcomers are quickly visited by personal home contacts. There is a spirit of expectation that the Lord is active and present with his people.[35]

Such was the observation of the Rev. Canon William Coyne, a member of the Mission Discernment Project Visiting Team. Quite simply, the Church of the Nativity works because it ranks high on any scale of the qualities of successful congregations. The Church of the Nativity ranks high, or is working towards, all twelve of Kennon L. Callahan's *Twelve Keys to an Effective Church*. Briefly these are specific, concrete mission objectives; pastoral and lay visitation; corporate, dynamic worship; significant relational groups; strong leadership resources; streamlined structure and solid participatory dicision-making; several competent programs and activities that serve, rather than use, people; open accessibility; high visibility; adequate parking, land, and landscaping; adequate space and facilities; and solid financial resources. Not that the Church of the Nativity has used Callahan's criteria in developing its ministry, it just looks that way!

Intuitively they seem to have understood Callahan's fourth key—"significant relational groups."

People search for community, not committees. People will put up with being on committees to the extent that they have discovered community. The search for community is the search for roots, place, and belonging—for a group of people in which significant relationships of sharing and caring take place . . . . People are not simply searching for contracts; they are searching for covenant . . . . They are searching for people with whom they can live out life together.³⁶

According to Kathy Eastham, "We try to discern God's will in everything we undertake."³⁷ Specifically the Mission Discernment Project identified the following factors that contribute to the Church of the Nativity's success in discerning its mission:

- **Bible-Based Ministry with Strong Emphasis on Teaching:** The Bible undergirds everything at the Church of the Nativity, from brief Bible reflections at the beginning of committee meetings to the official programs in Bible study. According to Lois Hummers,

   > Many opportunities for spiritual growth, both for children and adults, exist at Nativity.... Adults have an array of educational opportunities ranging from Basic Christianity, to Serendipity Bible Study Groups, to the new Sunday evening discipling course taught by the rector, to the Christian Foundations program, and various Advent and Lenten offerings. We believe that we are to "grow up into Christ" and encourage—and have an expectation—that parishioners will participate in one or more of these studies.³⁸

- **Constant Prayer:** One parish member wrote, "I think one reason Nativity is growing is that every day of the week someone is praying and fasting for Nativity's guidance."

   Members readily pray for each other and the rector. They pray individually. They pray in groups. They pray over the phone. Regarding her work in the Neurosurgery Department Office, Nancy Gove says, "60 percent of the time I just answer patients' questions. But sometimes I can see someone is distressed. I ask them if they have a faith. Then I ask them if they would like to have a prayer. It's always appreciated."³⁹ This is a typical scenario. There are many variations on this theme among Nativity's members.

- **Taking a Risk in Faith:** Members have taken a risk. They took a loan from the diocese, and they are contributing substantially in pledges for the building of the parish hall. They made the decision to build it themselves though not even one of the members was a professional builder. It was a risk taken in faith. In Kathy Eastham's words:

> We realize that we need to place all our cares at God's feet and He will guide us. It's a risky business. "Well, should we do this? Look at our budget over the last few years! Over the last few years we've hardly been able to keep things going. How are we going to be able to double everything? Triple everything?" It was God who reassured us that we needed to take the step. We needed to go ahead. It was God who said, "Go, do not worry about it." We probably still have doubts, but we were willing to take the Lord's hand and take the next step.[40]

- ■ *Newcomers Welcomed and Visited:* It would be hard to leave the Church of the Nativity on a Sunday morning unnoticed and ungreeted. Members go out of their way to meet visitors and talk with them, and follow up within twenty-four hours.
- ■ *Newcomers Incorporated Right Away:* A member since 1974 commented, "We were made to feel a part of the Body of Christ here immediately upon our arrival by being asked to work on groups within two months of our arrival." Indeed, many members of work crews, classes, and committees, even the vestry, are quite new to the church. They have gotten involved quickly.
- ■ *A Sense of Family:* Letitia Howe, for whom the congregation recently held a ninetieth birthday party, said, "They are my family," and almost every other member of any age would agree. Marie Campbell, a Roman Catholic from Worcester, who occasionally comes to the Church of the Nativity with friends who are members, said,

> The place that feels itself to be a family will open its doors to a stranger. In a large family there is always room for one more. This church feels like a family.[41]

- ■ *An Effective Interim Ministry:* This congregation's experience highlights the importance of interim ministry. In this case the interim pastor helped immeasurably in restoring the people's confidence in themselves and laid the groundwork for the changes that are in progress right now. As Marge Carlson noted, "Bob Ginn told us we were wonderful at a time when we weren't feeling good about ourselves [and] he was a catalyst for change."[42]

- **Clerical Leadership:** The Rev. Fred Goodwin is a young priest without a long track record. He has only been a priest since 1984, and this is his second parish, the first in which he has been rector; thus his effectiveness as a priest is not the result of the trials and errors of a long ministry.

    What is patently obvious is that Fred Goodwin is a secure and confident individual, but not proud or overconfident, without a trace of co-dependency problems. He is a high-energy hard worker, yet he still has a relaxed demeanor. The Rev. Canon William Coyne said simply, "There is a healthy family in the rectory."[43] Site Visitor Jane Cosby of the Diocese of Pennsylvania said of Goodwin:

    > He is genuinely called to the priesthood and to this ministry. He is a "servant priest." He is a consummate teacher. He motivates by putting members to work with the effect of stretching/achieving. He equips and by achievement increases the self-esteem of his people. He is knowledgeable (a trained evangelism consultant) and sees to it that his people are trained. He *sends* his people. He encourages the *authority of the laity*. He celebrates his priesthood from the point of view of the Priesthood of all Believers. He loves life—his, theirs, the church's. He prays and is prayed for. He fosters independence from himself so that the people will not falter when he is not there.[44]

- **Laity Ministering to Laity:** The laity give and receive ministry from each other. They do not hesitate to offer prayer for each other and to be present to each other in the practical circumstances of their lives. Furthermore, many of the members who have endured ineffective clerical leadership in the past have seen what can happen when too much reliance is placed on the priest and not enough on their own capabilities. As Michael Foust remarked, "It is the people who are the Church."

- ***Laity Living Lives of Ministry:*** Through small-group discussions, sermons, and education programs, parishioners are encouraged to view all of their lives as opportunities for ministry. And they do. As Frazier Glenn said,

  > I try to be a Christian and approach my job with Christian principles. I think "selfless service" is a kind of love. I try to be as patient as I can with people in this time of international turmoil.[45]

- ***Clerical-Lay Partnership:*** There is a good fit between priest and parish. They genuinely respect and trust each other. This makes it possible for them to work as a team. The adversarial relationship sometimes observed between priest and vestry is not present here. This priest has thrown his lot in with the people of the congregation in a collegial relationship.
- ***Broadly Based Responsibilities and Decision Making:*** Responsibilities are widely dispersed throughout the congregation. Many people are involved in the parish's decision-making processes. They are *shapers of ministry,* not merely passive recipients of it.
- ***Christian Education Programs for Children and Youth:*** With the church school, junior high and senior high youth groups, and the new nursery school for children that has just been launched, this congregation is bursting its seams with children and ministries to them. Christian formation has high priority and attracts parents who want their children to be well taught in the faith. Teens stay active through effective, upbeat, Bible-based programs. The Site Visitors commented that it is refreshing to be among healthy, outgoing, straightforward teenagers for whom the faith is alive and even exciting.
- ***Small Groups:*** People come looking for community and family at the Church of the Nativity. They come to know and to be known. This makes sense, since many, if not most, of the members have come to Northborough from other areas of the country to work in the area's high-tech industries, having left friends and family behind. Small groups afford the intimacy the members seek. They get it in Bible-study groups and adult education groups, through participation in the building crews, and other programs. Fellowship dinners in homes of the parishioners have recently been added. According to Angie

Trombley, coordinator of the dinners, "It's not the food, place setting, or dining area that's most important but the time to fellowship and get to know one another and who we are."[46]
- **Location and Geography:** The Church of the Nativity is well-placed and easily accessible to the several communities it serves. There is plenty of parking.

The Church of the Nativity is building God's house; it is building people's lives. Jane Cosby observed that "they have been down often enough and down far enough individually to know beyond a shadow of a doubt that Christ is the Answer."[47]

## AN ISSUE FOR THE CHURCH OF THE NATIVITY TO CONSIDER

The Visiting Team observed the need for pro-active planning for mission outreach: That 23 percent of the congregation's budget is directed outside the parish is encouraging, yet the Mission Discernment Team noted a lack of mission outreach planning.

The congregation responds generously to requests for assistance, and indeed they support an impressive array of causes and ministries, from helping a family whose home was destroyed by fire through supporting a prison ministry, to helping a Volunteer for Mission. Requests come to the Mission Outreach Committee, and they respond. Yet the committee does not, for the most part, look at the community, try to understand its needs, and plan outreach accordingly.

The financial commitment is there. Information is easily available, since the town administrator is a member of the congregation, as is a United Way staff member. There are others too who could help the congregation look at the community and help the members plan outreach effectively.

This issue will become more critical as the parish hall nears completion. When it is finished there will be a whole new space available, along with the energies of the people who are currently working on the construction. These will need to be redirected. Some of the builders have already mentioned that they would like to continue to use their skills to help those in need with home repairs. And some community needs are already being met—for example, by the newly initiated nursery school. So some of this thinking and some action have started to occur. Furthermore, since Northborough has very few persons of color and persons of other than Euro-American culture groups, special efforts will need to be made to reach out to those others who are different from Nativity's members, *for the congregation's own enrichment.*

## *AN ISSUE FOR THE EPISCOPAL CHURCH*

The Church of the Nativity is a lively, faithful, and growing church. It attracts and keeps its young members. There is a depth of commitment among its members. They are knowledgeable about the Bible and matters of faith. They are impressive.

When the Visiting Team was there, the senior high group was using a Bible study program developed by Youth for Christ USA. The popular adult Bible study uses the Serendipity format. The Christian Foundations Program developed by Trinity School for Ministry is unabashedly evangelical in emphasis.

The common thread running through these and other materials used by Nativity is *the authority of the Bible.* St. Stephen's Church in Oak Harbor, Washington, also part of the Mission Discernment Project, similarly uses materials that stress biblical authority from a wide variety of denominational traditions.

What is obvious is that some of our churches, such as the Church of the Nativity and St. Stephen's, Oak Harbor, will turn to other religious denominations for the resources they need. In the process of using them, such congregations often become very knowledgeable about the Bible. They readily apply it to everyday life, and they articulate the meaning of their faith with ease. The other side of this strength is often the corresponding thinness of resources and teaching materials in an Anglican framework.

Does this point to a need for resources reflecting both biblical authority *and* standard Anglican tradition?

## *RESOURCES*

For resources which have helped shape the style of ministry at the Church of the Nativity, parish leaders cite sources from the Alban Institute, Lyle Schaller's works on church management, resources from Peter Wagner's church growth work at Fuller Seminary, and those from Episcopal Renewal Ministries. Also cited are the following specific titles:

Coleman, Lyman. *Serendipity Bible for Groups.* Littleton, CO: Serendipity House, rev. ed., 1989.

Lovelace, Richard, *Renewal as a Way of Life.* Downer's Grove, IL: InterVarsity Press, 1985.

Yancy, Philip. *Where Is God When It Hurts?* Grand Rapids, MI: Zondervan, 1977.

---

## NOTES

[1] Ken Bishop, interview in Northborough, September 8, 1990.
[2] Fred Goodwin, interview in Northborough, September 8, 1990.
[3] Jim Baker, interview in Northborough, September 8, 1990.
[4] *Ibid.*
[5] Neal Weinstock, quoted in "Bay State Land Court Swamped with Filings for Foreclosures," by Arlene Levinson. Associated Press article in *The Day* (New London), September 12, 1990, p. C-4.
[6] Raymond Lambert *et al.*, "Planning for the Future, Responding to Needs," a Community Needs Assessment, sponsored by the United Way of Assabet Valley and United Way of Metrowest. No date; probably 1989.
[7] *Ibid.*, p. 31.
[8] *Ibid.*, p. 40.
[9] *Ibid.*, pp. 19-20.
[10] Bill Gagnon, interview in Northborough, September 8, 1990.
[11] Charlie Dexter, interview in Northborough, September 8, 1990.
[12] Ken Bishop, interview.
[13] Rob Robinson, interview in Northborough, September 8, 1990.
[14] Vestry Statement, August, 1990.
[15] Nancy Gove, interview in Northborough, September 8, 1990.
[16] Lois A. Hummers, report on the Christian Foundations Program, in "The Church of the Nativity: 30th Annual Report," January 21, 1990.
[17] Jane Glenn, interview in Northborough, September 9, 1990.
[18] Doug Cole, interview in Northborough, September 9, 1990.
[19] "Worship and Education at the Church of the Nativity," newcomer information packet.

[20] Barbara Dexter, interview in Northborough, September 8, 1990.
[21] Letitia Howe, interview in Northborough, September 9, 1990.
[22] Sharon Foust, handwritten statement for the Visiting Team, received September 8, 1990.
[23] Fred Goodwin, interview in Northborough, September 8, 1990.
[24] Sharon Foust, interview in Northborough, September 8, 1990.
[25] Marge Carlson, interview in Northborough, September 9, 1990.
[26] Bill Gagnon, "Church of the Nativity Annual Report," January 21, 1989.
[27] Mildred Swift, "The Church of the Nativity, Northborough, Mass.: A History, 1960-1965," p. 2.
[28] *Ibid.*
[29] J. Edward Putnam, "The State of the Mission—1973," one-page mimeographed report.
[30] Sharon Foust, interview in Northborough, September 9, 1990.
[31] Michael Foust, interview in Northborough, September 9, 1990.
[32] Nancy Kimball, interview in Northborough, September 9, 1990.
[33] Marge Carlson, interview.
[34] Ed Church, interview in Northborough, September 9, 1990.
[35] William H. Coyne, Site Visitor Report.
[36] Kennon L. Callahan, *Twelve Keys to an Effective Church: Strategic Planning for Mission* (San Francisco: Harper and Row Publishers, 1983), p. 35.
[37] Kathy Eastham, interview in Northborough, September 9, 1990.
[38] Lois A. Hummers, notes to the Visiting Team, August 28, 1990.
[39] Nancy Gove, interview.
[40] Kathy Eastham, interview.
[41] Marie Campbell, interview in Northborough, September 9, 1990.
[42] Marge Carlson, interview in Northborough, September 9, 1990.
[43] William Coyne, interview in Northborough, September 9, 1990.
[44] Jane Cosby, Site Visitor Report, September 12, 1990.
[45] Frazier Glenn, interview in Northborough, September 9, 1990.

[46] Angie Trombley, *News and Notes,* the parish newsletter, July 10, 1990, p. 2.
[47] Jane Cosby, Site Visitor Report.

*Visiting Team:* Jane Cosby and the Rev. Canon William Coyne
*Date of Visit:* September 8-10, 1990

> *The untrammeled individualist persists partly as a residue of the real and romantic frontiers, and also partly because runaways from more restricted regions keep reimporting him. The stereotype continues to affect romantic Westerners and non-Westerners in romantic ways, but it also affects real Westerners in real ways.*
>
> —Wallace Stegner,
> The American West as Living Space

## CHAPTER 12

# HIGH-COUNTRY CALLING

## STORY OF A CONGREGATION USING PROFESSIONAL CONSULTING SERVICES

### CHRIST CHURCH
### CODY, WYOMING

## *THE CONTEXT OF MISSION DISCERNMENT: CODY AND THE BIGHORN BASIN*

"This is high desert," according to Bob Ross, a geologist who is a land use specialist for the Bureau of Land Management (BLM) in the Cody Resource Area and a member of Christ Church:

> We have sagebrush, various grasses, livestock grazing. One third of the Bighorn Basin makes up the

> Cody Resource Area. We protect and manage over one and a half million acres of federal lands. What with the Shoshone National Forest to the west and various private lands, this is an area of about six million acres. It's home to me. If I come in by the Wind River Canyon or the eastern half of Yellowstone, I feel as if I'm back home.[1]

Pointing out the boulder fields on the way into Clark's Fork Canyon, Ross continues:

> Those rocks were once part of a low streambed. But over the ages they were raised to become this high land. We call it inverted topography—what was once low is now high. What was down is now up. Hey, this sounds a little biblical, doesn't it?[2]

One hundred and fifty years ago, Wyoming was a land of trails: the Oregon Trail, the California Emigrant Trail, the Mormon Trail—wagon ruts across the prairie and through the Rockies, the highroads of the Old West. In 1990, the centennial year of Wyoming statehood, sheep and cattle outnumber people ten to one, except possibly during the tourist season. Wyoming's population is less than 500,000, and half of the state is federal land. There is a lot of space. There is a lot of sky. Wyoming is a high state. Cody is 5,000 feet above sea level. Some mountain summits soar over 10,000 feet. To the west of Cody are the high mountains of the Absaroka Range, running north and south; to the south is Carter Mountain. In Cody itself, Heart Mountain dominates the vista.

This was the land of Indians, cowboys, mountain men, adventurers, dreamers, seekers, and outlaws. It still is. But to this list add miners, oil workers, migrant laborers, tourists. Cody is named for one such entrepreneur—Colonel William Frederick "Buffalo Bill" Cody, Pony Express rider, buffalo hunter, land developer, showman, promoter, and guide. Buffalo Bill first came to the area in the 1870s as a guide for a geological survey expedition. Over the next quarter of a century he led many hunting parties into the Bighorn Basin where, increasingly, he became interested in the agricultural potential of the area. But agriculture would only work with irrigation, and Cody was ultimately instrumental in bringing in both. Cody's associates suggested that the town be named for him, and he returned the compliment by naming the main streets after them.

Cody was an entrepreneur with an eye to the fast buck. While he cannot take credit for the establishment of the nation's first national park (Yellowstone in 1872) or first national forest (Shoshone in 1892), which are located just west of Cody, he certainly capitalized on the economic opportunities presented by the location of these federal sites. He was a prime mover in getting the Chicago, Burlington and Quincy Railroad to Cody in 1901, and he built hotels for the people to stay in once they got there. The Irma Hotel, named for Cody's sixteen-year-old daughter, still stands in downtown Cody at the corner of 12th and Sheridan.

Today people still come to Wyoming for what they can get out of it. According to Bob Ross, "Wyoming is an extractive state and its economy is tied to its resources."[3] It leads the nation in the mining of bentonite, a clay that resembles Silly Putty and is used in steelmaking and drilling oil wells, and trona, a mineral used in manufacturing glass, soap, and textile dyes. Wyoming has coal—enough of it to supply the entire United States for 300 years. It has uranium, gas, and oil. But according to Bob Ross, who spends time with people who have mining claims on the land, "Since 1983 when oil and gas started taking a plunge, a lot of people who used to work in these areas have moved on."[4] Now there is just one oil firm in town—Marathon, which is Cody's largest employer. The agricultural economy remains strong, with cattle, sugar beets, and grain the main products. Several farms produce a single crop—barley—for Coors Beer. Tourism, to offset the lagging oil industry, is being emphasized now as people in Cody take advantage of the town's position as the eastern gateway to Yellowstone Park.

Cody is still a small town. Its population is 8,000 by the most generous estimate, with 14,000 for the area. Its best attraction is its lovely environment. Residents and tourists alike prize Cody as a base for hunting, fishing, hiking, backpacking, and winter sports in the thousands of acres of park and wilderness lands. The nearest shopping mall is in Billings, 100 miles north in Montana, and Cody people go there to shop or just to get out of town and into an urban setting for a day or two. But the town itself has many advantages. Northwest College, a two-year college that is part of the state system, is located here. There are community concerts and plays. In the summer one can go to a rodeo every night of the week. Cody is a town full of artists, and their works are displayed in galleries and in the museums. The author James Michener once remarked that the Buffalo Bill Historical Center is "one of the finest museums in the nation." Indeed, the center is home to four museums which depict the art, artifacts, crafts, culture, traditions, and history of the American West. During the visit of the Mission Discernment Project Visiting Team, there was a special exhibit to mark the centennial of the Battle of Wounded Knee.

Cody also has churches and bars—twenty-two of each. Mormons predominate, and there are three Mormon "stakes" in town. There are also five Baptist churches, one Roman Catholic, and two Lutheran (one ELCA and the other Missouri Synod). According to Bob Ross, "The one down the hill is more like us. The one up the hill . . . well, they're so conservative, they don't even have women clergy."[5] But it's the Mormons who have the most pronounced effect on the community. They are a factor to be reckoned with. Some consider them conservative and unbending. According to Christ Church member K. T. Roes, "We tried to start a Planned Parenthood Clinic and there was so much dissension. I got telephone calls in the night. I was threatened. So I see a lot of conservatism here."[6] And according to Tina Jackson, another Christ Church member:

> Cody is very small town, very Mormon. And, as a result, there is no sex education in the schools, which is an issue which is very high on our list to do something about as a parish. You know there are thirty-two pregnancies in the high school and nobody knows about it officially. Nobody *wants* to know about it.[7]

But there are other voices. Hat McGee, one of Christ Church's members of longest standing, reflected:

> The Mormon Church is a way of life, not merely a religion. In every facet of life the church is part of that life. Look at their missionaries! What an example of dedication! They take care of their own. I think they will inherit the earth.[8]

Finally, the Rev. Warren Murphy expressed the view,

> There *is* a heavy Mormon influence, but the most controlling negative influence seems to come from "fundamentalist" congregations which proliferate on a regular basis. I still can't figure out who they are, but there is no shortage of them! Mormons tend to be more "establishment," while "fundamentalists" are on the outs.[9]

Cody has many faces. As Tina Jackson continued:

> This town has a split personality because there's the South Fork [of the Shoshone River, known locally as just "the South Fork"] with people who have their summer homes here and live in Miami or Long Island or Manhattan and come here for the summer. There's great wealth up there. *Town and Country* just devoted a whole issue to "Cody Country" in its August issue, and a Christ Church member was pictured on the cover. There is poverty in the community, but we're not exposed to it. It's well hidden, but it exists out in the country. There are a couple of trailer courts around here. Migrant workers working the [sugar] beet fields. That's sad.[10]

And, in K. T. Roes' words:

> There are a lot of people who are not psychically free. People in Cody—many of them—are very narrow. Many haven't lived in other parts of the world. I know people here who have never met a black.[11]

So Cody is very diverse, culturally if not racially. It's the home of 240 artists, about five of international reputation. There are writers, native Wyomingites and those who took John Soule's advice, popularized by Horace Greeley, "Go West, young man, go West." There are farmers, ranchers, dude ranchers, those in the tourist business, rich summer people, poor Mexican seasonal workers, government workers who manage federal lands, teachers, hospital workers, business people, the retired, and playboys.

But however outmoded it may be, the cowboy is the enduring and pervasive image of the area The contemporary novelist of the West Wallace Stegner suggested that:

> When youth run away from home, they don't run away to become farmers. They run away to become romantic isolates, lone riders who slit their eyes against steely distance .... The untrammeled individualist persists partly as a residue of the real and romantic frontiers, and also partly because runaways from more restricted regions keep reimporting him. The stereotype continues to affect romantic Westerners and non-Westerners in romantic ways, but it also affects real Westerners in real ways.[12]

Hat McGee should know:

> I was smitten with the West. I came out to Cody in 1946. We first came here when Al Simpson was an altar boy. It was just a small parish then. We all share certain common traits. Freedom and individualism are high values.[13]

It's a high-country calling.

## *CHRIST CHURCH:*
## *A CHURCH IN THE COMMUNITY*

Hat McGee said, "I feel that when I am in the community, I am the Church."[14]

Christ Church members understand ministry as primarily what they do during the week, as *being Christ* to others through the ordinary routines of their lives, as being the Church in the community. Joan Bray, chair of the General Convention's Standing Commission on Evangelism, who was a site visitor, commented:

> I don't get a personal pietistic approach as I listen to these people. What I get is faith informing their lives. It's not holy talk, it is holy lives. They have a sense of God empowering their daily life and ministry. It's been expressed by a number of

members: a world-famous artist, a florist, a resource specialist for the Bureau of Land Management, the owner of an irrigation company. I get it through teachers and from an addiction counselor. Through talking with them, I hear a clear connection between faith and empowerment.[15]

Thus the best way to introduce Christ Church's ministry is to introduce a sampling of members and hear how they describe their ministries.

Bob Ross works for the Bureau of Land Management. He is also a member of the church's Mission Committee (mission being understood here as community service). The committee recently started recycling in the parish and is now considering a sex education course to be offered to everyone in the town. This is how he talks about life and ministry:

> I think we're a group of people who are interested in social action. I am in church because of my religious beliefs, and I like to familiarize myself with other people who have an interest in social action. During my high school years growing up close to Washington, D.C., we used to just skip school, get on a bus and protest a war downtown. I always considered myself an activist, so I continue to ask myself, "What do I do?" I think we can make a difference with sex education, with working with the Bargain Box [a secondhand clothing store sponsored by the church], with recycling, with just being real active in the community. So that's what I like most about the church. I can acquaint myself with people who have the same interests and want to do the same kind of things to make a difference in the life of this community.
>
> Everyone in my office knows I'm an Episcopalian. I try to stay active in the humanizing influences on the job. I am on committees in my office that deal with employee issues—job sharing, maternity, paternity leaves, that type of thing. Through such means I brought recycling to the of-

fice and they're excited about it down in Worland [regional office of the BLM]. We have a small office here in Cody—about twelve people—but down in Worland there are about seventy-five people. There are all kinds of people—geologists, wildlife people, archeologists, clerical people, engineers—but they've really gotten interested in recycling. When I go down there, I just pick up their stuff for recycling and bring it back to Cody, where there is a company that handles it.

One of the committees I'm on deals with employee-generated initiatives and awards. Most awards, you know, come from managers. They come with money and plaques. But managers don't see everything. There are a lot of people who do important things who don't get those kinds of awards, so we're working to make sure some of those selections come from the employees themselves.

Considering my job directly . . . we deal with multiple use. We have to accommodate so many kinds of people, ideas, and uses, from those who want to use public lands for wilderness and solitude, to recreation, to those who want development. I consider myself like Jerry Ford, middle of the road. On the job I try to "toe the line" as a middle-of-the-road moderate. Like a lawyer, I understand that certain viewpoints have to be aired, whether or not I personally agree with them. So compromise is the name of the game in my job because we can't keep everyone happy. What normally happens is that we make everybody mad at us by taking the middle ground. Like the Cody Resource Management Plan—we had three protests from the environmental community and three from the development-commercial business industry—so we make both sides mad at us. One side says we protect too much, the other not enough. But I personally am very liberal. I really do want to know how best to manage and protect our million and a half acres. I am in this because I want to protect it.

I try to do some things with the church, and carry them forward in my work. I think we can see God in the poor people in particular and in our relationships with them. The Bible says you see God in the faces of the poor. I believe that. You've got to find God in other people. Those people are more likely to be the poor, and those who need your assistance.[16]

K. T. Roes, the mother of two small children, works as a bookkeeper for the business her husband owns, Mid-West Fence Company. She is also an EMT for the ambulance company in Cody and CPR instructor.

I used to work for the Patrons' Ball, the Frontier Festival—those social things—but I decided I wanted to channel my energies into something more useful than raising $40,000 for the Historical Society.

Working as an EMT . . . that's my ministry. When we're called in an emergency, our patients need someone to restore order for them. I feel that's where I should be.[17]

Don Kurtz was born in Cody and has been a member of Christ Church since 1968.

I'm in the irrigation equipment business—Pawnee Irrigation. Here it's mostly flood irrigation, and sprinklers, but we also pump out lakes, springs, and ponds. Most of our water comes from Buffalo Bill Dam. I also do landscaping, and I've got some greenhouses.

I love to hear the Bible stories and teachings of Christ, how he ministered to people. It's a model for my life, of how to live, of how to treat others.[18]

Kim Moser is a chemical abuse specialist at the Cedar Mountain Center, a family recovery center for addiction disorders (eating, drink, drugs), which is a unit of West Park Hospital in Cody. She is in charge of the eating disorders program, which serves inpatients and outpatients. Kim is convinced that physical recovery is directly tied to emotional and spiritual recovery. Although she is employed by a public hospital, she has instituted a twelve-step recovery program built on spiritual principles. It's the only way, she contends.

> People come here because they are addicted. They are unable to control their intake because of family, social, medical, or legal problems. And they come—whether they consider it or not—spiritually as well as emotionally bankrupt. So I believe that we have an obligation to teach them that abstinence and a spiritual way of life are necessary for long-term recovery.
>
> Anything they try on just a physical plane won't work, and I really believe that the source of addiction is spiritual deprivation. I think people use the substance to make up for the emptiness. They have to admit that they are responsible for their actions. It's not God's actions, or their parents', or whoever. They have to stop blaming. Then they are ready to believe in a greater power than themselves, which really means a power greater then their addiction. You see, for them addiction has become that high power.[19]

Kim went on to explain that she is herself a recovering alcoholic of six years as well as a recovering compulsive overeater, and she uses her experience of being "down" and recovering in working with her patients. "I am referred to here as 'the Dragon Lady' because I'm tough, but I do it with caring."[20]

Ann Model started a business making flower arrangements following a painful divorce and a bout with cancer five years ago. She has been highly successful, and her arrangements can be seen in several upscale Cody shops.

> All my life I've collected wild material. As a child growing up in Pennsylvania, I collected weeds. I've always loved fields, countryside, and landscapes. Creating with this wild material, it's like the landscape in your brain flowing through your head.

> At Mooncrest [the ranch outside Cody where she used to live], I frequently made huge bouquets of dried flowers. When I moved into town [following separation from her husband and divorce], I was numb, unhappy, and isolated. I was in a dehumanized state. I needed to sort myself out emotionally, so the idea to start arranging flowers was a need more than anything else. It wasn't something I needed to do for the money, but I felt this need to do something creative with what I was at that time in my life.
>
> Sometimes I wonder if creating doesn't come from inner chaos. Maybe I was trying to retain that connection with the land. I missed the ranch so much. Flower arranging was something I just did. I would go out there in the workshop. It was away from the telephone. I'd turn on classical music . . . . It's been part of my healing process. Hard times can give way to inner truth.
>
> I have this conviction that what you do in your life, really do it for someone else. If you make it, if you do it yourself, then it can become meaningful. I'm just creating it; I'm just doing it. It's an artistic expression, but because I've done it out of my own love it becomes more of a gift to the person who receives it.[21]

Harry Jackson is primarily a painter, but he started doing sculpture to improve his painting. Both his paintings and sculptures are on display in his studios in Cody and in Italy, as well as in museums and galleries around the world. One of the Mission Discernment Project Site Visitors asked a Christ Church member how Jackson feels about having his work compared with that of Frederic Remington. The reply was, "Harry's a gracious person, so wouldn't be insulted, but actually his work is more highly regarded than Remington's." When asked where he thought his artistic gift came from, the artist replied:

> From God. There's no question about it. I'm an incredible believer. I have no question about the Divine Providence. In no way, shape, or form. Nothing exists that is not of God. Nothing. *I know* that.

Every aspect of art is a reflection of the Divine Presence. The artist is a medium, a vessel, a channel, for the greater power. Without question. *Without question.* The artist is, in some small way, the vehicle through which the Divine is revealed.[22]

But he is wary of museums.

Museums are reliquaries. They keep fragments just like the Roman Catholic Church keeps the bones of saints. Museums are full of curators, dealers, and scholars. And they want to deny the living artist. They wish to do so because the living artist is messy. Messy. He speaks the truth as he sees it. Museums would rather deal with dead artists. The living artist is terribly threatening because he may speak what he sees. And it may not be terribly pleasant.[23]

Other Christ Church members also speak the truth as they see it. They express their faith through their daily living. Douglas Sunderland runs a catering business, "Because I don't paint or write. Cooking is a creative outlet for me."[24] Lolly Jolley is a high school librarian. Steve Dunn hangs wallpaper. Jim Hager is a public school music teacher who builds organs on the side. He has written a communion setting for Christ Church, where he is the parish organist. Steve Cranfill, the senior warden, is a local attorney who has just turned forty. The Christ Church community, he says, "keeps me honest." He has been a parole officer and a member of the Wyoming State Legislature. Carrie Gasch, the junior warden, was born and raised in Cody. She is a teacher's aide in the elementary school.

Mary Smith, a staff member who coordinates Christian education for the church, was born in Cambridge, Massachusetts. She left to be with "a childhood sweetheart who loved the West," and whom she married. Mary taught in a little school with only eight children on the South Fork of the Shoshone. In 1957 she started the first public kindergarten in Park County, in the cattle town of Meeteetse.

Tina Jackson, a musician and songwriter, according to K. T. Roes "could have a fabulous career as an entertainer. She's just that good."[25] Jane Dominick, who grew up in Virginia, says "I married a cowboy." Her family operates a guest ranch—the 7D Ranch—in the summer, and in the winter Jane is a high school English teacher. Alan Simpson is a U.S. senator. His family gave the land the church is built on. Shirley Lehman is a real estate agent and a member of the Cody School Board. Bill Garlow, a great-grandson of Buffalo Bill, is a local CPA and a motel owner. Gil Smith is a playwright and teacher. Daphne Grimes is an Episcopal priest who founded a retreat and conference center on her ranch in Cody.

Warren Murphy, who acknowledges that "I am big on Wyoming," has been the rector of Christ Church since December, 1989. It would appear that he and the parish are well matched. "This parish is ready to evolve into a new phase. They want to be challenged. I am a believer in putting the Gospel to work outside the parish setting."[26]

In the church there is a painting of the Wyoming landscape—a wide sagebrush valley, mountains, and an expansive sky. Superimposed on it is the outline of the Episcopal Church shield. One has to spend only a few days with the members of Christ Church to realize just how much that painting is a characterization of who Christ Church members are. They are Wyomingites by birth and adoption. They have great affection for their state. Its geography has left its mark on who they are. They are also Episcopalians by birth and adoption. The two go well together—Wyoming and Episcopalian. Lolly Jolley explains:

> I like to know all the borders, so the liturgy is very good for me. I don't need rigidity, but I do need borders, and liturgy allows for those, but there are choices. There is a lot of room in the Episcopal Church, but it's clear where the boundaries are.
>
> I honestly think some of this has to do with growing up in Wyoming, which is a state with very clear borders. If you think about the shape of our state, it is totally square and yet we have a lot of open space. We have a lot of mountains. We have great diversity within that, but those borders are very clear. The Episcopal Church is like the state of Wyoming.[27]

Steve Dunn and Don Kurtz stress the sense of freedom and individual choice, which are attractive to them. According to Steve:

> It's the lack of "thou shalts" and "thou shalt nots" that appeals to me. It's like Wyoming. I like the space of the Episcopal Church. I like the space of the great outdoors. There's freedom in both.[28]

And Don comments:

> I like the freedom of choice. Take this death penalty issue [Wyoming was expecting to have its first execution in twenty-five years two days after the visit of the Mission Discernment Project Site Visitors, and the rector, as chair of the statewide nine-denomination Wyoming Church Coalition, had taken a position against the death penalty, as had the Coalition as a whole]. Warren is a social activitist. He has a social conscience. I think his position on it is tied to the Bible. Scripture had to do with the shaping of his position. When he preached on it last Sunday, he put it in the context of the "seventy times seventy." So I have to respect that, even if I may personally disagree with it. I can live with it. It's his freedom of choice.[29]

Christ Church has 320 baptized members. On a Sunday morning, a total of 140 worship at one of the two services. During the summer months, the early service is held in "the Poker Church"—the congregation's first home—and the main service of the day is in the adjacent structure, which was built in 1965. Three of Harry Jackson's sculptures adorn the church, as do Ann Model's baskets of dried flowers. The congregation sings to Jim Hager's communion setting. Occasionally the children will sing songs composed and directed by Tina Jackson, who also serves as cantor. There is healing and anointing quarterly, performed following the Eucharist in a straightforward and understated manner. The rector, the Rev. Warren Murphy, is an effective preacher. He is also an adept teacher and—unless participants arrive on time—there is standing room only in his Bible-study class between the 8 and 10 o'clock services.

Children have a key place in the life of Christ Church. As Mary Smith explained, "Children learn about community first of all by *experiencing* community. They are drawn into full participation. They learn through their participation."[30] Curriculum is important too. The ideas of Howard Hanchey and John Westerhoff have influenced the development of a strong Christian education program. According to Mary Smith:

> Hanchey's idea is that less is more. The year is divided into five terms, plus Lent and Easter. In each term one theme is selected, and we really focus on it and immerse ourselves in it. This term it is sheep and shepherds (Luke 15: 3-7; Ezekiel 34: 11-16). We're going to take the children on a visit to a nearby sheep farm. They'll see what the sheep are like, and how they are cared for. We want to get across the idea that God is the shepherd who cares for us all. First-graders are relating this theme of caring to people who need special care.[31]

She expanded on this term's theme of sheep and shepherds:

> What does it mean to care for sheep? What are sheep like? What is the job of shepherd? Marshall Dominick and Gale Sunderland have arranged a trip to a sheep farm to do some "hands-on" activities with the children to answer some of these questions. They will show us something about the characteristics of sheep and the work of shepherds in Wyoming today. A class project that touches our lives in this community is [also] possible here. Are there ways we can take care of the "lost" and the outsider in Cody?[32]

The parish hall and nursery are well used. Christ Church is the center for Absaroka Headstart. On Thursdays the Bible Study Fellowship uses the whole building. Narcotics Anonymous has four meetings every week, Adult Children of Alcoholics two, and Emotions Anonymous meets once. The number of these groups and the frequency of meetings suggest another facet of life in Cody, for as Harry Jackson noted, "Drugs and alcohol are problems here because Cody is part of the United States of America. We have it coast to coast. It's the malaise of our century."[33]

The church sponsors the Bargain Box—a secondhand store in town—and the Wayfarers' Chapel, an outdoor chapel 40 miles outside of Cody, close to Yellowstone Park. This is a ministry to travelers and tourists, summer ranch hands, and clergy who take the services in return for accommodation and vacation time at a guest ranch. Christ Church provides services and pastoral ministry to the elderly who are residents of a local nursing home. The rector provides pastoral support for the twelve-step program at the Cedar Mountain Center. There is an active EFM group in the parish, which was started by Daphne Grimes in the late 1970s. Mary Smith has been the EFM mentor since 1988. Many members attribute their spiritual awakening and growth to those classes. Lay Eucharistic Ministry was introduced in May, and Lay Eucharistic Ministers (LEMs) are sent out at the conclusion of Sunday's main service with a prayer and blessing to visit the sick and shut-ins.

Structurally, the life of the congregation is organized around three committees: Parish Life, Worship, and Mission. The Mission Committee has been the most active lately.

In the spring of 1990 the Mission Committee started a recycling project. Every third Sunday is "Junk for Jesus" Sunday, and parishioners bring newspapers, aluminum cans, plastic, and glass for recycling. Douglas Sunderland has started writing an "environmental blurb" for the parish's monthly newsletter. In July it was about Styrofoam, in August toxic chemicals. In September, members started bringing their own coffee cups to church to avoid using Styrofoam cups.

The other issue that is receiving attention is the proposal that the parish sponsor a sex education course for children as a service to the town. Wyoming is third in the nation in teenage pregnancy, yet sex education is not given a high priority in the public schools. So the church believes that in making the offering, it will be responding to an important need in the community. K. T. Roes believes the program will be accepted. "Opponents to sex education in the town always say, 'Well, we want it done by the Church,' so here we are, we're a church and we're doing it!"[34]

Members of the congregation, for the most part, are hopeful and excited about what the future holds. Steve Dunn says:

I'm hopeful. This is no tight church. It is what I
was looking for. What I want is family-type stuff.
I want to have fun in the name of God. I want to
rock and roll. I want to have that warm feeling.
I want everyone to be glad they came here. I want
it to be that kind of warmth and family. I've craved
for that sense of family all my life. If people come
and share their joy, it can happen. Out of that sense
of family all kinds of good things can come.[35]

Mary Smith said, "Pat Keller [the former rector] said to me 'I think this congregation needs to start looking outside themselves, and Warren's the man who can lead them to do that.'"[36]

Warren Murphy is doing just that. Regarding Father Murphy's position on the death penalty, Lolly Jolley said, "I almost stood up and applauded Warren for addressing this issue from the pulpit. I hope we can get our state to look at the laws of our state and change this one."[37] And even though Steve Dunn says, "I'm not personally sure about the death penalty issue," he maintains,

I'm proud as hell Warren Murphy is down there
doing something. I want the Church to do something. I'm proud he's down there raising some
sand. I'm proud he's there with his collar on saying "This is my stand and this is my Church." I
salute what he's doing and what the Church is doing. I am proud of this church. I am proud that
Christ Church, Cody, will get its name in the paper
over this important issue. It's exactly where the
Church ought to be.[38]

K. T. Roes says, "I want to see the Church become a leader of political life and change in this community."[39] And so may it be . . . .

## UNDERSTANDING THE STORY

It all began at Purcell's Saloon at the turn of the century, when Cody was long on saloons and short on churches. Buffalo Bill Cody and George Beck, along with the local ranchers and barroom cowboys, were having their usual poker game. The pot grew larger as the night wore on. And as the game continued, Cody suggested that whoever won it should donate it for the building of the church of his choice. Beck won, and donated the pot to the Episcopalians.

For the previous two years, several women in town had worked at starting a church. One of them, Anna Peake, who had arrived in town with her husband, the editor of the *Enterprise* newspaper (still in operation) in 1898, was particularly important in the development of an Episcopal congregation. She contacted the closest bishop, James Funsten of Idaho, who came to Cody, talked with the women, and held a service in the little schoolhouse. He urged them to find a priest who would be willing to serve in this frontier outpost, build a church building, and get the men involved. It was a tall order, since most of the men in town were much more interested in the saloons that lined Sheridan than in establishing a church. Nonetheless, the women persisted, and probably more to placate his wife than anything else, George Beck handed over the poker proceeds to her. The women augmented the pot with what they could raise from bake sales, dinners, and the like, and a pretty church, built in the style of the day, was added to the Cody landscape in 1902. However much Christ Church members try to call it "the Little Church," it is still popularly known as "the Poker Church."

Through the years, "we've had our characters for clergy," according to Hat McGee. "In those early days someone could just come out here and hide out."[40] Nonetheless, the numbers increased beyond the capacity of the Poker Church, and a new church was built on the other side of town on land donated by Milward and Lorna Simpson, who were members of the congregation. "Building the church took a lot of faith, since we didn't have a lot of affluent parishioners,"[41] Hat McGee recalled. So various fund-raisers were held, and the Bargain Box, a used clothing store, was called into service to provide additional funds. The Poker Church, by this time a historic landmark, was moved to the new site. About the same time, the Wayfarers' Chapel was established by Christ Church with the cooperation of the National Forest Service as a summer ministry for those in the vicinity of Yellowstone Park.

The Rev. Patterson ("Pat") Keller became rector of Christ Church in 1971. He and his wife, Connie, were very much involved in the life of Cody. Father Keller was a member of the Cody School Board. "Loving," "active in the community," "there for us," are the phrases members use to describe the Kellers and their long ministry. Several told of their children's accidents—death in one case—in other areas of the state, and how Pat Keller arrived by plane to be with them.

In the mid-1980s a nursery wing was added to the church to accommodate the forty or so children in the church school. This attractive new space solved an overcrowding problem and also opened up new opportunities for ministry in the community. The church was then able to house Special Touch Preschool, for children with disabilities (which has since moved because it needed more space) and Absaroka Headstart, and provide more meeting space for groups that needed it.

Quite naturally, the Kellers were much missed when they left in 1988, and for a year the parish went through an interim period that started out being just this side of disastrous: an interim priest unsuited to the congregation, miscommunication, the natural grieving whenever any valued person departs, loss of numbers. Fortunately, Mary Smith had learned about CRW Management Services and about the Rev. Charles R. Wilson, an Episcopal priest who is a professional consultant and trainer. Wilson had written a small book called *Search,* a manual to guide search committees through the process of calling a new pastor, which Mary had read. With the agreement of the Bishop of Wyoming, Christ Church sought Wilson's help. According to Wilson:

> The congregation's first objective in approaching the search process is to create a congregational climate of vision, unity and sense of well-being. Put briefly, "a congregation empowered to make the best possible decision." Where a congregation fails to arrive at this state of affairs prior to the calling of their pastor, they are subject to manipulation by minority factions or external influences. And even if they escape those real hazards, their decision will be based on whims, unexplained premises or poorly defined criteria—hardly better than a random selection. The Holy Spirit will be their guiding light, of course, but we know that in corporate activity as well as personal

life the Spirit has greater access and influence where there is some degree of order and discipline.[42]

Wilson did indeed restore order and discipline; he helped create a sense of vision, unity, and well-being. He assisted members to identify conditions and issues in the community and parish that they felt they would like to address. Through the consultation process they identified goals. They wrote a community profile in which they looked at Cody—the context of their mission and ministry. They wrote a profile of Christ Church. On the basis of those two documents, they wrote a profile of the type of rector who should be called to serve the congregation. Commenting on the consultation process, K. T. Roes said:

> Once a month for about a nine-month time span, Chuck Wilson came up here. The first weekend he had an all-parish meeting. We had small group meetings between his visits. Everyone who had an interest had a chance to become involved. The process pulled us all together. One of the reasons it worked was that everyone felt they had a say.[43]

If "the proof of the pudding is in the tasting," if the proof of the consultation process is in the match between priest and congregation, then this has been a highly successful process. Many echo Harry Jackson's opinion that in Warren Murphy "We have a perfectly wonderful rector,"[44] and obviously one who is right for the congregation.

"This parish," already one with a great deal of going for it, "is ready to evolve into a new phase. People here want the challenge. They want to do something exciting. I am a believer in putting the Gospel to work outside the parish setting."[45]

Christ Church would like to share its experience with the rest of the Episcopal Church:

> 1. Our experience of how a small congregation in an isolated part of the country can do a first-rate ministry with limited resources;
> 2. How individual members can "be a Christian" by their life examples in the wider community; and

3. Being an inclusive community that reaches out to the needs of community people without all kinds of preconditions.[46]

It's a high calling, but this congregation is well on the way.

## DISTINCTIVE FEATURES

According to Joan Bray, herself a parish consultant in the Diocese of Connecticut,

> This congregation will continue to make a difference in its community. There is rugged individualism here, yet a sense of responsibility and community involvement. There is a clear evidence of prayer life, Scripture reading informing a sense of ministry, . . . a sense that it is God who calls.[47]

Perhaps members of Christ Church might not call it that, but the congregation has, in fact, been doing mission discernment in the community of Cody for quite some time. If one defines mission discernment as simply responding to the question, What are we being called to do in this time and place? individual members through their daily lives, and the congregation as a whole in its ministries, have been living out that answer. They have been discerning their mission and putting it into practice.

- **Varied Congregation:** This is a strong, varied, and interesting congregation. Individual members respect one another, bring out one another's strengths, and work well together. Members allow for differences of opinion and viewpoint. The Wyoming individualistic and independent spirit works well here.
- **Ministry in Daily Life:** Christ Church members have a lively appreciation of being engaged in ministry through the ordinary work of their lives. After visiting a few members of the congregation in their workplaces, Joan Bray concluded that "they don't talk a holy talk, they live holy lives."
- **Meeting Real Needs:** According to Harry Jackson, "Christ Church brings a steadying hand in this community. It brings a sense of pride. Narcotics Anonymous and all those other twelve-step groups meet at the church . . . . We have the

Bargain Box which has always been an Episcopal ministry. There is the Wayfarers' Chapel up at the North Fork . . . .'[48]

And the congregation continues to identify needs. Recycling and sex education are new. Kim Mosar has a phrase on the wall of her office at the Cedar Mountain Center: "To serve others is not a disposable luxury. For an apostle—it is a way of life."

Serving the needs of others is already a way of life for Christ Church members, and it is becoming more so.

- **Education:** Education for Ministry (EFM) has been an important influence in the development of this congregation. An atmosphere in which children are valued participants in the life of the congregation and a strong church school program have attracted new members.
- **Clerical Leadership:** For seventeen years Christ Church was served by a healthy, community-minded priest. Through the work of the Rev. Patterson Keller, the church was kept on a solid foundation, members were helped to understand their ministries, they were challenged and loved. As Hat McGee said, "Pat Keller was a really loving priest who was active in the community and on the school board. Connie [his wife] was also very active."[49] And the tradition of strong clerical leadership continues. Lolly Jolley noted that "In Pat Keller we had a priest who believes in community. Warren Murphy wants to increase that community."[50]

  In both cases, the priest has had a clear sense of ministry. In both cases it has been a good fit between congregation and priest.
- **Search Process:** The experience of this congregation illustrates the importance of the search process. During the interim period the parish was becoming divided. The atmosphere was not good. Members were starting to leave. Fortunately they had the good sense to obtain a professional consultant. The parish, not the diocese, paid for the service. It cost them something, but they wisely considered what might be the consequences if they did not have the "bailout" from the professional consultant. And that's what the Rev. Charles Wilson of CRW Management did initially: he bailed them out. Wilson helped create an environment in the parish that encouraged members to see the interim period as a creative time, a time to talk about

what they would like to do as a community, a time to define some goals, a positive and fruitful time, not a negative one.
- **Public Role:** Looking ahead, members see Christ Church assuming a more public role in the community, and they are enthusiastic about it. The rector, as chair of the Wyoming Church Coalition (WCC), will certainly encourage this development. In this past year the WCC, joining with other groups, has already been successful in lobbying the State Legislature to make Martin Luther King Day an official state holiday. Now the issue of the death penalty is current. People in this congregation feel they can and ought to influence these public matters. As Jane Dominick said, "The issues that face us as a community, face us as a parish."[51] And according to Steve Dunn, "This Church can probably be the spearhead for change in this community."[52]

It's a high-country calling. It's a calling to continue to be the Church in the community.

## RESOURCES

Dozier, Verna J. *The Authority of the Laity.* Washington, DC: Alban Institute, 1982.

Hanchey, Howard. *Christian Education Made Easy.* Wilton, CT: Morehouse-Barlow.

_____. *Creative Christian Education.* Wilton, CT: Morehouse-Barlow, 1986.

Hughes, Caroline, and Westerhoff, John H. *On the Threshold of God's Future.* New York: Harper and Row, 1986.

Kushner, Harold. *When Bad Things Happen to Good People.* New York: Avon Books, 1981; paperback edition, 1983.

Nelson, Gertrude M. *To Dance with God: Family Ritual and Community Celebration.* New York: Paulist Press, 1986.

Russell, Joseph P. *Sharing Our Biblical Story* Wilton, CT: Morehouse-Barlow, Rev. Ed. 1988.

Siegel, Bernie. *Love, Medicine and Miracles.* New York: Harper and Row, 1986.

Westerhoff, John H. *A Pilgram People.* Minneapolis: Winston Press, 1984.

_____. *Bringing Up Children in the Christian Faith.* Minneapolis: Winston Press, 1980.

_____. *Values for Tomorrow's Children.* Philadelphia: Pilgrim Press, 1973.

Wilson, Charles R. *Search*. Arvada, CO: Jethro Publications, 1985. Write to CRW Management Services, 6066 Parfet Street, Arvada, CO 80004.

## NOTES

[1] Bob Ross, interview in Clark's Fork Canyon, Wyoming, September 21, 1990.
[2] *Ibid.*
[3] *Ibid.*
[4] *Ibid.*
[5] *Ibid.*
[6] K.T. Roes, interview in Cody, Wyoming, September 22, 1990.
[7] Tina Jackson, interview in Cody, September 21, 1990.
[8] Hat McGee, interview in Cody, September 22, 1990.
[9] Warren Murphy, addition to the manuscript.
[10] Tina Jackson, interview in Cody, September 21, 1990.
[11] K. T. Roes, interview in Cody, September 22, 1990.
[12] Wallace Stegner, *The American West as Living Space* (Ann Arbor: University of Michigan Press, 1987), pp. 74 and 80.
[13] Hat McGee, interview.
[14] *Ibid.*
[15] Joan Bray, Site Visitor Report, September 24, 1990.
[16] Bob Ross, interview in Clark, Wyoming, September 21, 1990.
[17] K. T. Roes, interview in Cody, September 21, 1990.
[18] Don Kurtz, interview in Cody, September 22, 1990.
[19] Kim Moser, interview in Cody, September 21, 1990.
[20] *Ibid.*
[21] Ann Model, interview in Cody, September 21, 1990.
[22] Harry Jackson, interview in Cody, September 21, 1990.
[23] Harry Jackson, interview in Cody, September 23, 1990.
[24] Douglas Sunderland, interview in Cody, September 22, 1990.
[25] K. T. Roes, interview, September 22, 1990.
[26] Warren Murphy, interview in Cody, September 21, 1990.
[27] Lolly Jolley, interview in Cody, September 22, 1990.
[28] Steve Dunn, interview in Cody, September 22, 1990.
[29] Don Kurtz, interview in Cody, September 22, 1990.
[30] Mary Smith, telephone interview, November 14, 1990.
[31] *Ibid.*
[32] Mary Smith, memo, "Term Two: Thanksgiving/Advent/Christmas," Fall, 1990.

[33] Harry Jackson, interview, September 21, 1990.
[34] K. T. Roes, interview, September 22, 1990.
[35] Steve Dunn, interview.
[36] Mary Smith, interview in Cody, September 23, 1990.
[37] Lolly Jolley, interview.
[38] Steve Dunn, interview.
[39] K. T. Roes, interview, September 22, 1990.
[40] Hat McGee, interview.
[41] *Ibid.*
[42] Charles R. Wilson, *Search* (Arvada, CO: Jethro Publications-CRW Management Services, 1985), p. 1.
[43] K. T. Roes, interview, September 22, 1990.
[44] Harry Jackson, interview, September 21, 1990.
[45] Warren Murphy, interview in Cody, September 21, 1990.
[46] Warren Murphy, from the Site Visit Planning Sheet.
[47] Joan Bray, Site Visitor Report, September 24, 1990.
[48] Harry Jackson, interview, September 21, 1990.
[49] Hat McGee, interview.
[50] Lolly Jolley, interview.
[51] Jane Dominick, interview in Cody, September 21, 1990.
[52] Steve Dunn, interview.

*Visiting Team:* Joan Bray and Mary Hassell
*Date of Visit:* September 21-23, 1990

*We plow the fields and scatter
the good seed on the land,
but it is fed and watered
by God's almighty hand;
God sends the snow in winter,
the warmth to swell the grain,
the breezes and the sunshine,
and soft refreshing rain.*

—The Hymnal 1982
#291 (alt.)

## CHAPTER 13

# SOWING THE SEED YIELDING A HARVEST
### STORY OF A REGIONAL CLUSTER MINISTRY
#### HUDSON VALLEY MINISTRY
#### GREATER NEWBURGH, NEW YORK

## *THE CONTEXT OF MISSION DISCERNMENT: GREATER NEWBURGH*

Not far up the Hudson River from the Big Apple is real apple country. It's apple harvest season in apple country. You can pick your own or stop at any of the innumerable roadside stands for apples of every variety, for fresh apple cider, for squash and plump pumpkins galore. Kurt Borchert, a fruit farmer, who is a member of Christ's Church in Marlboro, says, "We grow apples all right . . . every imaginable kind. We also grow peaches, prunes, pears, strawberries, and cherries."[1]

The lush, tree-covered mountains that rise up from the west bank of the Hudson, the orchards yielding their fall harvests—all might give the impression that the Mid-Hudson region is a quiet pastoral paradise. Until, that is, one realizes that the city of Newburgh—the urban center of this area—ranks high in negative statistics: high in drugs, high in teenage pregnancy, high in numbers of persons with AIDS, high in numbers of the homeless, high in urban decay of all kinds. Until one understands that those who live here suffer much stress and have little time. Until one realizes that former country villages are now bedroom communities where residents may sleep in homes among the apple trees at night, but commute the hour and a half or so every day to the Big Apple, where they are New York City police officers and fire fighters, where they are teachers, businessmen and women, and bankers. David Laubheimer, senior warden of St. Anne's in Washingtonville, commutes daily to the South Bronx, where he is a junior high school teacher. Quite a few also commute to five IBM plants located throughout the area. And some, like Edith Gardner, also a member of St. Anne's, commute to Union Carbide in Danbury, Connecticut.

Orange County, the location of all but one of the six churches that make up the Hudson Valley Ministry (HVM), is a varied region of farming towns, suburban bedroom communities, and an urban center. They all sprawl together, punctuated by highways and shopping malls, fast-food restaurants, gas stations, and convenience stores. As New York City has expanded, more and more people have joined the exodus. Unable to afford the suburbs of Westchester and Rockland counties, they have spilled over into the Newburgh area. Orange County's population jumped 17 percent from 1970 to 1980, and increased by another 13 percent from 1980 to 1990. The striking anomaly, according to Robert Friedrich, who has studied the demographics of the area, is the city of Newburgh itself. It lost 10 percent of its population between 1970 and 1980 and another 11 percent in the next decade.[2]

The population of the city of Newburgh has leveled off now to about 25,000, but its composition has changed from mostly white to 50 percent black and Hispanic. It was once a prosperous town, but half the people now live below the poverty line. Two of the churches that make up the Hudson Valley Ministry are located in Newburgh—St. George's and the Church of the Good Shepherd.

St. George's was considered *the* church of the area, and its members, according to St. George's rector, the Rev. Wayne Schmidt, "held a lot of the wealth of the area."[3] But no more. According to Tess McCracken, the senior warden,

> Those ladies who are members of the world's oldest profession march right by the church parading themselves. They hang out at the corner all the time. Look, this is a rough neighborhood. Some of our members have been knocked out and attacked. They don't want to come in for meetings at night. They're afraid.[4]

The Church of the Good Shepherd was established as a mission of St. George's. It was a parish made up of British workers who came over to work in the Newburgh factories owned by the members of St. George's. According to the Rev. Kevin Coffey, principal pastoral and liturgical leader of the congregation, "It was very much a 'Yes, Father parish.'"[5] And in its hundred years, Good Shepherd has had only three rectors. At one time it had a Sunday school enrollment of 300. But, as Tess McCracken has suggested, the neighborhoods around these parishes have changed drastically. Now almost all of their members drive in to attend church on a Sunday monring, but they are leery of coming in the evening.

New Windsor adjoins Newburgh to the south. It is a suburb of 9,000 people and the location of the Hudson Valley Ministry Office at St. Thomas's Church. Condominiums are springing up alongside suburban subdivisions. The community is growing, and so is the church.

About 10,000 people live in Cornwall, where St. John's is situated. It is an affluent commuter community close to West Point, home of the United States Military Academy. Affluent though it may be, "People are feeling the pinch," according to member Ed Moulton, who is mayor of Cornwall-on-Hudson. "Locals are being forced out. People, particulary retirees, are getting so they can't afford to live here. They're moving south to Florida or north [to more northerly New York counties, which are still affordable]."[6]

Washingtonville, the site of St. Anne's, is, according to the Rev. Linda Strohmier, "a blue-collar town of about 5,000. It is a very Italian, very Roman Catholic area."[7] About 60 percent of the congregation's members are former Roman Catholics.

Christ's Church is in Marlboro, just across the county line into Ulster County. It's on the outer fringe of the Hudson Valley Ministry's area of ministry, and the people feel it. According to the Rev. Nancy Baillie Strong, Christ's Church's principal pastoral leader, "Marlboro is on the fringe and only just beginning to feel incorporated."[8] It is an area filled with people of Italian extraction, whose ancestors established orchards and vineyards like Borchert's Orchards, Kurt Borchert's family farm.

In a way, the Hudson Valley Ministry is like the fruit farm. All kinds and varieties of seeds are being sown in the soil of the five communities that make up the cluster. Seeds of every type of fruit are scattered here—every kind imaginable, as Kurt Borchert says of his apples. Kurt says he directs the acolytes and runs the youth group of his church just the way he runs his farm.

> I run the farm like I run the youth group. It takes patience to run a farm. Working closely with my family takes patience. And you have to keep yourself calm when you're dealing with people. Our fruit pickers come from every place. Right now we have five contract workers from Jamaica. At the farm across the street they're mostly Haitians. Sometimes I can't even understand a word they say. An Italian or a Mexican—they're speaking a whole other language. Even Jamaicans, even though they speak English, you can't understand them. But you know they want something, so you have to help them get it.[9]

And the same could also be said of the Hudson Valley Ministry as a whole. The field is plowed and seeds are scattered. The young plants are pruned and watered and fertilized. Working with the immediate family—the parish church—takes patience. Then there are others—other workers, who may speak a different tongue and are sometimes hard to understand. These others are in different congregations but still of the same farm. Members of the Hudson Valley Ministry, in their diverse ministries, want something, just like Borchert's Orchards' farmers and pickers. Just like farmers, with watchful eyes, with patience, with love and care, members of the Hudson Valley Ministry are beginning to yeild a rich harvest of faithful ministry.

## HUDSON VALLEY MINISTRY TODAY: SOWING THE SEED

Every Tuesday is clericus day for the clergy of the Hudson Valley Ministry. It is the day the ordained leaders who make up the regional ministry gather to talk about the week just passed. They'll discuss how the various meetings and programs went, and perhaps how they could have been better. Any problems that may have come up will be aired. They will discuss how they handled situations, and perhaps how they wished they'd handled them. They will toss ideas about and brainstorm over possibilities for the further development of the ministry they share. The meeting will begin with prayer, and at noon they will pause to celebrate the Eucharist using one of the Supplemental Liturgical Texts, and then continue with Bible study over lunch and on into the afternoon.

On the Tuesday during the Site Visit, the clericus meeting was held at the home of the Rev. Linda Strohmier, the rectory next to St. Thomas Church in New Windsor, and members of the Mission Discernment Project's Visiting Team joined them as they talked about themselves, their parishes, and their ministries.

Mother Strohmier is the program coordinator. It is her responsibility to coordinate the joint activities of the six congregations, and she herself is a program resource to the parishes. According to the Rev. David Stanway, the area missioner,

> Linda brought with her skills from her days of teaching theater and community organization. But most importantly, she brought energy and enthusiasm. She's got so much energy, it just leaks out everywhere. She carries the Holy Spirit in her and breathes it out all over the place.[10]

Mother Strohmier and Father Stanway are the only full-time clergy fully responsible to and paid for by the cluster. Mother Strohmier has pastoral and liturgical responsibility for St. Anne's Church in Washingtonville. St. Anne's, established in 1963, is the youngest of the six congregations. It is also the youngest in terms of the average age of its members. The focus of this 150-member congregation is families. Fifty-eight children are registered for church school. Vicki Richiuso said, "It was my son V.J. who picked St. Anne's. He said they were really friendly and they did fun things. That was four years ago when he was in the first grade."[11] David Laubheimer added, "Anyone who's going to preach here had better be prepared for distractions. We've got an army of 'screaming rug rats.'"[12]

The Rev. J. David Stanway, as area missioner, is responsible for the administrative oversight of the ministry. He is chair of the clericus and works with the vestries of all six congregations. He has pastoral and liturgical responsibility for St. Thomas in New Windsor. This church describes itself as,

> a small church with a big heart. We have only "survived" for several years—however, after becoming a part of the Hudson Valley Ministry and enjoying the Rev. David Stanway as our priest, we have nearly doubled in size . . . . We find joy in new babies, young families and the beginnings of a youth group . . . . We are most thankful that our parish has become much more far-reaching than the faithful who worship here on Sundays.[13]

There are two rectors in the regional ministry, the Rev. Wayne Schmidt, the rector of St. George's in Newburgh, and the Rev. Herman Badecker, the rector of St. John's Church in Cornwall. Both men have been in their parishes for about fourteen years and are supported financially by them. Both describe themselves as generalists, which indeed they have had to be, since theirs were regular one-parish, one-priest ministries until the establishment of the regional structure. Clearly both priests are thriving and are invigorated by the new arrangement. According to Father Schmidt, "I enjoy working with the group. It's new to me and I really enjoy the sharing of talents."[14] Father Badecker says, "I like to emphasize the practical. I like being with clergy who possess skills I don't possess."[15] But his colleagues are quick to point out that the skills he does possess are considerable, particularly his pastoral skills.

The Rev. Kevin Coffey works with the Hudson Valley Ministry as a "contract person" for thirty hours a week. He has pastoral and liturgical responsibility for the Church of the Good Shepherd in Newburgh. He likes these weekly clericus meetings because he has been a priest for only eighteen months and appreciates the help of his more experienced colleagues. At today's clericus meeting he describes how the parish's 100th birthday party went last weekend.

The Rev. Nancy Baillie Strong is also a "contract person," with pastoral and liturgical responsibility for Christ's Church in Marlboro, which she says "is the most charismatic" of the congregations. The parish had experienced rapid growth, then it dropped off. It has been growing again in these last eight months, owing to the stability provided by Mother Strong's leadership and the enrichment of the regional ministry. Both Mother Strong and Father Coffey have young children, who sometimes accompany them on visits to the nursing home to the delight of the residents. The Rev. Deborah Tammearu is also a contract person. She has been working part-time with the Hudson Valley Ministry to assist with education programs.

The clergy spend two-thirds of the year in the churches to which they are assigned, then they rotate to the others for the remaining third, except in Advent and Lent. According to Father Stanway, "Every six weeks we up and move. Every church sees every priest twice a year."[16] In this way, the strengths and skills of the various clergy are passed around. Members of the congregations can get to know them all, which is an advantage because they are bound to establish rapport with some more than others. Lieutenant Colonel Martha Bell, a member of St. John's, said of the arrangement, "I really enjoy having other rectors. I know Father Herman [Badecker, the principal priest in her own parish], but I have appreciated getting to know the other priests, especially the women."[17]

A body known as the Administrative Council acts like a vestry of the shared ministry. It is composed of all the clergy and representatives of the six churches, and is chaired by Father Stanway. There is also a Program Council, likewise composed of members of the six congregations. It is chaired by Mother Strohmier and is responsible for developing and planning the joint programs of the area ministry.

In 1989, the Program Council planned a joint Epiphany celebration. An original clown play, *The Visit of the Three Wise Guys,* was performed by minstrels and troubadors from five of the six parishes. Christmas trees from all six parishes made one huge bonfire, which lit up the valley. A festive supper followed.

On Holy Saturday, ninety children came together to experience in their own way the events of Holy Week. Jesus arrived on a very friendly and pattable donkey to a chorus of whistles, kazoos, and bells. This Last Supper consisted of tuna and peanut butter sandwiches as well as foot washing. The crucifixion was experienced in a darkened church. Jesus' resurrection was announced by trumpets, sunlight, Alleluias, and joy as the papers covering the windows were suddenly pulled down, flooding the whole space with light. During the day, the children made processional crosses for the congregations' two combined Easter vigils, and Easter communion bread for all six churches.[18]

A publication of the Hudson Valley Ministry describes the practical benefits of this style of ministry:

> These special events begin to show us the strength of area ministry: events impossible in just one small (or even medium-sized) church can happen as we work together. A newly-established youth group has bloomed . . . . Church school teachers meet together to support each other's ministries and plan ways to enhance local and area programs.
>
> Individuals and congregations are beginning to ask for programs they need and want. A weekly daytime Bible study will be joined this year by one or more evening Bible groups. Stewardship and new-member ministry programs are being developed at an area level. A singles group is in the planning stages, and special plans for health care workers are being developed.[19]

Reflecting on the energy that is erupting in the six congregations, Edith Gardner, former senior warden of St. Anne's Church, probably voices the sentiments of many:

> There is so much going on in the churches. There's something for everybody here. We go to the various functions all over the place. A service one place, a dance in another . . . . This is a beautiful concept and it's really working.[20]

In all the ministries of the Hudson Valley Ministry, as well as in the life of the individual congregations, which is also being enriched, Christian community is being developed and nurtured. But the acid test of all ministry is how it is carried out in the lives of the Church's primary ministers—its laity—in the ordinary structures of their day-to-day lives. Leaders in the Hudson Valley Ministry understand this and are beginning to address it. In the planning stage are "vocation days," during which members of various vocational groups will gather together to discuss "the spirituality, the sacrifice and the witness of their daily ministries . . . and to pray together for strength and support."[21] In announcing the vocation days, the HVM reminds its members, "'Vocation' isn't just a calling to ordination—every Christian is called to some particular task in life. Part of the work of the Church is to help its members identify their vocations, their ministries. Another part is to strengthen and support those members in their vocations."[22] Since there are a large number of teachers and health-care workers among HVM parishes, the first two vocation days are for them. According to the Rev. Linda Strohmier, "We're moving from lay ministry as something we do in church to lay ministry as something we do in our lives."[23]

Several members of HVM congregations discussed their daily work and the meaning of their ministries with members of the Mission Discernment Project Team. Others, such as Martha Bell and her family, who are members of St. John's in Cornwall, discussed why they are Episcopalians.

Martha is a lieutenant colonel in the U.S. Army. She is chief of the Department of Nursing at the sixty-five-bed Keller Army Community Hospital at the U.S. Military Academy at West Point. It is her task to supervise the 150-member nursing staff of the hospital, which serves West Point cadets and other members of the military community in the West Point general area. She and her husband, Dick, an instructor at the College of Aeronautics in New York City, are the parents of two school-age daughters. Martha spent one year in Vietnam and is concerned for three members of her department who "have their feet planted in the sand in Saudi Arabia, and are dealing with snakes, scorpions and camels wandering through their camps and spitting on them."[24] Martha is a former Roman Catholic who had been away from the Church for a while, but came back when she and her husband felt they should do something about the Christian nurture of their daughters.

Along the way we had become disenchanted with the Roman Catholic Church. It wasn't meeting the needs we had at the time. It wasn't helping me the year I was in Vietnam (which proved significant because that's where I met my husband). Actually neither of us felt the need to become closer to a church.

Then we started to have children. Our first daughter came along five and a half years after we got married, and she was baptized here at West Point in the Roman Catholic Chapel. Our other daughter was born five and a half years later, when we were in Alaska, and she too was baptized by a Roman Catholic priest. Even though I'd left the religion my folks raised me in, I still felt that it was an enormously important foundation, and Dick [son of a Methodist pastor] never felt comfortable with the Roman Catholic Church. He tried. Actually we both tried. We did from time to time go to church, but it just wasn't clicking. By the time we got to Fort Sam Houston [in San Antonio] in 1983 we felt we should do something about church for the children.

Our oldest daughter was in the first grade, and we were feeling the need to have some structure for her. I remember vividly the day. It was the Memorial Day they buried the Vietnam Unknown Soldier, so it was a significant watershed for both of us. So I said, "Well, Dick, I'm going to go to church." And I went to church—the Roman Catholic Church. And on that Sunday we prayed for migrant workers, we prayed for homeless people, for welfare mothers. We prayed for everybody except those in the armed forces, and this is not right. So I went home and said to Dick, "I'm never going to church again. I'm not going back because it just isn't right."

At the time I was working with a young man, and I told him how I felt about the service. He and his wife are close friends. Terry said, "Well, Marilyn and I went through this. She came from one religion and I came from another, and somehow we started going to the Episcopal Church. Why don't you just try it?" So we went with them to St. Luke's in San Antonio. We hauled the kids. We walked in, and an extraordinary thing happened to us. Someone actually introduced themselves to us and said, "I'm Linda Meyer. Welcome to our church." And during the service, when it was obvious that neither Dick nor I knew what the heck was going on, Linda guided us through the Prayer Book so we could follow it. She did the same with the hymnal. I mean they were really friendly, which was completely different than what I'd experienced in the Roman Church. There I never had anyone talk to me at a service. Never, ever. Another lady introduced herself to us and invited us to the coffee hour. Again, another completely new experience for us.

The next Sunday we went was the Sunday closest to the Fourth of July, and at the end of the service the last hymn sung was the National Anthem, and as I closed my hymnal I said Dick, "We have found our church."[25]

It was a thrilling discovery. They ultimately chose to attend St. John's Episcopal Church in San Antonio. The children greatly enjoyed the Sunday school, and their parents the adult education classes. The following November, Dick was confirmed and Martha received into the Episcopal Church. Dick joined a men's group. Martha joined a committee to develop a new-member ministry in the parish.

We just enjoyed being back in church again. We just basked in the fact of how nice it was to be able to go back to church again. There were people there who knew us, who wanted to get to know us, and who always welcomed us, even though it was a big church.[26]

What Martha has needed from her local church is support for her role in the military. She feels that she has found it, both in San Antonio and at St. John's in Cornwall, where the whole family is very active. Her faith governs every aspect of her work with staff and patients. Ever since mid-August, when the first troops started arriving in Saudi Arabia, Martha has written her former colleagues and enclosed small gifts to them. This week it's Kool Aid packets to "spike" canteen water and pressed autumn maple leaves to remind them of autumn in New York State.

Barbara Hynes takes pride in the accomplishments of Lieutenant Colonel Bell because she was her nursing instructor. Barbara, a member of St. George's in Newburgh, is semi-retired and works as an on-call hospice nurse.

> I have a special commitment to nursing. It's *caring* as distinct from curing. By the time you get to hospice, medicines have failed. But that's the point at which our loving and caring comes in. I usually do not know the people . . . I will visit in their homes, and I always say a prayer as I enter the home. I wouldn't impose prayer on the family, but I need it because I never know just what I'm walking into.[27]

Barbara recounted the story of one case on which she felt her ministry was particularly appreciated:

> On many of my nighttime visits to attend the death of a hospice patient, I have become increasingly concerned about the experience of young males in the family. On one such visit to a Hispanic family where the father had died, I found myself immediately involved with the wife who was crying but coping and then each of the three daughters who were crying and comforting each other and the mother in turn. The home was a trailer with a bedroom at each end and an open kitchen/living room area in the center of the trailer. The father was in the bedroom at the end of the trailer. A son in his late twenties sat quietly in the living room not talking with anyone. It was about 4:00 a.m., and we were waiting for the arrival of the funeral director. From time to time one of the daughters or the mother would go back to the

bedroom for another look or a "good-bye" to the father.

Finally the son got up and went quietly by himself down the narrow hall to the bedroom. Suddenly we heard the loudest, most terrible wailing coming from the room. A daughter jumped to run in, but I stopped her and said, "No, let him be."

The funeral director came. The son came out into the living room. What we usually do at this time is have the family go into another room as the body is removed. So the family went into the other bedroom. But the son came out into the living area where I was moving furniture to allow better access to the door. He asked me if the body would be removed in a bag. I answered, "yes." He then said to me, "I carried body bags in the service." As the funeral directors came out with the body, the son immediately assisted them all the way out to the car. I knew from then on that he could assume his masculine role throughout the coming days for his family. Somehow I felt he had grown in those moments.

Young men seem lost at these times. You cannot approach them directly. They simply move away. However during quiet moments they will usually talk to me when we are alone.[28]

Army Captain Kathy Coffey is the organist at St. Thomas in New Windsor. She and her husband, Kevin, the principal priest at Good Shepherd, are the parents of a three-year-old son and an eight-year-old daughter. She teaches English at West Point. Kathy feels privileged to be teaching "future leaders in America." Marriage and family are important to her, as are the unique demands the military makes on marriage and family. Helping cadets deal with these issues of life and lifestyle is a ministry to her. She shared her views with members of the Visiting Team:

The personal essay is part of the English course I teach to the plebes. A lot of them come to the Academy with strong opinions, but when you start questioning they're not really sure *why* they believe. They know *what* they believe, but they don't know why. No one's ever asked them or ever pushed them for an answer. So the personal essay gives them an opportunity to look at themselves. Ours is one of the few courses at the Academy that doesn't pretend to give answers. Cadets like to have everything wrapped up in nice packages. You do X, Y, and Z, and you'll get this result and be a success. But life's not quite that neat. So our course forces them to look at issues in a different way, and they see that everything isn't always tied up with the yellow ribbon at the end.

My role in that, besides getting themselves in touch with themselves, is very often that of listener. By . . . [writing] about personal experience, they often reveal themselves to us in ways that they would never . . . [do] to another person at the Academy. So I find out about their personal hurts and struggles. Often their writing doesn't improve, but they leave my office feeling better from having someone listen to them. So I try to give a listening ear.

Outside the classroom we have the Mentors' Program. Many of them are away from home for the first time. Life at the Academy is very regimented. They're not encouraged to express feelings, but they're supposed to—as they say—"suck it down," no matter how tough things get, don't show that emotion. I see part of my role there as showing them that sometimes you can't do it by yourself and you need to learn to evaluate what your strengths are and when you need help and not to be afraid to ask for that kind of help. The way we do that is to bring cadets into our homes so they get a chance to see us in a different dimension, not just the Army officer, not just the instructor in the classroom, but as a wife, as a mother, as a friend, so they can see how we work through some of our own family situations. It's important for them to see how you balance family and work, family and military. Some of these relations are mostly social, but there is a young woman in her second year with whom I've really become a friend. I am an officer but in some way a surrogate mother to her. I am someone she knows she can talk to when she has problems. Anytime the cadets reveal problems or concerns, I have contacts and can plug them in to someone who can help them if the problem's beyond something I can deal with myself. So that's how I see myself helping plebes.

I feel very strongly that they need to develop their values, to recognize what their values are. By doing Church History [as part of an advanced composition course on the literature of the Middle Ages] it gives them the opportunity to see how other people have developed values. How to judge, how to evaluate, etc. Soon we're going to move into the Sir Thomas More-Henry VIII dilemma. We're going to look at Sir Thomas as one who knew what he believed and was willing to die for it, because I think that's what our leaders need. Not just our military leaders, but *especially* our military leaders. To believe something, to know why they believe it, and what they're willing to do.

It's grueling—the preparation, the hours I spend with them . . . . It's draining, becoming part of their personal lives and personal hurts. But it's my ministry. People at the church sustain me by asking "How are you doing?" They care, and that really matters to me.[29]

Albert MacDowell is an attorney who was formerly a judge in the city of Newburgh. He practices law from a Christian perspective. He is also a member of the Church of the Good Shepherd, where he is the treasurer.

I'm a lawyer. For years I practiced in everything. For seven years I was acting city judge of Newburgh. For three years I was the judge. When I ran myself, I won against a guy who had never lost an election. I felt I did it . . . [because of] the value system I have. The people in the city want justice. I took the position that the poor shouldn't be locked up just because they're the accused. You see, the police like to feel someone gets punished. In law work, if you don't have a set of values, it's really hard to practice. You can read all the books and all the law, but they're not a set of values. For values you depend upon your church. Law is a business of trust and confidence, and in most situations all people understand is "Did I win?" or "Did I lose?" So I have an opportunity for Christian living every day in a quiet way. It gives me a good feeling at the end of the day when I feel I've done the right thing in each case.

What we deal with in the courts is unbelievable—drugs, murder, you name it. We see life at its happiest and at its saddest. Homelessness, abuse of women, abuse of neighbors. Then, of course, there are the traffic tickets. The light was yellow, wasn't it?!!

Newburgh is an experience in itself! One of the interesting things is that when you're in public life you get a certain view of the world. But you can be in private life and never see that other world. I live in the city. It's not a safe place. In 1983 my wife and I were attacked on our own front porch. My wife got her shoulder broken. It's dangerous all right. Look, I stay because they're not going to chase me out of my city. But I'm not mad at the people. I wasn't even mad at the person who attacked me. I look at this as society's problem. If they're mental cases, we [society] should have done something for them and not let them drift into situations where they have nowhere to go. If they're drug cases, we should have gotten them help. If they need employment, what can I say? . . . I look at the attack on my wife and myself as a part of the larger situation. What society needs is more prevention, not more punishments.

I'm being candid. When they [the defendants] were standing in front of me in the courtroom, I was with them. You see, the poor in the city never felt they got equal justice. I made it a point to always give everyone equal justice, irrespective of their backgrounds. I remember when I sentenced a black man to jail for fifteen days and his wife came up and thanked me, because she saw a white man sentenced that same day for the same charge for the same fifteen days. I had no double standard. To this day—and it was fifteen years ago when I was a judge—people stop me in the street and say, "Thank you."

But even in my law practice, I have the same opportunity to carry out my value system every day. There's too much you can do with the legal system to pervert justice, even in small ways, so it's up to the individuals involved—the lawyers—to do the fair thing. I feel that right is right and wrong is wrong. There's a lot you can do in the legal system if you want to practice your value system.[30]

Linda Muller, a member of St. John's Church, is director of the Red Cross in Goshen, New York. It's an agency with 126 programs and 700 volunteers. She chose this work after leaving a high-level management position in business. She has never regretted the decision.

I think God placed me here. I certainly don't do it for money. I mean it when I say that every day when I get home I have the knowledge that I somehow affected someone else's life in a positive way. I care for my fellow neighbor, I care to make a difference.

We need to get people out of the church and get them into the city of Newburgh. It's just seven and a half miles down the road, and we have to go into that other world and help the people. AIDS is a tremendous problem. It's one problem of many. We need to talk to kids. We have to be role models. We need to talk about alternatives. We need to offer hope. People need to see a way out. We need to make the connections and illustrate that the Church cares about the lives of people."[31]

Finally, Marianne Laurencell, a fifteen-year-old high school student who is a member of St. Anne's, says, "A lot of the churches talk about the future. But we're talking about youth now. We're talking about the Church of the present. We're talking about now."[32]

## UNDERSTANDING THE STORY

In Linda Muller's opinion,

> Cluster ministry is probably the greatest thing since motherhood and apple pie. We are a family of churches and a family of priests, and when your priest is on vacation—I know Linda Strohmier and I know Father Stanway and I know Herman, and I am comfortable to pick up the phone and say "help" to any of them. That's important to us.[33]

She is obviously sold on the concept of regional ministry. So is Ed Moulton, who like Linda is a member of St. John's in Cornwall. Their priest was one of the old-timers in the area from before the cluster was formed, and according to Ed, "Our rector has been re-energized and he brings it back to us."[34] And thus has the congregation become energized.

Edith Gardner of St. Anne's likes the arrangement for another reason. "Let me tell you—two and a half years as senior warden with no rector is no joke. It's very hard work."[35] And St. Anne's current senior warden, David Laubheimer, adds,

> The years Edith had to go through—this will never happen again. I'd like to see other churches go the same way. Regional ministry is good for the people, it's good for the community, it's good for the clergy.[36]

The Hudson Valley Ministry began in February, 1986, when Archdeacon Robert Willing invited the clergy of the area parishes to a meeting to discuss the concept. He indicated that within the archdeaconry the focus of late had been on planning and commissioning area approaches for the development of the mission of the Church. He assured them that he had no master plan in mind but rather a

> ... sincere interest in determining if: a) some sort of cooperative approach to ministry could become a reality, and b) if there are ventures in mission that we ought to be doing if we are not just to survive but grow.[37]

Then a study of the demographics of the Greater Newburgh communities was done, along with an analysis of ten Episcopal churches within the region.

In September, 1986, the vestries, wardens, and clergy of the ten parishes were invited by Archdeacon Willing to a joint meeting. Again they were reminded that the process was still "in an exploratory stage," and that

> the purpose of this meeting will be to assess parish strengths and needs, and to explore those avenues of ministry that can more efficiently be done in a collaborative fashion for the benefit of the mission of the church . . . . The primary focus will be to discover if God is calling us to an area approach for the development of mission and ministry.[38]

Clergy and vestries continued the discussion in their own congregations. Everyone had both time and opportunity to ask questions and to talk about the pros and cons of regional ministry. Will my parish lose its individual identity? If we have to share our priest with other congregations, won't that be our loss? But also they asked themselves, What can a group of congregations do that would be impossible for just our small parish to do by itself? Could a cluster get a youth group going, even though our own parish really doesn't have enough kids for one? Naturally they tried to visualize how regional ministry would work. They looked at models and examples that were already working. The Rev. David Stanway, coordinator of Tri-County Episcopal Ministry (TEAM), came to a meeting in March of 1987 to talk about TEAM and show slides of the five-congregation cluster he coordinated.

Ultimately six of the ten congregations decided to join the cluster, and a five-year cooperative plan was adopted by the parishes involved. They are a diverse group. Two of the parishes are urban, three are in small towns, and one is in a country village. In February, 1989—exactly three years after the first meeting to consider regional ministry was called—the Rev. David Stanway was hired as coordinator of the Hudson Valley Ministry. Three years from the inception of the idea to bringing the first staff person on board sounds like a long time, but as Father Stanway, a veteran of eighteen years of cooperative ministries in his native Canada and New York, emphasized, thoroughness and solid groundwork are of the utmost importance in developing regional ministry.

> It takes just that long for all the congregations to get everything "up front" that needs to get "up front." It takes just that long to deal with all the issues. If you don't do it right, if you don't take the necessary time someone's going to feel angry and left out.[39]

Stanway joined the two clergy who were already in the area, the Rev. Herman Badecker and the Rev. Wayne Schmidt. And they set about completing the building of the clerical team. Later in 1989 the Rev. Linda Strohmier arrived as program coordinator, and the Rev. Kevin Coffey joined them. The team was completed in January, 1990, with the addition of the Rev. Nancy Baillie Strong.

Growing into the concept of cluster ministry, even after it became official, has taken some time. But Nancy Strong, who is the principal priest at the most northerly parish, in Marlboro, says, "It was a little slow, but Christ's Church people are beginning to feel incorporated."[40] For the members of St. George's in Newburgh the benefits of the cluster became easily apparent last summer with the illness of the rector. As Tess McCracken explains, "Personally I was always enthusiastic, but not all of St. George's members thought it was so great. But then Father Schmidt was out sick for three months. You know there were weddings scheduled, there were all the regular services .... It would have been rough without the cluster, but as it turned out, not a single wedding had to be canceled."[41]

As the congregations grow into a regional identity, most of them are also coming into a greater appreciation of their own identities as parishes. In addition, according to David Laubheimer, the cluster has provided a sense of security and support so that "we're not worried about our survival needs any more. We're all in this together."[42] And they are growing. St. Thomas Church used to have fifteen people in the congregation on a good Sunday; now there are at least forty-five. Attendance is up 50 percent in Christ's Church, Marlboro. It's up by 25 to 30 percent in Washingtonville. The other congregations are holding their own.

The area ministry has given the confidence of laity and clergy alike a big boost. The clergy do not feel isolated. The laity feel empowered. Edith Gardner reflected:

> I remember when we were first talking about regional ministry. Some of the people were saying that they wouldn't have a pastor anymore. That was four years ago, when each parish had its own priest. Well, it just wouldn't work that way anymore. We could never go back. Now, the laity make a lot of decisions. They don't just say "Yes, Father," "Yes, Mother," the way they used to. We're not running a kindergarten anymore.[43]

With energy, stability, confidence, enjoying the increasingly rich harvest of ministry the members of Hudson Valley Ministry would like to do more in the communities around them. As Ed Moulton said,

> We've been together for just over a year. And look how much has been done! As a group we have so much more strength. Now I'd like to see us do more collective good as a group. We have the poor here, homelessness . . . . I'd like to see the churches sponsor some housing. We have a couple of spare acres right next to our church.[44]

In the fertile field that is the Hudson Valley Ministry, rich and delicious fruits are coming to harvest. And the concept of regional ministry is growing as others see and taste those fruits. Seeds continue to be sown. In 1981 there were four area ministries in the Northeast. Now there are fifty-one. Is regional ministry a wave of the future?

# *DISTINCTIVE FEATURES*

"The Hudson Valley Ministry," in the words of the Rev. John Rollins, Mission Discernment Project Site Visitor from New Jersey, "is an exuberant example of how a group of parishes can mobilize for ministry using a 'group practice' of talented clergy and the resources of gifted lay persons. Such a model can work especially well in urban or suburban settings. Of great value are the opportunities for lay persons to discover ministries in every facet of their lives and for clergy to work in a collegial style which shares their strengths in a much wider setting."[45]

It's an arrangement in which everyone benefits. As Joan Irving, a member of the Total Ministry Task Force, observed:

> The clergy are committed to *developing* ministry (within the people of God), not just *delivering* ministry (to the people of God).
>
> Clergy benefit from the collegiality and mutual support. They are able to use their own special gifts and also tap into each other's. They are able to be away for emergencies and times of personal growth.
>
> Many of the laity already had a sense of their ministry before the cluster. Some have a clear sense of ministry in the world and are very articulate! This will surely rub off on others.
>
> The parishes are developing a real sense of communal financial commitment. There are beginning signs of the realization that the parishes have a ministry in the community around them (not just individual laity but the parish as a whole reaching out).[46]

Other factors that contribute to the shaping and the success of this model are the following:

- ***Leadership Academy for New Directions (LAND) and the Example of Others:*** The Rev. David Stanway gives credit to LAND and those associated with it, who modeled a style of ministry different from what was usual in the Episcopal Church:

I was influenced by Boone Porter and Charles Winters. Winters was the resident theologian for New Directions. I first went to New Directions in 1975, where I met Bob Willing [currently archdeacon for the Mid-Hudson Region of the Diocese of New York and grandfather of this and several other regional ministries].

At LAND I met a wonderful person, David Brown from the Northeast Kingdom of Vermont [the congregations in the northeast corner of Vermont]. He has to be considered one of the pioneers in area ministry. I was just over the border and had more than a little interest in learning about how David set up a cluster ministry. There I was in the Province of Quebec with six congregations and me—the only ordained person. Do you think I was going crazy?

So we raised up lay pastors. I deliberately use the phrase "lay pastor," because it was they who did the pastoring. Now that's about as Roland Allen a concept as you can get! And you know something? Those places began to grow without the benefit of a resident priest.[47]

- **Careful Planning:** It took three years to plan the Hudson Valley Ministry. That much time was needed to do a demographic study of the area and a study of the Episcopal congregations, to present and discuss the concept in all the parishes, to look at clusters that were already established and working. It took that much time to take account of people's feelings and finally to create the structure for the cluster and obtain the required clerical leadership. Careful planning and no shortcuts—these are key.
- **Diocesan Support:** The initiative and the support for the establishment of the Hudson Valley Ministry was provided by Archdeacon Willing, who continues to guide it through its formation stages.
- **Congregations Chose the Cluster; It Was Not Chosen for Them:** The congregations were given a genuine choice of whether or not they wished to join the regional ministry, and indeed four of those originally approached decided against join-

ing. They were not forced into it by the diocese, or even by finances (although the cluster makes sense economically).

- *Beyond Survival:* A congregation concerned with just keeping its doors open or paying the priest is not likely to have a very productive ministry. A number of people mentioned this factor to the Visiting Team. The pooling of resources and the mutual support of parishes had freed members to look at the ministries and mission of the congregations in the town or city in which they are located.
- *Multiplication of Opportunities:* Training for specific ministries, adult education, new member strategies, stewardship, youth ministry—numbers might preclude a single parish from organizing a full program of such events and opportunities, but more is possible in a group of congregations.
- *Evaluation:* Programs, goals, and clergy are evaluated yearly. This keeps both clergy and congregations on track.
- *Broad View:* As the member congregations continue to live the concept of a shared ministry and mission across a region, they will be more inclined to look at the area as a whole, determine its needs, and work towards meeting those needs. Housing has been targeted as a need, as has Hispanic ministry.

## NOTES

[1] Kurt Borchert, interview at Borchert Farms, Marlboro, October 2, 1990.
[2] Robert E. Friedrich, Jr., "The Greater Newburgh Area Study," September 11, 1986, p. 2.
[3] Wayne Schmidt, interview in New Windsor, October 2, 1990.
[4] Tess McCracken, interview in Washingtonville, October 2, 1990.
[5] Kevin Coffey, interview in New Windsor, October 2, 1990.
[6] Ed Moulton, interview in Washingtonville, October 2, 1990.
[7] Linda Strohmier, interview in New Windsor, October 2, 1990.
[8] Nancy Baillie Strong, interview in New Windsor, October 2, 1990.
[9] Kurt Borchert, interview in Marlboro, October 2, 1990.
[10] David Stanway, interview in New Windsor, October 2, 1990.
[11] Vicki Richiuso, interview in Washingtonville, October 2, 1990.
[13] "Hudson Valley I.P.C.," a flier, p. 3.
[14] Wayne Schmidt, interview in New Windsor, October 2, 1990.
[15] Herman Badecker, interview in New Windsor, October 2, 1990.

[16] David Stanway, quoted in "Six Epsicopalian Churches Unite," *Mid Hudson Times,* September 26, 1990, p. 18.
[17] Martha Bell, interview at West Point, October 2, 1990.
[18] "Hudson Valley Program Life," flier, p. 4.
[19] *Ibid.*
[20] Edith Gardner, interview in Washingtonville, October 2, 1990.
[21] "Program News from HVM," an insert in the Sunday bulletins of the six parishes of the cluster, September 30, 1990.
[22] *Ibid.*
[23] Linda Strohmier, interview in Washingtonville, October 2, 1990.
[24] Martha Bell, interview at West Point, October 2, 1990.
[25] *Ibid.*
[26] *Ibid.*
[27] Barbara Hynes, interview in New Windsor, October 2, 1990.
[28] Barbara Hynes, "Hospice Story," fax, October 2, 1990.
[29] Kathy Coffey, interview in New Windsor, October 2, 1990.
[30] Albert MacDowell, interview in New Windsor, October 2, 1990.
[31] Linda Muller, interview in New Windsor, October 2, 1990.
[32] Marianne Laurencell, interview in New Windsor, October 2, 1990.
[33] Linda Muller, interview.
[34] Ed Moulton, interview.
[35] Edith Gardner, interview in Washingtonville, October 2, 1990.
[36] David Laubheimer, interview.
[37] Robert N. Willing, correspondence, February 18, 1986.
[38] Robert N. Willing, correspondence, September 11, 1986.
[39] David Stanway, interview in New Windsor, October 3, 1990.
[40] Nancy Baillie Strong, interview.
[41] Tess McCracken, interview in New Windsor, October 2, 1990.
[42] David Laubheimer, interview.
[43] Edith Gardner, interview.
[44] Ed Moulton, interview.
[45] John A. Rollins, Site Visitor Report.
[46] Joan Irving, Site Visitor Report.
[47] David Stanway, interview, October 3, 1990.

*Visiting Team:* The Rev. Dr. John T. Docker, Joan Irving, and the Rev. John A. Rollins
*Date of Visit:* October 2, 1990

*In every insult,
rift and war
where color,
scorn or wealth divide,
Christ suffers still,
yet loves the more,
and lives though ever crucified.*
—Brian A. Wren,
Hymnal 1982

## CHAPTER 14

# FAITH UNDER FIRE— A WITNESS OF HOPE

## STORY OF TWO CONGREGATIONS STAYING FAITHFUL IN A COUNTRY AT WAR WITH ITSELF

### CONGREGACIÓN SAN JUAN EVANGELISTA, SAN SALVADOR, AND CONGREGACIÓN SANTA MARÍA VIRGEN, ILOPANGO

### *THE CONTEXT OF MISSION DISCERNMENT: EL SALVADOR*

"Don't worry about the bombs you'll hear tonight," Ana Gómez assured Mission Discernment Project Site Visitors as she dropped them off at their hotel. "There's shooting every night. You'll get used to it."[1]

The atmosphere is tense. Army soldiers, dressed in camouflage fatigues, their fingers on the trigger of their assault rifles, are everywhere—on every street corner, patroling every block, standing watch behind makeshift sandbag barriers, poised in sentry towers, being transported through the city streets in the back of trucks. Looking closely into their dark eyes one notices a look of impending danger. Their youthful faces—many are only teenagers—are drawn. For these youngsters, participation in the regular army is compulsory. Garrisons "recruit" troops by carrying out sweeps through residential neighborhoods, rounding up boys as young as fifteen from bus stops and movie theaters and inducting them.

Right now the young soldiers are particularly jumpy, and for good reason. Just the week before, the FMLN (Farabundo Martí National Liberation Front) guerrilla units had assaulted several military installations in their campaign to push the government into serious negotiations with the FMLN. The United Nations-mediated peace talks between the government and the military on one side and the FMLN on the other are at a stalemate.

After over ten years of bitter fighting and 72,000 dead, both sides are tired of war. All the people of El Salvador are tired of living in fear in this militarized society. They have had enough.

El Salvador, the smallest Central American country (the size of Massachusetts), is the most densely populated country of the region, with a population of six million people. About one million Salvadoran refugees live outside the country (in the United States, Canada, Sweden, and Australia).

When the Spanish arrived to claim El Salvador in 1524, they found Indians of Mayan descent living peacefully on the fertile volanic plateau 2,000 feet above sea level. They were growing a wide variety of crops: beans, pumpkins, chilis, avocados, corn, guavas, papayas, tomatoes, cacao, cotton, tobacco, henequen, indigo, maguey, and elderberries.

In the first century of Spanish rule, 80 percent of the indigenous people died or were killed, along with many of the crops. Today the big three plantation crops—coffee, sugarcane, and cotton—dominate agriculture. Over 40 percent of the rural population are landless, and some 70 percent live in extreme poverty.

When Central America declared its independence from Spain in 1821, the large landowners formed the nucleus of El Salvador's oligarchy. By the 1880s, a second generation of immigrant coffee planters had added their names to the tightly knit group that held most of the country's arable land in its clutches.

El Salvador's coffee oligarchy moved rapidly in 1881 to privatize all communally held Indian lands; this increased the polarization between wealth and poverty. Peasant revolts broke out in 1880, 1885, and 1898.

To ensure and maintain control, the oligarchy began to build up the armed forces. In 1882, a rural police force was created. In 1890, a military school was opened. In 1912, the government created the National Guard, a special security force, to enforce the landlords' law.

When the depression of 1929 put El Salvador's ruling oligarchy in crisis, they turned to the military for help. In 1931, under increasingly deteriorating conditions, the army crushed a peasant revolt, killing 30,000 campesinos (peasants). Their power, based on force and shared with the ruling class, has continued unabated into the present. The army maintains order through force and political domination; the landed elite maintains control of the economy.

But this situation has gotten increasingly out of hand in this last decade. In 1980, the Salvadoran Army, Air Force, and Navy numbered 12,000. By 1990, they had grown to 55,000—even more if one counts the security and paramilitary organizations that operate under military authority.

Also linked to the Army are 11,000 Salvadoran police (National Police, Treasury Police, and the National Guard) and "security forces." These groups have a long and well-documented record of human-rights abuses. They patrol the countryside, provide intelligence networks, and constitute the nighttime death squads.

Recognizing that the war in El Salvador has its roots in poverty and repression, successive U.S. administrations have attempted to introduce moderate political and economic reforms. Washington sent military advisers to El Salvador to train the Army to function as professionals and to foster respect for human rights. Convinced that El Salvador was the front line in the battle against Communism, Congress overlooked the thousands of human-rights abuses and in the last decade poured at least $4 billion into the country, more than into any other nation in the hemisphere.

On the other side has been the FMLN—the Farabundo Martí National Liberation Front—a coalition of five political-military organizations which came together just as the country's social and political polarization was about to explode into civil war. Its decision to wage an armed struggle, along with political organizing, came after two decades of attempts to secure economic and political reform and a genuinely democratic government. Many have joined the FMLN after seeing their loved ones carried off and killed by the armed forces.

Completely polarized, Salvadorans of every political stripe live in fear, waiting for violence to erupt at any moment without warning.

A U.S. news correspondent says that El Salvador is the single most dangerous assignment in the world. Thirty members of the press corps have been killed in the last decade. He himself knows that his telephone is often bugged. One feels the tension in him. Before talking, he peers about to see who may be lurking around, then he speaks in whispered tones. A Salvadoran woman, one of the thousands who have fled their villages and joined the company of the displaced in San Salvador, will share her experiences with Site Visitors only if her name is not used. The same with a trade union official. They also talk in hushed tones in "safe" locations. A prominent business executive is also afraid. He scans the street and sidewalk before he gets out of his car to enter a restaurant. The car is a small, understated sedan with the windows blackened all around, except for a narrow band across the windshield. Many of his class routinely carry revolvers in shoulder holsters, which they feel they need to protect themselves.

In spite of it all, Salvadorans go about their daily rounds. Always the fear is there, but also the singing, the dancing, the laughter, the defiance of death. As the echo of bombs pierces the still December evening, they turn up the volume in the downtown discos. "Feliz Navidad, Feliz Navidad. We want to wish you a M-e-r-r-y Christmas" booms out of the speakers. "We get used to heavy bombs going off every night. People have to live their lives. We learn not to worry about tomorrow. We just try to live fully today,"[2] as one Episcopal Church official remarked.

In September, 1988, under the auspices of the Roman Catholic Church, some sixty-three grassroots organizations representing peasants, labor, students, and churches joined forces to press for a solution to the war. This coalition, the Permanent Commission for the National Debate for Peace in El Salvador, could be very influential.

On April 4, 1990, representatives of the Salvadoran government and the FMLN met in Geneva and formally committed themselves to United Nations-mediated negotiations to end the war. In September, 1990, the U.S. Congress voted overwhelmingly to halve U.S. military aid to El Salvador and to encourage a negotiated settlement.

These are all positive steps, yet the going is not smooth. The 1980 murder of Archbishop Oscar Romero is still unsolved, as are the 1989 murders of the six Jesuits and their helpers, to say nothing of the 72,000 other deaths in the intervening years. The Army is still out of hand. But the people are hopeful and expectant and joyful. The Church is hopeful, expectant, and joyful.

The churches support the peace talks. The various political parties have signed joint documents in support of a political solution. Trade unions across the political spectrum have united in a call for a negotiated solution to the conflict. Throughout El Salvador, the pressure for results is on. There is an increasing willingness to address the issues of democracy, the role of the military, and the economic development problems that underlie the military and social conflict.

In El Salvador, people know what it costs to be faithful to Jesus Christ. Their stories are real and immediate. El Salvador is the land of martyrs and saints, of witnesses and confessors. El Salvador—the Savior.[3]

## *THE EPISCOPAL CHURCH IN EL SALVADOR*

The Episcopal Church's first real presence in El Salvador began in 1957 with the establishment of the Mission of St. John the Evangelist in San Salvador. This was a chaplaincy-style ministry mainly to American and British businessmen and their families. The Rev. G. Edward Haynesworth (later Bishop of Nicaragua) was named archdeacon of El Salvador in 1963. In 1968 the present church building was constructed with a grant from the United Thank Offering.

In the 1970s the church became increasingly involved in medical and literacy projects. In 1973, a church organization named CREDHO (Concientización para Recuperación Espiritual y Económica del Hombre) was established by the Rev. Luis Serrano, the priest-in-charge of St. John the Evangelist. CREDHO developed a full range of aid programs and cooperatives. The ministry of the Diocese of El Salvador developed from its base at St. John the Evangelist. The diocesan office and CREDHO were both located there.

In 1983, the Archdeacon, the Ven. Victoriano Jimeno, established a small seminary for the training of priests for the diocese. The graduates of the program have gone out to establish congregations in the countryside and have been responsible for initiating substantial growth in the Church. Currently the diocese includes ten congregations and ten centers of mission.

Church members—like virtually everyone else in El Salvador—have suffered in the decade-long civil war. In 1982, nine members of La Florida, a church-sponsored model farm, were killed.

In November of 1988, the members of the Diocesan Convention affirmed their position on the state of the nation in a paper entitled "Official Document of the Episcopal Church in El Salvador in the Face of the Current Crisis." It states in part:

> God does not want humanity to suffer within Creation.... At no time did God establish an order whereby some would have more than others of the wealth that God created....
>
> Social well-being suffers from a deformation of justice. Breaking the natural order of equality, man has broken and destroyed his own wellbeing. In this moment when oppression is exercised most strongly against the weakest, one can see that the well-being of some is at the cost and evident impoverishment of others.
>
> The bad use of the wealth of God, which becomes a burden on others, is a social sin which is not part of the thought of God. Salvation is social and is not restricted to a concept of individual salvation.... The fruits of Creation must be at the service of all.
>
> In the face of the current Salvadoran situation, in which "anti-life" forces are put before human hope, the message of Jesus in John 10:10 comes to us with all its force: "This thief comes only to steal, to kill, and to destroy, but I have come

that you might have life, and that you might have it in all its abundance."[4]

In November, 1989, twenty-one church workers associated with CREDHO were seized and jailed. Josephine Beecher, a Volunteer for Mission who was among those jailed, observed that anyone working with the poor is regarded as subversive. "I suppose we are subversive because we are trying to subvert the existing order where the poor are so incredibly oppressed."[5]

Here in this country at war with itself the Episcopal Church has an important role in seeking to create a "middle ground" for those committed to negotiation and a peaceful resolution of conflicts, a middle way between the violence of the present government and that of the guerrillas.

The Ven. Victoriano Jimeno has been archdeacon of the Episcopal Church in El Salvador since 1980. Other diocesan staff members include Ana Emelia Gómez, the treasurer of the diocese, Virginia Bernal de Cabezos, director of the Office of Social Betterment, and the Rev. Santiago García, director of education. Until the Salvadorans elect their own bishop, the Rt. Rev. James Ottley, Bishop of Panama, serves as the appointed bishop of El Salvador.

Clearly this is a diocese that is growing. Archdeacon Victoriano Jimeno explains:

> Until 1987 we had only two regular priests. Until very recently we had seven priests. Now we are five priests, two deacons, and four seminarians.[6]

In a later interview, the Archdeacon outlined plans for the future:

> We are now working on a five-year plan. Our goal is to have fourteen to fifteen priests and twenty to twenty-five congregations.
>
> We are living in a country where 60 percent of the population is living in extreme poverty. The priest needs to incarnate him-herself in the reality of the total life of the people and deal with them holistically.
>
> Our vision is to change the traditional one priest-one parish structure of the Church. We

would like to see a system of parish centers—missionary centers—which would be centers for outreach ministries. Each center would have as its thrust five or six missions. I have a vision of multipurpose buildings, so that the church is not only the chapel but also has facilities for the community in which it is located.[7]

"This is a story," observed the Rev. Wilfrido Ramos, Mission Discernment Project Site Visitor,

of an emerging diocese with all the joy and excitement, yet growing pains, that come along in the process of coming of age. It is a story of beauty, yet also of suffering and hardship. It is the story of search for identity and affirmation of self, of witnessing and remaining faithful in the most difficult of human circumstances possible. The Episcopal Diocese of El Salvador is a Church in the making. It is a great story to be told and shared.[8]

## *THE LIFE AND MINISTRY OF TWO EPISCOPAL CONGREGATIONS, A MOTHER AND A DAUGHTER: CONGREGACIÓN SAN JUAN EVANGELISTA AND CONGREGACIÓN SANTA MARÍA VIRGEN*

San Juan Evangelista and Santa María Virgen illustrate the growth and change in mission in El Salvador, from being a chaplaincy to Americans abroad to becoming an almost fully contextualized ministry by Salvadorans to Salvadorans. They also present two distinct faces of ministry—the prophetic and the pastoral.

The seed was planted in San Juan, then St. John the Evangelist, the mother church of all Episcopal ministry in El Salvador. The mother church still looks more like the church of its founders than the Salvadoran Congregation of Santa María Virgen, yet it too has grown and changed and developed along with the changing circumstances of the country of El Salvador. San Juan's offspring—Santa María Virgen—is a young church. It is the rising church in El Salvador—more authentically Salvadoran, more a local expression of the faith, more a church of the poor, faster growing. As Wilfrido Ramos explains:

> San Juan is mother. From its womb, new missions and congregations have come into existence. Priestly vocations have been nurtured. New ministries of social service have been launched. Experiencing the social and prophetic witness of Father Luis Serrano and many of his parishioners at San Juan Evangelista brings one back to the faith and witness of the saints and martyrs of the early Church under persecution.
>
> As the mother congregation of most of the existing missionary work in El Salvador, San Juan represents roots, history, continuity, stability within instability, maturity of faith and understanding of mission, a response to vocation and a sense of commitment to an uncertain future. Its pastor, the Rev. Luis Serrano, embodies the figure of a prophet and suffering servant; a visionary yet often misunderstood; thought by some to be too radical for the times.[9]

Santa María, on the other hand, is

> a great example of evangelism at its best. The story of Santa María Virgen is a resurrection story. From nothingness and ashes suddenly grows a very vibrant congregation, full of hope and expectancy.[10]

- ***Congregación San Juan Evangelista in San Salvador:*** San Juan's pastor, the Rev. Luis Serrano, wrote the following in a Christmas letter to his friends and parishioners:

> Yesterday, December 24th, I celebrated the Holy Eucharist . . . . It wasn't the jail's chaplain who celebrated it. This time it was a prisoner priest. There was great fervor among the people, and at the moment I realized that God had given me the privilege to be a witness of real faith . . . .
>
> During seminary they never taught me about being in jail surrounded by 2,300 prisoners. But in our group we feel very close with each

other. We pray together, we share everything, even the oranges our families and friends bring us, some of them with tears in their eyes . . . . God blesses us every day. That same blessing is the one we ask for and wish to all of you, our Christian community.[11]

It had been a difficult year for San Juan's Luis Serrano, as it had been for the countless others whose daily work is that of seeking greater justice for the poor of the land.

On November 11, the FMLN had launched its largest offensive to date in the civil war, simultaneously attacking major military installations and holding territory in urban areas, including about one quarter of the capital city of San Salvador, for over a week. There had been many casualties. The government became nervous and more than usually defensive. Virtually anyone with a record of showing sympathy for the plight of the poor became suspect. Less than a week after the FMLN attack, on November 16, the Jesuits and their helpers were murdered at Central American University. On November 21, government forces broke into San Juan and seized twenty-one church workers. They were in San Juan taking care of 423 refugees from the November 11 offensive. That was their only purpose in being there.

The authorities claimed that the church workers were subversives, but according to the Presiding Bishop of the Episcopal Church, the Most Rev. Edmond L. Browning,

> The charges against them are false and without grounds . . . . Their only crime is to have befriended the poor and supported their cause for peace with justice.[12]

This chaotic November was a far cry from the old days of San Juan when it was called St. John the Evangelist, an English name for a very Anglo-American congregation. Then it was the parish of British and American Anglicans and Episcopalians whose businesses or embassy jobs took them to El Salvador. They built a lovely church in a pleasant area of the city. In 1963, the Rev. Jess Petty, a native of Ohio, became priest-in-charge of St. John's. By all accounts, he was a popular priest who built up a strong congregation. During his tenure a few Salvadorans joined the church, most of them well-placed in the San Salvador business world. In the early 1970s, the congregation consisted of about eighty English-speaking members and between twelve to twenty Salvadorans.

Petty left in 1972, amid a deteriorating economic and political climate in the country. Guerrilla armies were beginning to form. Between 1975 and 1980, hundreds of thousands of workers, peasants, students, teachers, and church activists formed themselves into popular organizations to work for reform. As opposition to the official regime mounted, repression increased, and military death squads began to kill and "disappear" large numbers of people.

In those dangerous days, the British and American members of St. John's began to depart. St. John's became increasingly a congregation of Salvadorans, Salvadorans with great affection for both their Church and their country.

The Rev. Luis Serrano, originally ordained as a Roman Catholic in his native Spain, had been working in Nicaragua and visited El Salvador in 1972. "I liked the country and the people. I thought I'd like to work in El Salvador. I visited St. John the Evangelist and liked it also."[13] So when Jess Petty left, Serrano took his place as priest-in-charge. Serrano had the advantage of being fluent in both English and Spanish, which was a distinct asset for this bilingual congregation.

Shortly after his arrival in El Salvador, Serrano visited two missions where the makeup of the congregations was markedly different from that of St. John's. The people were very poor, and this troubled Serrano. As he recalls:

> I remember saying to myself, "Here I am. I'm going to give bread and wine to these poeple, who don't even have bread and beans? I'm going to give the Holy Eucharist to people who have nothing?"
> 
> What does it mean to give Communion to people who have nothing? Right then and there I determined that I would not go back with the bread of the Eucharist unless I could also help people to improve their lives. This was the beginning of my social ministry.[14]

Serrano had not previously thought of himself as a social reformer, yet all of a sudden his vocation became clear:

I thought about these people. They needed to know how to plant better. They needed fertilizers and farming methods. We needed an agricultural school. I could also see that they needed to learn to read and write. They needed the tools to help themselves.[15]

Thus the seeds of CREDHO were sown. CREDHO was ultimately to become a large ecumenical social agency serving thousands of people every year through its five departments—legal aid, health, education, agricultural projects, and emergency services. Although CREDHO assumed its own separate legal identity in 1975, its offices were housed on the grounds of St. John's, and many members of the congregation participated in CREDHO's ministries. The diocesan headquarters was also situated at St. John's. And as the congregation became increasingly Salvadoran, St. John the Evangelist became San Juan Evangelista—a reflection of its Latino membership.

But in November, 1989, everything changed abruptly. The seizure of the church workers at San Juan distressed the members. Many believed that the church had been raided because the CREDHO workers were there. They became intimidated. They were suddenly fearful of attending church. So almost overnight, a full and vibrant congregation dwindled to a handful.

A year later, Father Serrano was still priest-in-charge of San Juan and the director of CREDHO, but the diocesan headquarters had been moved to another location and so had CREDHO. As a result, all parties were feeling a little more relaxed. Members are now returning to church. It was full on the Sunday the Mission Discernment Project Visitors were there. Wounds are beginning to heal.

On the Saturday of the visit to San Juan, the women of the congregation were involved in a one-day retreat. The topic was "Women in Society—Women in the Episcopal Church." About thirty participants of all ages gathered for meditations under the large *amate* tree in the churchyard. Several of the young mothers quite unselfconsciously suckled their babies as they listened to the talks and participated in small group discussions while their older children entertained themselves. Lunch was prepared and served from an outside kitchen, the women played parlor games, they danced to the music of tapes blaring from a "boom box" (in El Salvador they like their music loud), and celebrated the birthday of one of the members. There was great joy in the gathering. They were having fun.

A member of the youth group presented the Site Visitors with T-shirts the group was selling to raise funds. On the back of the shirt a laughing Jesus is pictured. It was explained that,

> We see the sad Jesus. We see the suffering Jesus.
> We see Jesus being crucified every day. But Jesus
> also laughs. Jesus sings. Jesus is happy.[16]

Indeed, all these members of San Juan have a great deal to be happy about. For one thing, they have survived. They are here and alive. For another, church members are coming back, and vitality is again reasserting itself. Then there are the solid accomplishments, such as the Salvadoran clergy whose priestly vocations were identified at San Juan. All of the Salvadoran priests who are now busy establishing congregations and mission centers in the outlying districts got their start at San Juan. Amanda Rivera is the mother of one of them and a leading member of San Juan. She explains:

> I am the mother of Father Edgar Rivera. The only thing I can say is that the Church is like my family. I've been a member since 1959. Before that I was a Roman Catholic. Once I came here I stayed forever. I like the community we have among ourselves. I love our Church.[17]

Another member, whom we'll call "María" to protect her identity, came to San Juan because of its social witness. María's father and husband, both farmers, were killed by the army. They were not members of the guerrillas but were thought to be, and for that reason were murdered. Afraid for herself and her three children, she fled with them to San Salvador.

> Before the war, I was very happy. We had corn and we had tortillas. We were all very happy people. When the war came, many people were killed. Father Rutilio Grande is from my hometown. He was always with the people. He came over to my house all the time. He enjoyed eating tortillas. He'd say, "Give me the big one." One day he said, "If

one time I die—it should be an inspiration for you to continue the struggle."

He was killed, and we have continued the struggle. Then Monseñor Romero was killed and the whole community gathered in vigil and prayer, and we came to the city to be present at his funeral.

I came to San Juan and Father Luis because he is so identified with the suffering of the people. I was seeking help, and here at San Juan they had people to help those of us who were displaced because of the war. It's important to be in solidarity with those who work for human rights. It's necessary to support the people in their struggles for liberation . . . . Here it's not just spirituality, but the whole person is taken into account.

Here it's like the early Church. We share what we have. Like the members of the early Church, we are persecuted, but we share. Thousands of people have been displaced. We live any place we can find. It's just survival. But we continue the struggle.[18]

Another member of San Juan, whose privacy also needs to be protected, is an officer of a trade union and a member of the Permanent Commission for the National Debate for Peace in El Salvador. "José," as we'll call him, told the Site Visitors:

In 1985 I became acquainted with the Episcopal Church. I came because I saw the Episcopal Church involved in Salvadoran society. I appreciated this and wanted to become a member. At San Juan, they're not disassociated from national realities. I'll tell you, it's a risk to come here. There are people around who'll say "Don't go to San Juan, because the police go over there and it's too dangerous."[19]

Here at San Juan the members know the price of being a Christian. Some even consider it dangerous to attend church services. Here faith is tested under fire, yet here also is the deep joy that comes through struggle. Here is a church of youth and hope. Juan Carlos Rivera (about fifteen years of age) is such a sign.

> As a young person, I see that the Episcopal Church is very alive. We are committed to the Good News of Christ and we are committed to the people. In spite of all the problems we are facing, I see our Church as growing and bearing a true witness.[20]

- ***Congregación Santa María Virgen in Ilopango:*** Luis Amaya Mejia, a teenage member of Santa María Virgen, recalls the congregation's beginning in 1986:

> We purchased an old house and we began in a very small room. We began with five members and two benches. That's all. With the charisma of Francisco [the former priest-in-charge], the church began to grow. It got so large, we couldn't fit into the little room anymore. So the people themselves tore down the wall and built a larger space. But this space filled up and we couldn't fit all the people inside. They had to stand outside the door, craning their necks to see inside. So we pushed out the wall again to make even more space.
>
> Our people are poor. Our church is poor, so we've done all the work ourselves. We've provided all our own labor and our own building materials. We all worked together, so finally we are able to have what you see now.
>
> Now we have about eighty members, and they just keep coming. Every week, more come.[21]

Ilopango is a rapidly growing community about 25 miles east of San Salvador. In one year the population rose from 10,000 to 15,000, as a result of the influx of war-displaced people. It is a town composed of workers, peasants, small business owners, and the unemployed. Maybell Flores, a sixteen-year-old Sunday school teacher, describes Ilopango, its people, and the church:

> We are very poor people. We have limited financial resources. There is a large, growing population around the church. Due to the conflict, a lot

of displaced people have moved into our neighborhood. Over there [she points], you can see the shantytown, the huts and cardboard cartons where people live.

It's when people are in these circumstances that they most need the Church. They need the Church for material help. They need the Church as a place where they find spiritual nurture. The people come here because this is a place where everyone is received and accepted.[22]

Clearly Santa María is a dynamic congregation that, until very recently, was served by a dynamic priest, the Rev. Francisco Guardado. Father Guardado tells his story to the Site Visitors:

When I was six years old I knew I wanted to be a priest. At seven, I started school, walking eight miles every day to get there and back home again. I knew I would have to study hard if I wanted to become a [Roman Catholic] priest. After I finished the sixth grade, my mother spoke to the priest about this, but he told her that a poor child could not study at the seminary.[23]

Guardado, however, persevered and was finally admitted to the seminary at the age of sixteen. He greatly enjoyed his studies but decided against ordination in the Roman Catholic Church because he wanted to get married and have a family. Thus he went to work for a commercial bank.

Then something wonderful happened to me. In 1982 I discovered the Episcopal Church through Archdeacon Victoriano Jimeno. I asked a lot of questions, and he listened to me. I joined San Juan and ended up being the church organist. I played the guitar as well.

In 1983, along with three other members of San Juan, I began to study in the new seminary Father Jimeno established. I also worked in the church. In 1985, I founded my first mission, Santísima Trinidad in San Martín. Afterwards, but in the same year, I left the bank and began to work full time for the Church, continuing to go to seminary on the side. In 1986, I founded missions in Soyapango and Ilopango.

Normally the way I go about it is to start in a house and get to know the people. The other way is to get to know the leadership of the community. This I did at Santísima Trinidad and San Andrés Apostol.

To start Santa María Virgen, I visited door to door and went to every house around the church. In Lourdes I started a mission in my house.[24]

Talking about evangelism at Santa María Virgin, Father Guardado says,

We're trying to develop a new evangelism system —"explosive evangelism." The church members all go through four months of training in discipleship. We train people to visit the homes and to bear witness to faith in Jesus Christ. Then each member has to commit him or herself to bringing in two new members every year to the Church. In this way, all members participate in evangelism. I may start it off at the beginning, but then every member takes up the responsibility.[25]

It is Francisco Guardado's opinion that "traditional evangelism is not effective." His understanding of "traditional evangelism" is that the priest takes the responsibility without relying sufficiently on members of the congregation to do their part. "In the traditional way you get very few committed people. In explosive evangelism, all the people do their part."[26]

Father Guardado is a no-nonsense priest. On the day the Mission Discernment Project Team visited Santa María Virgen, he greeted them in his Sunday dress—sneakers, old trousers, and T-shirt. These street clothes were also his liturgical vestments. Thus, by appearance, there was no difference between priest and parishioners.

If Francisco was tired from the previous night's all-night vigil on the eve of Advent Sunday, he did not show it. He greeted everyone who came with warmth and enthusiasm. Members greeted each other. They were obviously glad to be there. While people were still arriving, a gathering service began in a church full of the flowers the members had picked and brought in. Two youth members played the guitar and cello, and another trilled a tambourine. Father Guardado led the singing. Helpers kept bringing in more chairs from a back room until there was no more space and no more chairs. Then people started congregating outside the open door.

Newcomers stood up and were greeted with a song of welcome. Advent Sunday was explained by two engaging hand puppets. Announcements were made, and Sunday school students and teachers were identified and directed to their teaching areas. There was more singing. More greetings. Then the service of the day was about to begin.

With a baptism, worship, teaching, and fellowship, the members would be there for most of the day. But Santa María is not just church, however fulfilling the Sunday activities may be. Father Guardado explains:

> We cannot live divorced from the reality of our national and social situation. We are Christians and we are poor Salvadorans. We know that reality is hard and the government does not help the people. Our people are conscious of this injustice.
>
> We think the solution is dialogue between the government and the FMLN because we are tired of war. But we are also tired of injustice and the unequal distribution of wealth.
>
> We are Christians. We're of the Kingdom. But we are also creatures of this present time.[27]

Guardado poses the question:

> How do you preach the Gospel in a situation like this? This I know: You can't preach an empty gospel. You cannot ignore reality. But at the same time, we have to keep up the hope. We have to keep up the hope, the hope of Israel, the hope of the people of God.[28]

Part of preaching a gospel that is not empty is the demonstration, in concrete ways, of the truth that Christ does indeed care for the whole person. Maybell Flores explained that "we have an emergency fund and people come to us for help. We help with money and clothing. Whatever is possible, we do."[29]

A dressmaking project is just getting started. With a small donation from a parish in Ohio, six sewing machines have been purchased. Women will learn sewing and thus a way of supporting themselves and their families. This project was particularly attractive because the women can sew in their homes, and thus will not need child care. However, some of the members dream of establishing a day-care center as well as a clinic. The members see Santa María Virgen developing into the kind of multipurpose parish center that Archdeacon Jimeno envisions. By all appearances, they are well on their way.

Several youth members talked about their lives in the Episcopal Church in Ilopango. Blanca Cornejo, a young woman of about nineteen, is a volunteer secretary at Santa María. She told the Visiting Team,

> I was first invited to attend Santa María Virgen by a member of the congregation. More than anything else, I was impressed by how many people welcomed me. They asked me all kinds of questions—who I was, where I came from—I could see they were interested in me as a person. They made me fall in love with the Church.
>
> Also, I have found the biblical teaching very profound and in depth. Here there is a strong interest in giving you a solid foundation in the history, tradition, and biblical roots of the Church. The members know what the Church is, what the Church was, and what it should be now and in the future.[30]

Maybell Flores continues:

What attracted me to Santa María is the interest for me as a person and the Church's emphasis in providing its members a solid foundation in the faith. They make you aware of what a Christian should be and what Christianity is all about.

> We, the youth [ages fourteen to nineteen] of the Church, are not just puppets, but we are made to feel that we are very important members of the community. Before coming here, I was never a very religious person, but here I've come to feel Christ and to know Christ very deeply. Here they have helped me come to know myself and experience the Lord by the way we're treated as people, by the way we're accepted and taught about the faith.
>
> Yes, we have many young people here. We have a strong interest in serving the Church and serving others. We are very much aware that each person has a gift to share. And we have learned to put the gift at the service of the Church and God's people. This we have come to discover at Santa María.[31]

Hearing the many stories the people of Santa María Virgen told about themselves, their community, and their congregation, Wilfrido Ramos reflected,

> Santa María is the unfolding story of the ministry of San Juan Evangelista. Its priest-in-charge, Padre Francisco, a young, very creative and charismatic pastor, is himself a child of San Juan and the first fruit of the efforts of Archdeacon Victoriano Jimeno to raise a competent indigenous leadership.
>
> As a new, emerging congregation, Santa María Virgen is like a growing child that wants to affirm her own identity and personality and establish her own authenticity. San Juan is a little like the reluctant mother who hesitates in letting her child go on its own journey.
>
> The journey is a most promising one. The story of Santa María Virgen is the story of a church planting its own roots, flourishing, being faithful. The church is becoming the center of the life of the people in the community.[32]

# DISTINCTIVE FEATURES

The Episcopal Diocese of El Salvador is a story of life and vision, as an authentically Salvadoran expression of Anglicanism is taking root. Examples of faithful ministry abound everywhere. Mission Discernment Project Site Visitors have told the story of just two congregations. They could equally well have reported on the Hammock Project at Lourdes, where displaced families are participating in a church-sponsored, self-help cottage industry. They could have visited Congregación San Pedro y San Pablo in Sonsonate, where the priest-in-charge, the Rev. Edgar Rivera, who is also a veterinarian, and the people started a cattle project with seven cows. The families take care of the cows—which supply milk for their families—breed them, and give calves to other families. Father Rivera provides health care, inoculations, and the like for the herd, which now numbers fifty head of cattle. Members of San Pedro y San Pablo, most of whom are farmers, join together in farming a vacant lot the church owns. They call it the "Lot of the Lord," and its profits go to the support of the congregation.

Site Visitors could have told the stories of the two deacons, Ignacio Meza and Juan Alvarado, and the congregations they are building at Cojutepeque and Soyapango. They could have written about clinics, and the housing project for the war-displaced that Virginia Bernal de Cabezos is coordinating. They could have given the testimonies of the Episcopal peacemakers who are taking part in the National Debate for Peace in El Salvador.

How does the Diocese of El Salvador discern its mission? How do the congregations of San Juan Evangelista and Santa María Virgen discern what God is calling them to be and do at this time and place? In El Salvador these questions are essentially meaningless, since both the context of mission discernment and the appropriate responses are so obvious. At San Juan stress is placed on looking into the systemic causes of injustice and a prophetic response to the context. At Santa María, a pastoral response is emphasized.

Visiting the Church in El Salvador is nothing short of a converting experience. Through being with the people in this war-torn nation, one understands, in a dynamic way, just what full participation in the ministry of Jesus Christ as Lord and Savior really entails. In El Salvador one experiences the extent to which the forces of evil and sin and death will go. Yet one feels even more powerfully the forces of life and love, which will finally not let death prevail.

Specifically, a few factors were noted which contribute to the growth of the churches:

- **Church and Society:** Salvadoran Episcopalians expect the Church to deal with the political situation of their country. Virtually everyone prefaced his or her remarks with such phrases as "We cannot ignore the realities of our country." José, the labor union officer, for example, said, "I came because I saw the Episcopal Church involved in Salvadoran society. I appreciated this and wanted to become a member. At San Juan, they're not disassociated from national realities."
- **The Church Stands for Justice:** San Juan Evangelista has a prophetic ministry. Many people, including some of those interviewed by Site Visitors, have been attracted to the Church because it stands for social justice. María said, "It's important to be in solidarity with those who work for human rights. It's necessary to support the people in their struggles for liberation. They do that here."
- **The Whole Person:** These congregations understand the importance of spiritual nurture, yet they do not divorce spirituality from the rest of life. The Church gives material help; it sponsors clinics and self-help projects such as the hammock-making project, the dressmaking project at Ilopango, and the housing program for the displaced. The Church is also a place where members can laugh and play games and dance—as was the case at the women's retreat at San Juan.
- **Shared Ministry, Shared Evangelism:** There is the strong attitude, particularly at Santa María Virgen, that evangelism is the work of the whole Church and every member. Maybell Flores stated that "everyone has a gift to share and an opportunity to use it in the service of the Church and God's people."[33] Everyone shares the Good News, and everyone takes responsibility for bringing in new members.
- **Keeping Up the Hope of the People:** It is well understood that people need to be sustained by hope. Father Guardado mentioned that "we have to keep up the hope, the hope of Israel, the hope of the people of God." Indeed these Episcopalians seem hopeful.

- **Strong Teaching:** Members are well versed and articulate in matters of faith, the Bible, and the traditions of the Episcopal Church. Given this solid foundation, they are not shy about talking about the meaning of their faith.
- **Young Church:** Children are everywhere. In Ilopango, Site Visitors talked with more youth members (ages fourteen to nineteen) of the Church than adults, not because they particularly sought them out but because there were so many of them.
- **Strong Clergy:** Both the congregation of San Juan and that of Santa María have had the benefit of strong clergy who are effective leaders with strong personalities. They are creative. They share responsibility and they know how to bring people along with them. They are evangelistic, missionary priests.
- **Individuals Welcomed and Valued:** In one case newcomers were welcomed with songs of greeting, in another they were recognized and acknowledged. In both congregations it would have been difficult for the visitor to leave church unnoticed and unappreciated.
- **An Indigenous Church:** Faith in Jesus Christ imparted by Salvadorans to Salvadorans is powerful. The young church of Santa María Virgen makes no attempt to be like its Anglo mother. The music, the style of doing the liturgy, the appearance of the church—these are all distinctly Salvadoran. And the church is flourishing.
- **A Church of Martyrs and Saints:** It means something to be a Christian in El Salvador. Virtually everyone knows someone who has been jailed, tortured, or put to death for the sake of standing up for God's truth. The witness of the prominent clergy who have been murdered—Rutilio Grande, Archbishop Romero, the Jesuits—is very much alive, and it encourages those who are still struggling. They, and the 72,000 others who have died in this past decade, continue to cast a long shadow over life in El Salvador. Here, one appreciates the truth of the ancient saying, derived from a statement of Tertullian's, that "the blood of the martyrs is the seed of the Church."

El Salvador is a land of martyrs, confessors, and witnesses to faith in Jesus Christ. The witness of Salvadoran Christians has been a costly one. Theirs is a faith lived under fire. They are witnesses of hope. They are living proof that El Salvador—the Savior Jesus Christ—reigns and will prevail.

"Since we are surrounded by so great a cloud of witnesses... let us run with perseverance the race that is set before us" (Heb 12:1). Let us run in solidarity with our brothers and sisters of the faith in El Salvador and, like them, denounce all the forces and circumstances that hinder a true and abiding reconciliation between persons and nations, so that all people everywhere may live in freedom, justice, peace, and love.

## NOTES:

[1] Ana Emelia Gómez, interview in San Salvador, November 29, 1990.

[2] Virginia Bernal de Cabezos, interview in San Salvador, November 29, 1990.

[3] Note: The following sources were used to write this section: From El Salvador Public Information Campaign: "Basic Facts and Background Data," "The Jesuit Case and the Jakarta Plan," "U.S. Policy in El Salvador," "Alternatives to War—Negotiations," "Elections in El Salvador," "El Salvador's Key Players," "The Salvadoran Armed Forces," September, 1990; Tom Gibb and Frank Smyth, "El Salvador: Is Peace Possible? A Report on the Prospects for Negotiations and U.S. Policy," Washington Office on Latin America, April 1990; Lindsay Gruson, "In El Salvador Much Has Changed and Little," *New York Times,* November 11, 1990; Tom Barry, *Roots of Rebellion: Hunger and Land in Central America* (Boston: South End Press, 1987); CDHES, "Cronologia de Casos Relevantes Denunciados en la CDHES Durante el Año de 1990, Enero a Mayo, San Salvador," CDHES, May, 1990.

[4] The Diocese of El Salvador, "Official Document of the Episcopal Church of El Salvador in the Face of the Current Crisis," November 25, 1988, p. 3.

[5] Josephine Beecher, as quoted in *El Salvador Alert,* World Mission Information Office, Episcopal Church Center, January, 1990, p. 2.

[6] Victoriano Jimeno, interview in San Salvador, November 29, 1990.

[7] Victoriano Jimeno, interview in San Salvador, December 3, 1990.

[8] Wilfrido Ramos, Site Visitor Report, December 5, 1990.

[9] *Ibid.*

[10] *Ibid.*

[11] Luis Serrano, Christmas letter, written from jail in El Salvador, December 25, 1989.
[12] Edmond L. Browning, quoted in *El Salvador Alert,* January, 1990, p. 1.
[13] Luis Serrano, interview in San Salvador, November 30, 1990.
[14] *Ibid.*
[15] *Ibid.*
[16] A youth member of San Juan, conversation in San Salvador, December 1, 1990.
[17] Amanda Vuida de Rivera, interview in San Salvador, December 2, 1990.
[18] "María," interview in San Salvador, December 2, 1990.
[19] "Jose," interview in San Salvador, December 2, 1990.
[20] Juan Carlos Rivera, interview in San Salvador, December 2, 1990.
[21] Luis Aristides Amaya Mejia, interview in Ilopango, December 2, 1990.
[22] Maybell Flores Martínez, interview in Ilopango, December 2, 1990.
[23] Francisco Guardado, interview in San Salvador, December 29, 1990.
[24] *Ibid.*
[25] *Ibid.*
[26] *Ibid.*
[27] *Ibid.*
[28] *Ibid.*
[29] Maybell Flores Martínez, interview.
[30] Blanca Cornejo, interview in Ilopango, December 2, 1990.
[31] Maybell Flores Martínez, interview.
[32] Wilfrido Ramos, Site Visitor Report, December 5, 1990.
[33] Maybell Flores Martínez, interview.

*Site Visitor and Interpreter:* The Rev. Wilfrido Ramos-Orench
*Date of Visit:* November 29-December 3, 1990

> *True contextualization happens when there is a community which lives faithfully by the Gospel and in that same costly identification with people in their real situations as we see in the earthly ministry of Jesus. When these conditions are met, the sovereign Spirit of God does his own surprising work.*
>
> —Lesslie Newbigin,
> The Gospel in a Pluralist Society

## CHAPTER 15

# COMMON THREADS A DISCUSSION OF THE STORIES

### CYCLE OF DISCERNMENT

*To Seek and to Serve* is about how a congregation might discern its particular mission and empower its members to carry out that mission. It is about fourteen stories of mission discernment. Stories not only celebrate and affirm, they also help one learn about identity and about mission. The purpose of telling the stories of these congregations is not to declare, "Here is a model, you do this" or "This is a wonderful parish, and if you do what they have done, you're going to be what they are." *To Seek and to Serve to Mission* is not a resource that offers models. It rather contains *exemplars* that are descriptive but not prescriptive. The reader is invited to see some common themes and common determinants and draw some conclusions. As you read the stories, perhaps you found in them something that could apply to your congregation. Please take from them what you will.

These stories help to answer the question, What goes into a process of mission discernment? What are the common aspects of mission discernment? We see in them some clues.

Mission Discernment Project Site Visits began the first weekend in April in San Jose, California, and ended in El Salvador on the tenth anniversary of the murder of the four American church workers. In the intervening eight months, congregations in every province of the Episcopal Church were visited, from New England to the Pacific Northwest, from Wisconsin to Texas, from the city of Detroit to the South Carolina coastal community of Pawleys Island, from the single poorest county in the United States, to comfortable suburbs, to teeming urban centers. The size, style of ministry, location, and cultural and ethnic makeup of the congregations represent the strength and diversity of the Episcopal Church.

With few exceptions, all the congregations that successfully demonstrated a process of mission discernment share certain striking similarities in the way they went about their mission. So Santa Fe in San Antonio is like St. Luke's in Atlanta, which is like St. Philip's in San Jose, which is like St. Mark's in Plainfield (Indiana), which is like St. George's Church in Fredericksburg (Virginia), which is like St. Stephen's in Oak Harbor (Washington)—and so on—in certain basic ways.

The members of these congregations know their immediate mission field intimately. They know the *context* of their mission and ministry: They are knowledgeable about the community in which the church is located—its needs and hurts, its hopes and aspirations. They know a great deal about the lives of the individuals who make up the community of the congregation—their needs and hurts, their hopes and aspirations. The individual story and the community story are seen in light of *biblical tradition*. What is God, through God's Living Word, saying to the community of faith about the larger community? The biblical story is held in tension with the community story. What arises then is a *contextual theology* in which the question, What is God calling us to be and do in this time and place? is answered in the light of social analysis of the particular community and the insights drawn from study of *Scripture and biblical tradi-*

tion. The Rev. Antoine L. Campbell, director of Camp Baskervill at Pawleys Island, told Site Visitors,

> We have discovered for ourselves two basic truths:
> 1) . . . If you don't invest in community, the community won't invest in you. And the converse, if you invest in the community, the community will invest in you, and
> 2) The Gospel is true. If you don't offer the Gospel, you don't offer the best the Church has to offer.[1]

The *worship* (including worship space) of these congregations is shaped in relation to the hopes, hurts, needs, and aspirations of the community. Aspects of the community are incorporated into the worship—in the content of the prayers, in the language of the people, in their songs, art, and artifacts. Worship, in other words, is contextualized. Street and sanctuary are united. Worship, rather than sheltering its participants from the world out there, opens a doorway to empowerment in the wider community.

The whole could be called a "Cycle of Discernment," the elements in the cycle being context, Bible, contextual theology, and worship. The circle comes back to the context. Yet when the cycle of discernment comes around, the community is seen through new eyes and with renewed vision. Thus members of the congregation see not only needs, hurts, hopes, and aspirations but the concrete ways it can work in the community to meet its needs, relieve its hurts, encourage its hopes and aspirations. Thus the ministry becomes contextualized.

When the sites for the Mission Discernment Project were selected, even before one location was visited, project staff looked for a demonstration of mission discernment. In looking at the congregations that came to their attention, they saw housing co-ops, shelters for the homeless, a pump on an Indian reservation repaired by the Church. They saw neighborhoods that were supplied with bread and grapefruit. They saw congregations in which factory workers, farmers, secretaries, politicians, newspaper reporters, public figures—all saw their daily work as ministry and mission. In a myriad of ways, they saw fourteen stories of congregations and clusters of congregations making a decided difference in the lives of the communities in which they are located and in the lives of their members—and the members, in turn, making a difference in their daily lives. They saw the end—or rather the continuing—result of mission discernment. Looking backwards, the observer sees and understands that—in ways particular to each community and congregation—a process of mission discernment has been pursued, one that has these common threads. Lesslie Newbigin, in *The Gospel in a Pluralist Society*, corroborates, from his experience of forty years as a missionary, what Mission Discernment Project Visitors witnessed throughout the course of the project:

> If the Gospel is to be understood, if it is to be received as something which communicates truth about the real human situation, if it is, as we say, to "make sense," it has to be communicated in the language of those to whom it is addressed and has to be clothed in symbols which are meaningful to them. And since the Gospel does not come as a disembodied message, but as the message of a community which claims to live by it and which invites others to adhere to it, the community's life must be so ordered that it "makes sense" to those who are so invited. It must "come alive." Those to whom it is addressed must be able to say, "Yes, I see. This is true for me, for my situation . . . . "
>
> True contextualization accords to the Gospel its rightful primacy, its power to penetrate every culture and to speak within each culture, in its own speech and symbol, and the word which is both No and Yes, both judgement and grace. And that happens when the word is not a disembodied word, but comes from a community which embodies the true story, God's story, in a style of life which communicates both the grace and the judgement.[2]

What Site Visitors found in the fourteen locations was the wider community penetrating and shaping the life of the congregation, and the congregation—through its study of Scripture and coming to see itself in the light of biblical tradition, through its "doing theology" in relation to the context, through its worship—shaping the life of the community. So the life of the congregation is changed by the factors and issues emanating from the community in which it is located; *and* the life of the wider community is changed through the activity and influence of the congregation. The life of the congregation affects the wider community through its collective ministries as a congregation and also through the individual members whose ministries are lived out in the structures of society. Edward Jones, a member of St. George's Church in Fredericksburg, Virginia, expresses it well:

> ... the kinds of relationships built here help us go out ... in the community more responsibly. Here we see the ... different facets of the same issues and people. ... We have the educational opportunities to help us reflect upon the spirituality of it all.[3]

The following diagram suggests this interaction of community context and a congregation's process of mission discernment.

### *Cycle of Discernment*

*Congregation's Mission in the Community:*

| | |
|---|---|
| housing co-ops | street academy |
| soup kitchens | food for the neighborhood |
| clinics | |
| post office for the homeless | literacy programs |
| repair of neighborhood pump | rural homes |
| stimulations of community business ventures | neighborhood renewal political action, etc. |
| shelter for unwed mothers, for the war-displaced | |

*Initiating Factor:*
community issue
circumstance
chance/change
crisis
shift in leadership, etc.

# CONTEXTUALIZATION OF MINISTRY

A key question is, What triggers the cycle of discernment? What starts it off? Members of the Total Ministry Task Force, who read through the stories, noted that most of the congregations had a crisis, a change, a shift in leadership, a circumstance involving a member, a community issue, or the like, which caused them to look at the wider community in which they are located, or at their own ministry, or both, in a new way, with fresh vision. Can mission discernment be intentional? Are we passive victims having to wait for a crisis, or can we initiate action at any time? This question—What triggers the cycle?—invites further thought. It could be critical to understanding the whole process of mission discernment.

Indigenization, enculturation, enfleshment—these terms could also be used to describe this concept of ministry becoming imbedded in the life of the particular community. In varying degrees, depending upon the location, we came to understand ministry as partnership—partnership between members of the congregation and their clergy, and partnership between the community of faith and the wider community. When the partnership is functioning successfully, each party has a role of fostering and encouraging initiatives as well as correctives. Each party is enhanced. Anglican tradition is enhanced.

This idea of the contexualization of ministry is not new. It comes out of the world mission field, where the translation of a British or Northern Hemisphere expression of the faith (e.g., Anglicanism) has assumed particular power and dynamism in cultures very different from, say, the British Isles or New York City. It is easy to see and experience the contextualization of ministry in Africa and Latin America. But though more subtle, contextualization is also found in virtually every place where the local congregation sees itself in partnership with the wider community in which it is located.

Considering the congregations visited for this project, it is very easy to see the contextualization of an Anglican expression of the faith in predominantly black or Latino, Native American or Asian, congregations, where there is an obvious "owning" of the culture. It's not so obvious among European-American congregations, whose members often do not see themselves as coming from distinctive cultural traditions or who have become so much a part of a general melting pot they have long since lost any distinctiveness (art, music, verbal traditions). Yet it is an odd irony that the Episcopal Church, generally speaking, still looks more European-American than anything else.

As all ministry becomes more contextualized, as it is bound to, all culture groups ought to consider these matters of contextualization and consider how each tradition—as indeed each individual—contributes, or could contribute, to the rich tapestry of the whole. The Rev. Jerry Drino, speaking from the perspective of the multicultural congregation he serves in San Jose, California, points out a way towards our common future:

> We are co-creators of new religions forms. In the process, our understanding of God is expanded. We see an image of the human family as it is emerging. Something deep in the soul knows that this is the image God intends.[4]

## COMMON THREADS

We have alluded to some of the common factors that run through the fourteen stories. What follows is a closer look at them. Perhaps in your reading of the stories, you will have found other trends.

- ***The Contextualization of Ministry and Mission Is Critical:*** Nancy Cannon of the Church of the Messiah commented that:

> We had to ask ourselves whether we were going to be foreigners in our neighborhood.... There had been an almost subconscious transition to becoming a neighborhood church, *where the neighborhood altered what happened.*[5]

The neighborhood affects the congregation; the congregation affects the neighborhood. Such is the case in various ways in each of the congregations visited throughout the course of the Mission Discernment Project. Congregations have discovered—in ways particular to them and their situations—that immersion in their context is critically important. They have discovered for themselves what J. L. Segundo, a twentieth-century Latin American theologian, contends, that the practice of ministry in its context is first, and that reflection is second, in the process of doing theology.⁶

- ***The Laity Begin to See Daily Life as Ministry:*** Members of the congregations visited are seeking to make sense out of their daily lives. They want to know what their faith has to say about the ways they approach their regular work and community involvements. Most laity intuitively sense the connections, yet they often need the help of their congregations to voice them.

Sue Rohan, a member of the Wisconsin State Legislature and a member of St. Luke's in Madison, said:

> When I look at the issues, my faith enters in . . . . I apply the process of my faith to solve the problems we see working in society. Why not put money into prevention? Why not help parents?⁷

Albert MacDowell is an attorney and former judge in the city of Newburgh, and a member of Church of the Good Shepherd in Newburgh. He sees every day as an opportunity to do God's justice through his work:

> For values, you depend upon your Church . . . . I have an opportunity for Christian living every day . . . . What we deal with in the courts is unbelievable—drugs, murder, you name it. We see life at its happiest and at its saddest. Homelessness, abuse of women, abuse of neighbors . . . . I have the . . . . opportunity to carry out my value system every day . . . . There's so much you can do with the legal system to pervert justice, even in small ways . . . . There's a lot you can do in the legal system if you want to practice your values.⁸

Bruce Gunter, a member of St. Luke's in Atlanta, founded a social responsibility investment firm because, as he explained,

> For me . . . I was determined to make Christianity a part of my life. I got politically involved and determined to make faith a part of everything I did.⁹

The laity want to make connections in concrete ways; but in subtle ways too, their faith may inform their attitudes in approaching their daily lives. Bob Ross, a geologist for the Bureau of Land Management in Wyoming and a member of Christ Church, Cody, said:

> I try to do some things with the church, and carry them forward in my work. I think we can see God in the poor people in particular and in our relationships with them. The Bible says you see God in the faces of the poor. I believe that. You've got to find God in other people.[10]

- **Welcome, Newcomers' Programs, Hospitality:** Newcomers and visitors are welcomed and valued. Most of the congregations visited go well beyond the standard rector's greeting of visitors during announcement time. They have greeters who really do greet newcomers as they arrive at the church, they have newcomers stand up to be recognized during the service, they sing to them. There are all manner of "shepherding" and newcomer programs. Newcomers are telephoned and visited within the week of first appearing at the church; they are given gifts—like a freshly baked loaf of bread—from the congregation along with information about the parish's services and programs. Welcome Wagons take brochures about the congregation as they visit those who have recently moved into town. Members and clergy follow up. Doug and Diane Cole talked about their first visit to the Church of the Nativity in Northborough, Massachusetts:

> Brad Nutting and Fred [Goodwin, the rector] greeted us at the door. About eight people talked to us at the coffee hour. They said, "Welcome! How are you? It's great to have you!" After the next Sunday, Fred came over that afternoon. He joined us for lunch and stayed two hours. Now Diane's teaching first grade in the Sunday School, and the kids love it.[11]

Other congregations have no formal greeters or newcomers' programs, but still convey to visitors that they are genuinely wanted, valued, and appreciated. For example, Blanca Cornejo said of her first visit to Santa María Virgen in Ilopango, El Salvador, that,

> More than anything else, I was impressed by how many people welcomed me. They asked me all kinds of questions—who I was, where I came from—I could see they were interested in me as a person. They made me fall in love with the Church.[12]

- *Small Groups, Intimacy, Meeting of Personal Needs, a Sense of Family:* Opportunities for intimacy and small groups are features of most of the congregations visited. The Rev. Jerry Drino said of those who have come to St. Philip's, San Jose, and stayed: "Seldom do they come because they are looking for a multicultural parish. Rather they come to meet personal needs." Having met personal needs, members move on to participate in a whole range of ministries, yet the personal touch remains important.

Angie Trombley, coordinator of the fellowship dinners for the Church of the Nativity in Northborough, commented that "It's not the food or place setting or anything else that's important, but the time to fellowship and get to know one another and who we are."[13]

A sense of family, according to Steve Dunn, a member of Christ Church in Cody,

> ... is what I was looking for. What I want is family-type stuff .... I want to have that warm feeling. I want everyone to be glad they came here. I want it to have that kind of warmth and family. I've craved for that sense of family all my life. If people come and share their joy, it can happen. Out of that sense of family all kinds of good things can happen.[14]

Letitia Howe of the Church of the Nativity said of the congregation, "They are my family." Amanda Rivera said the same of her congregation, San Juan Evangelista, in San Salvador. So did Pat Castillo, a member of Santa Fe in San Antonio, "I'm part of a family. Here I feel like I've got ten moms and all the kids are like my little sisters."[15] Members of congregations as large as St. Luke's, Atlanta, and as small as Holy

Cross-Faith Memorial Church on Pawleys Island say the same of their congregations—'"This is my family." Mario Campbell, a visitor to the Church of the Nativity, remarked,

> The place that feels itself to be a family will open its doors to a stranger. In a large family there is always room for one more.[16]

- **Bible, Bible, and More Bible:** Bible reading, Bible study, Kerygma Bible study groups, Serendipity Bible study groups, formal and structured Bible study, informal Bible study, Bible study in homes, in the church, in local restaurants and diners, at members' work places, Bible study led by the clergy, Bible study led by the laity, Bible study in the early hours of the morning, Bible study over lunch hour, Bible study in the evening—Bible study of all kinds is seen by most congregations visited as crucial to the development and vitality of the congregations' life and ministry and the key to the empowerment of their members in their daily lives and ministries. One gets the sense that the Bible has come to life in the community of faith and that through Bible study, members come to see themselves and all of their lives and ministries in the context of biblical tradition.

In reflecting on the revival ministry at Santa Fe Church in San Antonio, the Rev. Carmen Guerrero said:

> . . . Life came when they began, as a congregation, to study the Scriptures in small groups. And one could find them studying in their homes, and studying in the church, and studying in the parish hall, and they did this at all hours. Sometimes they would do it in the evenings, and sometimes they would do it in the mornings, and sometimes during the week. Why, they even began to look at the Scriptures in the . . . county jail. And not only this, they also didn't seem to have any limits about who could be part of the study groups. There were groups of four-year-olds, and there were groups of senior citizens, and then one day the priest and vestry noticed that they didn't have enough room. There just wasn't enough room for all the

ministry that was happening. What had happened to the Church of the Holy Faith? They had become a scriptural community. They had entered into a dialogue. They had entered into conversation with Scripture. And as a result they began to give a different meaning to the people and the things in their lives.[17]

- ***The Clergy—Strong Leaders, of Obvious Faith and Collegial Style, Who Make Connections:*** Each congregation participating in the Mission Discernment Project was selected because of the ministry of the congregation, not the strength and talents of the clergy serving the congregations.

  As it turned out, the clergy, without exception, share certain common characteristics: They are people of obvious faith, with an obvious call to their ordained ministries. Their strength of character is apparent. They are steady and consistent. They have a sense of self. They share leadership easily, yet they are themselves strong and confident leaders. Berry Meaux, a member of St. Stephen's in Oak Harbor, Washington, said of his rector, that

  > The ability Jack Tench has is the ability to pick people. He brings out the best in people. And he says "Go ahead." So we have a real involved laity.[18]

  Most of the clergy are engaging preachers who, through their preaching, help the members of the congregation make connections between their lives of faith and the rest of their lives. Linda Grigsby in Fredericksburg, Virginia, said of the preaching of her rector, the Rev. Charles Sydnor,

  > Charles' preaching connects with me. He addresses reality. He relates to what you're doing in your own life through his teaching and preaching.[19]

  These clergy are involved in the life of the communities in which the church is located. They are in love with their work.

- ***Laity Initiate and Take Ownership of the Congregation's Ministries:*** A lay person, Jenny Pierson, initiated St. Luke's

Soup Kitchen in Atlanta when she started preparing sandwiches for the increasing numbers of people who had started to congregate in the church's back parking lot. A real estate broker, Fritz Leedy, went to his church—St. George's in Fredericksburg, Virginia—on a cold winter morning, to find a homeless man by the door.

> We arrived at the church on a miserably cold Tuesday morning at 7:00 for our Brotherhood of St. Andrew's Bible study. There we found Roger, crouched in the doorway. So we said, "Let's invite him in . . . ." He told us about the problems of homelessness and those who sleep under the Falmouth Bridge.[20]

Thus began St. George's shelter ministry.

The catechumenal program at St. Luke's, in Madison, Wisconsin, is run by lay teams. St. Philip's ministry to the Lao began when a laywoman, Barbara Somers, helped a Lao family plan the funeral of their son who had drowned. The laity initiate and take ownership of the congregation's ministries.

- ***Congregations Respond Quickly:*** Camp Baskervill offers a dramatic example of a quick response in a time of crisis. Hundreds of homes were suddenly swept away when Hurricane Hugo tore through South Carolina, ravaging everything in its path. Before the day was out, people were receiving help, meals, and medical attention at Camp Baskervill. Camp Baskervill soon became the official county relief center for the victims of the hurricane, and almost before they knew it, Camp Baskervill staff and volunteers were serving meals to 2,000 people in a four-county area.

The Church of the Messiah in Detroit began its housing co-op ministry when the apartment building across the street from the church caught fire and burned one winter's evening.

Most instances of quick response to need are less dramatic, but they have been just as effective in the building of ministry. Take the story of Bill Drake, a new arrival to the town of Plainfield, Indiana. Bill stopped by St. Mark's, distressed about his critically ill infant son in a Chicago hospital:

I saw the Episcopal Church sign outside and decided to stop in. It was on Friday, and I spilled the whole story to Millie [one of the members]. I came back on Sunday, and I was amazed to see William's name on the prayer list. Imagine that—from Friday to Sunday. They responded that fast.... They really cared.[21]

- ***Worship and Worship Space Reflect the Wider Community:*** The cultural and ethnic customs, traditions, and languages of the individuals who make up the congregations are often incorporated into the congregation's worship. What is outside the church is also found inside the church. Perhaps St. Philip's, San Jose, is the most conspicuous example of incorporating the cultures of the people into the halls of Anglicanism, but it occurs in other ways in the other congregations as well.

  Along with the *Hymnal 1982* and the Book of Common Prayer, many, if not most, of the congregations visited have compiled their own songbooks. They take the set prayers and generously add to them. The tone of the worship, wherever it is, feels like the tempo of life in the wider community. The service is personalized; it is enhanced to fit its location.

  Worpship space also reflects the life and cultures of the worshipers. Christ Church, Cody, for example is decorated with the sculptures of artist-member Harry Jackson and Ann Model's dried flower arrangements. The congregation sings Jim Hager's communion setting, and occasionally children will sing songs composed and directed by Tina Jackson. Santa María Virgen in Ilopango overflows with the lovely tropical flowers members pick from the countryside and bring in on a Sunday morning. Two of the congregations—St. Stephen's in Oak Harbor and the Church of the Nativity in Northborough—have made their own stained-glass windows.

- ***Congregations Make News, Not Only Publicity:*** Congregations are visible in their communities because they make news. Their service projects, housing programs, public acts, positions on public issues, and the like, make the news. The clown troupe of St. Mark's in Plainfield, Indiana, is often pictured in the local press making visits to prisons, group homes, and nursing homes. As Edward Jones, editor of *The Free Lance-Star* and a member of St. George's in Fredericksburg, said,

> I have an interesting problem in terms of telling our story in the community. It's a sort of conflict because, as managing editor, I have to almost bend over backward to make sure we're not giving our church favored treatment. But the Church just keeps making the news all the time.[22]

Of course, many of the churches that make news also do effective publicity. The members of St. Stephen's in Oak Harbor take a booth at the county fair. The clergy of the Episcopal Ministry in Pine Ridge, South Dakota, serve on the review stand for the annual powwow parade. Members of San Juan Evangelista march through the streets of San Salvador in the annual Independence Day parade carrying Episcopal Church signs and banners. Members of St. Luke's, Madison, drive around town with bright red bumper stickers on their cars advertising their church.

- ***Congregations Sing Well, Eat Well, Laugh a Lot:*** One wonders whether a quick barometer to guage the health of a congregation could be an affirmative answer to three simple questions: Do they sing well? Do they eat well? Do they laugh a lot?

  Almost without exception, one could answer yes to all three in the congregations visited throughout the course of the Mission Discernment Project. By singing well, we do not mean singing with any particular technical skill, but singing with heart. As for eating well, even the most economically depressed congregations are full of members who want to share the best they have—their favorite dishes, their most generous salads and delicious desserts—with their church family. And they do so often. They laugh a lot. To really laugh together with easy humor, people need to know each other well, feel relaxed together, and appreciate each other. Genuine laughter—the kind that is not just clever, cute, or sarcastic—is built upon knowledge of other persons and the joy of being together among friends and brothers and sisters.

- ***The Ministry Is God's Ministry:*** Many of the people in the congregations visited have an intuitive understanding that the ministry they are engaged in is God's ministry and that it is God who is doing this new thing in their midst. They see themselves cooperating in God's action. The Rev. Tony Campbell expressed what Site Visitors experienced in several settings:

We place radical trust in God and in God's strength. It's God's ministry, not ours, and we can step out into the water trusting that God, who called us to this, will be faithful. It's God's work through and through.[23]

- ***Empowerment through Storytelling:*** Each of the congregations visited had a story to tell of mission discernment—what God is calling them to be and do in this time and place. Individual after individual in congregation after congregation—they all told their stories in their own way. In every case, the storyteller was empowered (as were those who listened), for in the very act of telling the story, more hope, more resolve for mission, more vision, emerged to strengthen God's call to mission. Which brings us back full circle to where this Mission Discernment Project began. The Presiding Bishop's Task Force on Christian Education, of which this current work is a culmination, stated that,

    > ... we Christians are a story-formed people. Our consciousness and identity grow out of the salvation story as it is contained in Scripture.[24]

    Telling congregational stories and seeing them in light of biblical tradition empowers both storytellers and listeners, and enhances the missionary activity of each congregation in the community.

- ***Diocesan Involvement:*** The stories of the fourteen congregations do not often allude to diocesan assistance and support. Yet some receive financial support from their dioceses. Others, like the Hudson Valley Ministry and the Lutheran and Episcopal collaboration at Pine Ridge, are part of an overall diocesan planning strategy. Many dioceses stand ready to assist parishes in mission discernment.

- ***Growth in Membership:*** This Mission Discernment Project is not about increasing membership; it is about congregations' discerning their mission. However, as it happens, these congregations are growing, some of them dramatically. And the congregations growing the most are those in which the ministry is the most contextualized, where Anglicanism is most authentically filtered through the life and culture of the people, such as the Salvadoran Congregación Santa María Virgen.

So the people themselves tore down the wall and built a larger space. But this space filled up, and we couldn't fit all the people inside. They had to stand outside the door, craning their necks to see inside. So we pushed out the wall again . . . . [25]

---

## NOTES

[1] Antoine L. Campbell, interview at Pawleys Island, June 8, 1990.

[2] Lesslie Newbigin, *The Gospel in a Pluralist Society*. Grand Rapids, MI: William B. Erdmans Publishing Company, 1989, pp. 141 and 152.

[3] Edward Jones, interview in Fredericksburg, Virginia, April 27, 1990.

[4] Jerry Drino, interview in San Jose, April 1, 1990.

[5] Nancy Cannon, interview in Detroit, June 3, 1990.

[6] J. L. Segundo, *The Liberation of Theology* (Maryknoll, NY: Orbis Books, 1976), pp. 7-38.

[7] Sue Rohan, interview in Madison, May 6, 1990.

[8] Albert MacDowell, interview in New Windsor, New York, October 2, 1990.

[9] Bruce Gunter, interview in Atlanta, June 6, 1990.

[10] Bob Ross, interview in Clark, Wyoming, September 21, 1990.

[11] Doug Cole, interview in Northborough, Massachusetts, September 9, 1990.

[12] Blanca Cornejo, interview in Ilopango, December 2, 1990.

[13] Angie Trombley, interview in Northborough, September 9, 1990.

[14] Steve Dunn, interview in Cody, Wyoming, September 22, 1990.

[15] Pat Castillo, interview in San Antonio, July 10, 1990.

[16] Marie Campbell, interview in Northborough, September 9, 1990.

[17] Carmen B. Guerrero, presentation made on Scriptural Communities in Province VII, 1989.

[18] Berry Meaux, interview in Oak Harbor, Washington, August 18, 1990.

[19] Linda Grigsby, interview in Fredericksburg, April 26, 1990.

[20] Fritz Leedy, interview in Fredericksburg, April 26, 1990.

[21] Bill Drake, telephone interview, May 14, 1990.

[22] Edward Jones, interview in Fredericksburg, April 27, 1990.
[23] Tony Campbell, interview at Pawleys Island, June 10, 1990.
[24] *Report of the Presiding Bishop's Task Force on Christian Education in the Local Congregation*, November, 1987, p. 2.
[25] Luis Aristides Amaya Mejia, interview in Ilopango, December 2, 1990.

# Diocesan Stories
# Use Guides
# Resources
# and
# Project Documents

---
## APPENDIX 1
---

# DIOCESAN STORIES OF MISSION DISCERNMENT

Dioceses also seek to discern what God is calling them to be and to do. How does a diocese discern the mission of the diocese as a whole? How does a diocese connect itself to the mission discernment of congregations? In this chapter, we briefly summarize some of the ways dioceses are seeking to discern their mission. None of these stories is the whole story of any one diocese. They do suggest the rich experiences flowing from mission discernment. We tell them in a random order.

## *NORTHERN MICHIGAN: MINISTRY DEVELOPMENT*

In the Diocese of Northern Michigan, mission is not a side program or special commission. It is the focal point of everything that happens in the diocese. Under the leadership of the bishop, the diocese has been reoriented to develop the baptismal ministry of all church members. Since the diocese is small, the development of the ministry of the baptized is not just another program: it is central to everything. The diocese comprises 3,253 persons in thirty congregations. The annual diocesan budget is $347,000. Only seven congregations list over a hundred communicants, and only two congregations follow the one priest-one parish model. The diocesan council, the diocesan standing committee, and the commission on ministry include representatives from 60 to 70 percent of Northern Michigan's congregations. Hence, close contact is maintained. In ecumenical matters, there is dialogue with other denominations not only on the judicatory level, but in congregational circles as well. In some areas, the population is so sparse it makes little sense not to try to combine forces with other denominations. Even in places of greater population, ecumenical cooperation is encouraged as a creative and helpful approach.

Northern Michigan's mission strategy assumes that "the ministry of the Church in any place belongs primarily to the Church in that place."[1] Each of the thirty congregations is expected to assume responsibility for carrying on its own life and mission. Parochialism is avoided through strong regional, diocesan, and ecumenical relationships.

The diocese is divided into four regions, each with a regional council made up of representatives of each congregation and of the regional clergy. "Regional clergy" are seminary-trained clergy who are responsible for ministry development and support within each congregation in their region. They are assigned not to individual congregations but to entire regions.

An important focus of the work in the diocese over the last few years has been the covenant group process. The bishop, all fourteen seminary-trained clergy in the diocese, and other members of the diocesan family have been formed into a consultants' group. The consultants meet together to reflect on the unfolding process. They also prepare the curriculum for training local ministry-support teams. In addition, members of the group are assigned to work with the congregations participating in the covenant process.

The covenant process begins with the bishop or an appointee of the bishop visiting with a vestry or bishop's committee to present the possibility of refocusing the daily life and mission of a particular congregation from a priest-centered ministry to a ministry centered in all the baptized. When the vestry or bishop's committee agrees to this goal, a presentation is made to the full congregation.

If the congregation agrees, a consultant is selected. The consultant leads the "discovery process"—a series of four meetings for members of the bishop's committee or vestry, and any other leaders named by them. The full membership list of the congregation is reviewed to identify the specific gifts of the members and assign the various roles of the local ministry support team on the basis of those gifts. No one is invited to assume more than two roles. These roles include those of locally ordained priest (under Title III, Canon 9 of the Canons of the Episcopal Church, bishops may locally ordain priests, vesting them with authority to preside at the Eucharist and other sacramental functions in the congregations that have called them to this ministry); preachers; priestly ministry coordinators, who share in planning and training for worship; deacons; diaconal ministry coordinators; stewardship coordinators; education coordinators; and ecumenical coordinators.

The people identified as having the gifts suitable for these roles are *then* invited to join a covenant group. Those who accept their call covenant together to meet regularly for two years and to go through the curriculum that prepares them for these support roles in the congregation. At the end of the two- to three-year period they are commissioned, licensed, or ordained for their various responsibilities within the congregation. They become the local ministry support team.

This group does not minister to the congregation in the way the priest used to. Rather, all members of the congregation are engaged in ministry. Now more members of the congregation share responsibility for maintaining and ministering in their life together. New emphasis and support also are given to each individual's ministries of reconciliation (the priestly ministry), servanthood (the diaconal ministry), and oversight (the apostolic ministry) in their daily lives—in their homes, workplaces, and in all of their activities outside the walls of the church. In this way, the ministries of each congregation will directly reflect and grow from the community of which it is a part.

This has been a watershed year for the diocese's covenant process. There have already been five parish commissionings, and four persons have already been ordained to the priesthood, with another six to follow before the end of the year. In addition, seven have been ordained to the vocational diaconate, and another twenty-two have been licensed and commissioned for significant roles of ministry support in their congregations. These developments have, in effect, doubled the number of ordained clergy in the diocese and greatly enhanced a sense of local shared responsibility for the life and mission of the Church.

Northern Michigan hopes it is discovering a way to help congregations of any size carry on the work of the Church without being dependent on direct outside help or a resident professional. A whole new field of opportunity for genuinely new mission is opening for the diocese.

# LOS ANGELES: CONGREGATIONAL SELF-STUDY AND PLANNING FOR MISSION

In his address, "Adelante" ("Forward" in Spanish), to the 93rd Diocesan Convention in December, 1988, Bishop Frederick H. Borsch asked congregations, regions, organizations, institutions, commissions, program groups—every entity in the diocese—to think through and shape a plan for the mission of the diocese for the next five and the next ten years.

Out of the convention came a charge to the agenda and planning committee of diocesan council to implement a planning process. A committee of twenty-one persons was formed, representing the diversity of the diocese. Roughly half of this group became a subcommittee to deal with congregational planning, and the other half concerned itself with diocesan planning.

The committee believed strongly that congregations had to take some ownership of the future of their individual mission and ministry, and that out of this work would emerge a sense of where the mission and ministry of the diocese as a whole was heading. Congregations were to begin the process.

A pilot project involving fifteen congregations for the diocese's five regions was initiated. This project used a program developed and supported by Church Information and Development Services, an independent firm, and adapted it to the specific needs of the diocese. The program had previously been used for individual congregations, but had never before been applied on such a broad base. There are four segments to what became known as "Adelante 2000," the Diocese of Los Angeles' congregational self-study and planning process: Bible study, a congregational survey, a community analysis, and analysis of program and ministry.

The Bible study is led by the clergy and is used to explore mission and ministry. Examples of the lessons include a look at vision through Proverbs, Amos, and Jeremiah; an examination of the call to mission in Jesus' vision of God's reign in Luke 4; and an interpretation of the Church under the image of the vine and the branches from John 15. With the study series as a base, the planning process is undergirded by a biblical understanding of ministry and mission to guide the discernment of God's will for the congregation.

Each of the pilot congregations agreed to provide two persons for a forty-four-hour training program. Those two persons made a commitment to lead their congregation through the process and also committed themselves to helping other congregations in the planning process over the next two years. Each pilot congregation then created a committee of twenty to thirty people to oversee the work in their own congregation. The committee was broken up into various areas of responsibility for the three steps of the process. The two trained persons provided the leadership. Thus, local people participated in and led the project.

After much advance publicity, a single Sunday was selected for the entire congregation to take part in a survey during the worship service. The information gathered from the survey then went through a computer data-processing system at CIDS that produced a report to the congregation and the congregation's planning committee. The report gave a definition or profile of who they were as a congregation. The profile included items ranging from personal beliefs to participation in church life to straight demographic information.

The community analysis enabled the church to see what the needs of the community were and how the church was meeting those needs. This part involved personal interviews with community leaders and a demographic analysis of that community. These data gave planners a clear picture of the makeup of the surrounding community, including such information as age ranges, family makeup, and housing patterns. It gave them both a picture of the present and a five-year forecast of where the community was going. Because the community assessment was such an integral part of the planning process, the congregation could not fail to find out both the needs of the community and how the church was meeting or not meeting those needs.

The third part of the program analysis was done through home meetings. Here again, the entire congregation participated, this time in small group home meetings of ten and twelve persons. In these meetings, each group made a list of commendations, celebrating areas of current ministry effectiveness, and short-term recommendations to enhance the overall effectiveness of the church's life and work. All this information was then gathered together by the congregation's planning committee and put in a report to the vestry, with a plan for action.

With this report, the vestry and clergy went on retreat with a few representatives of their parish committee. The gathered information was presented by the committee members. The vestry and the clergy reviewed the data and developed a list of future directions in mission to be presented to the congregation. Sometimes this retreat was a painful experience. Sometimes a gap was seen between the leadership offered and the leadership the congregation senses it wants. However, what came out of the process was a better sense of direction for both congregation and clergy.

A great deal of excitement has been generated in the congregations participating in the project. The congregation members become a part of the process and see that they themselves will be part of the future ministry and mission of their congregation. Attendance and stewardship are up in almost all of the pilot congregations. Some report increases as high as 20 to 23 percent in stewardship and 10 to 15 percent in attendance.

After a presentation by some of the pilot project's participants at Los Angeles' 1989 diocesan convention, eighty-five congregations signed up for the project or are planning to participate in it in the future. Since then, twenty churches have had people trained to lead their congregations through the process. Another training session was scheduled for January of 1991. Training sessions are now projected for two to three times a year for the next few years until all the diocese's 152 congregations have participated. (Note: About 10 percent of the congregations used their own planning process. The diocese is not saying the diocesan system is the only acceptable one.)

For the diocese, the diocesan committee has just completed an analysis of questionnaires sent to program groups, commissions, and institutions. The information gathered from these questionnaires and the data from the congregations will become the base on which the plan for ministry and mission of the diocese for the next five to ten years will be built.

## *DELAWARE: MINISTRY OF THE LAITY*

The diocese believes it is in a historic time of transition. The Church is no longer a center of power and position in this post-Christian, pluralistic, and secular world of individualism.

The diocese believes, further, that God urgently calls all people to an active role in the ministry of reconciliation. The laity are God's primary ministers in the world. They are there in the world, where the primary theological issues and concerns of our day are experienced.

In response, the bishop and diocesan council have worked to encourage and assist congregations in becoming strong, financially self-supporting apostolic communities. Here the people of God gather for worship, strengthening, nurture, and conversation that prepare them to be agents of reconciliation in their communities, workplaces, homes, and beyond. Strong pastoral leadership is seen as essential to the work of the gathered communities of faith as places where people are received and prepared for empowerment. The ordained are encouraged and supported as the teachers, preachers, and preparers of the laity for their ministry in the world. This formation process is understood as a partnership. The laity bring their experience of the context in which they live into the churches for conversation and understanding informed by the Scriptures and tradition passed on by the ordained. The focus of the formation is a deepening understanding of the Gospel message, and it results in a living of the baptismal covenant.

Under the leadership of the bishop, the diocesan council has organized itself to be a strategic body, to identify and understand the issues facing the Church in this time and to empower responses to those challenges. The council has developed four commissions—pastoral leadership, congregations, formation, and mission—with lay and ordained members from both the diocesan council and the diocese at large, and has charged them to be specialists in their particular area. Their job is to be strategic planners, not program developers.

The commissions' work of the first two years has been to focus on the contextual issues in their areas and refine that focus by setting priorities among the challenges to be met. From this identification will come recommended responses, which may be implemented by task force groups in diocesan conferences, regional gatherings, resource assistance, and so forth. The job of the commissions remains always to be identifiers, recommenders, and reviewers.

To support the work of these commissions as parts of a whole and interdependent on each other, the staff members of each commission meet monthly with the bishop, his core staff, and his consultant, the Rev. James Anderson, of the College of the Laity, Washington, D.C. The commission chairs are also encouraged to come to council meetings. Commissions meet monthly and on occasion will schedule interactive meetings with one another. Their work has been shared with the diocese at large at the annual diocesan convention, where an audiovisual presentation was used to set up workshops led by the four commissions.

A stewardship task force committee operates as an integral part of the work of bishop and council to strengthen congregations to be apostolic communities shaping the laity for ministry in the world. The bishop and council have adopted a stewardship statement, supported a diocesan conference on stewardship, and continue to empower the stewardship committee in its work of educating the people of the diocese in an all-encompassing understanding of themselves as stewards of all of God's world. Paralleling and supporting this vision, an Episcopal Charities has been formed and is preparing to make its first annual appeal. The charities funds will be used to help support ministries that are common to the entire diocese—e.g., a nursing home, a day nursery, and an interfaith housing task force. The charities funds will also provide seed money for emerging ministries in the diocese. Work is also being done on developing existing conference and camp facilities as formation institutions for the work of the formation committee.

The bishop's visitations are planned with the same emphasis as the work of the council. At a meeting with a vestry, the bishop turns the focus of their work away from administrative tasks to that of a leadership body identifying the context of the communities they represent and developing ways to support their members in their ministries. Video aids such as *Faith on a Tightrope, Parts I and II,* produced by the Total Ministry Office of the Episcopal Church Center, and the *Field of Mission,* the piece produced for the annual convention, are getting people to talk about their own ministries. Teaching time with the congregation is also used to explain the current reality of the Church in a post-Christian age by reviewing history and underpinning it with an understanding of the Church in exile. Israel asked "how can we sing the Lord's song in a strange land" as it endured captivity in Babylon. Today's Christians are learning to sing the Lord's song in this strange new world of pluralism and secularism.

The consultant, the Rev. James Anderson, pointed out in an interview that "the issue is not the ministry of the laity. The issue is the mission of the Church. Given the kind of world we live in, it is the laity who must be the chief evangelists and missionaries. While the new Prayer Book and its baptismal service imply a new role for the laity, that simply is not the case yet. What we are going through is a massive transformation in the nature of the Church. It may take a hundred years."[2]

How ever long the task may finally take, the diocese's mission strategy has already had some positive effects in increased stewardship (up 23 percent in the last two years), heightened enthusiasm, and growing lay awareness of themselves as the chief ministers in the world, a world that cries out for the reconciliation of all people to God and to one another.

## *MILWAUKEE: LIVING OUR BAPTISMAL COVENANT*

At the Diocese of Milwaukee's 1986 diocesan convention, Bishop Roger White made this charge:

> It is my belief that the structure of the diocese needs to reflect the mission and ministry of the people of God . . . . I am concerned that the present structure does not enable the mission and ministry of the Church, but rather is a hindrance, and often is responsible for our poor planning, poor communication, and poor representation; it is in need of immediate examination.[3]

At the time of these comments, White had been diocesan bishop for a year, and had worked with the various groups in the diocese to assess where Milwaukee's strengths were and where changes might be needed to further the mission of the Church. The budgeting process had already been reorganized to reflect the baptismal covenant. However, it also became clear that major reorganization would be needed to focus the mission of the diocese and give it direction for the future. The Commission on Diocesan Restructure was created for that purpose.

This commission drafted a strong mission statement, which was adopted by the Diocesan Convention in 1987. The statement stressed three main objectives: to support and increase the members of the Church, the Body of Christ; to develop new and revitalized lay and clerical ministries; and to increase outreach. It reads as follows:

> The mission of the Episcopal Diocese of Milwaukee, as a part of the Body of Christ, is to live the Gospel of Jesus Christ in thought, word, and deed, as pledged in our baptismal covenant. We are called to pray and to offer worship, to be nourished by Word, Sacrament, and fellowship, and to empower and enable ministries for justice, peace and love.
>
> The Diocese is dedicated to support and increase the members of the Body of Christ, to develop new and revitalized parishes through evangelism and stewardship, and to increase outreach in service to human needs, thereby proclaiming Christ as Lord and Savior.[4]

Three steps were urged to carry out the three new objectives.

> 1. Strengthening the Deanery structure to strengthen spiritual, social, and administrative cooperation at that level of ministry.
> 2. Reorganizing the senior staff of the diocese to include an assistant with significant responsibilities in clergy deployment, pastoral care of clergy, and parish-to-parish problem solving.
> 3. Reviewing as necessary the reorganization of Departments and Commissions of the Diocese to help them become more accountable and more accessible to those in need of their services.[5]

To date, the mission statement has been fulfilled in the following ways.

> 1. As part of the development and growth of the diocesan program Living Our Baptismal Covenant, a catechumenal process has been adopted

throughout the congregations of the diocese, and serves as a widely known model throughout the Church for the formation of Christians in their faith. Twenty-five congregations out of sixty-four have adopted the process so far. Chapter 3 of this book is about one such congregation.

2. The Department of Congregational Development now encourages congregational financial self-sufficiency by providing specific consultation and support in close cooperation with congregations of all sizes in areas identified cooperatively.

3. Stronger programs in outreach include
- a growing number of outreach programs at the parish level, and diocesan financial support to begin and continue these programs through funds from Episcopal Outreach Ministries;
- continued leadership in "the Gathering," one of the largest and most adequate feeding programs in this metropolitan area;
- the recent upgrading of urban ministries in the Milwaukee metro area with new leadership and reorganized services, including diocesan funding for a new church building in downtown Milwaukee as an added base for worship and outreach;
- the recent development of a small intentional Christian community housed in a newly purchased Jubilee House in the central city;
- the development of St. Barnabas Center, a treatment program for troubled clergy and clergy families open to clergy from any diocese;
- initial efforts in Hispanic ministry in urban areas;
- the continuation of a large overnight shelter and food-supply program in a secondary urban area; and
- the development of housing for retired people in several locations in the diocese.[6]

The diocese believes these results are signs that it is fulfilling its main objective: Christians are being formed in faith and commitment, and being prepared for ministry where God has placed them so that they can be participants in God's mission.

## KANSAS: RELOCATING THE LOCAL BASES FOR MISSION

In 1987 the Diocese of Kansas adopted a long-range strategic mission plan, developed over a five-year period, to guide the diocese to the year 2000. The following is an outline of the strategic goals and some of the strategies developed to work toward those goals:

Goal 1: Stewardship formation and education
Goal 2: Evangelism
Goal 3: Developing new mission strategies
    Relocating poorly placed congregations
    Developing and redeveloping congregations
    Parish Action/Consultant Training (PACT)
    Developing a land bank for new start-ups
    New church start-ups
    New forms of ministries—e.g., regional ministries—for small churches and rural areas
    New Directions Diocesan Leadership Development
Goal 4: Developing the ministry of all baptized persons
    "Living into Our Baptism"
    "Ministry Exploration"
Goal 5: Spiritual development and Christian education
    Youth ministry
    Campus ministry
Goal 6: Communication
Goal 7: Outreach ministries and social concerns
    Episcopal social services
    Special concerns in society

This story tells only one part of Kansas' story of mission discernment.

In 1982, the diocese had commissioned the first of several demographic studies of Kansas City, Topeka, and Wichita. The consultant, Tex Sample of St. Paul's School of Theology in Kansas City, Missouri, discovered several churches poorly placed to serve their communities and attract new members. They had been built during the early 1950s, when suburban community life was focused on schools and churches. The enclosed shopping malls that have come along in later decades have become the new community centers. Populations now center around the malls rather than the schools and churches. These churches were now relatively invisible and isolated, a barrier to growth in ministry and evangelism.

The diocese took the lead in helping these congregations to relocate. Each convocation studied the situation of its churches in this predicament and recommended to the Long-Range Strategy Committee which congregations should move and where they should move.

Traffic arteries and feeder areas helped identify more visible locations. Adequate space and accessibility were considered as well. It was discovered that people are usually willing to spend up to twenty minutes traveling to church and that they more readily drive toward town rather than away from town. This favored new sites on the downtown side of suburban areas.

It was further discovered that 1.75 to 2.25 percent of people in suburban areas become members of Episcopal churches. The size of buildings and their location were chosen to serve the anticipated needs of their communities.

Normally, 80 percent of a congregation's members live within three miles of their church. The amount of debt incurred also needed careful study. A debt load requiring more than 25 to 30 percent of gross income makes a congregation maintenance-oriented rather than mission-oriented.

Since relocation involves a grief process, the first step was for a congregation to consider the new future a different location might bring them. Further, members needed to anticipate how new people might enter their relocated church community and how they might make room for them and share some of their accustomed roles with them.

To date, six churches have been relocated. The process is a demanding one. Nevertheless, increased vitality and membership have resulted.

# EASTERN OREGON: MUTUAL MINISTRY AND LOCAL RESPONSIBILITY FOR MISSION

In its Mission Strategy and Ministry Development Plan, the Diocese of Eastern Oregon states:

> The old, persistent (and unfulfilled) fantasy of a trained priest in every community and several ordained persons in larger churches has both directly and indirectly denied us the creativity and courage to develop wisely the skills for ministry which are available in each congregation, and to be responsive to those skills in terms of local and regional congregational needs . . . . In the process of working toward the wise development of ministry, we should examine every option, not as a stop-gap to weakness, but as a strategy for the development of the Servant Church which has the ability and will to move from survival to mission.[7]

The mission and ministry plan was developed over a two-year period by Eastern Oregon's Commission for Mission and Ministry Develpment. Made up of both clerical and lay representatives, the commission remains responsible for the oversight and implementation of the plan. One of its principal priorities is the establishment of regional strategies to make better use of diocesan resources. The development of clusters is one result. A cluster is a group of congregations in which each carries on its own mission and all come together for mutual support and share the services of one or more seminary-trained clergy. Another is that all the full-time diocesan seminary-educated clergy are released by their congregations to devote 20 to 25 percent of their time to diocesan work. This often means working in congregations that cannot afford full-time clergy. In addition, emphasis is placed on the ministry of the laity in the workplace and in the world.

Eastern Oregon sees its work growing out of the nature of Christian life in the rural Northwest. Eastern Oregon presents a number of unique challenges. Oregon is one of the most "unchurched" states in the country, with only 30 percent of the people in the state claiming any church affiliation. Further, there is no major city in the diocese to provide it with a strong organizing center. Some of the congregations are as much as 120 miles apart. The diocese believes the challenge before it is to recover some of the sense of excitement and vitality of the early Christian Church. It believes that one of the ways to achieve this is through mutual ministry.

Currently, the diocese is working with three of its twenty-three congregations on a project it hopes will serve as a model for future work. The first step is educational. It includes the history of what happened to the vision of the first Christians. Why did the Church become institutionalized and hierarchical, and what have been the positive and negative results? While the tightening up of church life brought survival, the cost was rigidity and a loss of intimacy and equality. Today we are recovering the importance of Baptism and the nature of genuine Christian community, in which each person's gifts for ministry are valued. This educational task has been led by each congregation's design committee, working in consultation with Helen Netos, the diocesan staff person for program.

In the two congregations where mutual ministry has developed the furthest, the education process remains ongoing. Teaching and sermons continue to emphasize the nature of Christian community. A series of theological topics also addresses the particular needs of each congregation in order to foster discussion of local ministry, both lay and ordained, and how it is lived out.

The final step in this process is the selection of a ministry support team. The support team is made up of ministers, both lay and locally ordained clergy, who support the congregation in carrying out its ministry. For example, a deacon will not only practice the traditional servant ministry of the diaconate, but will also organize others and bring the needs of the community to the attention of the congregation. Of the three congregations in this program, one has already named its ministry support team, and the second was scheduled to do so before the end of the year. The diocese is identifying additional congregations that seem to be ready to begin this process.

Several things have already been learned. This work will take a long time, and every congregation, every cluster, and every area needs to find its own special way of ministry. The diocese can be a resource, but the process will only work if every situation is treated as unique, because the responsibility for the mission of each congregation belongs to the people of that congregation.

# EAST CAROLINA: ANNUAL EVALUATION AND PLANNING FOR EACH CONGREGATION

The mission statement of the Diocese of East Carolina commits its people "to rejoice in being members of God's family, to affirm the diversity of gifts with which we are blessed, to serve with passion wherever God calls us into ministry, and to support this ministry with our time, talent, and money."[8] In response, Bishop B. Sidney Sanders has helped the diocese take servant ministry and mission discernment seriously. Clerical and lay leaders have also helped. The diocese's executive council, which drafted the mission statement, has developed a series of five-year goals for congregational development, stewardship, evangelism and renewal, the strengthening of black ministries, development of servant ministries, and leadership development.

The diocesan Department of Mission has initiated a plan for every congregation to review the dynamics of its mission and ministry to itself and to its community, and its shared ministry with other congregations in its region. Each is to evaluate its life over the past ten years and the life of the broader community of which the congregation is a part. Each congregation has been asked to annually determine its mission of servanthood, to evaluate its present potential and prospects, to choose goals appropriate to its restated mission, and to develop strategies to implement the new goals. The diocese provides trained consultants to assist congregations in evaluation and planning and training for ongoing leadership. The Rev. Ted McEachern of ACTS, the lead consultant, trains the consultants who work with the congregations. By the end of 1991, all but three of East Carolina's seventy-three congregations will have begun this annual mission review and planning. The costs are split between the diocese and the individual congregations.

The diocesan Stewardship Commission has made three videotapes over the past four years to communicate the vision and mission of the diocese and to share the stories of what is happening in some of East Carolina's congregations. The diocese's Evangelism Commission has involved ten congregations in an evangelism pilot program, which uses the congregation itself as the basic evangelizing unit. The congregation looks at itself in five different areas: how it proclaims the Gospel; new member ministry; lapsed members; renewal; and ministry to the community, which involves social outreach. The commission seeks to have twenty congregations participating by 1992, and from then on, to involve five new congregations each year.

Results can already be seen in the congregations that now provide basic services to the homeless and the poor. These include a day shelter in Wilmington supported by the area's churches; a "Shepherd's Staff" house in Belhaven ministering to poverty-stricken persons; and a $1.5 million retirement village for the poor in Belhaven called Pungo Village, which is soon to be duplicated in Hyde County. Stewardship support for the diocese has doubled over the past seven years, and a creative program has developed that supports various agencies and congregational outreach ministries with money from trust funds that formerly underwrote the diocesan operating budget. The agencies range from shelters for abused spouses to food pantries to farm worker day care. Over the last seven years, the diocese has given more than $500,000 toward these outreach programs. Thirty percent of East Carolina's annual budget is committed to outreach.

The whole thrust of the diocesan approach has been to help congregations move from maintenance to mission. The diocese believes that regardless of size, a congregation is not viable unless it is concerned with and responding to its surrounding community. The Diocese of East Carolina sees its role as not only raising awareness and holding congregations accountable, but also providing congregations with the teaching and resources necessary to address the needs of their communities.

## *SUMMARY*

East Carolina talks of moving from maintenance to mission. This theme underlies all of these stories. The same concern ran through the 1988 gathering in Lambeth, England, of the bishops of the twenty-seven national churches constituting the worldwide Anglican Communion, of which the Episcopal Church is a part. That conference, in Resolution 044, called for ". . . a shift to a dynamic missionary emphasis going beyond care and nurture to proclamation and service and, therefore, accepts the challenge this presents to diocesan and local church structures and patterns of worship and ministry, and looks to God for a fresh movement of the Spirit in prayer, outgoing love and evangelism in obedience to our Lord's command." The seven stories told here respond to this call.

Two other themes are threaded through the stories. One is the ministry of the laity. Today's world puts the laity in the primary places of mission. Their training and support are of the utmost importance.

The other theme is local responsibility for mission. The diocese cannot *do* mission for the local congregations; it *can* call for, encourage, and support local responsibility for mission.

These seven stories are not the only stories of dioceses moving from maintenance to mission. We regret we could not tell them all. New stories are forming. We want to tell more in the future. Dioceses and their congregations share the one mission to "restore all people to unity with God and each other in Christ" (BCP, p. 855).

---

## NOTES

[1] The Rev. James A. Kelsey, telephone interview, October 24, 1990.
[2] The Rev. James D. Anderson, telephone interview, November 16, 1990.
[3] The Rt. Rev. Roger J. White and the Rev. Canon Wyatt E. Stephens, draft of "Our Call to Mission," paper, Fall 1990, page 1.
[4] *Ibid.*
[5] *Ibid.*
[6] *Op. cit.*, White, page 2.
[7] "A Mission Strategy and Development Plan for the Episcopal Diocese of Eastern Oregon," a report of the Commission for Mission and Ministry Development to Diocesan Council, January 3, 1989; pp. 1-2. Revised and presented to Diocesan Convention, October, 1989.
[8] "Diocese of East Carolina Mission Statement," drafted by the Executive Council of the Diocese of East Carolina, 1989.

## APPENDIX 2

# Using This Book in Mission Discernment

To discern mission is to perceive, by the Holy Spirit, what a congregation is called to be and to do in its local community and beyond.

The Anglican Consultative Council, consisting of clergy and lay representatives from each church of the Anglican Communion, meeting in Badagry, Nigeria, in 1984, named elements of mission for a "mission audit" by every congregation. They are:

- Evangelism and initiation
- Worship, nurture, and teaching
- Service, and
- Social transformation.

These four areas are extremely useful for reference when a congregation seeks to discern its mission.

As a congregation faces the world, its mission has two dimensions. One dimension is what the congregation does as a body to minister in its community and the wider world. The primary ministries of the body as it faces the world are serving others in need, building a more just society, and making Jesus Christ known. The other dimension is what its members do as individuals to minister in their daily lives—in their workplaces, their homes, their communities; as citizens in their state and nation; and in their leisure—as well as in their churches. Some of the primary tasks in furthering the mission of the individual members are preparing the members for their mission, supporting them in their mission, and offering the means of holding one another accountable for faithfulness in mission.

The whole of mission discernment needs to be supported with individual and corporate Bible study and prayer. The lectionary passages for the period of mission discernment can be used for reflection, asking what do I/we learn here about mission and what do I/we sense God is saying to me/us about mission here, in this part of God's world. The lections for mission and ministry noted in pp. 929-30 of the BCP can also be reviewed for possible use.

A congregation needs to be sure there are special opportunities for group study and prayer and encouragement of private study and prayer. Prayer should open and close each meeting. Members should be encouraged to write down the reflections and ideas that come into their minds between meetings, to test them with other members, and to feed them into the group dialogue at meetings.

The congregation should also take time for silent prayer at moments during group planning meetings. Mission is discerned. Webster, second edition, 1946, says *to discern* is "to lay hold of with the understanding, especially that which is hidden or obscure." In a religious context, discernment is the work of the Holy Spirit. Its outcome has a rational coherence, but it is not necessarily the end result of a chain of rational argument.

The heart of mission discernment is theological reflection. A special committee of seven bishops was called together to review this book and its use. They identified a process for theological reflection with the help of one of their members, the Rt. Rev. Craig Anderson of South Dakota. Bishop Anderson describes the process as follows.

> In such movement, inductive methods which build on experience are appropriate for Anglicans. Those in a confessional tradition which tends to move from doctrine to experience will use other methods.
>
> The following method is offered as representative of "below to above" methodology. It is based on the Anglican model of theological authority for meaning and ministry as discerned in Scripture, tradition and reason. Sources that inform this method are: Gadamar, Hans Georg, *Truth and Method;* Farley, Edward, *Ecclesial Reflection;* Lonergan, Bernard, *Method in Theology;* Tracy, David, *Blessed Page for Order;* Whitehead, David

and Evelyn, *Method for Ministry;* and Lindbeck, George, *The Nature of Doctrine.*

These works draw on social phenomenology; trancendental Thomism, especially Karl Rahner; as well as contemporary Anglican theologians, e.g., John MacQuarrie and Urban T. Holmes. A more detailed account of the method, its relationship to the Anglican model, and its use for reflection and ministerial action is available if there is further interest.

"A Theological Method"
The direction is a hermeneutical circle.

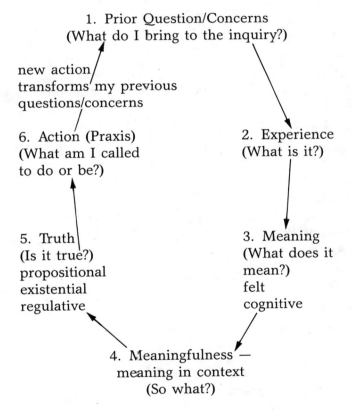

1. Prior Question/Concerns
(What do I bring to the inquiry?)

new action transforms my previous questions/concerns

6. Action (Praxis)
(What am I called to do or be?)

2. Experience
(What is it?)

5. Truth
(Is it true?)
propositional
existential
regulative

3. Meaning
(What does it mean?)
felt
cognitive

4. Meaningfulness —
meaning in context
(So what?)

—The Rt. Rev. Craig B. Anderson, Ph.D.

Bishop Anderson noted the tendency of contemporary theologians to stop at the meaning step and only make truth statements, thereby not making a strong contact with today's world. He also noted the tendency of nontheologians to move directly from experience to action and thereby miss the unique perspective of theological reflection and the unique chance that it offers for discerning God's will.

The method outlined above might be adapted as follows for using this book for theological reflection.

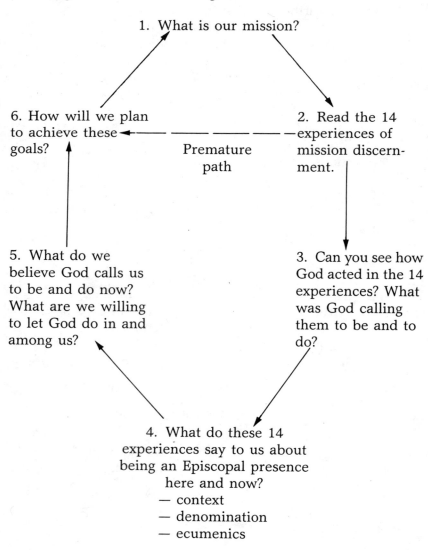

# SUGGESTED APPROACHES TO MISSION DISCERNMENT

For a congregation discerning its mission the first time, the following approach can be used.

1. Members prepare to explore what their mission is.
   a. Members, in prayer, plan how they will covenant with one another and God for individual and group Bible study and prayer throughout the discernment process.
   b. Members describe the mission of the congregation as they now see it and evaluate their present ministry.
2. Members review the chapters of this book.
3. Members work through the question, "How do we see God acting in these fourteen experiences? What was God calling each of the fourteen congregations to be and to do?"
4. Members work through the question, "What do these fourteen experiences say to us about being an Episcopal presence in our particular context here and now?" They include the implications for their work with other Christian communities in their area. Members may want to collect some of the information described in 6. a. iii from the more detailed planning step below as they consider these questions.
5. Members arrive at answers to the questions, "What do we believe God is calling us to be and do now? What are we willing to let God do in and among us?" This may result in so many calls to action that they have to choose among them. Useful criteria for these choices might be the depth of need, their ability to respond helpfully, and the level of challenge and excitement each alternative offers.
   a. Members develop plans to achieve their new goals for mission. (This step is described in greater detail later on.)
   b. Members evaluate how they worked together and give a final review to their goals (Are these the goals we believe God asks of us?) and plans (Are there better ways to achieve these goals?).
   c. As a congregation the group offers the goals and plans to God and asks God to adopt them where they are part of God's work and to correct them where they need correction.

This process is repeated every year or two with this book or a similar resource to provide the needed experience. After several years, their own experience in mission will become a more and more suitable subject for reflection.

This procedure assumes the family-size congregation (one with an average attendance of up to fifty). Larger congregations will use some combination of a representative task force and face-to-face meetings with as many of the members as possible. In both large and small congregations, be sure the mission discernment includes senior high school-age youth. If a college or university campus is nearby, be sure students and faculty are represented as well. Consultants with expertise in group work and planning and with a working Christian worldview may be used to help any size congregation in any or all of the six steps.

For congregations who are repeating the discernment process, the same procedure is followed, except for step 1. B., where the members evaluate their work to fulfill their present statement of mission.

The developing of action plans (step 6. a) can be oversimplified. The following is a more detailed description of the steps for planning. Congregations using these steps will find the basic elements of theological reflection coming up again and again. That is as it should be. Theology is implicit in every human activity.

6. a. Carefully consider these basic assumptions and criteria for your planning. Select those that will guide your mission discernment. Add your own.
   i. Examine some assumptions about mission.
      - For us the Church's ministry and mission are distinct but inseparable, yet the terms are often used interchangeably and vaguely.
      - A mission is a concise expression of an organization's purpose, specifying the fundamental reasons for its existence.
      - The word *mission* derives from the Latin *mittere* ("to send") or *missio* ("a sending") and implies being sent out with authority to perform a special duty.
      - The word *ministry* derives from the Latin *ministrare* ("to attend") and implies the performance of needed services within the context of a mission.
      - *Mission* implies missions, and *ministry* implies ministries.

- The fundamental mission of the Church is the restoration of all persons to unity with God and one another in Christ, the ministry of reconciliation.
- This ministry in general—and ministries in particular—is the Church's mission in general—and missions in particular.
- Mission points outward and leads us beyond ourselves.
- Mission has been accomplished only when effective ministry has been achieved.

ii. Consider some criteria for discernment.
- A mission—as the term is used here—is a planned response to a condition demanding attention, with the expectation of a specific result.
- The objective or goal of the mission is the future condition intended—not the activities involved, but the results wanted.
- A condition is merely a condition until it becomes an opportunity or a problem for someone, in which something is at stake.
- A condition demanding attention—one where something is at stake—confronts us with a choice, a crisis, a decision, to which we must respond.
- The choice or the crisis can lead to conflict between the memory of what has been and the vision of what might be.
- An issue involves two choices that are, ultimately, mutually exclusive.
- Needs can be met, and problems solved; but issues are never solved, only lived with. Issues are forever and for everyone; they involve us all and bespeak a dilemma of conflicting possibilities, each with its own cost and promise.
- Every condition demanding attention betrays issues that will emerge again to be resolved again in response to the final question, What is at stake for whom?
- Every issue before us is imbedded in the myths and legends and lives of the biblical people of God: their story is our story, and we are the story God tells.

*Examples:*

Tennessee used these criteria in developing its mission strategy in June, 1989. Two examples based on items 1 and 2 in Attachment 1 on p. 374 will illustrate.

1) One of the conditions faced in the Diocese of Tennessee is that there are twenty-one counties *without the presence of the Episcopal Church*. From the time of Bishops Otey, Quintard, and Gailor, the Diocese of Tennessee has discerned a call to provide an Anglican presence in Tennessee. In developing their strategy, they were making a choice of continuing to respond to this call originally discerned in the pioneer church.

    *Condition:* Twenty-one counties are without an Episcopal presence.

    *Stake:* We have commitment to an Anglican presence in Tennessee.

    *Choice:* We must choose to establish presence of some kind or continue present work only.

    *Conflict:* What has been—the comfort of present level—conflicts with what might be—increased cost in time and money.

    *Issue:* Shall we offer what we have in a new place vs. be effective where we are?

    *Mission:* Seek to establish some presence in the twenty-one counties.

2) In the Diocese of Tennessee we face a condition of the mixture of affluence and poverty throughout the diocese. We are making the choice in the development of our strategy to respond to this condition by including such a response in our development of total ministry. In addition, we are referring our understanding of this condition to the diocesan organization in social responsibility and asking them to be sensitive to it in their planning.

    *Condition:* Affluence and poverty are side by side.

    *Stake:* Poverty is painful.

    *Choice:* Shall we change the situation or accept the situation?

*Conflict:* What has been—the ease of an affluent lifestyle—conflicts with what might be—a change in the allocation of resources.
*Issue:* What can really be achieved when the problem is so great?
*Mission:* Reduce poverty.

Note: For each condition, the stakes, choices, conflicts, issues, and mission chosen can take a variety of forms.

iii. Collect some information about the world around you and about yourselves. The following questions are usually overlooked. Choose which ones you will seek to answer. Add your own.
- What human hopes and hurts touch you deeply, move you to act?
- Have you identified the needs of particular groups in your area, such as ethnic minorities, people with low income, youth (junior and senior highs), college students and faculty, young adults, singles and older adults?
- What do you have going for you, what gifts and talents?
- Who else in your congregation or diocese might have similar longings and competencies?
- What conditions among you and around you call out to be redressed?
- What have you, and others with you, to offer that might help?
- What is at stake for whom?
- What will you have to give up and risk losing along the way?
- What help might you need as you proceed, and where might you find it?
- What new conditions do you envision?
- How are they to be maintained and modified?
- What are your specific objectives in terms of concrete results?
- What biblical or credal rationale supports your conclusions?
- What, in descriptive terms, is your vision of the results of this mission?

- What kind of future are you building?
- What, succinctly, is God calling you to accomplish?

iv. Once you have collected the desired information to answer your questions, try to put it all together in a story. Then connect it with yourselves. Use these questions and others you may choose.
- What story does the condition at issue tell?
- Whose story is it?
- Where is a similar story told in the Bible?
- Where in myth, legend, or history has that story been told before?
- How is it your story?
- What is at stake for whom?
- What is the cost, for whom?
- What is the promise, for whom?
- What are you willing to risk?
- How might the story end?

v. Now, put into words the mission you hear, see, or feel God is calling you to take up.

a. Condition
- What specific dimensions of the condition you plan to address seem most significant? What further information about them do you need? How will you obtain it? Who is involved?
- Examples: Attachment #1—Conditions and Choices . . . in Tennessee, June, 1989.
  Attachment #2—Mission Opportunity Questionnaire. This questionnaire may be useful to help a congregation identify conditions they want to address and to prioritize them.

b. Objective
- What specific results are you after? What concrete changes will be needed in whom and by whom?
- Resource: Attachment #3—Force-Field Analysis. This inventory can help a congregation to clarify a condition or situation and to identify the forces to be dealt with in that situation.
  Attachment #4—Action—Objectives.

vi. Draw up your plan.
- What must be done? To gain commitment (orientation)? To gain competence (training)? To gain con-

fidence (consultation)? To gain cooperation (supervision)? To continue (evaluation)?
- Attachment #5—Planning: Its Reasons for Failure, Symptoms, and Cures.
- Attachment #6—Conflict-Resolution Styles. Conflict between different viewpoints may arise in discerning mission. This resource will provide some ways to work with conflict creatively. Recall too that conflict is part of life and a sign not of a problem but of vitality. Creative use of disagreement—perhaps a better name for conflict resolution—is essential in our fallen world where no one has a monopoly on the truth.

## *SOME FINAL NOTES*
1. Each congregation will need to adapt these steps to its own needs.
2. Each congregation needs to move through this process at its own pace. Try to avoid getting bogged down on the one hand, and on the other, moving so rapidly that nothing of significance occurs.

*Attachment #1*

# CONDITIONS AND CHOICES FOR MISSION STRATEGY

## DEVELOPED IN DIOCESE OF TENNESSEE MISSION STRATEGY WORKSHOPS, JUNE, 1989

1) One of the conditions we face in the Diocese of Tennessee is that we have 21 counties *without the presence of the Episcopal Church*. From the time of Bishops Otey, Quintard, and Gailor, the Diocese of Tennessee has discerned a call to provide an Anglican presence in Tennessee. In developing our strategy, we are making a choice of continuing to respond to this call originally discerned in the pioneer Church.

2) In the Diocese of Tennessee we face a condition of *the mixture of affluence and poverty throughout the diocese*. We are making the choice in the development of our strategy to respond to this condition by including such a response in our development of total ministry. In addition, we are referring our understanding of this condition to the diocesan organization on social responsibility and asking them to be sensitve to it in their planning.

3) One of the conditions we face in the Church is *a low level of expectation by many,* perhaps a majority, of laity and clergy, coupled with low financial support, a large fringe membership, and a lack of understanding of our own tradition. In the Diocese of Tennessee we are making the choice to respond to this condition through the development of the catechumenate, beginning in one parish and spreading through the Diocese. The mission strategy we are here developing will cooperate with the development of the catechumenate as a part of the development of total ministry in the Diocese.

4) One complex of conditions begins with the fact that *we tend to keep the Anglican heritage to ourselves,* with its gifts of freedom, powerful worship, and a reasonable approach to Scripture and doctrine. We live in a region with a pluralistic culture—with strong fundamentalist religion on the one hand and strong secular and humanistic values on the other, a region in which the attitude toward the Episcopal Church is a mixture of respect, ignorance, and condescension. As a diocese we are choosing to respond to this condition through the efforts of the Communications work-

ing group, but we realize that an adequate response requires additional energy, money, and effort. One such addition will be the inclusion of communications skills in the development of total ministry here contemplated. We also refer our understanding of this condition to the Evangelism working group as a challenge in their planning.

(These conditions, out of a total of thirteen, are reprinted by permission.)

*Attachment #2*

# MISSION OPPORTUNITY QUESTIONNAIRE*

This brief questionnaire is designed to elicit response to the data in our census report. It lists a number of projects and activities in which local churches are engaged and that may be possibilities for our church. Check the response that comes closest to your reaction to each possibility. There is room for you to note your own additional suggestions. You do not have to sign your name.

| | Not Needed in Our Community | Not Appropriate For Our Church | Low Priority At This Time | Only Moderate Priority At This Time | High Priority/ Needs Immediate Attention |
|---|---|---|---|---|---|
| 1. Set a goal for membership growth | ☐ | ☐ | ☐ | ☐ | ☐ |
| 2. Improve our church's outreach to young adults | ☐ | ☐ | ☐ | ☐ | ☐ |
| 3. Develop more effective outreach to young adults | ☐ | ☐ | ☐ | ☐ | ☐ |
| 4. Review our church's ministry to families and family members | ☐ | ☐ | ☐ | ☐ | ☐ |
| 5. Look for ways we can minister to persons in nontraditional families | ☐ | ☐ | ☐ | ☐ | ☐ |
| 6. Broaden our church's appeal to educational and income groups not now represented in our congregation | ☐ | ☐ | ☐ | ☐ | ☐ |
| 7. Examine ways our church can address problems of unemployment in our community | ☐ | ☐ | ☐ | ☐ | ☐ |
| 8. Consider more effective programs for the elderly and persons living alone | ☐ | ☐ | ☐ | ☐ | ☐ |
| 9. Review our congregation's stewardship potential in light of community income data | ☐ | ☐ | ☐ | ☐ | ☐ |
| 10. Review church staff salaries in light of community income data | ☐ | ☐ | ☐ | ☐ | ☐ |
| 11. Develop new ministries to single persons in our community | ☐ | ☐ | ☐ | ☐ | ☐ |
| 12. Consider ways our church can reach out to persons who are divorced and separated | ☐ | ☐ | ☐ | ☐ | ☐ |
| 13. Broaden our church's appeal to ethnic groups not now represented in the congregation | ☐ | ☐ | ☐ | ☐ | ☐ |
| 14. Do a better job of introducing newcomers in the community to the life and program of our church | ☐ | ☐ | ☐ | ☐ | ☐ |
| 15. Develop new ministries to military personnel living in our community | ☐ | ☐ | ☐ | ☐ | ☐ |
| 16. Strengthen our ministry to and with college students | ☐ | ☐ | ☐ | ☐ | ☐ |

|  | Not Needed in Our Community | Not Appropriate For Our Church | Low Priority At This Time | Only Moderate Priority At This Time | High Priority/ Needs Immediate Attention |
|---|---|---|---|---|---|
| 17. Do a better job meeting the needs of persons in local nursing homes | ☐ | ☐ | ☐ | ☐ | ☐ |
| 18. Consider new ministries with persons living in institutions such as prisons and mental hospitals | ☐ | ☐ | ☐ | ☐ | ☐ |
| 19. Improve our church's ministry to persons with disabilities | ☐ | ☐ | ☐ | ☐ | ☐ |
| 20. Look at our church building with a view to making it accessible to persons with physical handicaps | ☐ | ☐ | ☐ | ☐ | ☐ |
| 21. Find new ways to attract young people and families to our church school or church education program | ☐ | ☐ | ☐ | ☐ | ☐ |
| 22. Look for ways to appeal to young people who might be attracted to our church's youth groups | ☐ | ☐ | ☐ | ☐ | ☐ |
| 23. Explore the possibility of a vacation church school for neighborhood children | ☐ | ☐ | ☐ | ☐ | ☐ |
| 24. Explore the feasibility of a volunteer program to teach English to persons whose primary language is other than English | ☐ | ☐ | ☐ | ☐ | ☐ |
| 25. Convene a meeting of churches and other groups to look at problems in our community and ways we could address them together | ☐ | ☐ | ☐ | ☐ | ☐ |
| 26. Invite community leaders to meet with our church board to look at ways our church can work to address community concerns | ☐ | ☐ | ☐ | ☐ | ☐ |
| 27. Develop a "partnership" relationship with another (Episcopal) church or a group of churches facing pressing community needs | ☐ | ☐ | ☐ | ☐ | ☐ |
| 28. Consider the possibility of a church-sponsored day-care center for children of working parents | ☐ | ☐ | ☐ | ☐ | ☐ |
| 29. Examine the feasibility of our church sponsoring a housing project for the elderly or low-income families | ☐ | ☐ | ☐ | ☐ | ☐ |
| 30. Explore ways your congregation can work on environmental issues and their related issues of justice in your community | ☐ | ☐ | ☐ | ☐ | ☐ |
| 31. Explore ways your community needs to think globally as it acts locally | ☐ | ☐ | ☐ | ☐ | ☐ |
| 32. Explore ways your congregation might link itself with an Anglican congregation in another culture or country for mutual support and learning | ☐ | ☐ | ☐ | ☐ | ☐ |
| 33. Identify and use the experience of parishioners and/or community members who are from or have lived in another country | ☐ | ☐ | ☐ | ☐ | ☐ |
| 34. Establish or strengthen a committee that deals with world mission concerns | ☐ | ☐ | ☐ | ☐ | ☐ |

|   | Not Needed in Our Community | Not Appropriate For Our Church | Low Priority At This Time | Only Moderate Priority At This Time | High Priority/ Needs Immediate Attention |
|---|---|---|---|---|---|
| 35. Develop a partnership relationship with a congregation in another country | ☐ | ☐ | ☐ | ☐ | ☐ |
| 36. Initiate or increase involvement in our diocesan companion diocese relationship | ☐ | ☐ | ☐ | ☐ | ☐ |
| 37. Develop a global education program that expands our understanding of global issues | ☐ | ☐ | ☐ | ☐ | ☐ |
| 38. Review our church school program to see if it highlights world mission or Anglican partnerships | ☐ | ☐ | ☐ | ☐ | ☐ |
| 39. Support global mission through our contributions to the national Church apportionment, Good Friday Offering, Church School Missionary Offering, etc. | ☐ | ☐ | ☐ | ☐ | ☐ |
| 40. Support a Volunteer for Mission | ☐ | ☐ | ☐ | ☐ | ☐ |
| 41. Increase awareness of world mission by using the *Anglican Cycle of Prayer,* mission hymns, sermons and overseas visitors or missionaries during our liturgies | ☐ | ☐ | ☐ | ☐ | ☐ |
| 42. Develop a relationship with students from another country | ☐ | ☐ | ☐ | ☐ | ☐ |
| 43. Consider ways to be in solidarity with Anglican Churches as they address the needs of the poor, struggle for justice, evangelize, etc. | ☐ | ☐ | ☐ | ☐ | ☐ |
| 44. Organize study and action trips outside the U.S. for both young and old | ☐ | ☐ | ☐ | ☐ | ☐ |
| 45. Explore ways in which our congregation can develop a relationship with the national Church program and priorities | ☐ | ☐ | ☐ | ☐ | ☐ |
| 46. Study and develop local actions in response to General Convention or Executive Council actions | ☐ | ☐ | ☐ | ☐ | ☐ |
| 47. Explore ways to work ecumenically both locally and internationally | ☐ | ☐ | ☐ | ☐ | ☐ |
| 48. Explore ways to educate the congregation about our partner churches. This education process could include activities to allow the congregation to view the world through the partners' eyes, putting "our" selves into "their" place | ☐ | ☐ | ☐ | ☐ | ☐ |
| 49. Other _____ | ☐ | ☐ | ☐ | ☐ | ☐ |
| 50. Other _____ | ☐ | ☐ | ☐ | ☐ | ☐ |
| 51. Other _____ | ☐ | ☐ | ☐ | ☐ | ☐ |

*Numbers 1-29 and the format are reproduced from Carroll, Dudley, and McKinney, *Handbook for Congregational Studies,* Abingdon Press, p. 77.

Attachment #3

# FORCE-FIELD ANALYSIS INVENTORY*

PART I. Problem Specification

    Think about a problem that is significant in your "back-home" situations. Respond to each item as fully as necessary for another participant to understand the problem.

1. I understand the problem specifically to be that . . .

2. The following people with whom I must deal are involved in the problem:

    Their roles in this problem are . . .

    They relate to me in the following manner:

3. I consider these other factors to be relevant to the problem:

4. I would choose the following aspect of the problem to be changed if it were in my power to do so (choose only one aspect):

PART II. Problem Analysis

5. If I consider the present status of the problem as a temporary balance of opposing forces, the following would be on my list of forces *driving* toward change: (Fill in the spaces to the right of the letters. Leave spaces to the left blank.)

    _____ a. _____
    _____ b. _____

*Pfeiffer, J. William, and Jones, John E., *Handbook of Structured Experiences for Human Relations Training*, Vol. 2, University Associates, San Diego, pp. 82-84.

_____ c. _____

_____ d. _____

_____ e. _____

_____ f. _____

_____ g. _____

_____ h. _____

6. The following would be on my list of forces *restraining* change:

   _____ a. _____

   _____ b. _____

   _____ c. _____

   _____ d. _____

   _____ e. _____

   _____ f. _____

   _____ g. _____

   _____ h. _____

7. In the spaces to the left of the letters in item 5, rate the driving forces from 1 to 5.
   1. It has *almost nothing* to do with the drive toward change in the problem.
   2. It has *relatively little* to do with the drive toward change in the problem.
   3. It is of *moderate importance* in the drive toward change in the problem.
   4. It is an *important factor* in the drive toward change in the problem.
   5. It is a *major factor* in the drive toward change in the problem.
8. In the spaces to the left of the letters in item 6, rate the forces restraining change, using the number scale in item 7.

## Structured Experience 40

9. In the following chart, diagram the forces driving toward change and restraining change that you rated in items 7 and 8: First write several key words to identify each of the forces driving toward change (a through h), then repeat the process for forces restraining change. Then draw an arrow

from the corresponding degree of force to the status quo line. For example, if you considered the first on your list of forces (letter a) in item 5 to be rated a 3, draw your arrow from the 3 line in the "a" column indicating drive up to the status quo line.

**Restraining Forces**

```
       /a /b /c /d /e /f /g /h /
    5 /__/__/__/__/__/__/__/__/
    4 -----------------------------------
    3 -----------------------------------
    2 -----------------------------------
    1 -----------------------------------
```
**Status Quo** ─────────────────────────────
```
    1 -----------------------------------
    2 -----------------------------------
    3 -----------------------------------
    4 -----------------------------------
    5 /--/--/--/--/--/--/--/--/
      / a/ b/ c/ d/ e/ f/ g/ h/
```

**Driving Forces**

*PART III· Change Strategy*

10. Select two or more restraining forces from your diagram and then outline a strategy for reducing their potency.
11. Apply the following goal-setting criteria (the SPIRO model) to your change strategy:
    S—Specificity: Exactly what are you trying to accomplish?
    P—Performance: What behavior is implied?
    I—Involvement: Who is going to do it?
    R—Realism: Can it be done?
    O—Observability: Can others see the behavior?

*Attachment #4*

## ACTION-OBJECTIVES

When you write your action-objectives, remember that verbs control objectives. The following five principles will help you to select verbs that will move you out into action.

When you write objectives:
1. Avoid verbs that point to an outcome beyond the ability of the planner to achieve. Some of these verbs are:
   - request
   - invite
   - persuade
   - offer
   
   RECOMMENDATION: Don't use these verbs.
2. Avoid verbs that describe a process but *not* the outcome for which the process is undertaken. Some of these verbs are:
   - seek
   - try to
   - survey
   - discuss
   - review
   - continue
   - grow
   - deepen
   - advance
   - serve
   - encourage
   - influence
   
   RECOMMENDATION: Press for the verb that gives the reason *why* behind the process verb. Example: "Try to recruit three persons..." becomes "Enlist three persons...."
3. Avoid verbs that express results so vague that people cannot agree on what is meant.
   - appreciate
   - understand
   - know
   
   RECOMMENDATION: Don't use these verbs.
4. Avoid verbs that are limited to thinking rather than acting.
   - investigate
   - study
   - examine
   - think about
   - consider
   
   RECOMMENDATION: Save these verbs for first steps in your Program Plans.

5. Avoid verbs that express change *unless* you clearly state your starting point, the time period to be used, *and* the amount of change you want.

    increase                  support
    deepen                   maintain
    enhance                 decrease
    preserve                 reduce

RECOMMENDATION: Be sure you specify your starting point, the time period needed, and the amount of change you want. Example: "Increase our visiting teams" becomes "Increase our visiting teams from two teams to four teams in six months."

Attachment #5

# PLANNING: ITS REASONS FOR FAILURE, SYMPTOMS, AND CURES*

| REASONS FOR FAILURE | SYMPTOMS | CURES |
|---|---|---|
| 1) No Real Goals | • Do not reflect the church's purpose statement<br>• Talk about program plans<br>• Are vague—sound good; say little<br>• Completely beyond the reach of the church<br>• Not "owned" by membership | • Relate goal to purpose statement<br>• Rewrite goals so they describe end-states you want to reach or conditions you want to bring about<br>• Involve more persons in goal writing |
| 2) No Measurable Objectives | • Are not related to a goal<br>• Are not measurable, specific, or time-phased<br>• Do not contain action verbs | • Build each objective from a goal<br>• Answer in objectives such questions as: Who? How many? Where? When?<br>• Identify short-term and long-term objectives<br>• Use action verbs in the statement |
| 3) Failure to Anticipate Obstacles | • Excessive optimism<br>• Closing your eyes to conflicts<br>• Completion dates not met<br>• "Oops, I forgot!"<br>• Didn't get support when needed<br>• Crises are common | • Take time to list possible obstacles<br>• Prepare ways to overcome listed obstacles<br>• Be realistic in setting dates<br>• Check program plan details<br>• Talk to program plan manager<br>• Revise program plan or details |
| 4) Lack of Milestones and Progress Reviews | • Completion dates not set<br>• "It can wait", "I can remember that"<br>• "Let's play this by ear"<br>• Don't really know how you are doing<br>• Everything is short-term; no long-term aspects<br>• Don't remember when the last review took place<br>• No plans revised recently | • Set specific task milestones; stick to them<br>• See that the program plan manager is on the job<br>• Review your progress on the dates set<br>• Ask the question: Are we making enough progress toward the objective? |

| | | |
|---|---|---|
| 5) Lack of Commitment | • Putting things off<br>• Just doing daily, routine activities<br>• "I don't care what happens"<br>• Have not set priorities<br>• Planners skip meetings<br>• No reports submitted<br>• Pastor or lay members don't "own" the plan | • Involve others in the planning process<br>• Share proposed plans early so new ideas can influence their development<br>• Give the small groups of your church a chance to discuss proposed plans<br>• Talk with each team member to find out the level of his or her commitment<br>• Recruit replacements as necessary<br>• Celebrate successes you've had |
| 6) Failure to Revise Objectives | • Plans never change<br>• Being inflexible, refusing to face new facts that call for change<br>• No sense of movement toward objectives<br>• Help not sought when needed<br>• Waste time on programs that don't work<br>• Programs don't fit your priorities | • Deliberately seek feedback<br>• Compare feedback with your standards for achieving the objective<br>• Change emphasis and approach when it is appropriate<br>• Encourage program plan managers to alert planning task force when revision is needed<br>• Review progress more often |
| 7) Failure to Learn from Experience | • Lose sight of goals<br>• Repeat mistakes<br>• Feedback is ignored<br>• Evaluation standards are not used<br>• Face the same crisis again and again<br>• Unwillingness to change ways of doing things<br>• Never asking, "What did we learn this time?" | • Use milestones to review progress<br>• Have program units, task forces, etc., meet with the planning task force<br>• Keep a record of changes made as a result of evaluation<br>• Concentrate on results, not on giving reports for their own sake |

*Adapted from Timmons, Smollen, and Dingee, *New Venture Creation*, Richard D. Irwin, 1977, p. 45.

*Attachment #6*

## CONFLICT-RESOLUTION STYLES

There are five basic approaches to conflict resolution. They can be summarized as follows. Indicate the one you are most likely to use with followers with an [F]; with your peers, with a [P]; and with your supervisor, with an [S].

| STYLE | CHARACTERISTIC BEHAVIOR | USER JUSTIFICATION |
|---|---|---|
| Avoidance ☐ ☐ ☐ | Nonconfrontational. Ignores or passes over issues. Denies issues are a problem. | Differences too minor or too great to resolve. Attempts might damage relationships or create even greater problems. |
| Accommodating ☐ ☐ ☐ | Agreeable, nonassertive behavior. Cooperative even at the expense of personal goals. | Not worth risking damage to relationships, or general disharmony. |
| Win/Lose ☐ ☐ ☐ | Confrontational, assertive, and aggressive. Must win at any cost. | Survival of the fittest. Must prove superiority. Most ethically or professionally correct. |
| Compromising ☐ ☐ ☐ | Important all parties achieve basic goals and maintain good relationships. Aggressive but cooperative. | No one person or idea is perfect. There is more than one good way to do anything. You must give to get. |
| Problem Solving ☐ ☐ ☐ | Needs of both parties are legitimate and important. High respect for mutual support. Assertive and cooperative. | When parties will openly discuss issues, a mutually beneficial solution can be found without anyone's making a major concession. |

Review this chart with team members. Share the answers to test one another's perceptions. Discuss ways conflicts can be more effectively resolved in the team and with other units.

You and your team may find the following diagram helpful in discussing conflict-resolution styles.

```
         Assertive ↑
         | Win/Lose                    Problem Solving
         |
         |
         |
         |              Compromising
         |                   •
         |
         |
         |
         | Avoidance                   Accommodating
         ↓ Unassertive
           Uncooperative ─────────────→ Cooperative
```

Answer the following questions:

1. Which style is the most uncooperative and least assertive? _____.

2. Which style is characterized by assertive behavior, yet represents the maximum in cooperation? _____.

3. Which style is totally cooperative but unassertive?_____ _____.

4. Which style is totally assertive and uncooperative?_____ _____.

5. Which style takes the middle ground on assertiveness and cooperation? _____.

---

Answers to questions 1 through 5: 1. Avoidance; 2. Problem Solving; 3. Accommodating; 4. Win/Lose; 5. Compromising.

## APPENDIX 3

# SELECTED RESOURCES

*The resources in this section may be ordered from Episcopal Parish Services, unless directed otherwise. Episcopal Parish Services, Episcopal Church Center, 815 Second Avenue, New York, NY 10017, 800/223-2337; be sure to give order number. For further information from any of the following offices, write or phone the Episcopal Church Center, 212/867-8400 or 800/334-7626; 800/321-2231 (New York State).*

## ASIAMERICAN MINISTRY

*Women in Shadows.* Handbook prepared "to provide much-needed information about victims of domestic violence among Asian women"—especially those who are wives of U.S. servicemen. Contains helpful demographic data and descriptions of Asian values, as well as suggestions and recommendations of where to look for help; case studies and bibliography. #66-8708-1, $10.00.

*Episcopal Asiamerican Ministry.* Description of the history of and impetus for this ministry, its current activities, and its relationship to other Asian Churches. #61-0589, free.

*Korean Book of Common Prayer.* Contains the entire Book of Common Prayer, except for the Rite One versions of the various services. A number of special Korean festival collects and prefaces are appended. English and Korean text on facing pages. #66-8702-1 Leather edition, $60.00. #66-8703-1 Cloth edition, $20.00.

## EPISCOPAL COMMISSION ON BLACK MINISTRIES

*Linkage.* A yearly newsletter/journal, containing news items, articles of historical interest, commentaries about the Church at home and abroad, from the black perspective. #61-9011-1, free.

*Directory of Black Clergy.* Published annually, lists all black bishops, priests, and deacons of the Episcopal Church, black members of interim committees and commissions; black staff members at the Episcopal Church Center, vital statistics of black clergy (ordinations, necrology, etc.); summary of new ministries undertaken by black clergy; and other information. #61-9042-1, free.

*Special Publications* appear from time to time and include such titles as "Report of the Task Force for the Recruitment, Training and Development of Black Clergy"; *Lift Every Voice and Sing, II,* an Afro-American hymnal to be published by the Church Hymnal Corporation in 1992; "But We See Jesus," a pastoral letter from black Episcopal bishops; and "Black Bishops in the American Succession," a poster collection with biographical sketches. Other posters, brochures, and booklets for special occasions have also been published.

## CONGREGATIONAL DEVELOPMENT

*The New Church Development Notebook* series. A number of volumes that describe various aspects of new church development work. $2.00 per volume.
   1. *An Overview of a New Church Development Project.* #56-8831
   2. *A Diocesan Strategy for New Church Development.* #56-8832
   3. *A Biblical-Theological Foundation for New Church Development.* #56-8833

*Reshaping a Congregation for a New Future.* Examines the dynamics of a congregation in transition because of changes in size, life cycle, and community context. Offers an analysis of transitions and suggestions for dealing with these challenges. #56-8602, $3.00.

*Sizing Up a Congregation.* Offers four models for understanding the developmental history of a congregation in a sized progression. Outlines ways to attract and assimilate newcomers into congregations of all four sizes. #56-8801. $3.00.

*Further Resources.* For demographic studies of the area served by a congregation, for church and community seminars, and for other concerns, phone or write to the Congregational Development Office.

# EVANGELISM MINISTRIES

*The Catechumenal Process: Adult Initiation and Formation in Christian Ministry,* by Ann E. P. McElligott. A comprehensive overview that explains the process for adults seeking baptism, entering the Episcopal Church, or reaffirming their faith and for youth 16 and up making a mature profession of faith. It includes history, adaptations for congregations and dioceses, resources for leaders, and educational and liturgical procedures for the four stages of the process. *The Catechumenal Process* seeks to form Christians as effective missionaries and evangelists in word and deed in their daily environments. Order from the Church Hymnal Corporation, 800 Second Avenue, New York, NY 10017. 212/661-6700. $14.95.

*Handbook for Evangelism* (revised edition). An outline of Episcopal experiences and resources in proclamation by example and word, ministry to new members, ministry with the inactive or lapsed, founding new congregations, and parish revitalization and spiritual direction. #56-8914, $3.00.

*Proclamation as Offering Story and Choice,* by A. Wayne Schwab and William A. Yon. Experience-centered training based on the belief that Jesus Christ is already at work in the other person. The book is supplemented by two pamphlets, "The Drama of Anglicanism," by John Booty, and "An Anglican Evangelism," by Schwab. Adaptable for Sunday adult forums. #58-8821, $7.50 per set.

*Further Resources.* For further resources in working models in evangelism in congregations of all sizes, for training diocesan evangelism trainers, and for training in implementing the catechumenal process in congregations, phone or write the Evangelism Ministries Office.

# HISPANIC MINISTRIES

*Hispanic Demographic Profiles.* Report gives the state rankings by number of Hispanics and proportion of population: also includes the Hispanic profiles for the top twenty dioceses. Order from the Hispanic Office at the Episcopal Church Center, $15.00.

*The Spanish Book of Occasional Services.* Spanish version containing all the pertinent services found in the English version. Published by the Church Hymnal Corporation. Order from the Church Hymnal Corporation.

*El Reto Es Ahora.* Brief description of the purpose of the National Hispanic Office and the services available. Order from the Hispanic Office. Free.

## JUBILEE MINISTRY

*Jubilee Ministry, A Place to Serve: Linking Faith with Justice.* A resource that explains Jubilee Ministry, describes the work of eight Jubilee centers, and outlines ways for congregational leaders to study Jubilee Ministry and introduce it into a congregation's life. It maintains that community service and advocacy are indispensable to full proclamation by congregations of the good news of God in Jesus Christ. #61-8928, free.

## NATIVE AMERICAN MINISTRY

*Jamestown Commitment,* by Owanah Anderson. History of the relationship between the Anglican and Episcopal Churches and the Native peoples of North America. Order from Forward Movement Publications, 412 Sycamore Street, Cincinnati, OH 45202. 800/543-1813. Or contact the Native American Ministry Office at the Church Center directly.

*In the Spirit of the Circle.* A curriculum resource developed by Native Americans for church school or adult education. Series of 30 posters, photos, and illustrations, which depict stories of Native American history, ministry, and spirituality, linked to biblical stories and Episcopal tradition and practice. 32 pages, 12" x 17". #56-8901, $60.00.

*To Walk in Beauty.* Videotape of the consecration of the Rt. Rev. Steven Plummer, the first Navajo Bishop of Navajoland. This tape superbly captures much of what is important in Indian ministry today. 30 minutes. #50-343, $29.95.

*IKHANA.* Periodical newsletter, containing news items and stories about issues and events important in the work of Episcopal Native Americans throughout the country. Order from the Native

American Ministry Field Office, 924 North Robinson, Oklahoma City, OK 73102.

## *RURAL AND SMALL TOWN MINISTRIES*

*Reshaping Ministry: Essays in Memory of Wesley Frensdorf,* edited by J. Borgeson and L. Wilson. A major educational resource for anyone interested in the changing shape of the ministry. Book divided in three parts: the man and his vision; the experience; and synthesis and unfinished business. Challenges for the future based on a visionary past. 260 pp. Jethro Publications, 6066 Parfet Street, Arvada, CO 80004, 1990, 303/431-6436, $16.00 plus shipping.

*Faith in the Countryside: Report of the Archbishops' Commission on Rural Areas.* An excellent look at the state of rural communities and churches in England with much to be learned from its contents on this side of the Atlantic. Addresses main issues, reflects on where responsibility might lie, and examines the way the rural church has engaged them. Positive signs of growth and engagement that affect the working of the diocesan and national church are identified. Churchman Publishing, Ltd., 117 Broomfield Avenue, Worthing, West Sussex BN14 7SF. 1990.

*The Small Church Handbook,* by David Ray. An expansion and update of the author's classic work *Small Churches Are the Right Size.* When available in late 1991, this should prove to be most beneficial to anyone engaged in small church ministry or development. Pilgrim Press, The United Church Press, 475 Riverside Drive, 10th floor, New York, NY 10115, 212/870-3464.

*Choices for Churches,* by Lyle E. Schaller. Emphasis is placed on issues that must be addressed not only by congregations but by denominational leadership as well. Data, interpretation, insight and options are provided in an easily understood text. Anything by Schaller is worthwhile. 176 pp., Abingdon Press, 1990. Nashville, TN 37202, 800/672-1789. $10.95.

*Field of Churches: A Viable Option,* compiled by Thomas E. Sykes. Mission strategy for city and rural small congregations. This is an excellent study evolving from a Southern Baptist conference on "clustering." Much to be gained for anyone involved in "clustering." 119 pp., Home Mission Board, 1350 Spring Street, NW, Atlanta, GA 30367-5601, 1989. 404/898-7000, free.

## STEWARDSHIP

*The Hidden Treasure,* by Edward R. Rich III. Being a steward of time and talent in a demanding world is a full-time job. This book weaves Scripture, theology, and historical reflection into a background for practical exercises for individuals and groups. Readers will learn how to discover and deploy God-given talents for ministry. #52-8859, $3.00.

*Star System for Stewardship,* by Robert H. Bonner. This brief booklet outlines the five points of the stewardship-planning "star": the stewardship statement, the mission statement, the narrative budget, the line-item budget, and the action plan. Order copies for each stewardship planner well in advance of your congregation's annual campaign. #52-9038, $1.00.

*A Time for Vision: A Stewardship Handbook for Vestries,* by Robert H. Bonner and Stuart E. Schadt. The vestry that can consider the call of God to a given congregation can begin to pray and to dream, and to see God honor an intentional vision. This important and useful handbook is distilled from a series of workshops conducted in the field by Bonner, officer for congregational stewardship, and Schadt, former chair of the department of stewardship, Diocese of Texas. #52-8850, $2.00.

## WOMEN IN MISSION AND MINISTRY

*Women of Vision* is a training program empowering women for ministry in the world, the family and the Church, and for themselves. Eight modules in about 16 hours emphasize nurturing environments to support the acquisition of skills to help women manifest their Christian beliefs in the world. Sponsored by the Episcopal Church Women. For further information, phone the Episcopal Church Center, ext. 447.

*United in Leadership* is a similar training program to *Women of Vision* and is offered in Spanish for Hispanic women.

## ALBAN INSTITUTE

*The Empowering Church,* by Davida Foy Crabtree. Dr. Crabtree's small book is an account of how the congregations and pastors of combined Baptist and United Church of Christ congregations restructured themselves to support the lay people's ministries in the world. It answers the question posed by a longtime member of the congregation, "How do we connect the ministry of the laity with our church structure and with everything we do in the church and outside the church?" In the process of the restructuring, the congregation was renewed and invigorated, and it increased in members. The Alban Institute, 4126 Nebraska Avenue, NW, Washington, DC 20016; 1989, $9.95.

*Handbook for Congregational Studies,* edited by Jackson W. Carroll, Carol S. Dudley and William McKinney. How to gather and interpret data to evaluate current climate and programs, make long-range plans or develop a mission focus. The Alban Institute, 4126 Nebraska Avenue, NW, Washington, DC 20016, $19.95.

*The Life Cycle of a Congregation,* by Martin F. Saarinen. Traces the interplay of energizing factors, program, organizations and mission statements, and inclusiveness in the life cycle of a congregation. The Alban Institute, 4126 Nebraska Avenue, NW, Washington, DC 20016, $6.95.

## OTHER HELPFUL RESOURCES

*An Audit for the Local Church.* Prepared by the British General Synod Board for Mission and Unity on behalf of the Archbishop's Commission on Urban Priority Areas, this work outlines six stages for the parochial church council of a congregation seeking to become aware of the needs in its urban area and how it can cooperate with God in meeting them, 24 pp. Church House Bookshop, Great Smith Street, London SW1P 3NZ, England; $3 - 4.00 for shipping and handling.

*Association for Christian Training and Service,* the Rev. Ted McEachern, Director, 1001 18th Avenue South, Nashville, TN 37212. (615) 329-9973. McEachern is currently conducting mission discernment processes for congregations in the Dioceses of East Carolina and Mississippi.

*The Urban Christian,* by Raymond J. Bakke. Professor of Ministry at Northern Baptist Theological Seminary, and senior associate for large cities of the Lausanne Committee for World Evangelization, Bakke has developed a unique ecumenical approach to revitalizing clergy leadership for mission in urban centers. He has lived and worked in Chicago for over twenty years, and can be reached at International Urban Associates, 1043 West Madison, Chicago, IL, 312/850-9000. Inter Varsity Press, P.O. Box 1400, Downers Grove, IL 60515, 1987. $9.95.

*Church Growth and the Power of Evangelism,* by Howard Hanchey. Describes how churches can move from maintenance to mission and the place of evangelism, clergy leadership, education, and planning in the change. The author is professor of pastoral theology at Virginia Theological Seminary, and his suggestions ring with the authority of his own experience and that of others he knows. Cowley Publications, 980 Memorial Drive, Cambridge, MA 02138. $12.95.

*Congregations and Connections: Empowerment for Ministry.* Dateline series, May, 1990, Vol. 5, No. 5., by L. Roy Sells. Summary of a study of the General Board of Discipleship of the United Methodist Church on the need for congregations to work intentionally to help members see their daily living as opportunities for Christian ministry. Strong leadership and active congregations do not seem to help laity connect faith to daily life. Something more is needed.

*Ministry in Daily Life: A Study of Nine Congregations.* Nine congregations tell how they seek to help their members link faith and daily life. While intentional work to connect faith and daily life takes time and is difficult, progress can be made. Department for Research, Planning and Evaluation, Division for Parish Services, Evangelical Lutheran Church in America, 8765 West Higgins Road, Chicago, IL 60631, 1989.

"Mission" from *Bonds of Affection,* Proceedings of ACC-6 in Badagry, Nigeria, pp. 46-61, 1984. The mission audit names four areas for evaluation: (1) evangelism; (2) response and initiation; (3) Christian nurture and teaching (including, education and pastoral care); and (4) service and social transformation. Anglican Consultative Council, 14 Great Peter Street, London, SW1P 3NQ, England, 1984.

*Patterns of Parish Leadership: Cost Effectiveness in Four Denominations,* by Dean Hoge, Jackson Carroll and Francis K. Scheets. Roman Catholic, Episcopal, Lutheran, and Methodist churches were compared in terms of ordained and lay, professional and volunteer, leadership. Sheed and Ward, 115 East Armour Boulevard, P.O. Box 419492, Kansas City, MO 64141-6492, 800/333-7373.

*The Planning/Organization Workbook.* The basic resource of CRW Management Service (Charles R. Wilson, Director) outlines mission statements, goal-setting, action planning, organization, and policy planning. Jethro Publications, 6066 Parfet Street, Arvada, CO 80004.

*Faith, Focus and Leadership: Keys to Excellence in Six Episcopal Churches,* by the Rev. Peter A. R. Stebinger. Study by an Episcopal priest of six congregations, seeking to determine why they are successful. Although diverse in size and styles of ministry, he observed that in each of them faith is taught from the pulpit; the whole parish tries to live out the reality of being a community of faith; there is a unique and specific focus for the congregation's ministry, "self-differentiated" clergy leadership, and "self-differentiated" lay leadership. Forward Movement, 412 Sycamore Street, Cincinnati, OH 45202. 1990.

*Twelve Keys to an Effective Church,* by Kennon L. Callahan. A book, tapes, leader's guide, and workbook that discuss the characteristics of effective churches. Such churches have six relational characteristics (specific, concrete mission objectives; pastoral and lay visitation; dynamic corporate worship; significant relational groups; strong leadership resources; streamlined structure and solid participatory decision making) and six functional characteristics (several competent programs and activities; open accessibility; high visibility; adequate parking, land, and landscaping; adequate space and facilities; solid financial resources) in place. The author advises a congregation to work on nine of these characteristics (preferably five relational and four functional ones) to be an effective church, growing in mission and members. Callahan begins with mission and relates everything else to mission. That is his great strength over all the other books in this field. He says, "Jesus stands at the door and knocks, not to be let in, but to ask if you will come out and join him at work in the world." The tapes are the best part ($69.95), but you will also want all of the following: book, $14.95; Leader's Guide, $11.95; and Planning Workbook, $5.95. Order from the National Institute for Church Planning and Consultation, 15775 Hillcrest, #445, Dallas, TX 75248. 214/458-1511.

## APPENDIX 4

# DOCUMENTS OF THE MISSION DISCERNMENT PROJECT

## *A SUMMARY DESCRIPTION OF THE MISSION DISCERNMENT PROJECT*

In accordance with Resolution A 066a, the General Convention of the Episcopal Church, meeting in Detroit in July, 1988, resolved,

> That the Episcopal Church renew and strengthen its educational ministry by advocating a clear focus on mission at every level of its life faithful to the standard of biblical word and baptismal covenant, and . . . . That the Executive Council provide the necessary structures and funding so that the Missions Operations Team can enable congregations, with diocesan support, to continue or initiate a process of discernment, challenge, leadership and resource development, and action. (Res. A 066a)

Working to implement the resolution, the Education and Training Interunit Working Group developed working definitions of mission discernment, wrote to the dioceses of the Episcopal Church for input, resources and examples of mission discernment, and identified eleven types of congregations (family-size, program-size, Native American, cross-cultural, Hispanic, blue-collar, pastoral-size, corporation-size, African-American, Asian-American, college-university) for which models of mission discernment will be developed.

In order to develop the models, members of the Mission Discernment Project will visit congregations throughout the Episcopal Church from 2/90 to 6/90 in the eleven category groups in which mission discernment has been demonstrated as working.

This Mission Discernment Project is an opportunity for the Episcopal Church to celebrate its good news stories through the identification of concrete examples which will be drawn from what is *already working* and *already giving life and vision* in the Episcopal Church. The writer of Proverbs tells us that "Where there is no vision, the people perish" (Prov. 29:18a). So this project will be about a vision built and grounded in the reality of the actual experiences of congregations and parish members who are already engaged in effective mission. It is about God's total mission in the total congregation, in the total context of the diocese and the world for which our gracious savior Jesus Christ beckons us to love, to save, to heal, to transform and to renew.

Congregations to be considered as models are being carefully selected as a result of consultation with area and ethnic desks in the Episcopal Church Center, with bishops and Church leaders around the country. Visiting teams will consist of the coordinators of this phase of the project (Dr. Anne Rowthorn and either the Rev. A. Wayne Schwab, or the Rev. John T. Docker as they are able), and local representatives from the following groups: education and training network, the Executive Council and the Standing Commission on Evangelism.

The visits to specific locations where mission discernment is clearly demonstrated will include observing examples of how this discernment is actually put into practice. In the light of this, the visits will then be written up. The end result will be 10 to 12 carefully drawn models—along with accompanying resources and suggestions for use—which will be designed for testing in selected congregations throughout the Church from October 1, 1990, to January 3, 1991.

It is expected that following testing and revision of the models the project will be available to the whole Church in July, 1991, with ongoing support and evaluation until December 31, 1996.

A full description of the "Mission Discernment Project: A Plan for the Implementation of Resolution A 066a" is available upon request.

The Rev. A. Wayne Schwab, Project Director
Dr. Anne Rowthorn, Project Coordinator
The Rev. John T. Docker, Staff

# PLANNING GUIDE FOR SITE VISITS

Memo:     From Anne Rowthorn
To:        Congregations participating in the Mission Discernment Project
Re:        Planning for site visits

A. *Preliminary questions to focus the planning group:*
  1. What do you most want to share about your life as a congregation with the wider Episcopal Church? List.
  2. Who are the members of your congregation who most successfully make the links and the connections between their lives of faith and their lives outside of the parish walls? (Names and jobs or community roles.) Discuss this, and list several.
B. *Hearing the story:* List the names of those who can best tell the story of how your congregation got to where it is now.
C. *Seeing the story:*
  1. Congregation-sponsored examples (list):
  2. Laity in their workplaces or in the community (list):
D. *Schedule of visit* (times and activities for number of days that apply):
  Day 1:
  Day 2:
  Day 3:
E. Please list anything else the Visiting Team ought to see or do:

# GUIDELINES FOR SITE VISITS

The visiting team will consist of the project coordinators (Schwab, Rowthorn and Docker) accompanied by one or two local representatives from the following groups: Education and Training Network, the Executive Council and the Standing Commission on Evangelism.

Since Anne Rowthorn is charged with the responsibility of writing up the stories, she will visit each location and will be accompanied by either John Docker or Wayne Schwab as they are able. A key feature of the plan is the participation on the visiting team of individuals from the above mentioned bodies within the Episcopal Church. These persons will add local knowledge and insight, and this will spread out and enhance the impact of the project.

The visiting team will expect to spend approximately a day in each location to be visited. This procedure will include a brief gathering and orientation period for the members of the visiting team; the site visit itself, which will include the following segments—hearing the story, seeing the story, and reflecting on the story; and finally an opportunity for members of the visiting team to share their insights (understanding the story). These steps are described below:

## HEARING THE STORY

The visiting team will hear—in the words of the local parish leadership—about what exactly is happening in the congregation. In this segment of the visit they will first get an overview.

Following the overview they will explore, in retrospect, how the congregation got to this point. This portion of the visit will include a narrative of stories and journeys and pilgrimages. Hearing the stories of the people at each location is a particularly appropriate approach since—as the report of the Presiding Bishop's Task Force on Christian Education (of which this current work is an outgrowth) has so elegantly reminded us,

> ... we Christians are a "story-formed people." Our consciousness and identity grow out of the salvation story as it is contained in Scripture .... As long as the people of the Church are not intimately familiar with that story, we risk moving through the present with a hazy vision of who we are and where we are going rather than with a clear vision that Scripture provides, a vision of hope for the future and a vision that can lend meaning and direction to the present moment.*

## SEE THE STORY

In accordance with the adage that "seeing is believing," at each location the visiting team will want to see several concrete examples of how education for mission is working. This

---

*Report of the Presiding Bishop's Task Force on Christian Education in the Local Congregation, November, 1987, p. 2.

might mean visiting several lay members of the congregation at their workplaces, visiting a program or project sponsored by the parish, visiting a community or political leader who understands and is able to talk about his or her daily work as being a conscious working out of Christ's mission.

## REFLECTING ON THE STORY

Following visits to actual locations where mission is implemented, this portion of the site visit will be an opportunity for members of the congregation and the clergy of the congregation to reflect with members of the visiting team on the meaning of what has been seen and heard throughout the visit. It will be an opportunity to re-state and summarize what mission discernment means in that location and how it is carried out.

## UNDERSTANDING THE STORY

Following the conversations and visits at each site, the visiting team will talk about what they heard and saw and the concrete steps the congregation took—its discernment process—to build its educational ministry for mission. Through this sharing the team will look ahead to the next step of writing the model and to that end summarize where the congregation is with regard to its education for mission, its actual mission, exactly how it did and is doing it.

On the basis of conversation notes and audiotapes of the conversations, Anne Rowthorn will write up each visit.

## GETTING THE STORY—SITE VISITORS AS MIDWIVES

We will serve as midwives, as vehicles through which members of the congregation pass on their life, their vitality and their story. This is their show, their story, and our role is to help them tell it. Although there is a certain amount of factual data to obtain (preliminary section I), we'll want to move quickly in order to get into the "meat" of our time together. This outline is *suggestive only*.

The idea is to hear the story of this congregation and the stories of its members; to hear it in their own words and in their own way. We want to do everything we can to help them to showcase and celebrate what they have and through us to offer it to the Church. We want to stimulate their thoughts and imaginations—and then listen very carefully as they describe the steps they took to get there.

I. Preliminaries
   A. Brief description of the wider community in which the congregation is located:
      1. Population (Is it growing/losing population? Who is moving in? Ethnic/racial/cultural make-up of the community);
      2. Characteristics of the community. What's it like? Does it have a personality?
      3. Types of industry and employment.
      4. What are the key political/social/economic issues currently facing the community?
   B. Basics of the Congregation
      1. Where is the church located?
      2. How many members?
      3. Where do they live? (Around the church, or do they commute in?)
      4. What are their jobs?
      5. How do they spend their time?
II. Hearing the Story
   A. Describe the congregation as it is right now.
      1. What does the congregation do as a congregation?
      2. How does the congregation support its members in their daily life and living (job, community, political responsibility, family, leisure)?
   B. Tell us how this ministry evolved:
      1. Specific events and circumstances,
      2. Persons who made a difference,
      3. Processes, ideas, programs, issues and actions and events which touched and moved you and the life of this congregation.
      4. Were (or are) their any specific plans, mission or vision statements?
      5. Did you have any outside help or assistance?

III. Seeing the Story
   A. Visits with laity—work/community:
      1. Describe your regular work (or significant nonchurch-related or community activity).
      2. How do you express and live out your faith in your workplace through the channels of your daily work or community activity?
      3. How do you respond to the statement that, "The vocation of the laity involves the integration of spiritual values into the day to day decisions of life and work?"
      4. What is most exciting about your ministry right now? What do you most want to celebrate?
      5. In what ways does, and in what ways could, your congregation strengthen and support your ministry in the workplace and in the community?
         a) What do you need from your faith community?
      6. Are there any ways in which your faith comes in conflict with your work?
   B. Visits with laity—home/leisure:
      1. How do you see your home and family life as an arena for ministry? Or (depending on the situation), How do you see your household as a center for ministry?
      2. Who encourages and supports your ministry in your home (your marriage, your life as a member of the household, your role as a parent)?
      3. What is the greatest joy/satisfaction you experience in your ministry in daily life?
      4. What nurtures you personally? What feeds and refreshes your soul and spirit?
      5. Do you experience God's presence in leisure (either through specific leisure activities or leisure moments)? Can you explain?
      6. Do you see your leisure activities as avenues for ministry? In what ways?
      7. What would you say is the biggest tension you have run into in regard to your ministry in daily life?
      8. In what ways does, and in what ways could, your congregation strengthen and support your ministry in daily life and leisure?
         a) What do you need from your faith community?

- C. What the congregation does as a congregation:
    1. Do you see this neighborhood (area, town, city) as a mission field?
    2. How does the congregation make a difference in this neighborhood (area, town, city)?
    3. How have you determined this congregation's role in its wider community setting?
    4. What specific programs and/or strategies has this congregation developed to meet the needs of the neighborhood (area, town, city, community)?
        a) Have you cooperated with other churches/denominations/groups/bodies/governmental agencies?
    5. What are the joys of this outreach?
        a) What are the successes?
        b) What are the heartaches?
IV. Vision, Future, Sustaining Vitality
- A. Direction:
    1. What sustains the life and vitality of this congregation?
    2. What are the strengths of this congregation and its various ministries and programs?
    3. What does this congregation look forward to in the future?
        a) What are your hopes and dreams?
- B. Weaknesses:
    1. What's the downside? What hasn't worked?
    2. Why? (Briefly)
V. Resources which have been helpful to you. (Site visitors, be sure to get exact and complete references (title, author, publishing company, city, date of publication). List.
VI. Final reflections and sharing among congregation's leadership and team members. This is the last opportunity for members of the congregation to have their say. Listen up!!
VII. Debriefing among visiting team members: What do we most want to pass on (in our final report) about this congregation and this story?